The Short Story
in English

Walter Allen The Short Story
in English

Clarendon Press • Oxford
Oxford University Press • New York
1981

ISBN 0–19–812666–2
Library of Congress Catalog Number: 80-69569

Printed in the United States of America

To Peggy

Contents

Foreword

This book was several years in the writing. My views on the American short story were first adumbrated in the Sarah Tryphena Phillips Lecture delivered to the British Academy in 1973 and were developed in the seminars I conducted in my graduate course at the Virginia Polytechnic Institute and State University in 1974–5. It was there also that I first seriously applied myself to the question of Kipling. I have no doubt that I profited from my discussions with the students who attended. The first version of my survey of the short story in Ireland was a lecture given at a colloquium on Anglo-Irish writing held at York University, Toronto, in the spring of 1974, a later version of which appeared in the literary pages of the *Irish Press*, Dublin.

It remains for me to thank Kim Scott Walwyn, of the Oxford University Press, for the skilful and sympathetic editorial work exercised on my text in order to bring it down to publishable size.

Acknowledgements

The author and publisher gratefully acknowledge permission to use the following material.

Carson McCullers: Extracts from 'The Ballad of the Sad Café' from *Collected Short Stories & The Novel, The Ballad of the Sad Café*. Copyright 1955 by Carson McCullers. Reprinted by permission of Houghton Mifflin Company and the Executrix of the Literary Estate of Carson McCullers.

Sylvia Townsend Warner: Extracts from 'But At the Stroke of Midnight' from *The Innocent and the Guilty*. Reprinted by permission of the Author's Literary Estate and Chatto & Windus Ltd.

I

i

Everywhere in the world, whenever the short story is discussed, a handful of names crops up, Chekhov and Maupassant always, then Poe and Kipling and Joyce, and probably Katherine Mansfield and Hemingway as well. And this tells us two things. The short story as we think of it today is both an international form and a recent one, essentially a modern form. Poe, the earliest of the writers named, was born in 1809, Maupassant in 1850, Chekhov ten years later. It is against this background that the short story in English in all its manifestations throughout the world must be set.

But merely to make these statements is to be confronted with problems, of which the most obvious is that of definition. What makes a story modern? How does a modern story differ from one of the past? Men have been telling stories for thousands of years; telling stories and listening to them must be as old as language itself. Sometimes, of course, stories are called tales and, as etymology indicates, the tale was an oral form, composed to hold an audience, listeners not readers. Today, the words are interchangeable, and to attempt to make a formal distinction between stories and tales gets us nowhere. The stories or tales early men told one another have not, of course, survived, but we can guess what they were like from those that have come down to us from a much more recent past, from the *Arabian Nights' Entertainment*, the *Gesta Romanorum*, the *Decameron* of Boccaccio and so on. We still read and enjoy these but we do not confuse them with Chekhov's stories or Maupassant's. There seems a fundamental difference between them, one which quite transcends the difference between the spoken word and the written. Chekhov and Maupassant, Kipling and the rest, arouse in us quite other expectations than do Scheherazade and Boccaccio, and this we recognize by prefixing to Chekhov's and Kipling's stories and to those of other writers I have named the word 'modern'.

Such distinctions, of course, cannot be hard and fast ones. It is not difficult to find stories from the past that approximate to modern stories; the Old Testament story of Ruth is an instance.

And the oral tale is still very much with us, often in as primitive a form as it can ever have been. And I do not mean by this merely that it survives in those parts of the world where conditions are such that oral traditions of story-telling still exist, as in India, tribal Africa, and the Gaelic-speaking west of Ireland. The oral tale is still very much at home everywhere. Indeed, home is the operative word here, for the oral tale may be heard as a matter of course in every family circle, in every pub, wherever people come together in the ordinary traffic of life. We know it principally as the joke. The aim of the joke, any kind of joke, is to astonish us by a revelation of the unexpected or the incongruous or the disconcerting, and if we are astonished enough we show it by laughing.

Very few jokes, written down, would seem much like modern stories. They might very well, though, remind us of many of Boccaccio's tales in skeleton form. This throws light on the relationship of the modern story both to the joke and to tales of earlier times. It is similar to and of a piece with the relationship of the novel, which is about three hundred years old, to the kind of long fiction that preceded it, what we call romance. This is to put it too crudely, for the relationship is complicated by the fact that romance, or the romance, still survives, sometimes as an ingredient in the novel, sometimes in what seems its pure state. An example of the latter is the works of J. R. R. Tolkien, which are very evidently works of fiction but which cannot be called novels. For novels we equate with some degree of realism; we take it for granted that novelists give us more or less plausible representations of men and women as they behave in life. The romance, however, as Northrop Frye puts it, in his *Anatomy of Criticism*, does not attempt to create real people and '. . . that is why the romance so often radiates a glow of subjective intensity that the novel lacks, and why a suggestion of allegory is constantly creeping in around its fringes'. Here, Frye may very well be thinking not only of writers of medieval romance like Malory but also of later writers usually thought of as novelists, like Hawthorne. One may sum up from the glossary of *Anatomy of Criticism*, which defines the romantic as a 'fictional mode in which the chief characters live in a world of marvels (naive romance) or in which the mode is elegiac or idyllic and hence less subject to social criticism than the mimetic modes'.

The romance, then, is concerned with wonders. Obviously, it is not always easy to distinguish between novels and romances, but, compared with *Pride and Prejudice*, for instance, *Wuthering Heights* can be seen as more of a romance than a novel and is better understood in those terms.

Similarly, the short story, before the modern short story came into being, was a manifestation of the romance. Its province was the extraordinary; its aim, if not to astonish, was at least to surprise; its purpose, to entertain. Think of Scheherazade, who entertained the sultan so well, astonished him so successfully that literally she kept her head. Or think of Boccaccio's young ladies and gentlemen beguiling the time while in exile from plague-stricken Florence by telling stories to one another. No doubt the story-teller's wit, his elegance in the presentation of his material, his choice of words, his style generally, were all factors making for the appreciation of his art; but fundamental to everything was the listener's desire to be astonished.

An element of surprise is probably fundamental to any work of literature, but it is not now the first thing we ask for; and we assume that even the element of surprise must be in some sense accounted for and certainly that it will not be merely mechanical, the simple product of situation or of the juxtaposition of incongruities. Thomas Hardy said, primarily about the novel: 'A story must be exceptional enough to justify its telling ... Therein lies the problem – to reconcile the average with that uncommonness which alone makes it natural that a tale or experience would dwell in the memory and induce repetition.' In the modern short story we would expect what Hardy calls the uncommonness of the story to come from the special insight of the author or from discoveries made by the characters in the course of the story, not from the situation alone. Here is an example of what I mean.

In his *Sportsman's Sketches*, published in 1851, Turgenev, who was one of the founders of the modern story, has a story called 'Yermolai and the Miller's Wife'. The title suggests a story of sexual intrigue perhaps not very remote from Boccaccio. However, it is not the intrigue itself that interests Turgenev, who may be taken as the narrator of the story. He is out hunting with Yermolai, a serf who has been 'permitted to live where and how he likes' since he has been rejected 'as a man unfit for any work'. They seek somewhere to sleep the night, and a miller lets them have a shed a short distance from the mill. The miller's wife brings them food and the narrator realizes that she is 'neither a country wife nor a city dweller but a house serf. She looked about thirty; her gaunt and pale face still bore traces of a remarkable beauty.' Turgenev, half-asleep, decides that Yermolai and the woman, who is called Arina, are perhaps in love. A little later, the narrator realizes who Arina is, for he has heard of her from her former owner, a man called Zverkov. His wife's maids 'don't just live, but simply have heaven on earth'. She had, however, made it a rule not to keep any maids who married. After ten years Arina had asked permission to marry, which was indignantly refused, and six months later she confessed to being pregnant by her lover Petrushka the flunkey. As Zverkov tells Turgenev:

'Naturally, I immediately ordered her hair to be cropped, to dress her in coarse ticking, and to pack her off to the country! My wife was deprived of an excellent maid, there was no help for it; one cannot, under any circumstances, tolerate irregularity in a household. It's best to lop off a diseased limb at once. . . .'

Turgenev learns that Arina has been married two years, having been bought by the miller. As for Petrushka the flunkey, her lover, we learn his fate from Yermolai. 'Why, he was took for a soldier', he tells Turgenev; sold by his master, that is, into the Army. The story ends:

We were silent for a while.
'She doesn't seem to be in good health. What's the matter with her?' I finally asked Yermolai.
'No, you couldn't call her healthy! . . . Well, I guess we'll have a stand tomorrow. It wouldn't be a bad idea if you were to get some sleep now.'
A flock of wild ducks swept over our heads, whistling, and we heard them settling on the river not far from us. By now it had grown altogether dark and the air was becoming chill; a nightingale was sonorously trilling in a grove. We buried down in the hay and dozed off.

To retell Turgenev's story as I have done is, of course, to mangle it, for every word of it, everything that is not expressly stated but implied contributes to its total effect, which, like that of a poem, is scarcely capable of paraphrase. But what at the moment interests me is to see how what might have been a simple story of sexual intrigue is changed into or becomes the launching-pad for something quite other. It becomes an image of a woman's suffering, of callousness and hypocrisy, above all, of the evil of slavery. And the revelation of all this is contained almost in a single moment of time or at most in an interval between sleep.

The short story then deals with, dramatizes, a single incident and in doing so utterly transforms it. What we might call the basic anecdote is as it were dissolved in the multitude of implications that is apparent to the reader. These implications seem to me to be the hall-mark of the modern short story and its *sine-qua-non*. Yet, in the end, they cannot exist without the anecdote. This may be of the slightest, as far removed as the poet's

> My heart leaps up when I behold
> A rainbow in the sky.

Nevertheless, it is this sense we have of the short story being rooted in a single incident or perception that principally differentiates it from the novel. Certainly length alone does not, for the length of literary form has much more to do with commercial considerations than with theories of literature or aesthetics. But we recognize a short story as such because we feel that we are reading something that is the fruit of a single moment of time, of a single incident, a single perception.

I quoted above two lines from Wordsworth and now I have used the phrases 'a moment of time' and 'a single perception'. We are in a region where strict definition is scarcely possible, but something like these two concepts seem to have been in James Joyce's mind when in the *Stephen Hero* fragment he talks, through Stephen Dedalus, of the 'epiphany', which in Joyce's usage is the adaptation, near-blasphemous, of a theological expression to secular ends. The theory of epiphany, on which Joyce's work, his short stories *Dubliners* and his novel *Ulysses* alike, seems to have been partly based, is nowhere completely stated, and we know of it only from *Stephen Hero*, an earlier version of *A Portrait of the Artist as a Young Man* existing now only in a tantalizingly truncated form. There is, however, enough of it for us to know that it was a novel infinitely less closely wrought and therefore much more conventional than the *Portrait* as we have it now.

In it, we get this:

> . . . By an epiphany he meant a sudden spiritual manifestation, whether in the vulgarity of speech or of gesture or in a memorable expression of the mind itself. He believed that it was for the man of letters to record these epiphanies with extreme care, seeing that themselves are the most delicate and evanescent of moments.

These moments of epiphany are, as theory, akin to Ezra Pound's notion of the image. They can also be matched with similar moments of insight in Wordsworth's poetry, in *The Prelude* particularly. In addition, it may be worth while pointing out that many of the poems in *Lyrical Ballads* can be construed as short stories in verse, modern short stories at that. 'We Are Seven' is a good example.

I seem trembling on the verge of saying that the modern short-story writer is a lyric poet in prose; and indeed, the effect on the reader of many modern short stories, those of Chekhov conspicuously, is nearer to that of lyric poetry than to that of the novel or of older stories. But earlier, as a prototype of a short story which is always with us, one basically oral and non-literary, I instanced the joke, the story whose end is to astonish us. And I remember the stories of H. G. Wells, counterparts, except in brevity, of his scientific romances. I remember, too, stories which are strongly anecdotal but are none the less modern short stories. Kipling has many examples of this kind of story. So it seems reasonable to suggest that the modern short story can span the whole gamut from the astonishing – Wells – to that based on the almost mystical notion of the epiphany. In other words, any definition of the short story must be tentative, allowing for many apparent contradictions and some genuine ones.

I have suggested that the relation of the modern story to the older parallels that of the novel to the romance. In other words, we assume in the short story, as in the novel, that probability and realism, truth to psychology and to history, are pre-conditions of its being. In fact, as a form it was a later development in prose fiction than the novel, and it arrives more or less simultaneously in disparate literatures, and in English unequivocally in the nineteenth century. Many strands have gone to its making, a notable one being the impulse that made for journalism. In the early eighteenth century, we can see the *Spectator* Papers of Addison and Steele on the edge, as it were, of being short stories in the characterizations of Sir Roger de Coverley, Sir Andrew Freeport, and the rest, and we see something like this later in the century in some of Dr Johnson's *Idler* essays, in the account of Ned Drugget the shopkeeper, for instance. Here, the interest in characterization is much more finely focused than it was in the *Microcosmographie* of John Earle a century earlier.

For me, the first modern short story in English is by Walter Scott, whose fiction marks one of the great watersheds of literature. He was at once a writer of romance in the old style and of novels in the new. He adored the magical, the supernatural, the irrational, all that was sanctified by age and custom. But at the same time he was an extraordinarily acute observer of the behaviour of men in society and of men in specific areas of society. In the development of the novel this was of the greatest importance. In English writing George Eliot and Thomas Hardy both come very considerably out of Scott: his Scotland made Hardy's Wessex possible. Outside England, he taught novelists how to dramatize the life of their country in terms of character and institution and stands, therefore, as the great exemplar behind Balzac in France, Manzoni in Italy, Pushkin and Turgenev in Russia, Cooper and Hawthorne in America. It is fitting that the first modern English short story should be his.

It is 'The Two Drovers', which appeared in *Chronicles of the Canongate* in 1827. Not much more than 5,000 words in length, it is the nearest Scott ever came to writing tragedy, which in this instance arises from the clash of national traditions and temperaments. The two drovers are Robin Oig, a Scots Highlander, and Harry Wakefield, an Englishman from Yorkshire. Friends, they drive their herds together from Scotland south across the border. On the trek they have a misunderstanding about where they should pasture their cattle and they are forced, almost by public opinion as represented by the views of their fellow-drovers, to fight. Harry, having knocked Robin down, holds out his hand to

him in friendship. Robin rejects it; it is against his code to fight
with his fist, his weapon is the dirk, and having been knocked
down, he feels his honour has been besmirched. Next day, he
challenges Harry to fight him in the Highland manner and in
doing so, stabs and kills him. He surrenders to the police and
is tried, sentenced to death, and executed at Carlisle. We are
told:

He met his fate with great firmness, and acknowledged the justice of
his sentence. But he repelled indignantly the observations of those who
accused him of attacking an unarmed man. 'I give a life for the life I
took,' he said, 'and what can I do more?'

V. S. Pritchett has written in *The Living Novel* that 'the sense
and fair play of Wakefield, who cannot believe that enmity will
survive a little amateur boxing, are meaningless to the Highlander. Each is reasonable – but in a different way. The clash
when it comes is tragic; again two kinds of virtue are irreconcilable.' The clash of tradition and temperament is given a precise
focus in Scott. The basic anecdote is transcended, and at the end
we have learned something important about national character
which has been dramatized in speech and gesture.

Two years after 'The Two Drovers' appeared, Prosper Méri-
mée wrote 'Mateo Falcone'. Within two years, a comparable
story had been written in another language, and it is extremely
unlikely that the Frenchman had not read Scott. 'Mateo Falcone'
too is a story about honour in which personal honour mirrors a
national conception of honour: Falcone, the Corsican peasant,
shoots his ten-year-old son because the boy has betrayed the laws
of hospitality and for an official reward has handed over a fugi-
tive from justice to the police. It is a savage and unforgettable
story, written with an economy of words which Scott was incapable of.

Despite Scott's example, in England the short story as we now
know it was a late flowering compared with the story in the
United States, France, and Russia. In the United States in 1842,
reviewing Hawthorne's *Twice-Told Tales*, Edgar Allan Poe
offered a definition of the short story that is still valid. He
approves 'the short prose narrative, requiring from a half-hour
to one or two hours in its perusal'.

The ordinary novel is objectionable, from its length. . . . As it cannot be read at one sitting, it deprives itself, of course, of the immense force derivable from *totality*. Worldly interests intervening during the pauses of perusal, modify, annul, or counteract, to a greater or less degree, the impression of the book. But simple cessation in reading would, of itself, be sufficient to destroy the true unity. In the brief tale, however, the author is enabled to carry out the fulness of his intention, be it what it may. During the hour of its perusal the soul of the reader is at the writer's control. There are no external or extrinsic influences – resulting from weariness or interruption.

A skilful literary artist has constructed a tale. If wise, he has not fashioned his thoughts to accommodate his incidents; but having conceived, with deliberate care, a certain unique or *single* effect to be wrought out, he then invents such incidents – he then combines such effects as may best aid him in establishing this preconceived effect. If his very initial sentence tend not to the outbringing of this effect, then he has failed in his first step. In the whole composition there should be no word written, of which the tendency, direct or indirect, is not to the one pre-established design. And by such means, with such care and skill, a picture is at length painted which leaves in the mind of him who contemplates it with a kindred art, a sense of the fullest satisfaction. The idea of the tale has been presented unblemished, because undisturbed; and this is an end unattainable by the novel. Undue brevity is just as exceptionable here as in the poem; but undue length is yet more to be avoided.

Poe's statement can be criticized, especially for the way he seems to suggest that literary creation is a branch of technology, but it does set out the qualities that, after him, we take for granted in a short story; and these qualities are precisely those we do not find in the Victorian 'short prose narrative'. The passage suggests a reason for the late development of the short story in nineteenth-century England. Poe is obviously wrong when he asserts that the short story is a form superior to the novel; they are different, written and read to satisfy different demands. But the nature of the nineteenth-century novel in England was such as to make it very difficult for the short story as we know it to flourish or even to exist. It was too deeply entrenched in English cultural life; its supremacy was unchallenged. Even the novel's form, or its lack of form, worked against the short story. Disparagingly, Henry James called it a Gladstone bag, a convenient hold-all. Among other things, the short story or what was to be the short story could be crammed into it.

The case of Dickens is instructive here. Apart from his relatively short pieces like *A Christmas Carol* and *The Chimes*, he
wrote a fair number of brief prose narratives that are much less
well known than they deserve to be. They are authentic Dickens
and sometimes are as good as anything in the novels. But hardly
any are short stories in the modern sense and fewer satisfy Poe's
requirements. Most of them appeared in his own magazines
Household Words and *All The Year Round*, in which pride of
place was taken by his novels in their initial serial versions; the
shorter pieces were probably conceived of as little more than
'fillers'. They belong to the older tradition of story-telling in that
they set out to startle and astonish and of course they succeed in
their intentions. One of the most interesting is 'Mugby Junction', though part of its interest lies in that it seems to point
towards a minor category of the novel in the twentieth century, that which, like Thornton Wilder's *The Bridge of San Luis
Rey* and Vicky Baum's *Grand Hotel*, tells a number of disparate stories linked together by a setting in place and time
common to all. 'Mugby Junction' consists of three stories, of
which the first and third are mysterious and sinister, ghost
stories of the railway age, while the second, which is hardly a
story at all, is one of Dickens's most happy pieces of comic
writing, a satire on railway refreshment rooms and on British
attitudes to food as compared with the way such things are done
in France.

When the space at Dickens's disposal is such that selection is
forced upon him, as in *Sketches by Boz*, he seems to come closest
to the modern short story. Those in this collection belong to a
kind of journalism still with us, impressions of the world that are
not documentary only because the subject is seen through a temperament. It was a similar kind of writing through which, in
America half a century later, Stephen Crane and Theodore Dreiser came to fiction and the short story and, in England, Arthur
Morrison and Kipling himself. One of the sketches, 'Births. Mrs
Meek of a son', is a rendering of a universal situation, pride in
new-found paternity and the young father's resentment of his
domineering mother-in-law. It is touching, funny, and true; and
although Dickens wrote later that the tales were often 'extremely
crude and ill-considered, bearing obvious marks of haste and

inexperience', I cannot read it without being reminded of the young Chekhov, who, it is worth remembering, learnt his art in conditions not so unlike the young Dickens.

But Chekhov was fifty years ahead of *Sketches by Boz*, and during that time English writers had made only small progress towards the short story as we know it, as the practice of two of Dickens's greatest successors in the novel shows. In 1858, George Eliot published the three stories called *Scenes of Clerical Life*. They are prentice work and carry much too heavy a weight of authorial comment. These are defects that a novel may bear and remain memorable, but they sink a short story without trace. However, we do not read *Scenes of Clerical Life* as short stories. They are short novels and were written as such.

Then there is Hardy. Although his poetry includes many splendid short stories, a fact which in itself throws some light on the nature of the modern story, he was a traditionalist, and his views on fiction were old-fashioned even while he was writing his greatest novels. He did, however, publish four collections of stories, and they are at their best when at their furthest remove from the modern short story. The best is probably 'The Three Strangers', in which, on a wild March night in the eighteen-twenties, three men who are unknown to one another seek refuge from the storm at a christening party in a remote Wessex cottage. The three men are respectively the public executioner, his prospective victim, who has recently escaped prison and whom he will hang in a matter of days, and the condemned man's brother. The story has been criticized for relying too heavily on coincidence; but it is the coincidences, and the grimness of them, that give it a power of the wholly traditional kind and make it a story that once heard no man would forget and that any man, on the right occasion, would wish to tell to others. Here, Hardy's style is the counterpart of the speaking voice, repetitive, discursive. 'The Three Strangers' and such another story by Hardy as 'The Distracted Preacher' are reminders that the modern short story is not the only kind of story and that great things may still be done in the old 'oral' form.

But there are times when Hardy seems to be flirting with the newer story, and then problems arise; as with 'The Son's Veto', for instance. T. O. Beachcroft picks it out for special praise in his book on the short story *The Modest Art*, calling it 'a true example of the modern short story'. What has happened here, I think, is that Beachcroft, a fine short-story writer himself, is praising the story he has educed, in the light of his knowledge of modern stories, from Hardy's tale. The given situation could certainly be that of a modern story. Sophy is a country girl employed as a servant by a country clergyman's wife, because of whose illness Sophy rejects the proposal of a young gardener, Sam. After his wife's death, the clergyman, Mr Twycott, knowing he is committing 'moral suicide', marries her and they have a son. Mr Twycott dies and Sophy, with her son away at school, lapses into invalidism. By chance, she encounters Sam again, who is now a successful market-gardener. He proposes to her and she is willing to marry him. But her son, now a clergyman who has been educated into a snob, forces her to promise that she will not marry Sam. When she dies, her funeral procession passes Sam's shop outside London:

The man, whose eyes were wet, held his hat in his hand as the vehicles moved by; while from the mourning coach a young smooth-shaven priest in a high waistcoat looked black as a cloud at the shopkeeper standing there.

It is an effective ending, and there can be no doubt that Hardy handles the story, as Beachcroft says, 'with the greatest sympathy'. Yet the effect throughout is curiously muffled; Hardy seems to do little more with his material than report it. All the same, it is not difficult to get from the bare anecdote alone some feeling of how Chekhov would have handled it and what he might have made of it.

The change to the specifically modern short story in English writing was no doubt less sudden and dramatic than it appears now; but it can be dated fairly precisely. In October 1877, R. L. Stevenson, ten years younger than Hardy, published his first short story, 'A Lodging for the Night'. It is an imaginary account of the experiences of the French poet François Villon on a bitterly cold night in the Paris of November 1456. He is with 'some of the thievish crew with whom he consorted' when there is a sudden quarrel, and one of the company is stabbed to death. Villon flees into the deserted snow-bound streets and in the porch of a ruined house comes upon the corpse of a prostitute; 'she was freezing cold, and rigid like a stick'. Going through her clothes, he discovers two paltry coins hidden in her stocking and then, as he pockets them, finds that his friends have robbed him of his own money. In his rage he throws the coins he has taken from the dead body into the snow and, when he goes back to look for them, can find only one. He is penniless and shelterless, and wanders the streets in terror: he too may die of exposure, like the prostitute he has robbed. His terror is increased when he passes a street corner where, not so long before, a woman and her child had been devoured by wolves.

In the end, he is taken in by an old knight, the representative of the obsolescent values of chivalry which Villon despises. Waiting for the old man to bring him food, he assesses the room he is in. ' "Seven pieces of plate," he said. "If there had been ten, I would have risked it." ' With an insolent, cynical honesty, Villon tells the old warrior about himself; the old man is horrified and he ushers Villon out.

This is how the story ends:

> 'God pity you,' said the lord of Brisetout at the door.
> 'Good-bye, papa,' returned Villon, with a yawn. 'Many thanks for the cold mutton.'
> The door closed behind him. The dawn was breaking over the white roofs. A chill uncomfortable morning ushered in the day. Villon stood and heartily stretched himself in the middle of the road.
> 'A very dull old gentleman,' he thought. 'I wonder what his goblets may be worth.'

'A Lodging for the Night' is not a satisfying story. It is subtitled 'A Story of François Villon', but if we did not know this, would we find it so compelling? It depends for its effect on knowledge that is not derivable from the narrative. In other words, the story does not quite stand by itself, exist aesthetically in its own right.

All the same, 'A Lodging for the Night' is remarkable; as an evocation of intense cold, as a re-creation of late medieval Paris, as a rendering of a man of genius who was perhaps a revolutionary thinker and certainly in the world's eyes a great rogue. The rendering is everything; it fulfils utterly Conrad's definition of the writer's purpose: 'to make you see'. Indeed, the narrator as such seems to have disappeared from the story entirely. This may best be shown, perhaps, by a contrast with what is admittedly an extreme example of the narrator only too visibly at work, the first paragraph of Hardy's story 'For Conscience' Sake':

Whether the utilitarian or the intuitive theory of the moral sense be upheld, it is beyond question that there are a few subtle-souled persons with whom the absolute gratuitousness of an act of reparation is an inducement to perform it; while exhortation as to its necessity would breed excuses for leaving it undone. The case of Mr Millborne and Mrs Frankland particularly illustrates this, and perhaps something more . . .

Stevenson's place in English writing is a strange one. He was not a great novelist, except perhaps in *Weir of Hermiston*, which was unfinished at his death (at the age of forty-four), or a great poet, and he was a great short-story writer only once or twice. Yet it is difficult not to see him as a great writer. He brought even to his lightest works the scrupulousness of treatment and seriousness of execution that other writers have generally reserved for their most considered works. It is this that gives *Treasure Island*, for example, its classic status, its particular and altogether special eminence as a book for children. It was, it seems to me, his romantic temperament, his response to the past and antipathy to the prosaic present that prevented his being, except occasionally, a great writer of the modern short story, which is concerned very much with the immediate. Yet towards the end of his relatively short life he was ready and able to embrace the immediate; as is made manifest in his greatest short story, 'The Beach at Falesa'.

It brought a new theme into English fiction, one we associate both with Conrad and with Maugham, the interaction between the exotic, more precisely, the Pacific scene and its peoples, and the Western European. Stevenson wrote it on Samoa in 1891 and he knew exactly what he had done. It was, he wrote in a letter, 'the first realistic South Sea story',

> . . . I mean with real South Sea characters and details of life. Everybody else who has tried that I have seen, got carried away by the romance, and ended with a kind of sugar candy sham epic, and the whole effect was lost – there was no etching, no human grin, consequently no conviction. Now I have got the smell, and the look of the thing a good deal. You will know more about the South Seas after you have read my little tale than if you had read a library.

In other words, it is a work of realism, containing, among other things, a sexual frankness we find nowhere else in Stevenson and uncommon anywhere in English writing of the time. And, more than this, he expresses the contemporary world as it were through the speaking voice of that world. 'The Beach at Falesá' is a triumph of writing in the vernacular; or, rather, Stevenson most cunningly suggests the vernacular, for the story is told by a Mr Wiltshire, a trader who aims at making enough money to enable him to return to England and keep a pub.

Wiltshire goes to Falesá to manage the store there for his company. Before he disembarks he learns that all his predecessors have died mysteriously. Later, he meets Mr Case, the other white trader on the island, and through him a native girl, Uma, whom he marries against all his notions of proper behaviour by white men in the South Seas. Then he finds himself under a mysterious tabu; his trade is non-existent; and Case, who professes to fear the consequences of association with him, shuns him. In time, Wiltshire finds out that Case exercises a reign of terror over the natives in order to maintain his monopoly of the copra crop. The source of the man's power, he discovers, is that he is worshipped as a devil. He demolishes Case's 'shrine' with dynamite and kills him.

The story ends:

My public house? Not a bit of it, nor ever likely. I'm stuck here, I fancy. I don't like to leave the kids, you see; and – there's no use talking – they're better off here than they would be in a white man's country; though Ben took the eldest up to Auckland, where he's being schooled with the best. But what bothers me is the girls. They're only half-castes, of course; I know that as well as you do, and there's nobody thinks less of half-castes than I do; but they're mine, and about all I've got. I can't reconcile my mind to their taking up with Kanakas, and I'd like to know where I'm to find the whites?

What emerges from Wiltshire's self-told story is the portrait of a man uneducated, prejudiced, and ignobly decent, one of the first representations, as V. S. Pritchett has observed in his introduction to the Pilot Press's 1945 edition of *Novels and Stories* by Robert Louis Stevenson, 'of the very common, common man who has since become quite a figure; and has succeeded the gentleman'. As a story of colonial exploitation and its effects on exploited and exploiters alike, 'The Beach at Falesá' has links with stories by Kipling and Conrad. In the character of Mr

Case, Stevenson anticipates villains in Conrad such as Jones and Ricardo and even Kurtz. Rather more than fifty pages in length, 'The Beach at Falesa' is sometimes referred to as a short novel. It seems to me without question a short story: it has a double unity, that of theme, for everything is subordinated to the account of Wiltshire's defeat of Case, and that of tone, the speaking voice of Wiltshire.

How did Stevenson come to achieve what he did in 'The Beach at Falesa'? The answer, I suspect, has something to do with French writers and with Flaubert in particular. It is impossible to exaggerate the importance of Flaubert in the history of English and American fiction in the nineteenth century, for he changed the nature of prose narrative and changed by his example the attitudes of writers towards their craft; how, some quotations from his letters will show:

To desire to give verse-rhythms to prose, yet to leave it prose and very much prose, and to write about ordinary life as histories and epics are written, yet without falsifying the subject, is perhaps an absurd idea. . . . But may also be an experiment and very original. . . .

I don't agree with you that there is anything worth while to be done with the character of the *ideal Artist*; he would be a monster. Art is not made to paint the exceptions; and I feel an unconquerable repugnance to putting on paper something from out of my heart. I even think that a novelist *hasn't the right to express his opinion* on any subject whatever. Has the good God ever uttered it, his opinion? That is why there are not a few that choke me which I should like to spit out, but which I swallow. Why say them, in fact? The first comer is more interesting than Monsieur Gustave Flaubert, because he is more *general* and therefore more typical. . . .

I believe that the rounding of the phrase is nothing. But that *writing well* is everthing, because 'writing well is at the same time perceiving, thinking well and saying well' (Buffon). The last term is then dependent on the other two, since one has to feel strongly, so as to think, and to think, so as to express.

All the bourgeois can have a great deal of heart and delicacy, be full of the best sentiments and the greatest virtues, without becoming, for all that, artists. In short, I believe that the form and the matter are two subtleties, two entities, neither of which can exist without the other. . . .

The artist should be in his work, like God in creation, invisible and all-powerful; he should be felt everywhere and seen nowhere. And then art should be raised above personal affections and nervous susceptibilities. It is time to give it the precision of the physical sciences by means of pitiless method. For me the capital difficulty none the less continues to be style, form, the indefinable beauty, which is the result of the conception itself, and which is the splendour of truth, as Plato used to say. . . .

In these passages Flaubert is asserting the necessity of objectivity on the writer's part and the all-importance of style, in the sense of exactness of rendering. Implicit, too, is the contention that the writer's proper material is the ordinary. Contained in Flaubert's view of writing, then, is a theory of what was to be called Realism and, a little later, Naturalism. Flaubert's notions of art are classical and at extreme odds to what we normally consider romanticism and also, in fiction, at extreme odds with the novel as written both by mid-nineteenth-century English novelists and by the Russian masters, the kind of novel Henry James called fluid puddings.

Flaubert embodied his theories of art in *Madame Bovary* and *L'Éducation sentimentale* particularly, works marked, among other things, by what can only be called misanthropy, by a disgust with his age and with the people who lived in it. He called it the age of *muflisme*, which may be translated as swinishness and which he contrasted with the pagan and the Christian eras which had preceded it. But how could swinishness or, for that matter, the background of nineteenth-century industrialism, be made into art? The answer lay in treatment, by writing of ordinary life 'as histories and epics are written'. Treatment became almost everything and subject was relatively unimportant. The consequences of this for writing have been profound. Quite simply, it became possible for writers to deal with characters who were poor, humble, or afflicted as beings in their own right and not as eccentric, marginal, or comic figures. Here, Flaubert himself is the great innovator.

For, contemptuous as he was of the world he lived in and its values, which were enshrined especially in the *bourgeoisie*, the great middle class, he reserved his respect and his compassion for certain members of the poor whose lives exemplified fidelity, humility, endurance, and acceptance. The great illustration of this is his story, 'A Simple Heart', which begins:

For half a century the women of Pont-L'Evêque envied Mme
Aubain her maidservant Felicité.
In return for a hundred francs a year she did all the cooking and
the housework, the sewing, the washing, and the ironing. She could
bridle a horse, fatten poultry, and churn butter, and she remained
faithful to her mistress, who was by no means an easy person to get
on with.

In something like ten thousand words Flaubert tells the
story of the life of Felicité, a life in which, to the outside
world, nothing has happened. 'A Simple Heart' is a wonderful
example of Flaubert's art and the 'pitiless method' that produced it. It is steeped in memories from his own childhood.
He wrote it to show that he was capable, as Robert Baldick
has said in his introduction to his Penguin Classics translation,
of 'telling a tender, moving story in a detached, unemo-
tional style'. He was following that law which, according to
Wyndham Lewis in *The Writer and the Absolute*, 'in all the
arts that parallel nature', obliges the artist 'to a fanatical
scrupulosity, as it were a physical incapacity to depart from
nature's truths in exchange for any other'. We know that in
order to render Felicité's last illness accurately he consulted
a textbook on pneumonia; he took similar care with the details of the Corpus Christi procession; and from the museum
at Rouen he borrowed a stuffed parrot, which served as a
model for Loulou, Felicité's pet. The result is a complete
objectivity.

Flaubert died in 1880, the prose writer to whom serious
young writers in France and Britain alike put themselves to
school. His effect on English writing is apparent within a few
years of his death. It may be seen, I think, in Stevenson's Mr
Wiltshire in 'The Beach at Falesa'. With no pastoral background like Felicité's, and vulgar and ignoble in his circumstances, in the end, through Stevenson's intense focus on him
and him alone, he has the dignity that comes from an inarticulate decency.

Flaubert's example was reinforced by that of his disciple Guy
de Maupassant, who at the end of his relatively short life in 1893
was the most famous short-story writer in the world. It is worth
remembering that Chekhov himself was called by Tolstoy the

Russian Maupassant in that they shared a mastery of craft and fertility of imagination. In the Anglo-Saxon countries Maupassant's impact was immediate. The revolt against Victorian values, especially against the silence on sex, had begun, and among other things Maupassant was seen as a liberator.

He loses by being read in translation, for English tends to conventionalize his prose. What cannot be obscured even in translation is its speed; and this, no less than the liberation in subject-matter he offered, was influential in a quite vital way. Here *The Yellow Book*, the *avant-garde* magazine of the eighteen-nineties, is instructive. Among the new writers it published was Arnold Bennett, who was twenty-seven at the time. 'A Letter Home' is not an especially good story but it has its interest, as the first two paragraphs show:

Rain was falling – it had fallen steadily through the night – but the sky showed promise of fairer weather. As the first streaks of dawn appeared, the wind died away, and the young leaves on the trees were almost silent. The birds were insistently clamorous, vociferating times without number that it was a healthy spring morning and good to be alive.

A little, bedraggled crowd stood before the park gates, awaiting the hour named on the notice board when they would be admitted to such lodging and shelter as iron seats and overspreading branches might afford. . . .

The prose of these paragraphs has a speed and economy that sets it apart from the prose of the mid-nineteenth-century novelists. For Bennett, who by his own admission at this time knew the French literature of the century much better than he knew English, the derivation is certainly from Flaubert and Maupassant.

Another instance from the same time, interesting both for the manner of its prose and for its content, is Arthur Morrison's *Tales of Mean Streets*, published in 1894. 'Lizerunt', the first story in the volume begins:

Somewhere in the register was written the name Elizabeth Hunt; but seventeen years after the entry the spoken name was Lizerunt. Lizerunt worked at a pickle factory, and appeared abroad in an elaborate and shabby costume, usually supplemented by a white apron. She was something of a beauty. That is to say, her cheeks were very red, her teeth were very large and white, her nose small and snub, and her fringe was long and shiny; while her face, new-washed, was susceptible of a high polish. Many such girls are married at sixteen, but Lizerunt was belated, and had never had a bloke at all.

The stories are of low life in the East End and the prose is direct, colloquial, and ironical: Morrison is obviously not writing for an East End readership but for one that is consumed with curiosity about it. Morrison, indeed, is writing about scenes similar to those of writers in the United States who were almost exactly contemporary, Stephen Crane and Theodore Dreiser. Beginning as newspaper reporters, they had gone on, naturally as it were, to become short-story writers and novelists. What we see in their work, as in Crane's, is the influence of French Naturalism, as it is exemplified in the novels of Zola, with their emphasis on the importance of environment in the shaping of character.

The influence of Naturalism tied in with the influence of journalism. During the last decades of the century developments in printing, technology, and a mass increase in literacy went hand in hand. Together, these phenomena brought into existence the popular press in its daily, weekly, and monthly manifestations, which brought into existence a new kind of writer, often, though not necessarily, lower middle-class in origin. The classic document on this and on its effect upon writing and writers is George Gissing's novel *New Grub Street*, which treats among other things of the growing commercialization of literature. Typical of the new writers were H. G. Wells and Arnold Bennett; indeed, Bennett's first published works appeared almost simultaneously in *The Yellow Book* and in the weekly *Tit-Bits*, which culturally was the bottom of the new journalism. The new journalism, at whatever level, at once catered for and fostered curiosity about the ordinary, the immediate, the everyday. But so also, for quite different reasons, did the Naturalists. For the first time for generations popular writing and literature shared common territory and often a common content. Urban working-class life suddenly existed in literature in its own right, as it did not, for instance, even in Dickens's novels.

At the same time, the manner, the prose of the serious writer and especially of the short-story writer approximated in many ways more and more to that of the journalist. Indeed, the first great exemplar of this in British English had burst upon the astonished world some half a dozen years before Wells, Bennett, Morrison, and Stephen Crane and even Stevenson in 'The Beach at Falesa'. He was Rudyard Kipling.

In the United States the short story had been in being for a full half-century before Stevenson wrote 'The Beach at Falesá'. In 1837 it had established itself as a wholly idiosyncratic national art form with the appearance of Nathaniel Hawthorne's *Twice-Told Tales*; and after Hawthorne had come at least three other masters of the form by 1890. The reasons for this emergence of the short story in America, at once so dramatic and so triumphant, are necessarily obscure. Professor A. Walton Litz suggests in the introductory chapter of his *Major American Short Stories* that American writers

were led to the short story in part by what Henry James would have called the 'thinness' of American life, its lack of a rich and complex social texture: the brief poetic tale, rather than the sprawling novel of manners, seemed the natural form for their intense but isolated experiences. At the same time they were acutely responsive to the developments of English and European Romanticism. This collision of local and fragmented social experience with a cosmopolitan artistic vision proved ideal for the growth of the short story.

And we can say with absolute certainty that American writers in the nineteenth century were fortunate in having before their eyes the shaping example of Hawthorne's tales and the theories of the short story that Poe had derived from it. For the American writer the short story was, so to speak, 'there', already existing.

'If in any of my productions terror has been the thesis, I maintain the terror is not of Germany' – i.e., the Gothic – 'but of the soul.' Thus Poe, in the preface to his first volume of stories, *Tales of the Grotesque and Arabesque*, in 1840. Anglo-Saxon critics have often been pained by the nature of Poe's achievement as short-story writer and poet and by his enormous international reputation. By normal standards his prose is execrable; he seems to have no restraint and to write as it were at the top of his voice; his material is crude and sensational and his designs on the reader altogether too palpable. His readers in this century, R. P. Blackmur pointed out in his afterword to the New English Library edition of Poe, have been the young – and, he might have added, the uneducated; but as Blackmur also pointed out, 'great writers in France – Baudelaire, Rimbaud, Mallarmé, Valéry – made out of Poe a great figure and, indeed, a master craftsman'. He remains still to the Anglo-Saxon critic a formidably challenging writer.

Poe was the pioneer of what we call science fiction and the virtual inventor of the detective story. Stories like 'The Murders in the Rue Morgue' and 'The Purloined Letter' still delight by their concentration and their relentless use of ratiocinative logic, while their ingenuity was only equalled, and then not surpassed, by Conan Doyle's Sherlock Holmes stories half a century later. But his real contribution to the form was much more important than these. It was, precisely, the stories of the terror of the soul.

Some, it must be admitted, are pretty obvious constructions, ingenious machines for scaring unsophisticated readers. In his essay 'The Philosophy of Composition' Poe tells how he wrote his poem 'The Raven' beginning with the word 'nevermore' as the most mournful and chilling he knew and working backwards from that, devising his fable in the process. But this very obvious method of working is not by any means invariably Poe's way. Take 'The Fall of the House of Usher', probably his most remarkable story in that it seems to contain and sum up so much of him. It appears, at first sight, a farrago of extreme Romantic nonsense; but of course it is much more than that. Somewhere, W. H. Auden refers to the 'imaginary landscape' of Poe's poetry, and the landscape of the stories rarely mirrors that of North America. Indeed, the United States and its people scarcely exist in them. The detective stories are set in Paris, which Poe knew through the novels of Balzac and Eugène Sue. For the most part, though, the landscape is derived from that of the Romantic poets, Coleridge and Shelley in particular, and furnished with the accoutrements of the Gothic novel, ruined castles, dungeons, torture-chambers, and tombs. 'The Fall of the House of Usher' suggests Scotland as seen through the novels of Scott, an impression intensified by the name of the central character, Roderick Usher.

It is an almost empty, deserted landscape. No other house or habitation exists in the story. There are only three main characters, Roderick, his sister Madeline, and the narrator, whose name we never know. There are one or two references to peasantry, and to these we are indebted for a valuable piece of information:

I had learned, too, the very remarkable fact that the stem of the Usher race, all time-honoured as it was, had put forth, at no period, any enduring branch; in other words the entire family lay in the direct line of descent, and had always, with very trifling and very temporary variation, so lain ... it was this deficiency, perhaps, of collateral issue, and the consequent undeviating transmission, from sire to son, of the patrimony with the name, which had, at length, so identified the two as to merge the original title of the estate in the quaint and equivocal appellation of the 'House of Usher' – an appellation which seemed to include, in the minds of the peasantry who used it, both the family and the family mansion.

The house, then, may be seen as an outer integument, a body, in which the soul, the family, exists. It is, in other words, an exteriorization of a family marked for generations by extreme inbreeding and of which now only two members survive, Roderick and Madeline, twins between whom 'sympathies of a scarcely intelligible nature had always existed'. The suggestion of an incestuous relationship between them could hardly be plainer.

The narrator, an old friend of Roderick's, perhaps his only friend, comes to the house in response to an urgent summons from Roderick. Approaching it, he is oppressed as in a dream by the sense that 'about the whole mansion and domain there hung an atmosphere peculiar to themselves and their immediate vicinity – an atmosphere which had no affinity with the air of heaven, but which had reeked up from the decayed trees, and the grey wall, and the silent tarn – a pestilent and mystic vapour, dull, sluggish, faintly discernible, and leaden-hued'. He scans more narrowly 'the real aspect of the building'.

Its principal feature seemed to be that of an excessive antiquity. The discolouration of ages had been great. Minute fungi overspread the whole exterior, hanging in a fine tangled web-work from the eaves. Yet all this was apart from any extraordinary dilapidation. No portion of the masonry had fallen; and there appeared to be a wild inconsistency between the still perfect adaptation of parts, and the crumbling condition of the individual stones. . . . *Perhaps the eye of a scrutinizing observer might have discovered a barely perceptible fissure, which, extended from the roof of the building in front, made its way down the wall in a zigzag direction, until it became lost in the sullen waters of the tarn.*

I have italicized the last sentence of the paragraph because I think one may discern in it the key to the story and the unifying factor between the house and its inhabitants.

Entering the House of Usher, the narrator is led into a room 'very large and lofty' in which Usher is sitting. But the paragraph must be quoted:

The windows were long, narrow, and pointed, and at so vast a distance from the black oaken floor as to be inaccessible from within. Feeble gleams of encrimsoned light made their way through the trellised panes, and served to render sufficiently distinct the more prominent objects around; the eye, however, struggled in vain to reach the remoter angles of the chamber, or the recesses of the vaulted and fretted ceiling. Dark draperies hung upon the walls. The general furniture was profuse, comfortless, antique, and tattered. Many books and musical instruments lay scattered about, but failed to give any vitality to the scene. I felt that I breathed an atmosphere of sorrow. An air of stern, deep, and irredeemable gloom hung over and pervaded all.
Upon my entrance, Usher arose from a sofa. . . .

Vast though the chamber is, it surely suggests a dungeon and, beyond that, a tomb. The motif of the tomb persists throughout the story; in, for instance, the description of Usher's painting, which Poe, anticipating future developments in the visual arts by seventy years, calls an abstraction:

A small picture presented the interior of an immensely long rectangular vault or tunnel with low walls, smooth, white, and without interruption or device. Certain accessory points of the design served well to convey the idea that this excavation lay at an exceeding depth below the surface of the earth. No outlet was observed in any portion of its vast extent, and no torch or other artificial source of light was visible; yet a flood of intense rays rolled throughout, and bathed the whole in a ghastly and inappropriate splendour.

In 'The Fall of the House of Usher' immensity and confinement seem to be one.

After several days, Usher tells the narrator abruptly that the Lady Madeline is no more and that he intends to preserve her corpse for a fortnight within one of the vaults. The two men carry the coffin to its resting place. After the interment, Usher's condition deteriorates. 'There were times, indeed,' the narrator tells us,

when I thought his unceasingly agitated mind was labouring with some oppressive secret, to divulge which he struggled for the necessary courage. . . . It was no wonder that his condition terrified – that it infected me. I felt creeping upon me, by slow yet certain degrees, the wild influences of his own fantastic yet impressive superstitions.

When he retires to bed on the seventh or eighth day after the Lady Madeline's interment the narrator is feeling most deeply affected by these feelings, and Usher comes to his room, also agitated. The narrator attempts to soothe him by reading to him a medieval tale that seems uncannily to mirror the circumstances the two men are in. When he reads in the story that the silver shield hanging on the wall fell to the floor 'with a mighty great and terrible ringing sound', he becomes aware 'of a distinct, hollow, metallic, and clangorous, yet apparently muffled reverberation', while Usher, his eyes 'bent fixedly before him', speaks 'in a low, hurried, and gibbering murmur':

'. . . not hear it? – Yes, I hear it, and *have* heard it. Long – long – long many minutes, many days, have I heard it – yet I dared not – oh, pity me, miserable wretch that I am – I dared not – I dared not speak. *We have put her living in the tomb.*'

In a final outburst, he cries: 'Madman! I tell you that she now stands without the door!' As if in response to these words, the 'huge antique panels' draw slowly back and reveal 'the lofty and enshrouded figure of the Lady Madeline of Usher'.

There was blood upon her white robes, and the evidence of some bitter struggle upon every portion of her emaciated frame. For a moment she remained trembling and reeling to and fro upon the threshold, then, with a low moaning cry, fell heavily inward upon the person of her brother, and in her violent and now final death-agonies, bore him to the floor a corpse, and a victim to the terrors he had anticipated.

Again, there is the plain suggestion of an overmastering, unnatural love. The narrator flees the house:

Suddenly there shot along the path a wild light, and I turned to see whence a gleam so unusual could have issued; for the vast house and its shadows were alone behind me. The radiance was that of the full, setting, and blood-red moon, which now shone vividly through that once barely discernible fissure of which I have spoken as extending from the roof of the building, in a zigzag direction, to the base. While I gazed, this fissure rapidly widened – there came a fierce breath of the whirlwind – the entire orb of the satellite burst at once upon my sight –

my brain reeled as I saw the mighty walls rushing asunder – there was a long tumultuous shouting sound like the voice of a thousand waters – and the deep and dank tarn at my feet closed sullenly and silently over the fragments of the 'House of Usher'.

By any standard, the story is grotesquely overwritten. But it is not quite absurd. It is something more than a mere exercise in the pornography of death. So closely identified is the house of Usher with the family of Usher that when in the final paragraph of the story the fissure widens and splits the facade, we realize that what we have seen depicted is the disintegration of the human psyche. Poe, as D. H. Lawrence said, was a sort of scientist of the abnormal romantic mind.

The power of Poe's writing, and its influence, gave authority to a strain in American writing that has been constant in it since its beginning, what is called the Gothic. This had its origins in historical necessity, the situation in which the writer found himself in the first days of the United States, rather than in literary fashion, though that was a shaping contributory factor. When we look at the great European stories, those of Turgenev, Maupassant, Chekhov, Kipling, Joyce, Verga, Babel, Lawrence, O'Connor, Pritchett, we feel behind each one of them the presence and pressure of a whole society, dense, crowded, complex. We feel this no less strongly when the story is focused upon a single individual. We are conscious that he is linked to his fellows in a traditional, long established world by a thousand almost invisible threads.

We have the pronouncements of Cooper, Simms, and Hawthorne to show that nothing like this was possible in American writing in its early days. Hawthorne maintained that his fictions were romances, not novels, since in the absence of society in the English or European sense no one could write a novel. And, as Richard Chase showed in *The American Novel and Its Tradition*, the emphasis in American fiction from Cooper onwards has been on the solitary hero, who is often larger than life because he is solitary. These are the commonplaces of criticism, but they indicate a frequent divergence between American fiction and European that seems fundamental. Poe is important here because his stories often appear to represent a *reductio ad absurdum*. In 'The Fall of the House of Usher', for instance, there is no sense of an existing society at all.

Hawthorne, who was older than Poe by five years, was in every way a much finer writer. His writing seems so modern that, reading him today, it is impossible not to be struck by his affinity with Kafka. He seems to write as a man poised on the frontier between reality and dream, between his own times and the historical past.

His stories, then, are riddling and are capable of more than one interpretation. He explored and exploited the use of what Yvor Winters in *In Defence of Reason* called 'alternative possibilities', and seems to have inherited from his Puritan forbears, the guilt for whose sins he seems to have taken upon himself, a tradition of allegory, which he transmuted into something subtly different and infinitely richer, symbolism. As Daniel G. Hoffman has written in *Form and Fable in American Fiction*, 'Allegory was designed for the elucidation of certainty; they' – Hawthorne and Herman Melville – 'used it in the service of search and scepticism, and, at times, of comedic affirmation of human values. In the process they transformed allegorism into a symbolic method.'

The early story 'My Kinsman, Major Molineux' is characteristic of Hawthorne's method. It begins with a paragraph of necessary historical information, the first two sentences of which are:

After the kings of Great Britain had assumed the right of appointing the colonial governors, the measures of the latter seldom met with the ready and general approbation which had been paid to those of their predecessors, under the original charters. The people looked with most jealous scrutiny to the exercise of power which did not emanate from themselves.

That last sentence may be a clue to the interpretation, or to one interpretation of the story, which is set in New England in the early eighteenth century.

The story proper begins with the second paragraph: 'It was near nine o'clock of a moonlight evening when a boat crossed the ferry with a single passenger.' The river is not the Styx but it is obviously likely to be a boundary between two worlds or at any rate two ways of life. The single passenger is a youth of seventeen named Robin who has come to town in search of his distinguished kinsman Major Molineux and through him of a

fortune. He expects to profit by his kinsman's generous intentions, for, as he says, 'I have the name of being a shrewd youth.'

Robin's life, and his name suggests among other things
honesty and perhaps rustic naivety, has until now been passed in
a pastoral round of simple pieties, in what one might think an
idealized version of the frontier and of the founding fathers'
dreams. The city proves very different. Asking the way to the
house of his kinsman, Major Molineux, he is rebuffed, laughed
at, threatened with the stocks. He demands of a passer-by the
whereabouts of his kinsman. 'Watch here an hour,' the man answers, 'and Major Molineux will pass by', and he unmuffles his
face.

Robin gazed with dismay and astonishment on the unprecedented
physiognomy of the speaker. The forehead with its double prominence,
the broad hooked nose, the shaggy eyebrows, and fiery eyes were those
which he had noticed at the inn, but the man's complexion had under-
gone a singular, or, more properly, a twofold change. One side of his
face blazed an intense red, while the other was as black as midnight, the
division line being the broad bridge of the nose; and a mouth which
seemed to extend from ear to ear was black or red, in contrast to the
colour of the cheek. The effect was as if two individual devils, a fiend
of fire and a fiend of darkness, had united themselves to form this
infernal visage. The stranger grinned at Robin's face, muffled his
parti-coloured features, and was out of sight in a moment.

Robin settles himself on the church steps to await his kinsman
and is joined by a gentleman. They hear noises, the sound of a
trumpet, wild and confused laughter. The whole neighbourhood
is now aroused and a mighty stream of people rolls slowly towards the church, in the midst of them their leader, a single horseman in military uniform, holding a drawn sword. As he passes he
stares at Robin. He is, of course, the parti-coloured man whom
Robin had challenged an hour earlier. He thunders a command,
and the trumpets sound. The shouts and laughter die away.

. . . there remained only a universal hum, allied to silence. Right before
Robin's eyes was an uncovered cart. There the torches blazed the
brightest, there the moon shone out like day, and there in tar-and-
feathery dignity, sat his kinsman, Major Molineux.

He was an elderly man, of large and majestic person, and strong,
square features, betokening a steady soul; but steady as it was, his

enemies had found means to shake it. . . . His whole frame was agitated by a quick and continual tremor, which his pride strove to quell, even in these circumstances of overwhelming humiliation. But perhaps the bitterest pang of all was when his eyes met those of Robin; for he evidently knew him on the instant, as the youth stood witnessing the disgrace of a head grown grey in honour. They stared at each other in silence, and Robin's knees shook, and his hair bristled, with a mixture of pity and terror.

Though the question is not posed by Hawthorne, we are bound to pose it: who is at the centre of the ridicule? Robin, surely, as much as if not more than his kinsman. He hears laughter all about him, and it comes particularly, it seems, from the persons he has encountered and challenged in the town since his arrival from the country. The laughter grows. And then:

The contagion was spreading among the multitude, when all at once it seized upon Robin, and he sent forth a shout of laughter that echoed through the street – every man shook his sides, every man emptied his lungs, but Robin's shout was the loudest there.

The procession resumes its march, and Robin and the gentleman are left alone on the church steps. Here are the last lines of the story:

'Will you be kind enough to show me the way to the ferry?' said he, after a moment's pause.
'You have, then, adopted a new subject of inquiry?' observed his companion, with a smile.
'Why, yes, sir,' replied Robin, rather dryly. 'Thanks to you, and to my other friends, I have at last met my kinsman, and he will scarce desire to see my face again. I begin to grow weary of a town life, sir. Will you show me the way to the ferry?'
'No, my good friend Robin – not tonight, at least,' said the gentleman. 'Some days hence, if you wish it, I will speed you on your journey. Or, if you prefer to remain with us, perhaps, as you are a shrewd youth, you may rise in the world without the help of your kinsman, Major Molineux.'

'My Kinsman, Major Molineux' seems to me essentially a mysterious story, though some elements in it can be cleared up easily enough. Many of the rioters are dressed as American Indians, but this was a common device in colonial insurrections against the British, a means of disguise and also, perhaps, a sort of sympathetic magic by which normally law-abiding citizens could take on the savagery of the Indian. The man with the parti-coloured face can be explained similarly, even though Hawthorne himself seems to invite us to speculate upon his symbolic nature. What could be more natural than that the leader of a rising against authority would seek to remain unidentified and therefore don a mummer's guise? Taken at this level, the story deals with the adventures of a rustic youth who blunders into a civil disturbance. But questions remain.

Plainly, the story is one of initiation, initiation into the nature of the real world. This is to say, it is about the loss of innocence, for the town of the story is, we may think, a miniature Vanity Fair. Also and very obviously, it is about the necessity for a man to stand on his own feet: power, as Hawthorne suggests in the first paragraph of the story, should emanate from a man's self. By an extension of this, the story may be taken as a parable of the American colonies on the verge of the Revolutionary War; perhaps, even, a parable of what James called the 'complex fate' entailed in being an American, a significant part of which consisted in a 'superstitious veneration' for things English or European. But why is Robin's laughter the loudest of all? Is it a recognition that his pretensions and his naivety have put him in a false position? Is it ironical, an expression of disillusionment? Is it the delighted acknowledgement that a super-ego figure has been overthrown? Certainly, it seems to be a laughter of release. And who – or what – is the gentleman who waits with him on the church steps and who, we are told, accosts him 'in a tone of real kindness'?

A later story of more universal scope, richer in its ambiguities and perhaps Hawthorne's finest story, is 'Young Goodman Brown'. Again, it is an initiation story, initiation into sin. The setting is Salem at the end of the seventeenth century, the occasion All Souls' Eve, traditionally a time of terror throughout Christendom as it was in pre-Christian times, for it is the night when the dead rise and walk the earth. On this night, young Goodman Brown, a youth three months married, goes on a journey. It is a journey into the forest, and we know the associations the forest had for the Puritans of New England; indeed Brown seems to undertake his journey as though in a state of neurotic compulsion. His young wife Faith – the significance of the name needs no underlining, though its allegorical implications are never merely mechanical – pleads with him not to leave her on this night of all nights of the year. He is not to be dissuaded, but determines that 'after this one night', he will cling to her skirts and follow her to heaven.

Alone in the darkness of the forest, he is frightened, for the forest is the devil's province. Then he sees a man 'in grave and decent attire' waiting for him and who chides him for being late. 'Faith kept me back awhile', Brown explains, and we note the ambiguity of the statement. Brown protests his scruples about the venture that is at hand, saying that the Browns have been a race of honest men and good Christians since the days of the martyrs; to which the older man answers:

'Well said, Goodman Brown! I have been as well acquainted with your family as with ever a one among the Puritans; and that's no trifle to say. I helped your grandfather, the constable, when he lashed the Quaker woman so smartly through the streets of Salem; and it was I that brought your father a pitch-pine knot, kindled at my own hearth, to set fire to an Indian village, in King Philip's war. They were my good friends, both; and many a pleasant walk have we had along this path, and returned merrily after midnight. I would fain be friends with you for their sake.'

They walk on and meet other people, Goody Cloyse, 'a very pious and exemplary dame, who taught him his catechism in youth', and Deacon Gookin and the minister himself. (It may be noted that a Goody Cloyse was sentenced to death for witchcraft in 1692 by a court which included Hawthorne's great-great-grand-father.) Brown hears Goody Cloyse hale his companion as the devil, 'in the very image of my old Gossip Goodman Brown, the grandfather of the silly fellow that now is'. Realizing the identity of his companion and that Goody Cloyse is a witch and Deacon Gookin and the minister implicated in devil-worship, as he is too, by ancestral guilt, Brown sits down on a tree-stump and refuses to go further.

He passes into a hallucinatory state and finds himself in a multitude of the people of Salem. He cries: 'With heaven above and Faith below, I will yet stand firm against the devil.'

There was one voice, of a young woman, uttering lamentations, yet with an uncertain sorrow, and entreating some favour, which, perhaps, it would grieve her to obtain; and all the unseen multitude, both saints and sinners, seemed to encourage her onward.

'Faith!' shouted Goodman Brown, in a voice of agony and desperation; and the echoes of the forest mocked him, crying 'Faith! Faith!' as if bewildered wretches were seeking her all through the wilderness. . . .

'My Faith is gone!' cried he, after one stupefied moment. 'There is no good on earth, and sin is but a name. Come, devil; for to thee the world is given.'

Maddened with despair, he laughs loud and long; and we may recall Robin's similar response in the moment of recognition and perhaps disillusionment in 'My Kinsman, Major Molineux'.

A dark figure appears. ' "Bring forth the converts!" ' cries a voice echoing through the field and forest. Brown steps forward and approaches the congregation, 'with whom he felt a loathful brotherhood by the sympathy of all that was wicked in his heart'. Thither comes also the 'slender figure of a veiled female, led between Goody Cloyse, the pious teacher of the catechism, and Martha Carrier, who had received the devil's promise to be queen of hell'.

There follows, as the peak of the story, the devil's sermon:

'Welcome, my children,' said the dark figure, 'to the communion of your race. Ye have found thus young your nature and your destiny. My children, look behind you!'

They turned; and flashing forth, as it were, in a sheet of flame, the fiend-worshippers were seen, the smile of welcome gleamed darkly on every visage.

'There,' resumed the sable form, 'are all that ye have reverenced from youth. Ye deemed them holier than yourselves, and shrank from your own sin, contrasting it with their lives of righteousness and prayerful aspirations heavenward. Yet here they all are in my worshipping assembly. This night it shall be granted you to know their secret deeds: how hoary-bearded elders of the church have whispered wanton words to the young maids of their households; how many a woman, eager for widow's weeds, has given her husband a drink at bedtime and let him sleep his last sleep in her bosom; how beardless youths have made haste to inherit their fathers' wealth; and how fair damsels – blush not, sweet ones – have dug little graves in the garden and bidden me, the sole guest, to an infant's funeral. By the sympathy of your human hearts for sin ye shall scent out all the places – whether in church, bedchamber, street, field, or forest – where crime has been committed, and shall exult to behold the whole earth one stain of guilt, one mighty blood spot. Far more than this. It shall be yours to penetrate, in every bosom, the deep mystery of sin, the fountain of all wicked arts, and which inexhaustibly supplies more evil impulses than human power – than my power at its utmost – can make manifest in deeds. And now, my children, look upon each other.'

They did so; and, by the blaze of the hell-kindled torches, the wretched man beheld his Faith, and the wife of her husband, trembling before that unhallowed altar.

'Lo, there ye stand, my children,' said the figure, in a deep and solemn tone, almost sad in its despairing awfulness, as if his once angelic nature could yet mourn for our miserable race. 'Depending upon one another's hearts, ye have still hoped that virtue was not all a dream. Now are ye all undeceived. Evil is the nature of mankind. Evil must be your only happiness. Welcome again, my children, to the communion of your race.'

Listening to this revelation of the universality and omnipotence of sin, Goodman Brown and Faith stand side by side, 'the only pair, as it seemed, who were yet hesitating on the verge of wickedness in this dark world'. Looking round at the secret guilt manifested in the face of those about them, Brown cries: 'Faith! Faith! Look up to heaven and resist the wicked one.' Straightaway, he finds himself alone in the forest. Everything is normal and peaceful.

He returns next morning to Salem 'a bewildered man'. In the village street he passes the minister, from whom he shrinks as if to avoid an anathema. He sees Goody Cloyse standing at her lattice catechizing a little girl who has brought the morning milk, and he snatches the child away 'as from the grasp of the fiend herself'. Faith, in her ribbons, is waiting for him: he 'looked sternly and sadly into her face, and passed on without a greeting'.

Had Goodman Brown, asks Hawthorne, fallen asleep in the forest and only dreamed a wild dream of a witches' meeting? He does not answer the question. The consequences for Brown of the night's experience, whether dream or reality, are reported in the last paragraph of the story:

A stern, a sad, a deeply meditative, a distrustful, if not a desperate figure did he become from the night of that frightful dream. On the Sabbath day, when the congregation were singing a holy psalm, he could not listen because an anthem of sin rushed loudly into his ear and drowned all the blessed strain. When the minister spoke from the pulpit with power and fervid eloquence, and, with his hand on the open Bible, of the sacred truths of our religion, and of saintlike lives and triumphant deaths, and of future bliss or misery unutterable, then did Goodman Brown turn pale, dreading lest the roof should thunder down upon the grey blasphemer and his hearers. Often awaking suddenly at midnight, he shrank away from the bosom of Faith; and at morning or eventide, when the family knelt down at prayers, he scowled and muttered to himself, and gazed sternly at his wife, and turned away. And when he had lived long, and was borne to his grave a hoary corpse, followed by Faith, an aged woman, and children and grandchildren, a goodly procession, besides neighbours not a few, they carved no hopeful verse upon his tombstone, for his dying hour was gloom.

This riddling story rouses many questions but the principal fact seems to be that Brown is initiated into consciousness of sin as a universal experience, inescapable, transmitted from generation to generation, the great human heritage. Here Hawthorne is, of course, exposing the dark underside of Puritanism, perhaps of all religion. Two things in particular interest me. The first is Brown's alienation from society and from his family alike. He shrinks from the bosom of Faith, who is both his wife and his religious belief, because he has become aware of universal and fundamental hypocrisy as the great fact of life.

Yet the consequence of the realization of sin as a universal fact is not necessarily alienation. The realization could be comforting and a source of human sympathy, of consciousness of brotherhood with one's fellows. That this is not so for young Goodman Brown is a criticism on Hawthorne's part of the onesided and repressive nature of New England Puritanism. Hawthorne plumps for alienation, which is related to my second point. In a very real sense the story takes place as it were within young Goodman Brown himself. This Hawthorne himself underscores when he asks whether Brown's experience was contained in a dream. In other words, this great American short story is differentiated, as Poe's are, from the European story in general in that the emphasis is placed on the experience of the individual as individual and only in a peripheral way as a member of a community.

Similar characteristics are to be found in the stories of a no less remarkable American writer, Hawthorne's contemporary whom his practice greatly influenced, Herman Melville. 'Bartleby the Scrivener', for instance, is very mysterious indeed, though the setting is familiar enough, a lawyer's office in Wall Street in the eighteen-forties. It is reminiscent of the lawyer's offices we meet in Dickens's novels, and the story obviously owed much to Dickens.

The practice of the lawyer himself flourishes, and he engages another scrivener, Bartleby, whom he describes as 'pallidly neat, pitiably respectable, incurably forlorn!' As a scrivener, Bartleby gives satisfaction but he refuses to do anything apart from his strict job. His answer to any request, almost to any question, is, 'I would prefer not to.' The lawyer discovers that Bartleby has taken up residence in his office, and when ordered to quit, he replies: 'I would prefer *not* to quit you.' In the end, it is the lawyer who quits. He takes other offices, but Bartleby refuses to budge from his accommodation, though it is now tenanted by another lawyer. For reasons that he cannot explain to himself, though he justifies his feelings by references to Christian principles, his ex-employer feels responsible for Bartleby and when he learns that Bartleby has been forcibly removed, arrested, and sent to the Tombs, the New York City jail, he visits him there and offers to pay for his meals. Bartleby's response is: 'I prefer not to dine today. It would disagree with me. I am unused to dinners.' He turns to the wall. It is as though he is deliberately opting out of life, and he dies in the Tombs.

In the last paragraph, the lawyer vouchsafes some further information about Bartleby that has come his way after his death. It is rumoured that he had been 'a subordinate clerk in the Dead Letter Office at Washington' and had lost his job because of a change in administration. The lawyer comments:

Dead letters! does it not sound like dead men? Conceive a man by nature and misfortune prone to a pallid hopelessness, can any business seem more fitted to heighten it than that of continually handling those dead letters, and assorting them for the flames? For by the cartload they are annually burned. . . . On errands of life, these letters speed to death.

Ah, Bartleby! Ah, humanity!

The story has received many interpretations, and possible sources for Bartleby have been hunted down. He has been seen as being based on Henry Thoreau, who went to prison for not paying his taxes as a protest against the Mexican War. The story then becomes a parable of passive resistance. It has been seen, too, as a parable of Melville's own fate as a writer of works nobody wanted to read and who, rather than compromise with or concede to contemporary taste, said to society the equivalent of 'I would prefer not to.' By implication, the story then becomes a parable of the writer's situation in the modern world.

Yet this is to put the emphasis on Bartleby to an unwarranted degree. For there is another character in the story: the narrator, the lawyer who, it seems to me, is more than the symbol of an uncomprehending and bewildered though not necessarily hostile society in the presence either of the passive resister or the intransigent artist.

I am impressed by the notion of the duality of Bartleby and the lawyer. Bartleby appears almost as a protesting voice in the lawyer's mind, a psychological double whose role, to quote Mordecai Marcus's essay, 'Melville's Bartleby as a Psychological Double', is 'to criticize the sterility, impersonality, and mechanical adjustments to the world which the lawyer inhabits'. In this reading, the story appears to be a criticism of the repression of parts of the personality. And having said that, it is necessary to add that the richness of the story lies in the manifold interpretations that may be made of it, no one of which negates the others. All may be held in the mind simultaneously; for though I have used the word 'parable' for 'Bartleby the Scrivener' the story is rather a symbolic statement, necessarily ambiguous, of the human condition.

As riddling as 'Bartleby the Scrivener' but no less authoritative artistically is 'Benito Cereno'. In the year 1799 Captain Amasa Delano, of Duxbury, Massachusetts, commanding a general trading ship, is lying at anchor in the harbour of Santa Maria, a small uninhabited island off the coast of Chile. A strange ship sails into the bay. She is in a decrepit condition, flies no colours, and is being very badly navigated. Thinking the ship may be in distress, Delano orders the whale-boat to be lowered. When he reaches the ship he is further puzzled by, among other things, the spectacle of four elderly Negroes picking oakum and six others scouring rusty hatchets. The Spanish captain,

a gentlemanly, reserved-looking, and rather young man to a stranger's eye, dressed with a singular richness, but bearing plain traces of recent sleepless cares and disquietudes, stood passively by, leaning against the main-mast, at one moment casting a dreary spiritless look upon his excited people, at the next an unhappy glance toward his visitor. By his side stood a black of small stature, in whose rude face, as occasionally, like a shepherd's dog, he mutely turned it up into the Spaniard's, sorrow and affection were equally blended.... Sometimes the negro gave his master his arm, or took his handkerchief out of his pocket for him; performing these and similar offices with that affectionate zeal which transmutes into something filial or fraternal acts in themselves but menial; and which has gained for the negro the repute of making the most pleasing body-servant in the world; one, too, whom a master need be on no stiffly superior terms with, but may treat with familiar trust; less a servant than a devoted companion.

But Delano is still much bewildered by what he sees and, though an infinitely charitable man, cannot but be disturbed by the condition of the ship. He obtains from Cereno an account of what has happened. The ship had set out, well officered and well manned, with some fifty cabin passengers, a general cargo, and over three hundred Negro slaves, and had run into gales off the Horn which swept away officers and crewmen alike and caused the ship to be dismantled of all but immediate necessities. Then scurvy struck, 'carrying off numbers of the whites and blacks'. Then they were becalmed. And they ran out of water.

'But throughout these calamities,' huskily continued Don Benito, painfully turning in the half embrace of his servant, 'I have to thank these negroes you see, who, though to your inexperienced eyes appearing unruly, have, indeed, conducted themselves with less of restlessness than even their owner could have thought possible under such circumstances.... But it is Balbo here to whom, under God, I owe not only my own preservation, but likewise to him, chiefly, the merit is due, of pacifying his more ignorant brethren, when at intervals tempted to murmurings.'

'Ah, master,' sighed the black, bowing his face, 'don't speak of me; Balbo is nothing; what Balbo has done was but duty.'

So Delano passes his day on the Spanish ship, always bewildered, always rationalizing his bewilderment. He is puzzled that every Spanish sailor is accompanied by a Negro. He is puzzled that a huge black man in chains is paraded regularly before Cereno. He is constantly moved by the spectacle of the devotion to Cereno of the Negro slave, who happens to nick his master's throat while shaving him. The fondness the Negro women on board show to their offspring moves him to pious sentiments about the universality of the maternal instinct.

When Delano eventually steps down into the whale-boat to return to his own ship, Cereno suddenly jumps into it. 'The whole host of negroes, as if inflamed at the sight of their jeopardized captain, impended in one sooty avalanche over the bulwarks.' The American sailors pull away as fast as they can; and later, men of Delano's ship overpower the crew of the Spanish vessel, take her prisoner, and bring her into Lima.

That is the end of the first and longer half of the story. The second half is presented as a series of excerpts from the proceedings of a court of enquiry held in Lima. The *San Dominick* had been captured by the Negro slaves that were part of its cargo; their owners and the Spanish passengers had been murdered; Benito Cereno had been kept under duress, Balbo being in fact his jailer, a knife ready to stab him at any moment. The most cruel of all towards the captive whites had been the maternal Negro women. The humanitarian Delano had been completely deceived. His interpretation of what he saw was the very opposite of the facts.

'Benito Cereno' is a wonderfully sustained, intensely graphic piece of narration, which Melville took from an existing Spanish document. We cannot, of course, take it wholly at its surface value, for the main part of Melville's narration consists of Captain Delano's shifting impressions of the scene and action. We must first decide how we are to take Delano. He is, evidently, a man of good will, and high-minded, but a victim of his own propensity towards idealism. Melville, in fact, is drawing a picture of the American character, of the New England character particularly, similar to that first created by Henry James and familiar to us today in the novels of Graham Greene, in which American political gulli-bility and naivety appearing under the guise of idealism are shown to be fraught with disaster for those who possess them.

The point of this profoundly ironical story, which may be seen as a black farce, is, I believe, Melville's criticism of his fellow Americans. But there is more to it than that. It is a story of the relations between black and white and of a slave rising. It was published in 1855, six years before the Civil War broke out. What is Melville's attitude towards the black man? One thing we may be certain of: it was nothing like as simple as Captain Delano's. Delano is a Yankee, as Melville was, and he views the Negro through eyes distorted by senti-mentality; the Negro is seen as childlike, devoted to his master, of inferior intelligence, a happy child of nature or a sheepdog. The depositions at the Spanish court of inquiry at Lima say precisely the opposite: the Negro is treacherous, brutal, deeply cunning. I do not think we can attribute this view to Melville. He was obviously bound by the sources of his story and it was most likely enough for him in 'Benito Cereno', as in *Moby Dick*, to reveal the Janus-facedness of people, things, and institutions.

Melville's stories raise problems of the kind that confront us in his novels. If we knew Henry James only from his novels, with their finely discriminating analyses of conscience, consciousness, and motive, their 'princely expenditure' of language and their set pieces, we might have difficulty in believing that he could equally be a master of the short story. Admittedly, he often found the conventional short-story length of the time, 8,000 words or so, too limiting; all the same, he wrote more than one hundred and ten stories, all distinguished by the qualities that characterize his novels and yet, in my view, indisputably short stories. Certainly, the majority of them are long, what James himself called *nouvelles*.

James's stories are different in kind from those of most

American writers in that he was writing comedy of manners, a genre which implies of itself the necessity of a scope larger than the short story commonly offers. His concern was the behaviour of men and women in society, and he was especially fascinated by the behaviour of men and women who find themselves in societies foreign to them, societies in which the conventions and assumptions about behaviour are other than they are at home. He is the first and great exponent of what he called the International Subject, which comes down to the behaviour of Americans in Europe, the contrast between American and European manners – not morals; the distinction is important. His most famous treatment of the subject is probably the long short story 'Daisy Miller'. Daisy, an 'inscrutable combination of audacity and innocence', who behaves with the same kind of freedom in Italy as she does at home, disgraces herself in the eyes of the American community in Rome by being seen in the Colosseum at night with a young Italian who is plainly an adventurer and to whom she may or may not be engaged. She catches 'Roman fever' in the Colosseum and dies, protesting for the sake of the young American she loves and whose jealousy she has tried to arouse that she is not engaged to the Italian, who says at her funeral that Daisy was 'the most beautiful young lady I ever saw, and the most amiable . . . and the most innocent'.

'Daisy Miller' is a moving and also an amusing story, but the essence of James's treatment of the International Subject can be seen equally well in a story much less known, 'Miss Gunton of Poughkeepsie', a story which for James is very brief. The place-name in the title is significant. Poughkeepsie is a small town on the Hudson in New York State some sixty miles north of New York City, and we are to understand that Miss Gunton is a product of provincial America quite ignorant of European manners. While she is touring Europe, a young Roman prince falls in love with her. She flees to Paris and thence to London: if the prince pursues her there it will be proof he loves her. He does pursue her and proposes to her, whereupon she demands that his mother the princess, the great noble lady, shall write to her, welcoming her. Her English friend Lady Champer explains to her that the princess 'has never in her whole life made an advance, any more than anyone has ever expected it of her'. But, as Lady Champer also explains to the prince:

'Lily's rigidly logical. A girl – as she knows girls – is "welcomed", on her engagement, before anything else can happen, by the family of her young man; and the motherless girl, alone in the world, more punctually than any other. Then the girl goes and stays with them. But she does nothing before.'

Here we have a clash of conventions, of sets of socially right behaviour, each proper in the context of its own society but irreconcilable with the other. Lily goes back to the States, and the prince prevails upon his mother to swallow her pride and make the necessary advances to Lily. Her letter crosses with Lily's to the prince announcing her engagement to an American. 'I've become,' says the prince, later, to Lady Champer, 'for my mother a person who has made her make, all for nothing, an unprecedented advance, a humble submission,' and he adds, of Lily: 'And I believed she loved me!' To which Lady Champer retorts: 'I didn't. No – it was all the rest; your great historic position, the glamour of your name, and your past. Otherwise what she stood out for wouldn't be excusable. But she has the sense of such things, and *they* were what she loved.'

In 'Miss Gunton of Poughkeepsie' James has not the space to do more than illustrate his moral, certainly not enough to develop his characters. All the same, it is a rewarding study of the clash of cultures as seen in manners. The last words are Lady Champer's: 'With Americans one is lost!' The cry echoes and re-echoes through the novels and stories on the International Subject. It rings through 'Madame de Mauves', one of James's finest novellas, written twenty-five years earlier. It has a splendid opening set piece evoking the impression made by Paris on a sensitive young American, a passage which, as always with these Jamesian set pieces, enhances the story, its milieu, and its characters.

The young American is Longmore. Through his friend Mrs Draper he meets another lady, who 'was perhaps not obviously a beauty nor obviously an American, but essentially both for the really seeing eye'. From Mrs Draper he learns that she is

Madame de Mauves, that she lives in Saint Germain and is very unhappy. A letter from Mrs Draper tells him Madame de Mauves's story:

'. . . It is the miserable story of an American girl born neither to submit basely nor to rebel crookedly marrying a shining sinful Frenchman who believes a woman must do one or other of those things. The lightest of *us* have a ballast that they can't imagine, and the poorest a moral imagination that they don't require. She was romantic and perverse – she thought the world she had been brought up in too vulgar or at least too prosaic. To have a decent home-life isn't perhaps the greatest of adventures; but I think she wishes nowadays she hadn't gone in quite so desperately for thrills. M. de Mauves cared of course for nothing but her money, which he's spending royally on his *menus plaisirs*. I hope you appreciate the compliment I pay you when I recommend you to go and cheer up a lady domestically dejected. . . .'

There follows an account, of sustained beauty, of Euphemia, Madame de Mauves. The young American girl was educated at a convent in Paris for high-born ladies and had fallen in love with an idealistic vision of aristocracy:

She dreamed of marrying a man of hierarchical 'rank' – not for the pleasure of hearing herself called Madame la Vicomtesse, for which it seemed to her she would never greatly care, but because she had a romantic belief that the enjoyment of inherited and transmitted consideration, consideration attached to the fact of birth, would be the direct guarantee of an ideal delicacy of feeling. She supposed it would be found that the state of being noble does actually enforce the famous obligation. . . . She was essentially incorruptible, and she took this pernicious conceit to her bosom very much as if it had been a dogma revealed by a white-winged angel. . . . She had a mental image of that son of the Crusaders who was to suffer her to adore him, but like many an artist who has produced a masterpiece of idealization she shrank from exposing it to public criticism. It was the portrait of a gentleman rather ugly than handsome and rather poor than rich. But his ugliness was to be nobly expressive and his poverty delicately proud.

Against the protests of her family, Euphemia marries the brother of a convent friend, M. de Mauves, a descendant of the Crusaders, a 'quiet, grave, eminently distinguished' man, who, it turns out, sees women as objects not essentially different from lavender gloves which, soiled in an evening, are then thrown away. Euphemia, with her fine idealism, is quite without the 'pliant softness and fine adjustability' de Mauves's conception of women demands. Her marriage is doomed to unhappiness to be borne stoically.

Longmore, also an American idealist, is not so much a passionate lover as a connoisseur of the Puritan conscience. It is made delicately plain to him by de Mauves that if he were to become Euphemia's lover it would be more welcome than not, but his scruples, which come out in the following, will not allow this:

> Longmore sank back with a sigh and an oppressive feeling that it was vain to guess at such a woman's motives. He only felt that those of this one were buried deep in her soul and that they must be of the noblest, must contain nothing base. . . . 'She has loved once,' he said to himself as he rose and wandered to the window; 'and that's for ever. Yes, yes – if she loved again she'd be *common*. . . .' He must see everything from above, her indifference and his own ardour; he must prove his strength, must do the handsome thing, must decide that the handsome thing was to submit to the inevitable, to be supremely delicate, to spare her all pain, to stifle his passion, to ask no compensation, to depart without waiting and to try to believe that wisdom is its own reward.

He returns to the United States. He hears nothing of Madame de Mauves. When he learns that Mrs Draper has come home he immediately calls on her, and she tells the following strange story:

> M. de Mauves had *fait quelques folies* which his wife had taken absurdly to heart. He had repented and asked her forgiveness, which she had inexorably refused. She was very pretty, and severity must have suited her style; for, whether or no her husband had been in love with her before, he fell madly in love with her now. He was the proudest man in France, but he had begged her on his knees to be re-admitted to favour. All in vain! She was stone, she was ice, she was outraged virtue. People noticed a great change in him; he gave up society, ceased to care for anything, looked shockingly. One fine day they discovered he had blown out his brains.

That is the penultimate paragraph of the story. The last one is:

> Longmore was strongly moved, and his first impulse after he had recovered his composure was to return immediately to Europe. But several years have passed, and he still lingers at home. The truth is that, in the midst of all the ardent tenderness of his memory of Madame de Mauves, he has become conscious of a singular feeling – a feeling of wonder, of uncertainty, of awe.

James shows the American girl to be more truly aristocratic, more truly 'noble' than her nobly born husband. But is this his final judgement on her? Light on this is thrown by the last paragraph of the story. Longmore does not return to France to seek her out, for he is plainly scared of her. Her behaviour reveals her as a woman either too good to be true or a woman morally monstrous in her unrelenting refusal to forgive, a woman imprisoned in a monstrous self-regard. She is the victim, James shows, of her excessively romantic temperament. As much as Flaubert's Emma Bovary, she is invincibly ignorant of the real world, the facts of life as they are. And this is true of Longmore also, who is revealed as a refined sentimentalist, as much a monster, perhaps, in his delicate sensationalist's way as Euphemia.

The dénouement also throws light on and explains what otherwise would seem a totally irrelevant though admittedly very beautiful episode in the story. One day Longmore goes walking in the country. He lunches at an inn, and the landlady invites him to smoke his cigar in the garden behind the house. From there he observes a young painter and his girl, who reads the poetry of André Chenier to him as he paints. The whole episode is an idyll, an evocation of normality, of happiness, of fruitfulness, of what James himself calls in his description of the scene seen from the window of the inn, 'the unperverted reality of things'. And it is anything but irrelevant, for it provides us with a standard by which we may judge both Euphemia and Longmore.

Conrad called James 'the historian of fine consciences', a superb phrase the richer for its ambiguity, since there is some doubt whether Conrad was using 'conscience' in its normal English sense or with its French meaning of perception, consciousness. 'Madame de Mauves' is a comparatively early story but it is typical of James in the subtlety of the analysis of character and of what may be called fine consciences in the English and French senses alike. This makes his work all of a piece and makes attempts to categorize his stories somewhat stupid except for the sake of convenience. His stories on the International Subject overlap with his stories about art and the artistic life and with those about the supernatural.

Of the stories on art, some, like 'The Lesson of the Master', are on the inevitable corruption of the artist by society; others are on the nature of art itself and on its relations with and differences from life. Of these latter, 'The Real Thing' is particularly fascinating because it dramatizes a truth about art which could have been expressed in no other way.

The narrator is a portrait painter and book-illustrator who is visited by a Major and Mrs Monarch, impoverished gentlefolk looking for work as artists' models. The Major pleads that he and his wife are 'the real thing', with the implication that if a painter wishes to portray ladies and gentlemen who better than them as models?

From a combination of pity, embarrassment, and perhaps curiosity he agrees to try them. They are not satisfactory, not nearly so good, not nearly so convincing as ladies and gentlemen in his illustrations as his professional models. A friend and fellow-artist condemns the illustrations and tells the narrator that the Major and his lady are the sort of people one must get rid of. The situation is embarrassing. 'If I went a little in fear of them it wasn't because they bullied me, because they had got an oppressive foothold, but because in their really pathetic decorum and mysteriously permanent newness they counted on me so intensely.'

He breaks the news to them that he can no longer use them as models and, having told them, discovers they have been washing his china, cleaning his cutlery, polishing his silver. 'They had accepted their failure, but they couldn't accept their fate.' The story ends:

Then, with the Major and his wife, I had a most uncomfortable moment. He put their prayer into a single sentence: 'I say, you know – just let *us* do for you, can't you?' I couldn't – it was dreadful to see them emptying my slops; but I pretended I could, to oblige them, for about a week. Then I gave them a sum of money to go away, and I never saw them again. . . . My friend Hawley repeats that Major and Mrs Monarch did me a permanent harm, got me into false ways. If it be true I'm content to have paid the price – for the memory.

In the irony and ambiguities of its resolution 'The Real Thing' is one of James's most deeply disturbing stories.

II

In nineteenth-century American literature, as for that matter in English, Henry James was very much a man on his own. He lived more than half his life in England, never quite an Englishman; and behind him, in the States, American literature was developing in ways more predictable than his had taken. It was the age of expansion; the frontier was pushed back to the Pacific Ocean; new states and therefore in a small way new nationalisms, new regional literatures, came into being. The expansion, the increasing diversity of the American scene was reflected in what was being written. Perhaps the most spectacular, melodramatic manifestation of this expansion had been the discovery of gold in California in the eighteen-forties, which drew to the old Spanish colony people from all over the world. One such was the boy Francis Bret Harte, who at the age of fifteen left his birthplace, Albany, New York, to follow his widowed mother to California where she married again. At various times he was engaged in school-teaching, mining, printing, and journalism and in 1868 became editor of the newly-founded *Overland Monthly* of San Francisco, in early issues of which appeared his stories 'The Luck of Roaring Camp' and 'The Outcasts of Poker Flat'. They attracted immediate attention on the eastern seaboard and in England. They remain his most famous stories. Life in the mining settlements was raw and conditions brutal, but that was not how Harte presented it. His stories are flagrantly sentimental: prostitutes have hearts of gold, professional gamblers the feelings of gentlemen. As a short-story writer and poet, Harte has been forgotten by critics, yet the stories still have a certain charm; the sentimentality, though gross, is in its way on the side of humanity. Despite enormous differences in the scenes portrayed, there is a kinship with Dickens, and Harte's vast popularity in America and in England, where he spent the last years of his life, is understandable.

An early disciple of Harte was Ambrose Bierce, whose first story was published in the *Overland Monthly*, but Harte's influence was soon displaced by that of Poe, which is seminal, as may

be seen not only from Bierce's stories but also from his definition, in his debunking work, *The Devil's Dictionary*, of the novel
as a padded short story, lacking unity or totality of effect. This
is obviously a re-statement of Poe's theories on the short story,
and when one looks at his stories with his definition in mind one
can see that Bierce was writing in terms of a consistent aesthetic.
No doubt they are often and too much disfigured by gimmickry;
nevertheless, Bierce's stories are, in my view, unduly neglected
and underrated. As a delineator in fiction of the Civil War, in
which he fought, he is second only to Stephen Crane in *The Red
Badge of Courage*. The surfaces of his stories are much more
realistic than Poe's, but, like Poe, he is obsessed with the terror
of the soul that feeds on death. The real world the stories describe should not prevent us from seeing how solipsistic the
stories are. It is significant that his favourite figure is the man
on his own, the loner, and, in 'One of the Missing', the scout.
Searing's orders are to 'get as near the enemy's lines as possible
and learn all that he could'. Accordingly, he makes his way
through the forest, crawls across the terrain beyond and hides
himself in a ruined shed in a derelict plantation. He sees that the
enemy is withdrawing.

Searing had now learned all that he could hope to know. It was his duty
to return to his own command with all possible speed and report his
discovery. But the gray column of infantry toiling up the mountain
road was singularly tempting. His rifle – an ordinary 'Springfield', but
fitted with a globe sight and hair trigger – would easily send its ounce
and a quarter of lead hissing into their midst. That would probably not
affect the duration and result of the war, but it is the business of a
soldier to kill. It is also his habit if he is a good soldier. Searing cocked
his rifle and 'set' the trigger.

There follows a disquisition on determinism remarkably like
that of Hardy's poem 'The Converging of the Twain' in spirit.
It opens: 'But it was decreed from the beginning of time that
Private Searing was not to murder anybody that bright summer
morning, nor was the Confederate retreat to be announced by
him.' As he is about to fire, 'a Confederate captain of artillery,
having nothing better to do while awaiting his turn to pull out
and be off, amused himself by sighting a field piece obliquely to
his right at what he took to be some Federal officers on the crest

of a hill, and discharged it. The shot hit its mark.' It hits, in fact, the shed in which Searing is concealed. He is knocked unconscious by the blast and when he comes to, realizes that he is pinioned by the debris above him, he cannot move but he is unhurt. His right arm is partly free, and cautiously he attempts, with little success, to wriggle beneath the weight above him. Then:

... his attention was arrested by what seemed to be a ring of shining metal immediately in front of his eyes. It appeared to him at first to surround some perfectly black substance, and it was somewhat more than a half inch in diameter. It suddenly occurred to his mind that the blackness was simply shadow and that the ring was in fact the muzzle of his rifle protruding from the pile of debris. He was not long in satisfying himself that this was so – if it was a satisfaction ... He was unable to see the upper surface of the barrel, but could see the under surface of the stock at a slight angle. The piece was, in fact, aimed at the exact centre of his forehead.

The rifle is cocked, the trigger is set; even if he can disentangle himself from the debris that pins him down, his struggles will only mean that the rifle goes off.

Perceiving his defeat, all his terror returned, augmented tenfold. The black aperture of the rifle appeared to threaten a sharper and more imminent death in punishment of his rebellion. The track of the bullet through his head ached with an intenser anguish. He began to tremble again.

Suddenly he became composed. His tremor subsided. He clenched his teeth and drew down his eyebrows. He had not exhausted his means of defence; a new design had shaped itself in his mind – another plan of battle. Raising the front end of the strip of board, he carefully pushed it forward through the wreckage at the side of the rifle until it pressed against the trigger guard. Then he moved the end slowly outward until he could feel that it had cleared it, then, closing his eyes, thrust it against the trigger with all his strength! There was no explosion; the rifle had been discharged as it dropped from his hand when the building fell. But Jerome Searing was dead.

'One of the Missing' is a sensational story. I believe it is much more, but even at that level it is interesting to see the way in which the feeling of personal isolation, of man existing without reference to the community of his fellows, has by this time invaded popular American fiction. As in Poe, we see life confined to the thoughts and sensations within a single skull; and part of Bierce's importance is that he helped to reinforce the Poe tradition in American fiction.

Short stories in the opposed European tradition continued of course to be written and two names in this end-of-the-century period should be mentioned, those of Frank Harris and Hamlin Garland, both of whom wrote about the Middle West. Harris, perhaps because of the odour of notoriety which clings to him, has been much neglected. He was born in Ireland, migrated to the United States at the age of fourteen, graduated in law at the University of Kansas, and returned to England by the time he was forty to become editor of the *Saturday Review*, the friend of Wilde and Shaw and the patron of Wells. But in his time in the States he contrived to write some interesting stories of Kansas and the states beyond in the first decades of statehood. They are not, it must be admitted, good as short stories but their historical interest is real, they contain vivid vignettes of life on what was no longer the frontier and their sense of raw life goes some way towards redeeming their technical clumsiness. The faults of the story 'Elder Conklin', for example, are plain in that there is no one centre of interest. Instead, there are at least four disparate themes clamouring for attention and Harris lacks the art to fuse them into one, so that the story reads like a novel in synopsis. But still there is a strange impressiveness. The author has something important to say and does not know how to say it; that it is something important we do not doubt.

Harris's best American story is 'The Best Man in Garotte'. It is very short, so that it is not more than a dramatization of a single incident. It is a story of the frontier and begins:

Lawyer Rablay had come from nobody knew where. He was a small man, almost as round as a billiard ball. His body was round, his head was round; his blue eyes and even his mouth and chin were round; his nose was a perky snub; he was florid and prematurely bald – a picture of good humour. And yet he was a power in Garotte.

Rablay has the art of composing quarrels, even, by his wit and vivacity, of preventing them.

Lawyer Rablay was to Garotte what novels, theatres, churches, concerts are to more favoured cities; in fact, for some six months, he and his stories constituted the chief humanizing influence in the camp. Deputations were often dispatched from Doolan's to bring Rablay to the bar.

Then, one afternoon, a notorious 'bad man', Bill Hickock arrives in camp. He refuses to be charmed by the lawyer and forces a fight upon him. Rablay refuses to fire, drops the revolver on the floor, and flees from the room. Hickock, a score of revolvers covering him, is forced to crawl, on hands and knees, out of Garotte.

Lawyer Rablay, too, was never afterwards seen in Garotte. Men said his nerves had 'give out'.

Unlike Harris, Garland was a native of the Middle West, born in Wisconsin and a school teacher in Iowa. His best-known story, 'The Return of the Private', from his first collection *Main-Travelled Roads*, is probably his best. Garland's earliest memory was of his father returning from the Civil War, and 'The Return of the Private' describes, very simply, the last stages of a journey back to Wisconsin from the South of a party of demobilized Union soldiers. It focuses on one man. His wife and family do not know when he is returning, and his coming takes them by surprise. In terms of anecdote, that is all. The last words are:

The common soldier of the American volunteer army had returned. His fight with the South was over, and his fight, his daily running fight with Nature and against the injustice of his fellow-men, was begun again.

The story is told with simple dignity. Its theme is family life, community life, the willing, loving return to the duties of husband, father, citizen. It could well have been written anywhere and at any time after a war. It plainly transcends the purely regional. In one meaning of the word, it is classical.

By far the greatest of the American short-story writers and novelists who came out of daily journalism was Stephen Crane. How great he might have been it is impossible to say, for he died at the age of twenty-nine. His prose is an adaptation of the prose of the daily newspaper; his stories are news-stories transmuted into art. Of the most famous, 'The Open Boat', Conrad said that 'by the deep and simple humanity' it seems 'somehow to illustrate the essentials of life itself, like a symbolic tale'.

The story has a sub-title: 'A Tale Intended to be after the Fact: Being the Experience of Four Men from the Sunk Steamer *Commodore*'. Crane was one of those four men, a war correspondent at the time, sailing on a steamer that was running arms from Florida to the rebels in Cuba. The steamer foundered, and Crane – in the story he appears simply as the Correspondent – got away in a ten-foot dinghy with the captain, who had been injured, and two members of the crew. After a day and a night they reached Florida, but one of the men, the oiler, was drowned in the surf. That is what happened and that in essence is the story of 'The Open Boat'. Crane's newspaper report of the foundering of the *Commodore* appeared in the *New York Press* of 7 January 1897.

In the newspaper report the experience in the open boat is ignored. In the tale it is put under the microscope of Naturalism.

It begins:

None of them knew the colour of the sky. Their eyes glanced level, and were fastened upon the waves that swept towards them. These waves were of the colour of slate, save for the tops, which were foaming white, and all the men knew the colours of the sea. The horizon narrowed and widened, and dipped and rose, and at all times its edge was jagged with waves that seemed thrust up in points like rocks.

This is a remarkable because unexpected opening for we should expect men in an open boat to be almost abnormally conscious of the sky. But the reality, which Crane evokes, is that the four men, because of their situation, can be conscious only of water, of waves and the sea.

The second paragraph is similarly surprising:

Many a man ought to have a bathtub larger than the boat that here rode the sea. These waves were most wrongfully and barbarously abrupt and tall, and each froth-top was a problem in small-boat navigation.

What is stressed here is the sense of outrage that the four men feel, in a sense the *unfairness* of the situation. And this irony is stressing the fact that in the last analysis, when alone against the elements and the primordial things, men have no rights. In this respect, 'The Open Boat' is a chastening story.

Crane's manner is that of Naturalism. The story is told as though by an impersonal omniscient narrator with a God's-eye view. The action is rendered in the simplest of language, for the most part in words of one syllable; and never have monosyllables been used with more telling effect, as this extract, chosen almost at random, shows:

Canton-flannel gulls flew near and far ... One came, and evidently decided to alight on the top of the captain's head. The bird flew parallel to the boat and did not circle, but made short sidelong jumps in the air in chicken fashion. His black eyes were wistfully fixed upon the captain's head. 'Ugly brute,' said the oiler to the bird. 'You look as if you were made with a jack-knife.' The cook and the correspondent swore darkly at the creature. The captain naturally wished to knock it away with the end of the heavy painter, but he did not dare to do it, because anything resembling an emphatic gesture would have capsized this freighted boat; and so, with his open hand, the captain gently and carefully waved the gull away.

The gulls, perfectly at home on the waves, almost insolently rebuke human pretension as the narrator's irony mocks the competence of the boat's crew, that of the correspondent included. 'They will not be able to summon much except courage and endurance to save themselves,' says John Berryman, to whose masterly analysis of the story I am much indebted. 'The Open Boat' is one of the great heroic stories of the sea, but the heroism is conspicuously played down. And as Conrad saw, it is also a metaphor of life.

Crane is sometimes called an Impressionist, and perhaps the word is as exact as parallels between the different arts can be. Impressionism was contemporary with Naturalism and shared similar principles, the parts played by the environment and heredity in the literary movement being taken by light, shade, and atmospheric conditions in the equivalent paintings. To me, his work resembles generally the movement in painting as exemplified in Matisse, Dufy, Derain, Vlaminck, and Othon Friesz that succeeded Impressionism, that of *Les Fauves*, rather than Impressionism strictly. The outlines of things are more sharply defined in Crane, the lighting is more intense, a greater degree of drama is permitted, than is normal to Impressionism. One sees this in 'The Blue Hotel', the story of a quarrel and a murder that take place in a small hotel in Nebraska. One sees it too in 'The Bride Comes to Yellow Sky', a story that came out of a tour of the American West and Mexico that Crane made for journalistic purposes in 1895. It begins with a newly-married couple travelling to their new home:

The man's face was reddened from many days in the wind and sun, and a direct result of his new black clothes was that his brick-coloured hands were constantly performing in a most conscious fashion. From time to time he looked down respectfully at his attire. He sat with a hand on each knee, like a man waiting in a barber's shop. The glances he devoted to other passengers were furtive and shy.

The bride was not pretty, nor was she very young. She wore a dress of blue cashmere, with small reservations of velvet here and there, and with steel buttons abounding. She continually twisted her head to regard her puff sleeves, very stiff, straight, and high. They embarrassed her . . . The blushes caused by the careless scrutiny of some passengers as she had entered the car were strange to see upon this plain, underclass countenance, which was drawn in placid, almost emotionless lines.

They were evidently very happy . . .

They reach their destination, the small town of Yellow Sky on the Mexican border, where Frank Potter, the bridegroom, is the town marshal. As they make their way to their new home,

A man in a maroon-coloured flannel suit . . . rounded a corner and walked into the middle of the Main Street of Yellow Sky. In either hand the man held a long, heavy, blue-black revolver. Often he yelled, and these cries rang through the semblance of a deserted village, shrilly flying over the roofs in a volume that seemed to have no relation to the ordinary vocal strength of a man. . . . These cries of ferocious challenge rang against walls of silence.

The whole town is barred against Scratchy Wilson, who, when sober, is 'kind of simple – wouldn't hurt a fly – nicest fellow in town'. Scratchy, the world turned against him, silently refusing him a fight, remembers Jack Potter and decides to go to his house and challenge him.

Such is the situation when Potter and his bride turn the corner to the house. Their new state has made them self-conscious; Crane tells us that they walk 'sheepishly' and laugh 'shamefacedly'. Then there is the confrontation with Scratchy, revolver in either hand. It is wonderfully well realized, the consternation on both sides and especially Scratchy's when he realizes that Potter for once is unarmed and that the woman at his side, scarcely noticed before, is his new bride.

'Is this the lady?' he asked.

'Yes, this is the lady,' answered Potter.

There was another period of silence.

'Well,' said Wilson at last, slowly, 'I s'pose it's all off now.'

'It's all off if you say so, Scratchy. You know I didn't make the trouble.' Potter lifted his valise.

'Well, I 'low it's off, Jack,' said Wilson. He was looking at the ground. 'Married!' He was not a student of chivalry; it was merely that in the presence of this foreign condition he was a simple child of the earlier plains. He picked up his starboard revolver, and, placing both weapons in their holsters, he went away. His feet made funnel-shaped tracks in the heavy sand.

So the story ends, a grimly sardonic rendering of how order came to the West, the final ironical comment on Bret Harte's stories of the gold rush.

In the early years of this century the short story in America seemed to be in danger of disappearing altogether or, rather, into the swamps of daily journalism and magazine fiction. The great name was that of O. Henry, who had an enormous and mainly bad influence for many years on writers on both sides of the Atlantic. In his own country he was a kind of popular poet of New York City, which he celebrated as the modern Babylon. He wrote more than six hundred stories, and although this may remind us of Chekhov's beginning, he never graduated beyond Chekhov's early stage. A typical story is 'While the Auto Waits', the action of which takes place in a quiet, small park in New York City. A young man and a girl meet by chance there and sit on the same bench. Outside the park gates a car is waiting with a chauffeur; from her talk the girl is very rich, the young man poor. The following is an exchange between them:

'I have always liked,' he said, 'to read and hear about the ways of wealthy and fashionable folks. I suppose I am a bit of a snob. But I like to have my information accurate. Now, I had formed the opinion that champagne is cooled in the bottle, and not by placing ice in the glass.'

The girl gave a musical laugh of genuine amusement.

'You should know,' she explained, in an indulgent tone, 'that we of the non-useful class depend for our amusement upon departure from precedent. Just now it is a fad to put ice in champagne. The idea was originated by a visiting Prince of Tartary while dining at the Waldorf. It will soon give way to some other whim. Just as at a dinner party this week on Madison Avenue a green kid glove was laid by the plate of each guest to be put on and used while eating olives.'

The young man confesses that he works in the restaurant with the brilliant electric sign in the street on the other side of the park, not as a waiter but as a cashier. Dusk descends, and the girl must go to her social engagement. She forbids the young man to accompany her, for Pierre the chauffeur is waiting for her. When she reaches the car, she dashes across the road into the restaurant and takes her place in the cashier's desk. The young man dallies for ten minutes and then rises to go. He walks to the car, steps into it and says two words to the chauffeur: 'Club, Henri.'

The story is an example of formula-writing. O. Henry was the master of what has been called the trick-ending. He was not its inventor but he taught thousands of magazine writers in the United States and Britain for a generation or more how to do it. He reduced the short story precisely to a trick, his reward being the naive reader's gasp of surprise at the end.

James, who had known Flaubert and Turgenev, called Rudyard Kipling 'the most complete man of genius (as distinct from fine intelligence) that I have ever known'. T. S. Eliot, years later, in his introduction to *A Choice of Kipling's Verse* called him 'the most inscrutable of authors . . . a writer impossible wholly to understand and quite impossible to belittle'. On the face of it, Eliot's judgement is an extraordinary one to pass on a writer who as a very young man had captured the public imagination and enthusiasm as no other author since Dickens.

Rudyard Kipling was born in 1865 in Bombay and was sent to England at the age of six, to suffer a cruelly unhappy childhood at the hands of foster-parents. Out of memories of this came 'Baa Baa, Black Sheep', a terrifying story marred by sentimentality. At seventeen he returned to India to be a reporter first on the Lahore *Civil and Military Gazette* and then on the Allahabad *Pioneer*. It was the *Gazette* that featured most of the stories in *Plain Tales from the Hills*, one of the seven volumes he had published by the age of twenty-three. These were written under the conditions of journalism and in part as journalism, but the author had put himself to school with Maupassant and was, moreover, a prose-writer with, as V. S. Pritchett says in his essay on him in *The Working Novelist*, 'the gaiety of the word in his veins'. The stories have the laconic directness of first-rate reporting, and Kipling appears as a 'special correspondent for posterity', to use the phrase Bagehot applied to Dickens. He brings to life in all its variety the Anglo-India of the late nineteenth century, the society of an alien class ruling a native population.

One of the most striking things about *Plain Tales* is its range. One feels that there is nothing Kipling does not know about the society he is describing. 'Knowing' is a word critics have applied to him from the earliest days and in part it is derogatory, suggesting the almost insolent assurance of his style. But there is a positive side too. He really does persuade us that he *knows*; as in 'Tod's Amendment', in which a little English boy is instrumental in altering the course of legislation by unconsciously showing more insight into the Indian mind and needs than his elders possess. The stories are uneven, as though Kipling cannot yet recognize differences in levels of seriousness. 'A Friend's Friend', for instance, opens on altogether too high-pitched a note of facetiousness. Tranter 'of the Bombay side' has passed on to Kipling a traveller named Jevon, who gets very drunk at a ball. His behaviour redounds on Kipling, who is held responsible for him. Jevon passes out, and, when the ball is over, the men set to work on him:

> We corked the whole of his face. We filled his hair with meringue-cream till it looked like a white wig. To protect everything till it dried, a man in the Ordnance Department, who understood the work, luted a big blue paper cap from a cracker, with meringue-cream, low down on Jevon's forehead. This was punishment, not play, remember. We took gelatine off crackers, and stuck blue gelatine on his nose, and yellow gelatine on his chin, and green and red gelatine on his cheeks, pressing each dab down till it held as firm as gold-beater's skin.

He is wrapped up in sixty feet of carpet and then hoisted on to one of the bullock-carts that has come to take away the borrowed furniture in the hall. The story ends with a glance back to the first paragraph: 'Wherefore, I want Tranter of the Bombay side, dead or alive. But Dead for preference.'

The gusto and the gloating and the detail with which Kipling describes Jevon's humiliation are unmistakable. The whole thing is nasty, but nasty in a typically Kiplingesque way, and it is something we must learn to accept in him.

What is more important is the range of sympathy that *Plain Tales* shows. There is 'Lispeth', for instance, the story of a hill girl brought up by a missionary and his wife, 'westernized' by them, a triumph one would think of conversion to Christianity. She falls in love with an Englishman who passes through the district, assumes – and she has had some encouragement – that he loves her and will return to marry her. When she learns that she has been deluded she says to the missionary's wife:

> 'How can what he and you said be untrue?'
> 'We said it as an excuse to keep you quiet, child,' said the Chaplain's wife.

'Then you lied to me,' said Lispeth, 'you and he?'

The Chaplain's wife bowed her head, and said nothing. Lispeth was silent too for a little time . . .

'I am going back to my own people,' she said. 'You have killed Lispeth. . . . You are all liars, you English.'

'Lispeth' is at once objective and compassionate, a study of mutually uncomprehending racial codes and of Anglo-Saxon hypocrisy. Here it is worth while pointing out that Kipling's attitude towards misalliance between the races, in which his sympathy goes out especially towards the coloured partner, the woman, is markedly compassionate.

'Lispeth' was the first story in *Plain Tales*, and the stories that follow show Kipling's range. 'Thrown Away' is the story of a young subaltern in India who has been reared under 'what parents call the "sheltered life" system'. The Boy – as he is called throughout the story, with an unfortunate suggestion of sentimentality – cannot understand why he is not treated in the regiment with 'the consideration he received under his father's roof. This hurt his feelings.' One day he disappears, and Kipling and a kindly major go after the boy only to find that he has committed suicide by shooting himself. The story then relates how they save the boy's reputation by putting it out that he died of cholera and inventing the circumstantial evidence necessary to convince his colonel and his parents. In fact, in the ingenuity with which the suicide is transformed there is a strong element of the practical joke. The story ends:

The saddest thing of all was the letter from the Boy's mother to the Major and me – with big inky blisters all over the sheet. She wrote the sweetest possible things about our great kindness, and the obligation she would be under to us as long as she lived.

All things considered, she was under an obligation, but not exactly as she meant.

The fifth story in *Plain Tales* is in Kipling's knowing, cynical vein. Phil Garron comes out to India to become a tea-planter, leaving behind him Agnes, his fiancée. After two years, he is still too poor to marry her, and under family pressure she marries a man more eligible, writing to Phil that 'she should never know a happy moment all the rest of her life', which, Kipling says, 'was a true prophecy'. Phil marries a hill-girl, Dunmaya; as Agnes discovers when, suddenly widowed and rich, she comes to India to seek him out:

Now the particular sin and shame of the whole business is that Phil, who really is not worth thinking about twice, was and is loved by Dunmaya, and more than loved by Agnes, the whole of whose life he seemed to have spoilt.

Worst of all, Dunmaya is making a decent man of him; and he will ultimately be saved from perdition through her training.

Which is manifestly unfair.

I have taken these stories from the first half-dozen in *Plain Tales*. They vary greatly in seriousness and achievement and are not fully representative of Kipling's range in the volume. They do not include any of the stories about children or about the three private soldiers Mulvaney, Ortheris, and Learoyd, the best of which is probably 'The Taking of Lungtungpen', in which a Burmese village is captured by a British platoon, entirely naked. Nor do they include two stories which are completely *sui generis* and therefore stand apart from the others: 'To Be Filed for Reference', the story of an educated Englishman, an alcoholic gone native, who leaves behind him on his death a manuscript of which Strickland the policeman says 'the author was either an extreme liar or a most wonderful person'; and 'Gate of Sorrows', a remarkable rendering of the experience and condition of opium-addiction. No moral judgements are made in either of these stories; they are completely objective, and they link up, it seems to me, with the stories of the supernatural or at any rate the irrational or scientifically inexplicable that were to follow and that are at odds with conventional ideas of Kipling as a conventional man.

What they all do is to show the brilliance of Kipling's prose, which to an extent beyond any of his coevals in British English is based on the vernacular, on speed and directness of narration, on an unerring eye and economy of means.

They illustrate, too, his values, which were profoundly conservative in the purest sense, though, to see them at their most explicit, we have to turn to his books for children and young people, to *Stalky & Co.*, and to the *Jungle Books*, where they are expounded in the form of fables. Very briefly, he hated and

feared all those things that would damage or weaken the social
fabric and was the impassioned supporter of all those that imposed obligations upon individuals, organized religion, conventional morality, the ethics of what we now call in-groups. For
him, the great human safeguards were the concepts of duty,
obedience, and work. He was the advocate, one might say the
celebrant, of generic man. It is here, in fact, that the final
criticism of his work possibly lies.

In all this, there is an obvious kinship with Conrad, who, without
being an Imperialist, was as profoundly conservative. But Conrad's
was the more complex personality, perhaps because as a Pole he
belonged to a people that had for generations been in revolt, while as
a middle-class Englishman Kipling was one of those who ruled as
though by right of birth. Beneath Conrad's conservatism, and no
doubt its cause, was a passionate apprehension of the forces of
nihilism within man. Conrad had himself plunged into the heart of
darkness: Kipling, one feels, shrank back from it.

But he had at least looked into it from a distance. When he moved
to the Allahabad *Pioneer* it contained, he tells us, a whole page of
'syndicated serial-matter bought by the running foot. . . .
Henceforth no mere twelve-hundred Plain Tales . . . but three- or
five-thousand-word cartoons once a week.' These allowed an astonishing growth in the complexity of Kipling's work, as can be seen
from two stories dating from as early as 1885 and 1888, 'The Strange
Ride of Morrowbie Jukes' and 'The Man Who Would be King'.

In the first of these, Jukes, a civil engineer, finds himself,
while suffering from fever, marooned in a kind of crater at the
bottom of a valley. He has stumbled into 'a town where the dead
who did not die but may not live have established their headquarters'. Jukes is in a kind of limbo which is inescapable. The
irony is, Morrowbie Jukes, as his name may indicate, is very
much the pukka Englishman highly conscious of bearing the
white man's burden – the phrase, incidentally, was Kipling's invention. In the crater he meets an Indian he had known four
years earlier, Gunga Dass, changed almost beyond recognition
into a withered skeleton, who explains:

'There are only two kinds of men, sar. The alive and the dead. When
you are dead you are dead, but when you are alive you live . . . If you
die at home and do not die when you come to the ghat to be burnt, you

come here ... In epidemics of the cholera you are carried to be burnt almost before you are dead. When you come to the riverside, the cold air perhaps makes you alive, and then, if you are only little alive, mud is put on your nose and mouth and you die conclusively. If you are rather more alive, more mud is put; but if you are too lively they let you go and take you away. I was too lively, and made protestation with anger against the indignities that they endeavoured to press upon me. In those days I was Brahmin and proud man. Now I am dead man and eat' – here he eyed the well-gnawed breast-bone with the first sign of emotion that I had seen in him since we met – 'crows and other things. . . .'

Cast away among the almost dead and the utterly dehumanized, Jukes is 'overmastered completely' by a 'sensation of nameless terror'. Although he is eventually, unconvincingly rescued, we are in the process shown an exceedingly powerful vision of hell or something like it.

'The Strange Ride of Morrowbie Jukes' began, one guesses, as a farcical story of the downfall and discomfiture of a prig whom Kipling disliked but it becomes more than this and haunts one as an intensely imaginative metaphor for the horror of life.

Much more successful since it is more considered is 'The Man Who Would be King'. On a stifling Saturday night in June Kipling, the young newspaperman, is putting the paper to bed alone. Suddenly two adventurers, Dravot and Carnehan, appear. They tell Kipling what they want:

'We have been all over India, mostly on foot. We have been boiler-fitters, engine-drivers, petty contractors, and all that, and we have decided that India isn't big enough for such as us ... Therefore, such *as* it is, we will let it alone and go away to some other place, where a man isn't crowded and can come into his own. We are not little men, and there is nothing that we are afraid of except Drink, and we have signed a Contrack on that. *Therefore*, we are going away to be Kings.'

'Kings in our own right,' muttered Dravot.

They have decided that the only place now in the world that 'two strong men can Sar-a-*whack*' is Kafiristan:

'We shall go to those parts and say to any King we find – "D'you want to vanquish your foes?" and we will show him how to drill men; for that we know better than anything else. Then we will subvert that King and seize his Throne and establish a Dy-nasty.'

Two years go by. On a hot summer night Kipling is again putting the paper to bed.

At three o'clock I cried, 'Print off', and turned to go, when there crept to my chair what was left of a man. He was bent into a circle, his head was sunk between his shoulders, and he moved his feet one over the other like a bear. I could hardly see whether he walked or crawled – this rag-wrapped whining cripple who addressed me by name, crying that he had come back. 'Can you give me a drink?' he whimpered. 'For the Lord's sake give me a drink!'

It is Peachey Taliaferro Carnehan. Broken in body, half-crazed – 'my head isn't as good as it might be' – Carnehan tells his story; how he and Dravot had imposed themselves on the warring tribes of Kafiristan, made themselves all-powerful kings, and fallen through Dravot's weakness of will or dynastic ambition. He had broken the 'contrack' which provided against women as well as drink and taken a wife, 'a queen to breed a king's son for the king'. When he kissed her in public she bit him, drawing blood. It was the end; he had been shown not to be a god and merely human; and his subjects rose against him. Dravot was forced to walk across a river on a rope bridge, which was cut while he was on it. As for Carnehan:

'But do you know what they did to Peachey between two pine-trees? They crucified him, sir, as Peachey's hands will show. They used wooden pegs for his hands and his feet; and he didn't die. He hung there and screamed, and they took him down next day, and said it was a miracle he wasn't dead. They took him down – poor old Peachey that hadn't done them any harm that hadn't done them any —'

He rocked to and fro and wept bitterly, wiping his eyes with the back of his scarred hands and moaning like a child for some ten minutes.

'They was cruel enough to feed him up in the temple, because they said he was more of a God than Old Daniel that was a man. Then they turned him out in the snow, and told him to go home, and Peachey came home in about a year, begging along the roads quite safe; for Daniel Dravot he walked before and said: "Come along, Peachey. It's a big thing we're doing." '

Then he produces from the 'mass of rags round his bent waist' the dried, withered head of Dravot.

'The Man Who Would Be King' is a great story. We are made

aware of the nearness to the heart of darkness of civilized man.
It is also a heroic story; we do not for a moment doubt the
courage, the resource, the shaping dream, of Dravot. J. I. M.
Stewart's remark, from his admirable book on Kipling, is apt
here:

It is a world in which Daniel Dravot's dream of empire is one with
Alexander's (he founds much hope on the fact that his subjects are so
light of skin, and Alexander's actual armies may have set their stamp
upon them.) – and one also with that greater Raj in which Kipling so
fervently believed, and of which in his finest poem, 'Recessional', he
was so majestically to sing the dirge, without quite knowing what he
did. *The captains and the kings depart. . . .* They depart, very horribly,
very horribly, in 'The Man Who Would Be King'.

It is a comment, even a parable, on empire and empire-building.
Dravot and Carnehan are petty adventurers living by their wits,
but Kipling makes explicit the comparison between them and the
honoured empire-builders such as Sir James Brooke in Sarawak.
    To the events narrated and their implications Kipling main-
tains a neutral attitude, and much of the force of the story comes
from this neutrality. It is a great and wonderful story and yet
one has reservations. 'The Strange Ride of Morrowbie Jukes' is
the story of a man who has been in hell and has been left un-
moved by it; at the most, 'he grows very hot and indignant when
he thinks of the disrespectful treatment he received'. This
reduces the story to little more than a horrific anecdote. 'The
Man Who Would Be King' is much richer, but even here Kipling refuses to venture upon the great generalizations that are
forced upon Conrad in 'Heart of Darkness'. One may say that
Kipling deliberately evades the metaphysical horrors implicit in
his story.
    Without disparaging the Indian stories, it is safe to say that
Kipling's imagination gained in freedom once he was outside the
influence of India and things Indian. It was no longer bound by
the naturalistic. Eliot's words are borne in on one: 'the most
inscrutable of authors . . . a writer impossible wholly to understand and quite impossible to belittle'. This can be illustrated
again and again. There is the astonishing 'Wireless', which is set
in a provincial chemist's shop on a cold December night in the
very early days of wireless telegraphy. In the back room an

amateur enthusiast is trying to get in touch with Poole harbour, while in the shop itself are the chemist's young assistant, Mr Shaynor, who is tubercular, and the narrator, whom we may think of as Kipling. As for the chemist's shop on this December night:

Across the street blank shutters flung back the gaslight in cold smears; the dried pavement seemed to rough up in gooseflesh under the scouring of the savage wind, and we could hear, long ere he passed, the policeman flapping his arms to keep himself warm. Within, the flavours of cardamoms and chloric-ether disputed those of the pastilles and a score of drugs and perfume and soap scents. Our electric lights, set low down in the windows before the tun-bellied Rosamond jars, flung inwards three monstrous daubs of red, blue, and green, that broke into kaleidoscopic lights on the faceted knobs of the drug-drawers, the cut-glass scent flagons, and the bulbs of the sparklet bottles. They flushed the white-tiled floor in gorgeous patches; splashed along the nickel-silver counter-rails, and turned the polished mahogany counter-panels to the likeness of intricate grained marbles – slabs of porphyry and malachite. Mr Shaynor unlocked a drawer, and ere he began to write, took out a meagre bundle of letters. From my place by the stove, I could see the scalloped edges of the paper with a flaring monogram in the corner and could even smell the reek of chypre. At each page he turned towards the toilet-water lady of the advertisement and devoured her with over-luminous eyes. He had drawn the Austrian blanket over his shoulders, and among those warring lights he looked more than ever the incarnation of a drugged moth – a tiger-moth as I thought.

This is wonderful writing; as Randall Jarrell comments, 'no one ever again will have to describe a drugstore', and the description, with its reminiscences of Keats's 'The Eve of St. Agnes', is part of the very groundwork of the story. It is not merely a piece of virtuosity.

The narrator mixes a drink from the spirits and drugs the shop offers and gives some to Mr Shaynor, who passes into a kind of trance; 'all meaning and consciousness die out of the swiftly dilating pupils'. As the radio amateur in the inner room makes contact with Poole harbour, the narrator realizes that Mr Shaynor is writing, composing poetry. He is, in fact, composing 'The Eve of St. Agnes'. It is as though the spirit of the apothecary's assistant John Keats had taken possession of the apothecary's assistant Mr Shaynor, who has never heard of Keats. By an imaginative leap Kipling has identified wireless, the new invention by which sounds are transmitted over great distances through the air, with telepathy or some form of what we now call extra-sensory-perception.

There are remarkable stories in quite different modes, those in which Kipling exercises his mythopoeic gift, a gift that seems to be linked with his love of Sussex. It is seen most conspicuously in 'Friendly Brook' and 'The Wish-House', which are masterpieces, besides, of dialogue and the rendering of character through speech. 'Friendly Brook' begins:

The valley was so choked with fog that one could scarcely see a cow's length across a field. Every blade, twig, bracken-frond, and hoof-print carried water, and the air was filled with the noise of rushing ditches and field-drains, all delivering to the brook below. A week's November rain on waterlogged land had gorged her to full flood, and she proclaimed it aloud.

It would be impossible to overpraise either the uncanny accuracy of the observation of the scene and of country crafts or the words and rhythms through which the observation is expressed. It is, of course, another aspect of the Kipling that in *Plain Tales from the Hills* manifested itself as knowingness.

As they work, the two labourers Jabez and Jess discuss the strange behaviour of Jim Wickenden, whose haystack and cottage are in danger of being flooded by the brook when in full spate but who will not take any action to save them. His strange story emerges through their talk. Jim Wickenden has a foster-daughter, and the girl's real father has been blackmailing him by threatening to claim the girl back. When the man came at flood-time Jim made him drunk, so that, crossing the rickety, half-broken plank bridge in front of the cottage, he had missed his footing and fallen into the brook and been drowned.

'Let be how 'twill, the brook was a good friend to Jim. I see it now. I allus *did* wonder what he was gettin' at when he said that, when I talked to him about shiftin' the stack. "You dunno everythin'," he ses. "The Brook's been a good friend to me," he ses, "an' if she's minded to have a snatch at my hay, *I* ain't settin' out to withstand her." '

'I reckon she's about shifted it, too, by now,' Jesse chuckled. 'Hark! That ain't any slip off the bank which she's got hold of.'

The Brook had changed her note again. It sounded as though she were mumbling something soft.

In those last lines the brook is personified; we realize that for Wickenden it is something like a local deity to be placated and propitiated; and we remember similar local gods in Latin poetry. 'Friendly Brook' must strike one now as an intensely pagan story: it is as thought the pre-Christian, pagan deities of Rome have been naturalized in Sussex.

'The Wish House', which is no less remarkable an imaginative feat, is also based upon and largely told in rustic speech. Mrs Ashcroft has a bad leg, and is visited by an old friend. The two women reminisce. They have lived long, and behind them we feel the shadowy presence of earlier women of the people in literature, notably Chaucer's Wife of Bath, Juliet's nurse, and the old women of Hardy.

Mrs Ashcroft tells her friend about the Wish House. One day, as a cook in London, she was 'half mad with the 'eddick', which had disappeared when a little girl visited a Wish House on her behalf:

'Sophy said there was a Wish 'Ouse in Wadloes Road – just a few streets off, on the way to our greengrocer's. All you 'as to do, she said, was to ring the bell an' wish your wish through the slit o' the letter-box.'

That summer, Mrs Ashcroft, on holiday in her native village in Sussex, sees her old lover Harry Mockler 's'runk and wizen: 'is clothes 'angin' on 'im like bags, an' the back of 'is neck whiter'n chalk.' He had cut his foot with a spade while 'muckin' out the old pond at Smalldene. There was poison in de dirt, an' it roshed up 'is leg, an' come out all over him.' Back in London, she goes to the Wish House.

'Fourteen, Wadloes Road, was the place – a liddle basement-kitchen 'ouse, in a row of twenty-thirty such, and tiddy strips o' walled garden in front – the paint off the front doors, an' naun done to naun since ever so long. . . . I stooped me to the letter-box slit, an' I says: "Let me take everythin' bad that's in store for my man, 'Arry Mockler, for love's sake . . ." '

That night, Mrs Ashcroft knocks her leg just above the ankle against an old roasting-jack. When the injury becomes worse her employers send her off to Sussex to recover. But we know that, back in the village, unable to work and pensioned off, she has a cancerous leg and her time is short. 'I saw 'Arry once or twice in de street,' she tells Mrs Fettley, 'wonnerful fleshed up an' restored back', and a little later, she says that Harry 'got 'is good from me 'thout knowin' – for years and years'.

This story of self-sacrifice, of the willing taking on of another's suffering, seems to me Kipling's most beautiful story, and it is completely unsentimental. Mrs Ashcroft's action is one with her maternal, earthy, racy nature; and that, indeed, is the guarantee as it were of its authenticity. As invented folk-lore, the notion of the wish-house is breath-takingly brilliant and because of its very feel of folk-lore it carries with it no sense of strain.

I have called 'The Wish House' Kipling's most beautiful story, but how can one choose between it and the very different 'They', the most mysterious and haunting of his works and one which profoundly influenced Eliot in the writing of 'Burnt Norton'? These stories illustrate what Professor Andrew Rutherford, in his preface to the Penguin edition, has described as the evolution in Kipling's work 'of that complex, closely organized, elliptical, and symbolic mode of writing which ranks him as an unexpected contributor to "modernism" '. The most remarkable example of this seems to me 'Mrs Bathurst', which was written in 1904, either in South Africa, where Kipling had been a war correspondent, or soon after his return. The story is a masterpiece of allusiveness, impressionism, and indirection; the realistic detail is handled with unerring skill; and the dialogue not only sharply personifies the characters but also evokes a whole way of life, for the presence of the Royal Navy is felt in the story all the time. It is an extraordinarily complex and subtle piece of writing which demands many readings and in a curious way it seems to look forward, not so much to later prose, for none has gone beyond it in subtlety, as to the kind of poetry Pound and Eliot were to be writing ten years later.

The story arises out of the chance meeting at the Cape between Kipling, an old friend, Hooper, who is an inspector of railways, another old friend, Pyecroft, a naval petty officer, and

Pritchard, sergeant of marines, whom Kipling is meeting for the first time. They retire to an empty railway coach in a siding, drink beer, and reminisce. Each is individualized in his own unique personality through his speech. They talk, or rather, Pyecroft and Pritchard do, of a Mrs Bathurst, a widow who keeps a bar much frequented by sailors in Auckland, New Zealand. Her mystery and power are evoked in the following snatch of dialogue:

'How many women have you been intimate with all over the world, Pritch?'

Pritchard blushed plum colour to the short hairs of his seventeen-inch neck.

' 'Undreds,' said Pyecroft. 'So've I. How many of 'em can you remember in your own mind, settin' aside the first – an' per'aps the last – *and one more?*'

'Few, wonderful few, now I tax myself,' said Sergeant Pritchard, relievedly.

'An' how many times might you 'ave been at Auckland?'

'One – two,' he began. 'Why, I can't make it more than three times in ten years. But I can remember every time that I ever saw Mrs B.'

'So can I – an' I've only been to Auckland twice – how she stood an' what she was sayin' an' what she looked like. That's the secret. 'Tisn't beauty, so to speak, nor good talk necessarily. It's just It. Some women'll sit in a man's mind if they once walk down a street, but most of 'em you can live with for a month on end, an' next commission you'd be put to it to certify whether they talk in their sleep or not, as one might say.'

'Ah,' said Hooper, 'that's more the idea. I've known just two women of that nature.'

'An' it was no fault o' theirs?' asked Pritchard.

'None whatever. I know that.'

'An' if a man gets struck with that kind of woman, Mr Hooper?' Pritchard went on.

'He goes crazy – or just saves himself,' was the slow reply.

'You've hit it,' said the Sergeant. 'You've seen an' known somethin' in the course o' your life, Mr Hooper. I'm lookin' at you!' He set down his bottle.

The conversation then turns by association to a warrant-officer of Marines called Vickery, nicknamed 'Click' because of his ill-fitting false teeth, who has disappeared into the interior, has

presumably deserted. Sergeant Pyecroft tells how he went with
Vickery on five successive nights to a cinematograph exhibition
in Cape Town, and he describes the show. It must, incidentally,
be one of the earliest descriptions of a film in literature and it
shows again how Kipling's imagination was quickened by tech-
nological invention:

'Vickery touched me on the knee when the number went up. "If you
see anything that strikes you," he said, "drop me a hint"; then he went
on clicking. We saw London Bridge an' so forth, an' it was most inter-
estin'. I'd never seen it before. You 'eard a little dynamo-like buzzin',
but the pictures were the real thing – alive an' movin' . . .

'Then the Western Mail came into Paddin'ton on the big magic lan-
tern sheet. First we saw the platform empty an' the porters standin' by.
Then the engine came in, head on, an' the women in the front row
jumped up; she headed so straight. Then the doors opened and the
passengers came out and the porters got the luggage – just like life.
Only – only when anyone came down too far towards us that was
watchin', they walked right out o' the picture, so to speak. I was 'ighly
interested, I can tell you. So were all of us. I watched an old man with
a rug 'oo'd dropped a book an' was tryin' to pick it up, when quite
slowly, from be'ind two porters – carryin' a little reticule an' looking'
from side to side – comes our Mrs Bathurst. There was no mistakin'
the walk in a hundred thousand. She came forward – right forwards –
she looked out straight at us with that blindish look which Pritchard
alluded to. She walked on and on till she melted out of the picture . . .,
an' as she went I 'eard Dawson in the tickey seats be'ind sing out:
"Christ. There's Mrs B!" '

Hooper swallowed his spittle and leaned forward intently.

'Vickery touched me on the knee again. He was clickin' his four false
teeth with his jaw down like an enteric at the last kick. "Are you sure?"
says he. "Sure," I says; "didn't you 'ear Dawson give tongue? Why, it's
the woman herself." "I was sure before," he says, "but I brought you
to make sure. Will you come again with me tomorrow?" '

Vickery's abandonment of ship, his disappearance into the
interior, is bound up, one infers, with his obsession with Mrs
Bathurst. The dénouement – but that is to put it altogether too
crudely – comes when we learn that Hooper, the inspector of
railways, has discovered the dead body of Vickery in a teak
forest on the edge of the line in Rhodesia. It was entirely blackened, turned into charcoal, for Vickery had been struck by light-

ening, identifiable only by his four false teeth, which Hooper ıas in his waistcoat pocket.

Kipling's are the most complex stories in English and the most varied, the least predictable and the most challenging and disturbing. Take 'Mary Postgate', which every critic has praised for its technical brilliance and many have been repelled by, assuming Kipling's own attitude towards the central event to be Mary Postgate's. A lady's companion, middle-class, middle-aged, watches without compunction or intervention a shot-down German airman die in agony – her mistress's son, a pilot in the Royal Flying Corps, whom she has doted upon, having recently been killed in combat. Coming into tea immediately after, she strikes her employer suddenly as 'quite handsome'. It is an appalling and unforgettable story, but the Kipling who could make his Tommy say, 'You're a better man than I am, Gunga Dinn,' cannot be equated with Mary Postgate.

In England, the flowering of the short story in the last years of
the nineteenth century and the early years of the twentieth seems
to be summed up in Kipling. He gave the form prestige, so that
it became entirely proper for writers of fiction to take the short
story as seriously as they did the novel. New magazines and per-
iodicals came into existence that both exploited and furthered its
prestige. One such was *The Strand Magazine*, the first number
of which appeared in 1891. It was founded, significantly, by
George Newnes, who had earlier founded *Tit-Bits* and was as
essentially middle-class as *Tit-Bits* was working-class. According
to Reginald Pound, its last editor, it 'projected the sense of responsibility that was closely related to the moral temper of the
founding years, when "Mr Editor" was a vastly respected entity,
infallibly wise and just, and always in the people's fancy, be-
nignly bearded.' Over the years, the names of Conan Doyle,
H. G. Wells, W. W. Jacobs, and P. G. Wodehouse were particularly associated with it. The stories of none of these writers
are quite what we mean by modern short stories, but most of
them have a common quality of incidental realism. In Doyle's
stories, for example, besides the obvious fascination of watching
the working of Sherlock Holmes's mind, his solving of the apparently insoluble, which are the elements of wonder, there is
also a real sense of the London of the period.

W. W. Jacobs, who produced sixteen books, the majority of
them collections of short stories, was an exquisite minor artist.
Born in Wapping on London River, he set his stories mainly on
the Thames; his characters are skippers and mates and sailors on
coastal schooners, lightermen and watchmen of wharves, and
their women, wives, daughters, and sweethearts. Realism was not
his aim. He was a master of artificial comedy and of his own
mannered dialogue, which was based on Thames speech. He
wrote with the utmost economy. Everything is dramatized. Farce
may be present as the basic element of his stories, but it is
always modulated by an extremely subtle, low-keyed humour.

Within these limits, which are admittedly very narrow, Jacobs is a master. We read his stories partly to savour the skill and freshness with which he deploys material of a kind that has entertained men and women at all levels of sophistication since the birth of language. His success is evident in the comic fairy-land he created.

Well's first reputation was as a writer of scientific romance, and his short stories, of which he wrote five volumes, fall gener-ally under that head. The finest of the scientific romances in that it is the most profoundly imaginative and the most deeply felt is *The Time Machine*, a work about eighty pages long, the first version of which he wrote when he was still a student at the Imperial College of Science. It becomes almost the prose equiva-lent of the great poem on nineteenth-century science the poets of the time never wrote. In it, the most vivid imagination of the age is electrified by the shock upon it of contemporary theories of evolution and economics. Darwin and Marx are miraculously brought together in the vision of the Eloi and the Morlocks, the degenerate descendants of the *rentiers* and the proletariat, and Wells rises to even greater heights of imagination in the last pages of the story, in his contemplation of an earth thirty million years hence almost bereft of life. It is, it seems to me, a Shel-leyan imagination; and though *The Time Machine* is often crude in circumstantial details, in what the eighteenth-century critics called the machinery of the fable, this matters little compared with the intensity of its imaginative vision.

Scientific speculation offered Wells a world of wonders which both delighted and terrified him, and reading Wells's scientific romances and stories, one is reminded of the way Swift plays with ideas in *Gulliver's Travels*. 'The Plattner Story' is a good example. A young schoolmaster, experimenting with some green-ish powder one of the boys has come across on the Sussex Downs, causes an explosion in which he disappears. Plattner, whom the Narrator meets and interviews after his return, had been blown into the twilight world of the Fourth Dimension, a world parallel with ours but unseen by us, inhabited by impotent spirits of the dead who are constantly observing human acti-vities. He had been propelled out of space. The Proof? 'His entire body had had its left and right sides transposed.'

There follows an impressive display of what might be called Wells's scientific sleight-of-hand:

There is no way of taking a man and moving him about in *space*, as ordinary people understand space, that will result in our changing his sides. . . . Mathematical theorists tell us that the only way in which the right and left sides of a solid body can be changed is by taking that body clean out of space as we know it, taking it out of ordinary existence, that is, and turning it somewhere outside space. This is a little abstruse, no doubt, but anyone with a slight knowledge of mathematical theory will assure the reader of its truth. To put the thing in technical language, the curious inversion of Plattner's right and left sides is proof that he has moved out of our space into what is called the Fourth Dimension, and that he has returned again to our world. Unless we choose to consider ourselves the victim of an elaborate and motiveless fabrication, we are almost bound to believe that this has occurred.

This passage precludes any account of the explosion or of Plattner's adventures in the Fourth Dimension; and this gives the story something very much like the form of a theorem in geometry. Beyond this, something else is apparent in 'The Plattner Story': we are in the presence of one of the oldest types of story, the ghost story.

Thus, Wells's stories generally approximate to old forms. He sets out to chill or to shock or to make us laugh. There is 'The Lord of Dynamos', with its notably brisk beginning:

The chief attendant of the three dynamos that buzzed and rattled at Camberwell and kept the electric railway going, came out of Yorkshire, and his name was James Holroyd. He was a practical electrician but fond of whisky, a heavy red-haired brute with irregular teeth. He doubted the existence of the Deity but accepted Carnot's cycle, and he had read Shakespeare and found him weak in chemistry. His helper came out of the mysterious East, and his name was Azuma-zi. But Holroyd called him Pooh-bah. Holroyd liked a nigger help because he would stand kicking – a habit with Holroyd – and did not pry into machinery and try to learn the ways of it. Certain odd possibilities of the negro mind brought into abrupt contact with the crown of our civilization Holroyd never fully realized, though just at the end he got some inkling of them.

Azuma-zi begins to worship the largest dynamo as a god and gives Holroyd to it as a human sacrifice. In the end, he is killed by it himself and the story ends:

So ended prematurely the worship of the Dynamo Deity, perhaps the most short-lived of all religions. Yet withal it could at least boast a Martyrdom and a Human Sacrifice.

It is, it seems to me, a story Kipling might have written, and I think one can detect his influence in it.

Others, like 'The Stolen Bacillus', are deplorably facetious. A bacteriologist shows a visitor to his laboratory what he describes as a preparation of cholera bacillus and is surprised by the visitor's unhealthily excited curiosity. He tells the man:

'Yes, here is the pestilence imprisoned. Only break such a little tube as this into a supply of drinking-water, . . . and death – mysterious, untraceable death, death swift and terrible, death full of pain and indignity – would be released upon this city. . . .'

He is called away for a moment and when he returns he finds the visitor has gone, and has taken the cholera bacillus with him. Pursued by the bacteriologist, the thief is cornered but he cries: ' "Vive l'Anarchie! You are too late, my friend. I have drunk it. The cholera is abroad!" ' He has, in fact, as the bacteriologist knows, merely drunk a culture of the bacillus that produces blue patches on certain monkeys.

Here, we are in the presence of the material of children's comic papers; yet the story is carried through with great zest. The spirits may be preternaturally high, but there is still, as in Wells generally, the actualization of the scientific. In stories of this kind, he may be said to have domesticated science.

Wells was a vigorous but not markedly sensitive writer of prose, and his attempts at the avowedly poetic in prose are generally more embarrassing than successful. However 'The Door in the Wall' does seem to succeed. An eminent politician tells how throughout his successful but circumscribed life he has been haunted by a door in a wall in West Kensington which as a small child he passed through, to find himself in a paradise of love and happiness. In later days, he had glimpsed it from time to time, but always at a time when the press of the world's business has been such that he cannot enter. His narrative ends with these words:

'Let me tell you something, Redmond. This loss is destroying me. For two months, for ten weeks nearly now, I have done no work at all, except the most necessary and urgent duties. My soul is full of un-appeasable regrets. At nights – when it is less likely that I shall be recognized – I go out. I wander. Yes. I wonder what people would think of that if they knew. A Cabinet Minister, the responsible head of the most vital of all departments, wandering alone – grieving – sometimes nearly audibly lamenting – for a door, for a garden!'

That is not the end of the story:

They found his body very early yesterday morning in a deep excavation near East Kensington Station. It is one of two shafts that have been made in connection with the extension of the railway southward. It is protected from the intrusion of the public by a hoarding upon the high road, in which a small doorway had been cut for the convenience of some workmen who live in that direction. The doorway was left unfastened through a misunderstanding between two gangers, and through it he made his way.

'The Door in the Wall' is not a difficult story. It seems to call for a more sensitive prose than Wells was capable of, but all the same it is a haunting story. It is as though what one would normally think of as a de la Mare story had been written by Wells.

Though Wells never entirely abandoned scientific romance, from about 1900 it was more and more displaced by novels of social criticism. However, from time to time the world of the scientific romances does overlap that of the social novels, and his most satisfying short stories are probably those that are the fruit of a fusion of his observation of lower middle-class life and his powers of speculation. To the point here is 'The Man Who Could Work Miracles', with its brilliant beginning:

It is doubtful whether the gift was innate. For my own part, I think it came to him suddenly. Indeed, until he was thirty he was a sceptic, and did not believe in miraculous powers. And here, since it is the most convenient place, I must mention that he was a little man, and had eyes of hot brown, very erect red hair, a moustache with ends that he twisted up, and freckles. His name was George McWhirter Fotheringay –not the sort of name by any means to lead to any expectation of miracles – and he was clerk at Gomshott's. He was greatly addicted to assertive argument. It was while he was asserting the impossibility of miracles that he had his first intimation of his extraordinary powers. This particular argument was being held in the bar of the Long

Dragon, and Teddy Beamish was conducting the opposition by a monotonous but effective 'So *you* say', that drove Mr Fotheringay to the very limit of his patience. . . . 'Looky here, Mr Beamish', said Mr Fotheringay, 'Let us clearly understand what a miracle is. It's something contrariwise to the course of nature done by power of will, something what couldn't happen without being specially willed.'

'So *you* say,' said Mr Beamish, repulsing him.

The reader's curiosity is immediately piqued by this, and the satisfaction of it is tantalizingly delayed.

'For instance,' said Mr Fotheringay, greatly encouraged. 'Here would be a miracle. That lamp, in the natural course of nature, couldn't burn like that upsy-down, could it Beamish?'

'You say it couldn't,' said Beamish.

Mr Fotheringay inverts the lamp, which to his consternation continues burning. His attempt to disprove the possibility of miracles has merely proved to him that he can work them.

He passes the night in his room, experimenting with miracles. He is satisfied he can perform them but is not entirely happy about his power, and next evening, performing an entirely innocent miracle, he comes up against the law. He consigns the policeman to San Francisco and thereafter feels guilty. On Sunday evening after chapel, he consults the Congregationalist minister, Mr Maydig, who tests Fotheringay's powers until Fotheringay, noticing it is now three o'clock and that he has to be at business by eight, says he must be going. Mr Maydig suggests he puts the clock back by stopping the rotation of the earth. Mr Fotheringay does so, and there follows a wonderful description of the consequences. As he finds himself flying head over heels through space at a truly astronomical speed he has enough wit to will that he comes down safe and sound. 'He willed it only just in time, for his clothes, heated by his rapid flight through the air, were already beginning to singe.'

This experience cures Mr Fotheringay of any love of miracles and he decides to perform a final one to restore himself and everything else to their condition before he inverted the lamp in the Long Dragon. Immediately, he finds himself standing at the bar, listening to a familiar voice saying 'So *you* say.'

In this story, which seems to me his happiest, the two sides of Wells's genius come together perfectly.

Wells was one of the first English reviewers to recognize the genius of Conrad, who was ten years older than him but began writing some years later. Less technically accomplished than Kipling's, his work serves to remind us that technique is not an end in itself but a means to an end. His view of life was well stated by Bertrand Russell, who, talking of him in a memorable broadcast, said: 'I felt ... that he thought of civilized and morally tolerable life as a dangerous walk on a thin crust of barely cool lava which at any moment might break and let the unwary sink into fiery depths.'

And yet, despite this, Conrad often followed techniques that render credibility more difficult. Thus, 'Heart of Darkness' is told in the first person by a character named Marlow, who recounts an experience he has had as a young man up the Congo. Conrad got the device, I suspect, from *Blackwood's Magazine*, for which he wrote the story. Stories of adventure told after dinner by men over their port were almost a speciality of *Blackwood's*; we find John Buchan using the same formula in its pages twenty years later.

It must be admitted that the device makes for heavy weather. Marlow and his validity have first to be established. A group of successful middle-aged men are staying on a yacht in the Thames estuary. It is to these men that Marlow tells his yarn, as he inappropriately calls it.

Before he begins to do so, Conrad comments:

The yarns of seamen have a direct simplicity, the whole meaning of which lies within the shell of a cracked nut. But Marlow was not typical (if his propensity to spin yarns be excepted), and to him the meaning of an episode was not inside like a kernel but outside, which brought it out as a glow brings out a haze, in the likeness of one of those misty haloes that sometimes are made visible by the special illuminations of moonlight.

It is only after this introduction that the story can begin, so Conrad would seem the last man in the world to be a short-story writer. The truth is, the power of his imagination, the depth of his insight, and the commensurate grandeur of his prose are such as to compel us to accept the conventions within which the stories are written. After reading 'Heart of Darkness', one forgets what may be called the scaffolding of the story and remembers Marlow's experience only.

Conrad told Edward Garnett: 'Before I went to the Congo I was just a mere animal.' He meant he was still innocent, and 'Heart of Darkness' throws much light on the remark. It can be summarized very briefly. Marlow secures command of a river boat on the Congo. Once there he finds that all civilized values, together with the white man's integrity, are threatened by what had been called the 'orgiastic native life' and by the enormous power imperialism gives to the white man. Marlow hears rumours of a man named Kurtz, who had begun in Africa as a good liberal; he had truly hoped to bring civilization to the Dark Continent, to which end he had written a report for the International Society for the Suppression of Savage Customs on the problems that Africa poses. But Africa betrays him, or rather the heart of darkness, which is at once the darkness of Africa and the darkness in the heart of man, does so. He exploits the white man's power over the superstitions of the natives in order to screw more and more ivory out of them. He realizes what is happening to him and scrawls on his report 'Exterminate all the brutes' and when he dies he whispers 'The Horror! The Horror!'

On one level, the story shows the other side, as it were, of the aspirations of Kipling's Carnehan and Dravot in 'The Man Who Would be King'. But it is much more than this. At bottom, it is a story of the double. Marlow identifies himself with Kurtz: Kurtz is the man he might himself have become had he not been alerted in time by the awful warning of Kurtz's example.

Conrad was haunted by the notion of the double, by the notion that by some trick of fate or nature, and for him they are very nearly the same thing, the good man, the honourable man, may be turned into his opposite. Tony Tanner expresses it thus in his monograph on *Lord Jim*:

... he explored this possibility that a hidden part of a man committed to order and the rules of society might suddenly embrace and identify itself with a being, a presence, an apparition which seems most antipathetic to his own conscious self, a walking reminder of all that inner darkness and weakness which civilized man has suppressed in order to make group life possible.

In his short story 'The Secret Sharer' Conrad pursues this same theme. It may not be as great as 'Heart of Darkness', lacking as it does what may be called the public or political dimension of the other, but it is technically a much better story, more economical both in structure and in language, and with a greater clarity.

The narrator is a young sea-captain who has just got his first command at a Far Eastern port. Conscious of his new responsibilities and of his inexperience, he feels himself insecure. 'But what I felt most,' he tells us at the beginning of the story, 'was my being a stranger to the ship; and if the truth must be told, I was somewhat of a stranger to myself.' On the night before the ship sails he finds that the rope side-ladder has not been hauled in and is annoyed, 'for exactitude in small matters is the soul of discipline.' He proceeds to get in the ladder himself and is startled to find a naked swimmer at the end of it trying to climb on board. He helps the man up; 'It was, in the night, as though I had been faced by my own reflection in the depths of a sombre and immense mirror.' The stranger tells his story. His name is Leggatt, and he has escaped from the ship on which he was mate and to which he has been confined because he has killed a sailor who had panicked at a time when orderly action was essential for the ship's safety. He has escaped not to save himself but to avoid the ignominy of trial. The captain identifies himself with Leggatt, who under stress has behaved as he himself might have done. Leggatt is in a sense his *doppelganger*.

At great hazard, the captain conceals Leggatt in his cabin and eventually puts his ship close inshore in dangerous, because unknown, waters to give Leggatt a chance of swimming unseen away. It is in this test of himself that he gains mastery of his ship, his officers and crew, and himself.

Conrad's most famous short fiction, I imagine, is still 'Typhoon'. Rather less than 20,000 words in length, it is unequivocably a short story, and is the most straightforward, the least ambiguous statement of Conrad's creed, which, at its simplest, is that a man must do his duty. Captain MacWhirr, of the steamer *Nan-Shan*, brings his ship through the typhoon; he restores order to the cargo of coolies, and is able to do so because he has 'just enough imagination to carry him through each successive day and no more'.

'There are few novels in our period,' H. G. Wells wrote, 'to be put beside *The Old Wives' Tale* and *Riceyman Steps* and few short stories to equal "The Matador of the Five Towns".' On the novels Wells is obviously right, on "The Matador of the Five Towns", though it is the best of Bennett's short stories, I am not so sure. If 'Heart of Darkness', 'The Secret Sharer', and 'Typhoon' were taken away from the body of Conrad's work the loss would be great indeed; insofar as short stories and novels can be compared, they possess a like authority to *Nostromo* and *Lord Jim*. By contrast, the relation of 'The Matador of the Five Towns' to *The Old Wives' Tale* is very much that of a foot-note; the short story could be merged into the novel without strain.

Bennett, who was nothing if not a professional writer, established a pattern for the novelists who followed him. He wrote almost thirty novels and five volumes of short stories. We now take it for granted that a novelist will write the occasional short story and publish the occasional volume of them; and there can be few good novelists who have not written on occasion good stories. Some, indeed, are memorable, as, for instance, Aldous Huxley's 'Young Archimedes' and Graham Greene's 'The Basement Room', but there is obviously a difference between the novelist who is an occasional short-story writer and the novelist like Conrad or Lawrence whose short stories add another dimension to his work.

A writer who was an occasional novelist rather than an occasional short-story writer – he published five collections of stories to two novels – was 'Saki' (H. H. Munro). His provenance has been indicated by V. S. Pritchett, who has written, in his essay on him, 'The Performing Lynx', in *The Working Novelist*, that he 'belongs to the early period of the sadistic revival in English comic and satirical writing – the movement suggested by Stevenson, Wilde, Beerbohm, Firbank, and Evelyn Waugh – the early period when the chief target was the cult of convention.' One may throw in, the more closely to define Saki's position, the names of two or three other writers with whom he had affinities, the Belloc of *A Bad Child's Book of Beasts*, the Harry Graham of *Ruthless Rhymes* and, above all perhaps, the young Kipling, with whom he shared a similar background and upbringing. He was born in Burma in 1870 and sent home to Devon, where he was brought up by an aunt whom he found detestable. He returned to Burma as a young man and joined the Burma Police; but ill health compelled him to resign and return to England, where he began to write for newspapers like the *Westminster Gazette*. Many of his short stories appeared there. They are very rarely more than four or five pages long and are wholly *sui generis*.

It is scarcely possible to speak of development in Saki's art; it remained all of a piece, and characteristic of it is his story of the detested aunt, 'Sredni Vashtar', which appeared in the volume *The Chronicles of Clovis* in 1911. The style in which it is written is one of finely contemptuous disdain. The aunt, Mrs de Ropp, would never, we are told,

in her honestest moments, have confessed to herself that she disliked Conradin, though she might have been dimly aware that thwarting him 'for his good' was a duty which she did not find particularly irksome.

Conradin's haven from 'the Woman', as he calls Mrs de Ropp, is a disused tool-shed behind the shrubbery which has for him the aura both of a playroom and a cathedral, for he has peopled it not only from his imagination but with 'two inmates of flesh and blood'. One is 'a ragged-plumaged Houdan hen, on which the boy lavished an affection that had scarcely another outlet', the other a large polecat ferret, his most treasured possession, of which he is 'dreadfully' afraid and which he kept behind close iron bars in a large hutch. 'Its very presence in the tool-shed was a secret and fearful joy, to be kept scrupulously from the knowledge of the Woman.' He devises a name for it, Sredni Vashtar, which from that moment 'grew into a god and a religion'.

His absorption in the tool-shed attracts the Woman's attention, and one morning she announces that the Houdan hen has been sold and taken away. After this, Conradin prays nightly in the tool-shed to the ferret: 'Do one thing for me, Sredni Vashtar.' Mrs de Ropp surprises him one day in the tool-shed and demands to know what is in the hutch, answering her own question: 'I believe it's guinea-pigs. I'll have them all cleared away.' She enters the shed and without hope, he prays to the ferret for her defeat:

He knew that the Woman would triumph as she triumphed now, and that he would grow ever more sickly under her pestering domineering and superior wisdom, till one day nothing would matter much more with him and the doctor would be proved right. And in the sting and misery of his defeat, he began to chant loudly and defiantly the hymn of his threatened idol:

Sredni Vashtar went forth,
His thought were red thoughts and his teeth were white.
His enemies called for peace, but he brought them death.
Sredni Vashtar the beautiful.

While the maid lays the table for tea Conradin watches at the window.

Hope had crept by inches into his heart, and now a look of triumph began to blaze in his eyes that had only known the wistful patience of defeat. Under his breath, with a furtive exultation, he began once again the paean of victory and devastation. And presently his eyes were rewarded; out through that doorway came a long, low, yellow-and-brown beast, with eyes a-blink at the waning daylight, and dark wet stains around the fur of jaws and throat. Conradin dropped on his knees. The great polecat ferret made its way down to a small brook at the foot of the garden, drank for a moment, then crossed a little plank bridge and was lost to sight in the bushes. Such was the passing of Sredni Vashtar.

The maid summons her mistress to tea and Conradin toasts himself a slice of bread, buttering it and eating it with slow enjoyment. He listens to the silence of the house and then 'the loud foolish screaming of the maid'.

'Whoever will break it to the poor child? I couldn't for the life of me!' exclaimed a shrill voice. And while they debated the matter among themselves, Conradin made himself another piece of toast.

So 'Sredni Vashtar' ends. It is flawless, a masterpiece of the psychology of a lonely, emotionally neglected, and imaginative childhood, the more powerful because the boy's passionate wish for revenge, though controlled by the disdainful tone of the prose, is carried through to the end. Generally, Saki is content to present an artificial universe approximating in the magic of its nonsense to Wilde in *The Importance of Being Earnest*. But artificial though it may be, the comedy is never quite irrelevant to the world as we know it, as we see in the delightful 'Tobermory', which recounts a disconcerting incident at Lady Blemley's house-party on a 'chill, rain-washed afternoon of a late August day, that indefinite season when partridges are still in security or cold storage, and there is nothing to hunt – unless one is bounded on the north by the Bristol Channel, in which case one may lawfully gallop after fat red stags'. Mr Appin, most unprepossessing and unpromising of house-guests, announces to the astonishment of all that he has discovered how to teach animals to talk and that his first successful pupil has been none other than Lady Blemley's pet cat Tobermory. At which point, Tobermory enters the room. Constraint becomes panic when it is apparent from his replies to questions that Tobermory is a cat that enjoys telling home-truths. 'Why did I ever come down here?' Agnes Resker asks dramatically. Tobermory is not slow to tell her:

'Judging by what you said to Mrs Corbett on the croquet-lawn yesterday, you were out for food. You described the Blemleys as the dullest people to stay with you knew, but said they were clever enough to employ a first-rate cook; otherwise they'd find it difficult to get anyone to come down a second time.'

'There's not a word of truth in it! I appeal to Mrs Corbett –' exclaimed the discomforted Agnes.

'Mrs Corbett repeated your remark afterwards to Bertie van Tahn,' continued Tobermory, 'and said, "That woman is a regular Hunger Marcher; she'd go anywhere for four square meals a day", and Bertie van Tahn said . . .'

V. S. Pritchett isolates the essential Saki when he characterizes him as 'this gifted lynx so contemptuously consenting to be half-human' and sums up one side of his talent when he writes that although his characters are 'done in cyanide, the deed is touched by a child's sympathy for the vulnerable areas of the large mammals'. The artificiality of Saki's world, the frivolity of his manner, cannot mask a threat; which is to say that Saki's is an old world, the familiar world, the real world, ever so slightly rearranged.

That the Edwardian age was a haunted period in writing can be seen quite clearly by a recital of names. Arthur Machen, M. R. James, Algernon Blackwood, Lord Dunsany, Walter de la Mare were writers of very different orders of talent and achievement but all were concerned with the world of fantasy.

This may be merely another way of stating the truism that prose fiction always leans either to history or to poetry, to realism or romance in Northrop Frye's sense of the word. Of these haunted writers the most distinguished is always remembered first as a poet in the literal sense. As a short-story writer, Walter de la Mare closely resembles Henry James, specifically the James of what are sometimes called the supernatural stories. His prose is almost as dense as James's and as resonant, the stories no less 'difficult'. Their fabric is no less of the material world than James's; they are rooted in a solid and palpable, if mundane, reality, and de la Mare writes very much as a man of his time and as a master of its common speech, exploiting both with delightful humour. For example, 'A Revenant' has Edgar Allen Poe attending, as a revenant, a lecture on himself in a provincial town. It is at once a brilliantly subtle exposure of academic pretension, an absorbing consideration of the nature of poetry, and a remarkably convincing recreation of Poe. The milieu depicted is as well 'documented' as James's, but the equation between the setting of the story and its dénouement and deducible moral is not easily determined. Here, de la Mare's stories are of a piece with his poetry, with 'The Listeners', for instance: they are perfectly comprehensible but disturb the mind nevertheless by overtones sensed rather than understood.

On this aspect of de la Mare's stories no one has written with more insight than Graham Greene, who, after a paragraph on de la Mare's prose ('unequalled in its richness since the death of James, or, dare one at this date, say Robert Louis Stevenson'), concludes his essay in *The Lost Childhood*:

> With these resources at his command no one can bring the natural visible world more sharply to the eye: from the railway carriage window we watch the landscape unfold . . . we are wooed and lulled sometimes to the verge of sleep by the beauty of the prose, until suddenly without warning a sentence breaks in mid-breath and we look up and see the terrified eyes of our fellow-passenger, appealing, hungry, scared, as he watches what we cannot see – 'the sediment of an unspeakable obsession'.

To illustrate Greene's thesis I choose 'The Trumpet'. Two boys, Philip, the rector's son, and his friend Dick, decide to spend that night when, according to superstitition, ghosts walk, in the village church:

> The minute church, obscurely lit by a full moon that had not yet found window-glass through which the direct beams could pierce into this gloaming, was deserted and silent. Not a sound, within or without,

disturbed its stony quiet – except only the insect-like rapid ticking of a clock in the vestry, and the low pulsating thump of a revolving cog-wheel in the tower above the roof. Here and there a polished stone gleamed coldly in the vague luminous haze – a marble head, a wing-tip, a pointing finger, the claws and beak of the eagle on the brazen lectern, the two silvergilt candlesticks flanking the colourless waxen flowers upon the altar. So secret and secluded seemed the church within its nocturnal walls that living creature might never have been there at all – or creatures only so insignificant and transitory as to have left no perceptible trace behind them.

Like a cataleptic's countenance it hinted, moreover, at no inward activity of its own. And yet, if – fantastic notion – some unseen watcher through the bygone centuries had kept it perpetually within gaze, he might at last have concluded that it possessed a *sort* of stagnant life or animation . . .

The two boys sit side by side in a pew daring and out-boasting each other. Philip, conscious of his superiority in class and religious status, is especially aggressive, and when Dick goes outside to watch for ghosts, sucking jujubes, he stares at 'the monument that not only dominated but dwarfed the small but lovely chancel'.

The figure of the angel was now bathed with the silver of the moon. With long-toed feet at once clasping and spurning the orb beneath them, it stood erect on high. Chin thrust out, its steadfast sightless eyes were fixed upon the faded blue and geranium red of the panelled roof. Its braided locks were drawn back from a serene and impassive visage, its left hand lay flat upon its breast, and with the right it clasped a tapering, uplifted, bell-mouthed, gilded trumpet held firmly not against but a little distance from its lips.

Philip is risking a lot in being alone with the angel now, among other things a beating from his father and the humiliation of its being discovered that he has been beguiled into the adventure by a village boy about whom he feels curiously ambivalent. Dick is described as being 'like a mysterious and unintelligible little animal, past taming, and possessed of a spirit of whose secret presence he himself was completely unaware'.

The boy now returns, and they both contemplate the angel. At last, Philip dares Dick to climb the monument and blow the angel's trumpet. The monument, which is surmounted by the angel, is loftier than Philip has thought, and as Dick climbs he pleads, cajoles, orders 'in helpless fear and fury' the other to come down. ' " It's wicked! It's *my* angel, it's *my* trumpet! I hate you! Listen! – I tell you! I command you to come down!" '

'His adjurations,' de la Mare tells us characteristically with an echo of seventeenth-century prose, 'had become as meaningless as is now the song the Sirens sang', for suddenly there is 'a rending snap, abrupt as that of a pistol shot'. The angel's wooden trumpet has broken under Dick's grasp, and he falls.

The solid pendulum had resumed its imperturbable thumping again, the fussy vestry clock its protest against such indifference. By any miracle of mercy, *could* this be only yet another of this intrepid restless little Yorick's jests? The sharp-nosed crusader continued alabaster-wise to stare into the future. The disgraced angel, breast to lock-crowned head, stood now in shadow as if to hide her shame. Her mute wooden trumpet remained clutched in a lifeless hand. . . . No.

'Dick! Dick!' an anguished stuttering voice at last contrived to whisper. 'I didn't mean it. On my oath I didn't mean it. Don't let me down . . . Dick, are you dead?'

But since no answer was volunteered, and all courage and enterprise had ebbed into nausea and vertigo, the speaker found himself incapable of venturing nearer, and presently, as thievishly as he had entered it, crept away out into the openness of the churchyard, and so home.

Thus ends this astonishingly complex and richly-wrought story. It demands the kind of analysis a great poem receives, though, like a great poem, it is ultimately recalcitrant to analysis. It is, one feels, such a story as Poe might have dreamed of but never succeeded in writing.

The settlement of Australia began in 1788. More than half a century passed before anything like a literature emerged and even then it was a literature that deferred to England and established English patterns. It was not until the eighteen-eighties that a consciously Australian writing, recognized as such both in Australia and in London, came into being. For this, the *Bulletin*, a Sydney weekly newspaper, was largely responsible. Among other things, it sought to foster democratic nationalism and those anti-authoritarian, anti-Establishment, Populist tendencies perhaps endemic to Australia because of the manner of its foundation.

In the short story, the most famous of the writers associated with the *Bulletin* was Henry Lawson. He was born in 1867 in the goldfields of New South Wales, the son of a Norwegian sailor-turned-bushman and an ambitious, literate mother, and spent an unhappy childhood on an impoverished farm. The character, Mitchell, who appears in a number of his stories, appears to be speaking for Lawson himself when he says, in a story called 'The Lost Souls Hotel', which is the depiction of a daydream:

'I'd have good cheerful books of the best and brightest sides of human nature – Charles Dickens, and Mark Twain, and Bret Harte, and these men. And I'd have all Australian pictures – showing the brightest and best side of Australian life. And I'd have all Australian songs.'

Bret Harte, indeed, is Lawson's closest affinity, and he has a similar easy sentimentality and – its obverse – an easy cynicism, qualities probably inseparable from populist attitudes and encouraged, no doubt, by the conditions of journalism in which he wrote. Nevertheless, even at their most sentimental, his stories pulsate with the sense of something like Burns's 'A man's a man for a' that', the sense of democracy as a passionately held creed.

This is apparent in the story 'The Union Buries Its Dead', which is simply an account of how a local trades union branch looks after the funeral of one of its members, who is drowned one afternoon in a billabong and buried the next day.

We walked in twos. There were three twos. It was very hot and dusty; the heat rushed in fierce dazzling rays across every iron roof and light-coloured wall that was turned to the sun. One or two pubs closed respectfully until we got past. They closed their bar doors and the patrons went in and out through some side or back entrance for a few minutes. Bushmen seldom grumble at an inconvenience of this sort, which is caused by a funeral. They have too much respect for the dead.

In content and in manner of telling, 'The Union Buries Its Dead' is a hymn to democracy. It is also an exercise, as it were, in telling the truth, particularly the truth of feeling. As such, it sets out not merely to avoid sentimental pieties but to expose them. Thus, after the description of the interment, we have this:

I have left out the wattle – because it wasn't there. I have also neglected to mention the heartbroken old mate, with his grizzled head bowed and great drops streaming down his rugged cheeks. He was absent – he was probably 'outback'. For similar reasons I have omitted reference to the suspicious moisture in the eyes of a bearded bush ruffian named Bill. Bill failed to turn up, and the only moisture was that which was induced by the heat. I have left out the 'sad Australian sunset', because the sun was not going down at the time. The burial took place exactly at midday.

The dead bushman's name was Jim, apparently, but they found no portraits, nor locks of hair, nor any love-letters, nor anything of that kind in his swag – not even a reference to his mother; only some papers relating to union matters. Most of us didn't know the name till we saw it on the coffin; we knew him as 'that poor chap that got drowned yesterday'.

Lawson is pleading, very effectively, a rough-and-ready democracy of which anonymity is almost the essential condition. But then control slips. The last paragraphs read:

It turned out, afterwards, that J. T. wasn't his real name – only 'the name he went by'.

Anyway, he was buried by it, and most of the 'Great Australian Dailies' have mentioned in their brevity columns that a young man named James John Tyson was drowned in a billabong of the Darling last Sunday.

We did hear, later on, what his real name was; but if we ever chance to read it in the 'Missing Friends Column', we shall not be able to give any information to heart-broken Mother or Sister or Wife, nor to anyone who could let him hear something to his advantage – for we have already forgotten the name.

This suggests callousness that is as inadequate a response to life and death as overt sentimentality.

In fact, Lawson's sentimentality is generally inoffensive, disinfected as it is by humour, as in 'Send Round the Hat', which narrates the doings of a bushman known as the Giraffe, a man of compulsive good nature who can never resist passing the hat round for anyone who attracts his pity. No question, it ends sentimentally enough:

And, as I sit here writing by lamplight at midday, in the midst of a great city of shallow social sham, of hopeless, squalid poverty, of ignorant selfishness, cultured or brutish, and of noble and heroic endeavour frowned down on or callously neglected, I am almost aware of a burst of sunlight in the room, and a long form leaning over my chair, and:

'Excuse me for troublin' yer; I'm always troublin' yer; but there's that there poor woman . . .'

And I wish I could immortalize him!

But before reaching the end, we have been entertained by such irreverent stories about the Giraffe as:

They say that when a new Governor visited Bourke the Giraffe happened to be standing on the platform close to the exit, grinning good-humouredly, and, the local toady nudged him urgently and said in an awful whisper, 'Take off your hat! Why don't you take off your hat?'

'Why?' drawled the Giraffe, 'he ain't hard up, is he?'

And they fondly cherish an anecdote to the effect that, when the One-Man-One-Vote Bill was passed (or Payment of Members, or when the first Labour Party went in – I forget on which occasion they said it was) the Giraffe was carried away by the general enthusiasm, got a few beers in him, 'chucked' a quid into his hat, and sent it round. The boys contributed by force of habit, and contributed largely, because of the victory and the beer. And when the hat came back to the Giraffe, he stood holding it in front of him with both hands and stared blankly into it for a while. Then it dawned on him.

'Blowed if I haven't bin and gone and took up a bloomin' collection for meself!' he said.

Lawson may be seen at his full stature in such a story as 'A Child in the Dark', which is autobiographical, his 'Baa-Baa, Black Sheep', as it were. It begins:

New Year's Eve! A hot night in midsummer in the drought. It was so dark – with a smothering darkness – that even the low loom of the scrub-covered ridges, close at hand across the creek, was not to be seen. The sky was not clouded for rain, but with drought haze and the smoke of distant bushfires.

Down the hard road to the crossing at Pipeclay Creek sounded the footsteps of a man. Not the crunching steps of an English labourer, clodhopping contentedly home; these sounded more like the footsteps of one pacing steadily to and from, and thinking steadily and hopelessly – sorting out the past. Only the steps went on. A glimmer of white moleskin trousers and a suggestion of light-coloured tweed jacket, now and again, as if in the glimmer of a faint ghost light in the darkness.

The man reaches his hut. On the kitchen table a school exercise book lies open at a page bearing a poem headed 'Misunderstood', written in a woman's hand. In the bedroom, he finds his wife, 'a big, strong, and healthy-looking woman', sleeping in a four-poster bed with a baby in a cradle beside her.

There was a plate, a knife and fork, and egg-shells, and a cup and saucer on the top of the chest of drawers; also two candles, one stuck in a mustard-tin, and one in a pickle-bottle, and a copy of *Ardath*.

In another room, sleeping on a mattress on the floor, is a boy, 'a child almost', who wakes up when his father comes in and tells him that he must sleep on the sofa for 'Mother's bad again with her head'. He says that he had started to wash up and clean the kitchen when he became sick. He has also brought in a load of wood and given the baby her tea. Then the woman calls out:

'Nils! Nils! Are you there, Nils?'
'Yes, Emma.'
'Then for God's sake come and take this little child away before she drives me mad. My head's splitting.'
The father went into the child and presently returned with a cup of water.
'She only wanted a drink,' the boy heard him say to the mother.
'Well, didn't I tell you she wanted a drink? I've been calling for the last half-hour, with that child screaming, and not a soul to come near me, and me lying here helpless all day, and not a wink of sleep for two nights.'
'But, Emma, you were asleep when I came in.'
'How can you tell such infernal lies? I –. To think I'm chained to a man who can't say a word of truth! God help me! To have to lie night after night in the same bed as a liar!'

At four o'clock Nils sets out for his day's work in the nearby town. Later, the boy gets up and milks the three cows. His mother calls and he goes to her:

'Why didn't you answer when I called you? I've been calling for the last three hours. Is your father gone out?'

'Yes, mother.'

'Thank God! It's a relief to get rid of his ever-lasting grumbling. Bring me a cup of tea and *The Australian Journal*, and take this child out and dress her; she should have been up hours ago.'

And so the New Year began.

'A Child in the Dark' is the presentation of a domestic situation made as simply as possible. There is no sentimentality, and the pathetic is allowed to remain implicit. The clue to its effect, and to the point of view from which the situation is seen, is contained in a single-sentence paragraph half-way through the story. The father has been called into her bedroom by his wife. Lawson writes:

The child in the front room lay quaking with terror, dreading one of those cruel and shameful scenes which had made a hell of his childhood.

'A Child in the Dark' must be one of the best stories ever written. Lawson reached comparable heights only rarely but he never failed to illuminate the Australian working scene of his day with humour and humanity.

III

D. H. Lawrence saw himself primarily as a novelist but in fact expressed himself in almost all the literary forms current in his time and with the like distinction in each, although it has been argued that in fiction he was at his best in the short story. H. E. Bates writes in *The Modern Short Story*, comparing the stories and the novels:

His stories are always the expression of a more direct, more controlled, and more objective art. . . . Lawrence is for once bound to say what he has to say within reasonable, even strict, limits of time and space.

I am not at all certain of this. The value of a literary work rests ultimately on something beyond method and technique which we can only call, clumsily, depth of insight. Lawrence, whatever form he chose to write in, was of a piece, no writer more so, and he wrote novels and stories side by side throughout the twenty-five years, more or less, of his writing life. However closely related, the novels and stories are not in competition with each other. As a short-story writer, though they are so different in kind that comparison between them would be absurd, Lawrence, it seems to me, must be judged second only to Kipling in English writing.

His first volume, *The Prussian Officer*, appeared in 1914. F. R. Leavis, who has done so much for the recognition of Lawrence as a master of the short story, finds the title-story characterized by an 'unpleasant kind of power'. But this is inseparable from his genius, and although 'The Prussian Officer' may be unpleasant, it is not uncharacteristic. Lawrence's customary theme is that of relationship and what it may symbolize; 'The Prussian Officer' treats of the relationship between a professional soldier, a cavalry captain, and his conscript orderly. It would be altogether too naive to see the captain as a simple sadist. He kicks and brutalizes his orderly because he is in the grip of emotions he cannot recognize or, one guesses, put a name to. He is a man who has mistresses but he is plainly, though the word is not used, caught up in an unconscious homosexual passion for the young man which distorts his being. His very acts of sadism towards the youth may be interpreted as acts taken as it were in self-defence, though they lead to his death at the hands of the orderly. The story is a daring dramatization of abnormal psychology. It is as much a 'thought-adventure', to use his own phrase, as his novels.

As such, it reminds me of another of his stories; I refer to 'The Woman Who Rode Away', probably Lawrence's most remarkable and convincing rendering of the religious values of the Mexican Indians, a triumph of the empathic imagination. The woman of the title is married to a Dutchman who has risen from nothing to become the owner of silver mines in Mexico. The story opens:

She had thought that this marriage, of all marriages, would be an adventure.

In reality, she has found herself virtually a prisoner in a barricaded hacienda in a remote Mexican province. Her husband, who is the essence, as it were, of the Protestant work-ethic, is very vividly rendered:

He was a man of principles, and a good husband. In a way, he doted on her. He never quite got over his dazzled admiration of her. But essentially he was still a bachelor. He had been thrown on to the world, a little bachelor, at the age of ten. When he married he was over forty, and had enough money to marry on. But his capital was all a bachelor's. He was the boss of his own works, and marriage was the last and most intimate bit of his own works.

He admired his wife to extinction, he admired her body, all her points. And she was to him always the rather dazzling Californian girl from Berkeley, whom he had first known. Like any sheikh, he kept her guarded among the mountains of Chihuahua. He was jealous of her as he was of his silver mines: and that is saying a lot.

At the beginning, the woman is presented in general terms; we are left to infer her dissatisfaction and sense of frustration. She is eventually sparked off by a visiting engineer who says to her husband: 'I wonder what there is behind those great blank hills.' He is not satisfied by the man's comments on the Indians who live beyond the hills and he presses the question:

'But don't you suppose it's wonderful, up there in their secret village?'

'No. What would be wonderful about it? Savages are savages, and all savages behave more or less alike: rather low-down and dirty, unsanitary, with a few cunning tricks and struggling to get enough to eat.'

'But surely they must have old, old religions – it must be wonderful, surely it must. . . .'

And this particular vague enthusiasm for unknown Indians found a full echo in the woman's heart. She was overcome by a foolish romanticism more unreal than a girl's. She felt it was her destiny to wander into the secret haunts of these timeless, mysterious, marvellous Indians of the mountains.

One day when her husband is away she gives way to her Bovaryism, saddles her horse and rides away into the mountains. The rest of the story, the evocation of her long ride and of the mountains and of her capture by the Indians, who 'could not see her as a woman at all', and of her ultimate destiny and the long weeks of preparation before being sacrificed to the sun on the shortest day of the year, is sheerly magical. The woman is in a semi-trance, under a spell, as the reader is under the spell of Lawrence's prose. The evocation is utterly convincing, so specific and vivid is the detail. 'The Woman Who Rode Away', as Leavis says, 'imagines the old pagan Mexican religion as something real and living', and Lawrence transmits his sense of this reality and vitality to the reader. The story is the fine fruit of Lawrence's experience of Mexico and also his astonishing ability to translate into imaginative reality the works of anthropology that he is known to have been reading at the time.

'The Woman Who Rode Away' is, of course, fully mature Lawrence. This 'The Prussian Officer' may not be, but what cannot be disputed is the quality of the writing. Witness the first paragraph, which, without introducing either the captain or the orderly, frames the action:

They had marched more then thirty kilometres since dawn, along the white, hot road where occasional thickets of trees threw a moment of shade, then out into the glare again. On either hand, the valley, wide and shallow, glittered with heat; dark-green patches of rye, pale yellow corn, fallow and meadow and black pine woods spread in a dull hot diagram under a glistening sky. But right in front the mountains ranged across, pale blue and very still, snow gleaming gently out of the deep atmosphere. And towards the mountains, on and on, the regiment marched between the rye-fields and the meadows, between the scraggy fruit-trees set regularly on either side of the high road. The burnished, dark-green rye threw off a suffocating heat, the mountains drew gradually nearer and more distinct. While the feet of the soldiers grew hotter, sweat ran through their hair under their helmets, and their knapsacks could burn no more in contact with their shoulders, but seemed instead to give off a cold prickly sensation.

There is nothing immature about that. It is a good example of Lawrence's prose, with its strong and subtle rhythms, its careful and cunningly placed verbal repetitions, its empathy into physical experience.

And the two short stories, for all their differences, have one thing in common very rare in short stories. They are conceived 'from an enormous height', as Forster said of Hardy's novels. This means that though there are large areas of Lawrence's characters of which we know nothing, yet we do know enough about them for them to be able to take on the proportions of potentially tragic figures. Their individuality, their idiosyncrasy, may be stripped away; because of that, they remain fundamentally human.

This is apparent even in Lawrence's first accepted, though not first published, short story, 'Odour of Chrysanthemums', which appeared in Ford Madox Hueffer's *English Review* in June 1911. It was collected in *The Prussian Officer*, and it may be useful to quote the first paragraph:

The small locomotive engine, Number 4, came clanking, stumbling down from Selston with seven full wagons. It appeared round the corner with loud threats of speed, but the colt that it startled from among the gorse, which still flickered indistinctly in the raw afternoon, outdistanced it at a canter. A woman, walking up the railway line to Underwood, drew back into the hedge, held her basket aside, and watched the footplate of the engine advancing. The trucks thumped heavily past, one by one, with slow inevitable movements, as she stood insignificantly trapped between the jolting black wagons and the hedge; then they curved away towards the coppice where the withered oak-leaves dropped noiselessly, while the birds pulling at the scarlet hips beside the track, made off into the dusk that had already crept into the spinney. In the open, the smoke from the engine sank and cleaved to the rough grass. The fields were dreary and forsaken, and in the marshy strip that led to the whimsey, a reedy pit-pond, the fowls had already abandoned their run among the alders, to roost in the tarred fowl-house. The pit-bank loomed up beyond the pond, flames like red sores licking its ashy sides, in the afternoon's stagnant light. Just beyond rose the tapering chimneys and the clumsy black headstocks of Brinsley Colliery. The two wheels were spinning fast up against the sky, and the winding machine rapped out its little spasms. The miners were being turned up.

No need to comment on the quality of the prose or the author's acute perception of detail; every word carries weight.

My immediate reason for quoting the passage is to indicate that most of the stories in *The Prussian Officer* are products of Lawrence's day-to-day experience in the Nottinghamshire and Derbyshire coalfield. The first paragraph of the story might be thought to be slow, since we are always being told about the necessity of speed in the opening of a story. But beside setting the scene and giving us information which we shall recognize is crucially important, it is plainly conceived to distance the events of the story; it is one way by which Lawrence can be seen to be creating from an enormous height.

In his story, Mrs Bates, a woman of natural dignity, pregnant again, is waiting for her husband to return from the pit. The colliers have been wound up, and she sees them pass her door. When her husband does not come she decides that he has slunk off to the public house. We have the picture of an embittered woman, neglected by her husband. Then his dead body is brought into the cottage by his mates: he has been killed in an accident at the coalface. She is joined by her mother-in-law, who helps her prepare the body. Bates's mother sees her son in a very different way from his wife's:

'He went peaceful, Lizzie – peaceful as sleep. Isn't he beautiful, the lamb? Ay – he must ha' made his peace, Lizzie. 'Appen he made it all right, shut in there. He'd have time. He wouldn't look like this if he hadn't made his peace. The lamb, the dear lamb. Eh, but he had a hearty laugh. I loved to hear it. He had the heartiest laugh, Lizzie, as a lad—'

Later, looking at her husband's body, Mrs Bates has a revelation:

For as she looked at the dead man, her mind, cold and detached, said clearly: 'Who am I? What have I been doing? I have been fighting a husband who did not exist. *He* existed all the time. What wrong have I done? What was that I have been living with? There lies the reality, this man.' And her soul died in her for fear; she knew she had never seen him, he had never seen her, they had met in the dark and had fought in the dark, not knowing whom they met or whom they fought. And now she saw and turned silent in seeing. . . . She looked at his naked body and was ashamed, as if she had denied it. After all, it was itself. . . . She had refused him as himself. And this had been her life, and his life. She was grateful to death, which restored the truth. And she knew she was not dead. . . .'

What might be called the local stories in *The Prussian Officer* include two other of Lawrence's finest stories. Very different in manner and content, they indicate something of the extent of his range. *The White Stocking* is a story of a young husband's discovery that his pretty little wife has been accepting presents from her former employer. It is a story of jealousy and reconciliation; we are convinced of the husband and wife's love for each other. We are convinced, too, that the young woman means no harm: she cannot resist pretty things, tributes to her sexual attractiveness. It is a wonderful portrait of a flirtatious young woman unaware, perhaps, that her behaviour could be misconstrued, since for her it exists on the level of play. The story, it seems to me, can be compared only with Chekhov, with such a story as 'The Darling'.

'The Daughters of the Vicar' is the first version of a theme that Lawrence was many times to dramatize, the theme of upper-class sterility and the saving of an upper-class woman by the vitality and superior human values of a working man. The vicar and his wife and family live in a mining village in virtual exile, ignored by the miners, few of whom are Anglicans. Their poverty is intensified by their determination to keep up appearances traditional to their position. They can be saved only by the two daughters making good marriages. One succeeds: she marries a wealthy young clergyman, Mr Massy, a representative of the intellect rendered sterile because of the absence of other qualities and a creation comparable, as Graham Hough pointed out in *The Dark Sun*, with that of Casaubon in George Eliot's *Middlemarch*. Mary marries Massy without love:

If she had let herself, she would have hated him, hated his padding round the house, his thin voice devoid of human understanding, his bent little shoulders and rather incomplete face that reminded her of an abortion. But rigorously she kept her position. She took care of him and was just to him. There was also a deep, craven fear of him, something slave-like.

There was not much fault to be found with his behaviour. He was scrupulously just and kind according to his lights. But the male in him was cold and self-complete, and utterly domineering. Weak, insufficient little thing as he was, she had not expected this of him. It was something in the bargain she had not understood. It made her hold her head to keep it still. . . .

Louisa, the other daughter, makes no such good marriage. In the course of her parochial duties she comes to nurse an old village woman, Mrs Durrant, and meets her son Alfred, a collier. Like all Lawrence's males who marry women of a higher social class, he is presented as a rather superior working man; he reads books and is interested in Fabianism. In Mrs Durrant's last illness, since she can no longer perform it, it is Louisa who enacts the female role in a miner's home: she washes Alfred's back when he comes up from the pit. She falls in love with him, and obviously the contrast between him and the Revd Mr Massy must not be forgotten.

The final scene, in which Alfred goes to the vicarage to ask for Louisa's hand, is especially brilliant in its delineation of the nuances of class-embarrassment and class-awkwardness. The dialogue is superb. The marriage becomes the less unwelcome to the vicar and his wife when Alfred says:

'I was thinking of emigrating,' he said.
'To Canada? Or where?'
'I think to Canada.'
Again there was a pause.
'We shan't see much of you then, as a son-in-law,' said the mother, roughly but amicably.
'Not much,' he said.

Although Lawrence spent years of his literary life in near poverty, his genius was early and widely recognized, so that he was soon moving in social circles far removed from those of a miner's son at Eastwood and an elementary school teacher at Croydon. The range of scene and class dealt with in the novels and stories after the very early fiction was greatly expanded, and this was reinforced by the circumstances of his life from 1919 onwards, when he became a wanderer over the face of the earth. So in some sense the stories change. Often they become less obviously realistic. Sometimes they take the form of what one can only call fable, as in 'The Man Who Loved Islands', which F. R. Leavis brilliantly relates to 'Hawthorne's kind of fable, which is psychological, moral, and philosophical'. The man in question is a man in search of self-sufficiency who progresses, or deteriorates, from island to island, each further removed from human contact, until he ends his life alone on a bare rock in the Atlantic.

I have called the story a fable, but no moral is deduced or appended. It is not necessary that it should be, for it cannot be stressed too much that Lawrence's moral, for he was always a moralist, is there in the texture of the prose, the wonderful evocations, visualized in all their detail, of the islands the man inhabits.

More often, the later stories are extremely penetrating studies of character, as in 'Jimmy and the Desperate Woman'. A comic, indeed a satirical story, it begins:

'He is very fine and strong somewhere, but he does need a level-headed woman to look after him.'

That was the friendly feminine verdict upon him. It flattered him, it pleased him, it galled him.

Having divorced a very charming and clever wife, who held this opinion for ten years, and at last had got tired of the level-headed protection game, his gall was uppermost. . . .

'I am not,' he said to himself, 'a poor little man nestled upon some woman's bosom. If I could only find the right sort of woman, she should nestle on mine. . . .'

As the editor of a literary magazine, Jimmy is intrigued by the poems submitted to him by a Mrs Emilia Pinnegar, 'who wrote from a mining village in Yorkshire'.

Jimmy had always had a mysterious feeling about those dark and rather dreadful mining villages in the north. He himself had scarcely set foot north of Oxford. He felt that those miners up there must be the real stuff.

He and Mrs Pinnegar correspond: 'she was, of course, unhappily married.' And since he had to lecture in a town nearby on 'Men in Books and Men in Life', he decides to visit her.

There is a splendidly ironical description of the country he finds himself in:

It was February, with gruesome patches of snow. It was dark when he arrived at Mill Valley, a sort of thick, turgid darkness full of menace, where men speaking in a weird accent went past like ghosts, dragging their heavy feet and emitting the weird scent of the coal-mine under-world. Weird and a bit gruesome it was. . . .

After much weary walking and asking, he entered a lane between the trees, in the cold slushy mud of the unfrozen February. The mines, apparently were on the outskirts of the town, in some mud-sunk country. He could see the red, sore fires of the burning pit-hill through the trees, and he smelt the sulphur. He felt like some modern Ulysses wandering in the realms of Hecate. How much more dismal and horrible, a modern Odyssey among mines and factories, than any Sirens, Scyllas, or Charybdises.

He meets Mrs Pinnegar, 'a tall woman with a face like a mask of passive anger', and dares to invite her and her small daughter to come to live in London. Her husband returns from the shift, and Jimmy watches him being washed before the fire by his wife. For Jimmy, 'it was a new experience . . . to sit completely and brutally excluded from a personal ritual'. Later, the two men talk. Pinnegar is a man of some education but angry and bitter, in revolt against his wife. The two seem implacable enemies, each demanding what the other refuses to give. In the end, things are arranged, despite Jimmy's increasing reservations: Mrs Pinnegar will join Jimmy in London. He meets her at the station and

a sickly grin came over him as he held out his hand. Nevertheless, he said:

'I'm *awfully* glad you came.'

And as he sat in the taxi, a perverse but intense desire for her came over him, making him almost helpless. He could feel, so strongly, the presence of that other man about her, and this went to his head like neat spirits. That other man! In some subtle, inexplicable way, he was actually bodily present, the husband. The woman moved in his aura. She was hopelessly married to him.

'Jimmy and the Desperate Woman' is a story of great subtlety. Throughout, the tone of the narration is sardonic. In part, the story is about the old division in England between the north and the south, and the south is seen in some sense as an intruder, as Jimmy is between the Pinnegars. It is also about the exposure of a man who is governed by an inescapable impulse to dramatize himself and who cannot resist the temptation to experiment with his own feelings and with those of others, a man, one might say, who is congenitally incapable of sincerity, a man who also perhaps confuses life and literature. Lawrence does not need to tell us what the consequences of this particular action of Jimmy's will be. He is self-doomed, and we know he will glory in self-destruction.

In his last years, Lawrence wrote a number of stories which one can only call supernatural, since they describe events that are inexplicable. They carry the greater conviction because Lawrence makes no attempt to explain them. Among them are 'Glad Ghosts', 'The Last Laugh', and 'The Rocking-Horse Winner', which is the most remarkable. Paul is a boy born into a middle-class family always impoverished because always living beyond its means. The house is haunted by the phrase, 'There must be more money.' When Paul asks his mother why the family has no money she tells him it is because they have no luck. He proves that *he* is lucky by mounting his rocking-horse, riding it at a gallop, and coming out with the name of a winning horse in a forthcoming race. Helped by the gardener and a sporting uncle, Paul, galloping on his rocking-horse, names the winners of the classic races time and again, amassing a fortune before he rides himself to death.

Then there are the 'short novels'. One is immediately struck by the extreme and effortless naturalness – which is by no means the same as naturalism – of the telling of 'The Fox'. The flow of life seems to have been set down without any tampering on the part of the author. This quality of naturalness comes out in the first paragraph:

The two girls were usually known by their surnames, Banford and March. They had taken the farm together, intending to work it all by themselves: that is, they were going to rear chickens, making a living by poultry, and add to this by keeping a cow, and raising one or two young beasts. Unfortunately, things did not turn out well.

Although these women have decided to share the farming,

Banford is the real boss. She has the major financial stake in the enterprise because her father, 'who was a tradesman in Islington, gave his daughter the start, for her health's sake, and because he loved her, and because it did not look as if she would marry'. She and March set upon the enterprise 'quite gallantly', but their series of small disasters is precisely chronicled, and we are soon made to realize that, because it is the nature of things as they are, nothing can turn out well for them. The symbol of this is the fox that preys on their poultry. In vain March tries to shoot it. She is haunted by it: 'She looked for him unconsciously when she went towards the wood. He had become a settled effect in her spirit, a state permanently established, not continuous, but always recurring.'

A young soldier turns up, and they give him temporary house-room. He shoots the fox and for March becomes the embodiment of it, exerting in her the fascination the animal had. He is an intruder into the life of the farm as the fox had been, a symbol, on another plane, of the natural. He proposes to March and she agrees to marry him, despite her love and devotion to Banford, who, the boy realizes, must be disposed of before March can become his. He kills her, in a brilliantly executed device of Lawrence's which enables the death to be seen either as premeditated or as the fulfilment of an unconscious wish. What does not obtrude itself into the reader's mind is any moral consideration: the boy behaves naturally, as much *sui generis*, as the fox had in stealing the chickens.

Once again, everything, the moral of the story and Lawrence's own attitude towards the events he is narrating, is articulated in the language of the story. The dramatization is complete.

E. M. Forster was born five years before Lawrence and survived him by forty. At first glance, they would seem to have practically nothing in common, but when Lawrence died in 1930 and was attacked by the obituary writers of the literary Establishment, Forster declared in a letter to the *Nation*: 'All that we can do . . . is to say straight out that he was the greatest imaginative novelist of our generation.'

Forster published two volumes of short stories in his lifetime, *The Celestial Omnibus* in 1911 and *The Eternal Moment* in 1928, and there is also *Life to Come*, a posthumous volume. The stories in this last volume are interesting rather for the light they throw on the merits and weaknesses of those in the earlier volumes than as achievements in their own right. They were written, many of them, not for publication but for Forster's own pleasure and that of his friends. He was therefore able to dispense with the mythological, which characterized his life's work, and this was not always an advantage. One sees this in the story 'Arthur Snatchfold', a story of the consequences of a brief sexual encounter between a wealthy business man and a milkman. It is obviously powerful but equally obviously propaganda.

In *The Celestial Omnibus* Forster calls his stories 'fantasies', and often they are curiously unsatisfactory, for they tend to be fusions of delightful and very perceptive social comedy and symbolism, and the symbolism, because too 'literary' and so too obvious, is less successful than the social comedy. Very often, too, they are based on Greek myth.

This is so in 'The Story of a Panic' which according to Forster himself was the first story he wrote. A group of wholly conventional, wealthy middle-class English people, among them a boy of fourteen named Eustace who is represented by the stuffy narrator as utterly graceless, are visiting Italy. They go on a picnic in a chestnut wood, in the course of which something strange happens:

Then the terrible silence fell upon us again. I was now standing up and watching a cat's-paw of wind that was running down one of the ridges opposite, turning the light green to dark as it travelled. A fanciful feeling of foreboding came over me; so I turned away, to find to my amazement, that all the others were also on their feet, watching it too.

It is not possible to describe coherently what happened next; but I, for one, am not ashamed to confess that, though the fair blue sky was above me, and the green spring woods beneath me, and the kindest of friends around me, yet I became terribly frightened, more frightened than I ever wish to become again, frightened in a way I have never known, either before or after. And in the eyes of the others, too, I saw blank expressionless fear. . . .

They panic, they flee from the wood, and when they are in control again realize that Eustace is not with them. Returning to the wood, they find him asleep. When they wake him he says he is very happy.

He stepped out manfully, for the first time in his life, holding his head up and taking deep draughts of air into his chest. I observed with satisfaction to Miss Mary Robinson that Eustace was at last taking some pride in his personal appearance.

And yet from then on Eustace behaves impossibly; he escapes from his bedroom and refuses to return. In the end, they have to invoke the help of Gennaro the waiter, who brings him to the foreground of the hotel.

I reached the terrace just in time to see Eustace jumping over the parapet of the garden wall. This time I knew for certain he would be killed. But he alighted in an olive tree, looking like a great white moth, and from the tree he slid to the earth. And as soon as his bare feet touched the clods of earth he uttered a strange loud cry, such as I should not have thought the human voice could have produced, and disappeared among the trees below.

'He has understood and he is saved,' cried Gennaro, who was still sitting on the asphalt path. 'Now, instead of dying he will live!'

He dies, of course.

In 'The Story of a Panic' Forster is attempting two things simultaneously, to expose the smugness of the middle-class narrator and to present Eustace, the graceless boy who becomes the embodiment of possession by Pan, the boy in touch with the irrational, the primitive. Behind the story is Forster's eternal message, stated in *Howards End*: 'Only connect – the poetry and the prose.' Here, the prose is unfortunately more convincing than the poetry; and one has to contrast the story with Lawrence's 'The Last Laugh', which is also about possession.

Lawrence's story is much more mysterious than Forster's, for the irrational is not pinned down. Lawrence, rather, recreates the state of being in which we may suppose the original notion of Pan had its birth. In other words, he has himself made a myth parallel with the myth of Pan, not simply used a convenient shorthand expression for the truth the myth embodies. A poet's revivifying imagination has been at work, by comparison with which Forster is merely indulging in reminiscences of classical studies.

Forster's best short story, which I take to be 'The Eternal Moment', avoids the mythological altogether. The beginning is Forster at his most brilliant, with the kind of comic, deflating juxtaposition of images that is his speciality:

'Do you see that mountain just behind Elizabeth's toque? A young man fell in love with me there so nicely twenty years ago. Bob your head a minute, would you, Elizabeth, kindly. . . .'

An elderly maiden lady, who is plain-spoken and therefore unconventional, Miss Raby is a novelist whose ambition, Forster's irony implies, exceeds her achievement. Years earlier she had written a best-selling novel that made the fortune of Vorte, a village in what seems the Austrian Tyrol, and which she is re-visiting for the first time. It has changed and she is stricken with guilt, for it is she who is responsible for the change.

She seeks out the poor boy, the baggage porter who had fallen in love with her and whom she had rebuffed. He is now the distinguished concierge of the most fashionable hotel in the resort; he speaks 'all languages fluently, and some well' and is putting on weight. He is terrified when Miss Raby reminds him of their previous meeting, and protests his innocence.

She did not attend. She was watching Feo. His alarm had subsided; and he revealed a new emotion, even less agreeable to her. . . .

She realized that only now was she not in love with him: that the incident upon the mountain had been one of the great moments of her life – perhaps the greatest, certainly the most enduring: that she had drawn unacknowledged power and inspiration from it, just as trees draw vigour from a subterranean spring. Never again could she think of it as a half-humorous episode in her development. There was more reality in it than in the years of success and varied achievement which had followed, and which it had rendered possible. For all her correct behaviour and ladylike display, she had been in love with Feo, and she had never loved so greatly again. A presumptuous boy had taken her to the gates of heaven; and though she would not enter with him, the eternal remembrance of the vision had made life seem endurable and good.

That is not the end of the story but it indicates Forster's abiding belief in the importance of the life of impulse and of sexual love. In the hotel concierge, he has found the symbol adequate to express his vision, adequate because it engages his wit, and not his poetry.

The most influential figure in the short story in English during the second and third decades of this century was almost certainly James Joyce, consideration of whom is made the more complicated by the fact that he belongs not only to the short story in English but also to the Irish story in English and is obviously its greatest figure. From one point of view, he is a regional writer; and the first thing to be determined is what makes Irish writing Irish and what distinguishes it from English.

It is a question that would have received short shrift from Matthew Arnold. He commented:

I have seen advertised *The Primer of American Literature*. Imagine the face of Philip or Alexander at hearing of a primer of Macedonian Literature! Are we to have a Primer of Canadian Literature too, and a Primer of Australian? We are all contributaries to one great literature – English literature. The contribution of Scotland to this literature is far more serious and important than that of America has yet had time to be; yet a *Primer of Scotch Literature* would be an absurdity.

Arnold, of course, is trailing his frockcoat. The point is that we do today, ninety years after he wrote, talk habitually and as a matter of course about American literature, Canadian literature, Australian literature, Caribbean literature, and by this mean far more than merely that the authors of the literatures in question happen to be United States, Canadian, Australian, or West Indian nationals. It seems to us self-evident that a literature is shaped as much by the history and experience of the people to whom the author in question belongs as by the language in which it is written, and although one suspects Arnold of being disingenuous, at the time he was writing Canadian and Australian, for example, scarcely existed as national literatures and were still analogous to regional writing in England. There has to be some sense of nationhood or at least of separate identity before we can speak of a specific literature.

Looked at this way, the Irish story defines itself. According to Frank O'Connor, the first serious collection of modern Irish stories is George Moore's *The Untilled Field*, published in 1903. In an English context Moore appears as one of a galaxy of writers – Stevenson, Gissing, Kipling, Morrison, Conrad, Bennett – who were all greatly influenced by the French and by Turgenev and were, largely, Naturalistic in their approach to their material. They wrote objectively and therefore appeared to write critically. Moore, however, stands apart from his English contemporaries in the nature of his criticism. Gissing and Morrison criticize the quality of the working-class; but Moore goes beyond this. Take 'Home-Sickness', perhaps his finest story, a study of the effects of exile. An Irish barman working in New York is ill, and since the doctor advises a sea-voyage, he goes back to Ireland, to his native village. There, he meets a girl and decides to marry her. But he does not; instead, he flees back to New York, flees perhaps principally because of the puritannical tyranny of the Irish clergy.

He took a wife, she bore him sons and daughters, the bar-room prospered, property came and went; he grew old, his wife died, he retired from business, and reached the age when a man begins to feel there are not many years in front of him, and that all he had to do in life has been done. His children married, lonesomeness began to creep about him in the evening and when he looked into the firelight, a vague, tender reverie floated up, and Margaret's soft voice and name vivified the dusk. His wife and children passed out of mind, and it seemed to him that a memory was the only real thing he possessed, and the desire to see Margaret again grew intense. But she was an old woman, she had married, maybe she was dead. Well, he would like to be buried in the village where he was born.

There is an unchanging, silent life within every man that none knows but himself, and his unchanging, silent life was his memory of Margaret Dirken. The bar-room was forgotten and all that concerned it and the things he saw most clearly were the green hillside, and the bog lake and the rushes about it, and the greater lake in the distance, and behind it the blue line of wandering hills.

The stories in *The Untilled Field* are dramatized criticisms of Irish life. Moore is concerned especially with what seem to him the dominant features of that life at the turn of the century: the fact of emigration and a dwindling population caused not only by poverty but also, he thought, by a lack of joy owing to the tyranny of the priesthood. Despite the beauty of the countryside and the loyalty of its people, Ireland in the eighteen-nineties is not a place for a man who has known freedom.

The criticism is continued, much more fundamentally, by Joyce, who was Ireland's most intransigent critic. He too saw Ireland from outside, as an exile in Europe and as a writer who had schooled himself in the European traditions of Flaubert and Ibsen. *Dubliners* was published, after many delays, in 1914 and Joyce executes his stories with, as he told his brother Stanislaus in a letter, 'a scrupulous meanness' of language. The anecdotal basis that is in most modern short stories tends to disappear almost completely; on the surface, they are 'slices of life' in the Zolaesque sense, slices, as Harry Levin has said, 'sliced thin'.

They represent the furthest reaches of Naturalism in English. But here a *caveat* is necessary. In England at least Naturalism has been seen as the drab opposite of symbolism when, in fact, it is the other face of symbolism. Joyce's great achievement in *Dubliners* is to have replaced the anecdotal basis of the story with a structure of symbolism. It is this that gives significance to stories like 'A Little Cloud' and 'A Painful Case', stories which although at first reading seem very close to works by Gissing, are not only poignant but representative in the fullest sense.

They are, to use his own words, epiphanies, and it may be interesting to look at the penultimate story of *Dubliners*, 'Grace', in the light of the word. It begins:

Two gentlemen who were in the lavatory at the time tried to lift him up; but he was quite helpless. He lay curled up at the foot of the stairs down which he had fallen. They succeeded in turning him over. His hat had rolled a few yards away and his clothes were smeared with the filth of the floor on which he had lain, face downwards. His eyes were closed and he breathed with a grunting noise. A thin stream of blood trickled from the corner of his mouth.

A drunk who has fallen down the stairs that lead from the pub to the lavatory is taken home to bed. His friends plan to reform him by persuading him to go into a religious retreat. One evening, four of them sit round his bed drinking. Cunningly, they talk about religion or at least about matters to do with religion as an institution and unerringly Joyce catches the ignorance, pretentiousness, and inanity of the nonsense men talk in pubs and clubs when conscious that they are dealing with the profound and sublime:

Mr Power again officiated. Glasses were rinsed and five small measures of whiskey were poured out. This new influence enlivened the conversation. Mr Fogarty, sitting on a small area of the chair, was especially interested.

'Pope Leo XIII,' said Mr Cunningham, 'was one of the lights of the age. His great idea, you know, was the union of the Latin and Greek Churches. That was the aim of his life.'

'I have often heard he was one of the most intellectual men in Europe,' said Mr Power, 'I mean, apart from his being Pope.'

'So he was,' said Mr Cunningham, 'if not *the* most so. His motto, you know, as Pope, was *Lux upon Lux* – Light upon Light.'

'No, no,' said Mr Fogarty eagerly, 'I think you are wrong there. It was *Lux in Tenebris*, I think – *Light in Darkness*.'

'O yes,' said Mr M'Coy, '*Tenebrae*.'

'Allow me,' said Mr Cunningham positively, 'it was *Lux upon Lux*. And Pius IX, his predecessor's motto was *Crux upon Crux* – that is, *Cross upon Cross* – to show the differences between their two pontificates.'

The inference was allowed. Mr Cunningham continued.

'Pope Leo, you know, was a great scholar and a poet.'

'He had a strong face,' said Mr Kernan.

'Yes,' said Mr Cunningham, 'He wrote Latin poetry.'

'Is that so?' said Mr Fogarty.

And so on. The retreat they go to is a retreat for business men held at the Jesuit Church in Gardiner Street where the preacher

told his hearers that he was there that evening for no terrifying, no extravagant purpose; but as a man of the world speaking to his fellow-men. He came to speak to business men and he would speak to them in a business-like way. If he might use the metaphor, he said, he was their spiritual accountant; and he wished each and every one of his hearers to open his books, the books of his spiritual life, and see if they tallied accurately with conscience.

For Joyce, in Edwardian Dublin the grace of God is equated with a business transaction. Religion is reduced to an appalling vulgarity. According to his brother Stanislaus, Joyce based the story on Dante's *Divine Comedy*, the underground lavatory in the pub corresponding with Hell, the sickbed in a suburban house in Dublin to purgatory, and the church in Gardiner Street to Heaven; and Frank O'Connor, who sees the story as an exercise in the mock heroic, suggests that the four men round Mr

Kennan's bed must be the four evangelists, Matthew, Mark, Luke, and John. These are surmises, but what is certain is that through his selection of detail and his style of scrupulous meanness Joyce extracts from his story wider and more deeply disturbing implications than we should expect to find in a Naturalistic story of an incident in a drunk man's life.

Dubliners was Joyce's only volume of short stories and it has a greater unity than is common in a collection of stories, greater than in any collection until we come to Anderson's *Winesburg, Ohio* and Hemingway's *In Our Time*. O'Connor, in *The Lonely Voice*, has suggested that the stories are arranged 'rather in the way a poet arranges lyrics in a book, to follow a pattern that exists in his own mind'. This view would seem to be vindicated in that the last story in the collection, 'The Dead', may be seen as a coda to what has gone before, a final summation.

'The Dead' is one of the supreme stories in literature. It recounts the events during and after the Misses Morkan's annual dance, which is held near the New Year. The Misses Morkan are famous older music teachers of Dublin, and never once, we are told, had their dance 'fallen flat'. On this particular occasion it is snowing all over Ireland. Miss Kate and Miss Julia are awaiting the arrival of their nephew Gabriel Conroy and his wife Gretta. Gabriel, as is customary, is to act as master of ceremonies; and when he appears becomes the story's centre of consciousness. He is a graduate of the National University, a schoolmaster and a minor man of letters, self-conscious, self-absorbed. He is not slumming precisely but he has the comfortable feeling that his aunts' middle-class guests are his social and intellectual inferiors. However, the surface of his mind is ruffled when dancing with a young woman who has been a fellow-student. She is a nationalist. They are talking of holidays:

'Well, we usually go to France or Belgium or perhaps Germany,' said Gabriel awkwardly.

'And why do you go to France and Belgium,' said Miss Ivors, 'instead of visiting your own land?'

'Well,' said Gabriel, 'it's partly to keep in touch with the language and partly for a change.'

'And haven't you your own language to keep in touch with – Irish?' asked Miss Ivors.

'Well,' said Gabriel, 'if it comes to that, you know, Irish is not my language.'

Their neighbours had turned to listen to the cross-examination. Gabriel turned left and right nervously and tried to keep his good humour under the ordeal. . . .

'And haven't you your own land to visit,' continued Miss Ivors, 'that you know nothing of, your own people, and your own country?'

'O, to tell you the truth,' retorted Gabriel suddenly, 'I'm sick of my own country, sick of it.'

He does not recover his composure or feel fully at ease until he is called to carve the goose at supper. 'He was an expert carver and liked nothing better than to find himself at the head of a well-laden table.'

The party ends; the guests begin to go. It is still snowing, and while Gabriel is waiting in the hall for a cab to be found he stares up the stairs at his wife, who is standing on the threshold of the drawing-room listening to the singing of Bartell D'Arcy the tenor. He is deeply affected by the sight of his wife on the stairs, listening:

A wave of yet more tender joy escaped from his heart and went coursing in warm floods along his arteries. Like the tender fire of stars moments of their life together, that no one knew of or would ever know of, broke open and illuminated his memory. He longed to recall to her those moments, to make her forget the years of their full existence together and remember only their moments of ecstasy. For the years, he felt, had not quenched his soul or hers. Their children, his writing, her household cares had not quenched all their souls' tender fire.

Desiring his wife, in the hotel bedroom, he is excited and gratified by what he construes as her initial response to his approaches but when he asks her what she is thinking about she bursts into tears: 'O, I am thinking about that song, "*The Lass of Aughrim*".' And she tells him about the young man Michael Furey, of whom he had known nothing before this, and how he used to sing the song to her when she was a girl. He was 'very delicate'. 'I think he died for me', she says.

Gabriel felt humiliated by the failure of his irony and by the evocation of this figure from the dead, a boy in the gasworks. While he had been full of memories of their secret life together, full of tenderness and joy and desire, she had been comparing him in her mind with another. A shameful consciousness of his own person assailed him. He saw himself as a ludicrous figure, acting as a pennyboy for his aunts, a nervous, well-meaning sentimentalist, orating to vulgarians and idealizing his own clownish lusts. . . .

Gretta sobs herself to sleep and we approach the end of the story:

Generous tears filled Gabriel's eyes. He had never felt like that himself towards any woman, but he knew that such a feeling must be love. The tears gathered more quickly in his eyes and in the partial darkness he saw the form of a young man standing under a dripping tree. Other forms were near. His soul had approached that region where dwell the vast hosts of the dead. He was conscious of, but could not apprehend, their wayward and flickering existence. His own identity was fading out into a grey impalpable world: the solid world itself, which these dead had one time reared and lived in, was dissolving and dwindling.

A few light taps upon the pane made him turn to the window. It had begun to snow again. He watched sleepily the flakes, silver and dark, falling obliquely against the lamplight. The time had come for him to set out on the journey westward. Yes, the newspapers were right: snow was general all over Ireland. It was falling in every part of the dark central plain, on the treeless hills, falling softly upon the Bog of Allen and, farther westward, softly falling into the dark mutinous Shannon waves. It was falling, too, upon every part of the lonely church yard on the hill where Michael Furey lay buried. . . . His soul swooned slowly as he heard the snow falling faintly through the universe and faintly falling, like the descent of their last end, upon all the living and the dead.

'The Dead' has been called an 'evocation of the union of all the living and the dead', and the unifying image is that of snow. At the beginning, it is palpable snow. By the end of the story it has become the symbol of the oblivion that falls on and buries all men and all things.

The story is most beautifully woven. Its various moods co-exist in a continuum: merriment, festivity, music are shown as part of the fabric of life that complements the greater fact of oblivion. The first pages are studded very subtly with images of mortality. Lily the maid is 'literally run off her feet'. Miss Kate and Miss Julie are old ladies who have lived in the house on Usher's Island ever since their brother died. Gretta takes 'three mortal hours to dress herself'. All these lead to Gabriel's final recognition that 'the time had come for him to set out on his journey westward'. And the unity of the whole, which moves from the representation of men and women in society to the lonely man's recognition of the truth about himself and about the human condition, is never broken.

During the first decades of the century it seemed that the domination of American art and culture by the eastern seaboard exemplified in Boston and New York was yielding to domination by the Middle West with Chicago as its centre. Mark Twain, William Dean Howells, Ambrose Bierce, and Hamlin Garland were the precursors of what by the twentieth century was to be a positive regiment of writers from the states watered by the northern Mississippi and its tributaries. Some of these writers were of recent immigrant stock, others of families old in American terms which over the generations had pressed steadily west. Typical of these latter was Willa Cather. Of the same generation as Dreiser, Anderson, and Sinclair Lewis, she inherited an altogether richer patrimony which made her differences from them much more pronounced than her resemblances. She was born in 1873 in the mountains of north-west Virginia, where her family had farmed for almost a century, but when she was six the Cathers moved to a ranch in Nebraska, a state not then twenty years old and settled largely by German, Norwegian, and Czech immigrants, the celebration of whose lives was to be one of the principal themes of her fiction. Later, when the family moved into the town of Red Cloud, she was able to go to high school. An English storekeeper taught her Latin and Greek. At the University of Nebraska she discovered Virgil, discovered especially that among other things Virgil was the poet of the rural neighbourhood, the locality. Graduating, she became a journalist in Pittsburgh, was a schoolteacher for a time, and then became a magazine editor, a career which gave her opportunities for travel in Europe.

Her first book was published in 1905, a collection of short stories called *The Troll's Garden*. These are stories of the life of art and of life among the artists, which remain interesting but do not bear comparison with James's treatment of the subject. She comes into her own when she brings the artist, or the person of innate sensitivity and imagination, into juxtaposition with life in

Nebraska, the frontier. Three stories stand out, 'The Sculptor's Funeral', 'A Wagner Matinee', and 'Paul's Case'.

The first describes the return in his coffin of a famous sculptor to be buried in his birthplace, a little town in Kansas. One of the sculptor's disciples, a young man from Boston, accompanies the coffin. He discovers from the totally uncomprehending, unsympathetic comments of the dead man's family and neighbours all that the sculptor had had to contend with in a community dedicated to the crudest materialism. It is not a particularly subtle story; the townsfolk depicted are no more than types, exposed and denounced by Jim Laird, the friend of the sculptor's boyhood and now a highly successful lawyer and a drunk. He has made the compromise the sculptor never did. His harangue over the coffin concludes with the words:

'And we? Now that we've fought and lied and sweated and stolen, and hated as only the disappointed strugglers in a bitter, dead little Western town know how to do it, what have we got to show for it? Harvey Merrick wouldn't have given one sunset over your marshes for all you've got put together, and you know it. It's not for me to say why, in the inscrutable wisdom of God, a genius should ever have been called from this place of hatred and bitter waters; but I want this Boston man to know that the drivel he's been hearing here tonight is the only tribute any truly great man could ever have from such a lot of sick, side-tracked, burnt-dog, land-poor sharks as the here-present financiers of Sandy City – upon which town may God have mercy!'

The note sounded in this grimly bitter story is the closest Willa Cather gets to the anger of disillusionment with American commercial life that we find in the works of Dreiser, Masters, Anderson, and Lewis. Though constant in her attitude towards America, it was never again so intransigently expressed. It should be observed that the denounced inhabitants of Sandy City are not pioneers or immigrants but commercial exploiters and, moreover, Anglo-Saxons.

A much more sympathetic story and much more typical of its author is 'A Wagner Matinee'. It describes the visit to Boston of a Nebraska farmer's wife who as a young woman has taught music at Boston Conservatory. Her niece takes her to a Wagner concert:

The concert was over; the people filed out of the hall chattering and laughing, glad to relax and find the living level again, but my kins-woman made no effort to rise. The harpist slipped his green felt cover over his instrument; the flute players shook the water out of their mouthpieces; the men of the orchestra went out one by one, leaving the stage to the chairs and the music stands, empty as a winter cornfield.

I spoke to my aunt. She burst into tears and sobbed pleadingly. 'I don't want to go, Clark, I don't want to go!'

I understood. For her, just outside the door of the concert hall, lay the black pond with the cattle-tracked bluffs; the tall, unpainted house, with weather-curling boards; naked as a tower, the crook-backed ash seedlings where dishcloths hung to dry; the gaunt, moulting turkeys picking up refuse about the kitchen door.

Often Willa Cather seems to idealize her pioneers and immi-grants but she never sentimentalizes them. She was not a disciple of Flaubert for nothing and she never forgot the deprivation for the individual person the pioneering life often involved.

'Paul's Case' is set in Pittsburgh.

Several of Paul's teachers had a theory that his imagination had been perverted by garish fiction, but the truth was that he scarcely ever read at all. The books at home were not such as would either tempt or corrupt a youthful mind, and as for reading the novels that some of his friends urged upon him – well, he got what he wanted much more quickly from music; any sort of music, from an orchestra to a barrel organ. He needed only a spark, the indescribable thrill that made his imagination master of his senses, and he could make plots and pictures enough of his own. It was equally true that he was not stage-struck – not, at any rate, in the usual acceptation of that expression. He had no desire to become an actor, any more than he had to become a musician. He felt no necessity to do any of these things; what he wanted was to see, to be in the atmosphere, float away on the wave of it, to be carried out, blue league after blue league, away from everything.

The life of the theatre and the concert room is more real to him than that of the lower middle-class family and the great industrial and commercial city in which he lives; it is only to the aesthetic, and that in its cruder manifestations, that he responds. When he leaves school it is to become a clerk, and the second part of the story begins within a train a mile out of Newark, New Jersey, bound for New York City: he has stolen a thousand dollars of the firm's money. In New York he buys new clothes, including a frock coat and dress clothes, and a scarf pin at Tiffany's, and puts himself up at the Waldorf. He has come into his own.

When Paul went down to dinner the music of the orchestra came floating up the elevator shaft to greet him. His head whirled as he stepped into the thronged corridor, and he sank back into one of the chairs against the wall to get his breath. The lights, the chatter, the perfumes, the bewildering medley of colour – he had, for a moment, the feeling of not being able to stand it. But only for a moment; these were his own people, he told himself. He went slowly about the corridors, through the writing rooms, as though he were exploring the chambers of an enchanted palace, built and peopled for him alone. . . .

He was not in the least abashed or lonely. He had no special desire to meet or to know any of these people; all he demanded was the right to look on and conjecture, to watch the pageant. The mere stage properties were all he contended for. Nor was he lonely later in the evening, in his lodge at the Metropolitan. He was now entirely rid of his nervous misgivings, of his forced aggressiveness, of the imperative desire to show himself different from his surroundings. He felt now that his surroundings explained. Nobody questioned the purple; he had only to wear it passively. He had only to glance down at his attire to reassure himself that here it would be impossible for anyone to humiliate him.

On his eighth day after his arrival in New York he discovers from a newspaper that his theft has been made public in the Pittsburgh press, that his father has refunded the money, that the minister and his Sabbath-school teacher have expressed the hope 'of yet reclaiming the motherless lad', that it is rumoured he has been seen in a New York hotel, and that his father has gone East to find him and bring him home. Paul's money is almost at an end but he remains calm: 'He had a feeling that he had made the best of it, that he had lived the sort of life he was meant to live.' He takes a cab to the station and catches a train, which he leaves at Newark to plunge through the snow-covered fields.

The carnations in his coat were drooping with the cold, he noticed their red glory was over. It occurred to him that all the flowers he had seen in the glass cases that first night must have gone the same way, long before this. It was only one splendid breath they had, in spite of their brave mockery at the winter outside the glass. . . .

He jumps from a railway bridge into the river below and drops back, in Willa Cather's words, 'into the immense design of things'.

Reading 'Paul's Case', we cannot help but be reminded of Dreiser's *An American Tragedy*, though Paul is given greater dignity than Clyde Griffiths, both by the symbolism that attends his death and because his tragedy springs essentially from what Johnson, in *Rasselas*, called 'that hunger of the imagination which preys incessantly on life'.

The stories of *The Troll's Garden* were a memorable first appearance in American writing, though, as we can now see from Willa Cather's later work, which was mainly in the novel, not wholly characteristic for she had not quite discovered her true vein. That happened in about 1908, when she met Sarah Orne Jewett, who greatly influenced her. Miss Jewett was born in 1848 in South Berwick on the Maine coast and though she travelled fairly widely both in America and in Europe, South Berwick remained her home all her life, which was devoted to recording with faithful realism the lives of fishing and farming families who were neighbours in a community that had once known economic greatness but was now in decay. She was a conscious artist whose model, like Willa Cather's, was Flaubert, one of whose famous sentences, *Ecrire la vie comme on écrit l'histoire*, she kept pinned to the back of her desk. Her most famous book, *The Country of the Pointed Firs*, shows that it was a statement of what she herself was attempting. Like many collections of what in fact are short stories, *The Country of the Pointed Firs* is sometimes called a novel, since it is divided into chapters, each of which is a separate character-sketch of South Berwick, which she calls Dunnet Landing. The sketches, from which plot is almost entirely absent, are held together by being the impressions of the countryside and its people as received by a summer visitor. It is the least sensational of writing, but a culture and a history are brought to life with unemphatic vividness. The following paragraph, where the visitor is taken to a nearby island by her landlady, will convey something of Miss Jewett's quality, among other things her ability to render vernacular speech:

On a larger island, farther out to sea, my entertaining companion showed me with glee the small houses of two farmers who shared the island between them, and declared that for three generations the people had not spoken to each other even in times of sickness or death or birth. 'When the news came that the war was over, one of 'em knew it a week, and never stepped across his wall to tell the others,' she said. 'There, they enjoy it: they've got to have somethin' to interest 'em in such a place; 'tis a good deal more tryin' to be tied to folks you don't like than 'tis to be alone. Each of 'em tells the neighbours their wrongs; plenty likes to hear and tell again; them as fetch a bone'll carry one, an' so they keep the fight a-goin'. I must say I like variety myself; some folks washes Monday an' irons Tuesday the whole year round, even if the circus is goin' by!'

Since for the most part Willa Cather wrote novels of the early years of Nebraska and, later, of French Quebec and New Mexico, her canvases were obviously much larger than Sara Orne Jewett's; her novels became by implication the history of the American frontier wherever it might be; but she did from time to time write memorable stories of Nebraska life that, though more widely ranging than Miss Jewett's, are essentially character sketches.

The most famous is probably 'Neighbour Rosicky' which Maxwell Geismer, in *The Last of the Provincials*, calls an 'agrarian idyll'. The story is about Rosicky's coming to terms with old age after a life of hard work, and inevitably it is predictable: Rosicky dies because he insists upon 'stealing a march on Doctor Ed' and raking the thistles for his young American daughter-in-law. But between the doctor's telling him he had a bad heart and his death he has relived his life. He and his wife had lived in the city before fulfilling their desire to work the land, and then

they had been at one accord not to hurry through life, not to be always skimping and saving. They saw their neighbours buy more land and feed more stock than they did, without discontent. Once when the creamery agent came to the Rosickys to persuade them to sell him their cream, he told them how much money the Fasslers, their nearest neighbours, had made on their cream last year.

'Yes,' said Mary, 'and look at them Fassler children! Pale, pinched little things, they look like skimmed milk. I'd rather put some colour into my children's faces than put money into the bank.'

The agent shrugged his shoulders and turned to Anton.

'I guess we'll do like she says,' said Rosicky.

So in his semi-retirement he contemplates his lot. Like all farmers, he has suffered from the hazards of the climate; he has not made much money; but he has a wife he loves and five contented sons. From the story the portrait emerges of a good man, painted by himself as he works on his farm and remembers his life, and also by Dr Burleigh, who enters the action from time to time as a privileged observer and whose role is very much like Willa Cather's own in the immigrant community of her youth. Burleigh, indeed, has the last paragraph of the story. On his way to visit the family some weeks after Rosicky's funeral he stops his car at the cemetery.

For the first time it struck Doctor Ed that this was really a beautiful graveyard. He thought of city cemeteries; acres of shrubbery and heavy stone, so arranged and lonely and unlike anything in the living world. Cities of the dead, indeed; cities of the forgotten, of the 'put away'. . . . Nothing could be more undeathlike than this place; nothing could be more right for a man who had helped to do the work of great cities and had always longed for the open country and had got it at last. Rosicky's life seemed to him complete and beautiful.

Writing on 'Neighbour Rosicky', Geismer finds that the accent on gaiety is a little forced in the account of Papa Rosicky's 'special gift for loving people'. One can accept this. It seems to me that Willa Cather was partially defeated, as all but the greatest writers have been, by her attempt to describe a positively good man; but more important, perhaps, was her increasing antagonism to the modern American world. There is an ideological bias in the story; it is a dramatization of her idea of the good life and the conditions in which it is possible to live it.

Willa Cather saw her intensely local scene in the light of two thousand years of European literature. By comparison, Sherwood Anderson was uneducated or, more properly, self-educated, and critics have always tended to patronize him. Yet he is one of the first American writers whose work links up with that of Joyce, Lawrence, and Virginia Woolf in Europe. No Americans, he said, 'lived, felt, or talked as the average American novel makes them live, feel, or talk and as for the plot short stories of the magazines – those bastard children of de Maupassant, Poe, and O. Henry – it was certain that there were no plot short stories ever lived in any life.' The statement strikes one as a less sophisticated version of Virginia Woolf's famous comments on the novel in *The Common Reader*. Anderson's achievement seems the product of a native, determined, and perhaps muddled honesty, and one of its components was a revulsion from the materialism of American life. Born in Ohio in 1876, Anderson was a successful business man until in 1912 he walked out of his paint-manufacturing business and his family to begin his life over again. The first and perhaps the most important fruits of this spiritual rebirth were the short stories published in 1919 entitled *Winesburg, Ohio*. 'It is as though,' A. Walton Litz has written in the commentary accompanying his selection in *Major American Short Stories*, 'Poe's powerful gothic imagination, softened and domesticated through the influence of naturalism and psychoanalysis, were applied to the desperate prisoners of provincial life.'

The stories focus on crucial moments in the lives of men and women living in the small town of Winesburg. They have been seen as examples of what has been called the revolt from the village, and there are obvious affinities between Anderson and contemporaries like Dreiser and Sinclair Lewis. The date of publication seems significant: there was a popular American song of that early postwar period, 'How you gonna keep 'em down on the farm now that they've seen Paree?' In fact, the time of the events described in *Winesburg, Ohio* is some ten years before the First World War.

The stories are linked together by a character common to all, George Willard, a reporter on the *Winesburg Eagle* and the son of the proprietor of the town's hotel. One of his roles is to be the confessor of the other characters, and it is difficult not to think of him as Anderson. He, too, wishes to be a writer; in the last story he leaves the town to seek his fortune on a big city newspaper; and one suspects that the book he is destined to write is *Winesburg, Ohio*.

Anderson prefaces the collection with a description, which on the face of it seems to have nothing to do with Winesburg, of an unpublished book called 'The Book of the Grotesque'.

... The thought was involved but a simple statement of it would be something like this:

That in the beginning when the world was young there were a great many thoughts but no such thing as a truth. Man made the truths himself and each truth was a composite of a great many vague thoughts. All about in the world were the truths and they were all beautiful.

The old man had listed hundreds of the truths in his book. I will not try to tell you all of them. There was the truth of virginity and the truth of passion, the truth of wealth and of poverty, of thrift and of profligacy, of carelessness and abandon. Hundreds and hundreds were the truths and they were all beautiful.

And then the people came along. Each as he appeared snatched up one of the truths and some who were quite strong snatched up a dozen of them.

It was the truths that made people grotesques. The old man had quite an elaborate theory concerning the matter. It was his notion that the moment that one of the people took one of the truths to himself, called it his truth, and tried to live his life by it, he became a grotesque and the truth he embraced became a falsehood.

When we turn to the stories proper we find that Anderson is dealing with men and women frozen into postures of estrangement and alienation, from which they attempt to break away, generally through some effort to communicate with George Willard, who appears to them as a sort of absolving priest or at any rate a free spirit as they are not. I assume that in Willard Anderson is describing what seems to him the function of the writer in modern life. The people who 'confess' to him are cut off from communion with their fellows; they are drunks, homosexuals, voyeurs, frigid women, religious maniacs. But despite the distortion they suffer from their alienation from the society in which they live, they are at the same time, Anderson seems to suggest by his sympathetic treatment, superior to their fellow-citizens who acquiesce and accept, who are 'normal'.

'Hands', the second story in the volume, is typical. Wing Biddlebaum has been the 'town mystery' ever since he arrived in Winesburg twenty years earlier. He lives alone, and his only friend is Willard. He is the quickest and best strawberry-picker in the town, the growing of soft fruits being Winesburg's chief industry. He seems to live in terror of his hands; he keeps them in his pockets or hides them behind his back. He has in fact – and this is the core of the story – been a school teacher in a small town in Pennsylvania, a dedicated teacher, and in his fervour as a teacher he would caress and fondle the boys, until one day he is beaten up by angry parents and driven out of town as a pervert. So he comes to Winesburg.

Some characters in these stories do achieve a sublimation of a kind. Anderson was writing very much under the influence of Freud. There is the Revd Curtis Hartman in the story 'The Strength of God'. He is married to a frigid woman and he struggles against his carnal desire for Kate Swift, the school teacher into whose bedroom he can peep from the belltower of his church. Although he laments the unfairness of this burden of desire, he breaks a hole in the stained glass window of the belfry the better to watch Kate Swift, and one night sees her naked on her bed, weeping, and kneeling in prayer. He rushes out to seek George Willard in the newspaper office:

He began to advance upon the young man, his eyes glowing and his voice ringing with fervour. 'I have found the light,' he cried. 'After ten years in this town, God has manifested himself to me in the body of a woman.' His voice dropped and he began to whisper. 'I did not understand,' he said. 'What I took to be a trial of my soul was only a preparation for a new and more beautiful fervour of the spirit. God has appeared to me in the person of Kate Swift, the school teacher, kneeling naked on a bed. Do you know Kate Swift? Although she may not be aware of it, she is an instrument of God, bearing the message of truth.'

Though the stories of *Winesburg, Ohio* plainly spring from a criticism of American small-town existence, of its narrowness, its conformity, its emptiness, its preoccupation with commercial values, it is equally plain that they go beyond this. Despite their realistic surface, they are not primarily realistic. Anderson is dramatizing what seems to him the essence of the human condition: the individual is at odds with his society, which is another way of saying that society is the enemy of the individual.

Anderson is a flawed writer. He was a *naïf* and at times it is difficult not to think he was a *faux naïf*. Certainly his simplicity often appears to be what Matthew Arnold called *simplesse*. He claimed to have been influenced in his style by Turgenev in *Sportsman's Sketches*. Much more obvious are the influences of Gertrude Stein and of the Bible. At his best, he captures in his prose the rhythms of American common speech, as Mark Twain did. His influence on later American writing has been great; on Hemingway, who repaid him by parodying him in *Torrents of Spring*, and on Faulkner. When one reads him today, one sees how much he is at the centre of one American tradition of short-story writing: later writers like Carson McCullers and Flannery O'Connor went on to explore his theme of alienation and incommunicability through characters who are almost freaks.

Ring Lardner came to the short story from journalism and wrote all his life in the tradition of a long line of American humorists who exploited slang and the illiteracies of vernacular speech for comic ends. The greatest of them, of course, was Mark Twain, who entirely transcended his medium, and when Lardner's collection *How to Write Short Stories* appeared in 1924, it was as the successor of Mark Twain that Edmund Wilson hailed him. He had begun as a baseball writer on an Indiana paper, taking over in 1913 the 'In the Wake of the News' column in the *Chicago Tribune*, in which appeared his Jack Keefe letters, purported to be written by an oafish, semi-literate baseball player who through his own words exposes himself in all his obnoxiousness. Published in 1916 as an epistolary novel, *You Know Me, Al*, they brought him to the notice of a wider than local public. He was admired, for instance, by Scott Fitzgerald as well as by Wilson, and *How to Write Short Stories* brought him a nationwide reputation. The title of the volume has been seen as evidence of Lardner's inability to believe that he was a serious writer, and reviewing the book, Wilson commented on the discrepancy between the stories and the jokey way in which they were presented. 'What one finds in *How to Write Short Stories*,' he said, 'is a series of American types almost equal in importance to those of Sherwood Anderson and Sinclair Lewis.'

Lardner is transmuting what was initially a stock comic device into an instrument of satire, while at the same time his sensitivity to the spoken word was contributing to the liberation of American prose from the tyranny of its English heritage. This was one of the great movements of the time. Mencken's enormously influential book *The American Language* was published in 1919, and there were two revised editions within the next four years. It was a movement bound up, obviously, with realistic fiction; one recalls that when Sinclair Lewis's *Babbitt* appeared in 1922 a glossary of specifically American words was appended to the English edition. Round about this time, too, there was a novel published in America called *Talk United States*. There is no need to postulate missionary endeavour in Lardner's exploitation of

the vernacular; as Wilson was to write later: 'Relatively uneducated writers like Ring Lardner and Mark Twain have had so
poor a literary vocabulary that they were likely to seem bald or
thin when they attempted straight English prose, and they could
only express themselves adequately by having their story told by
a character who spoke some form of illiterate dialect or special
slang.' Nevertheless, one must emphasize the part Lardner
played in the liberation of American prose by bringing back into
it the rhythms of American native speech.

There is a characteristic story in *How to Write Short Stories* in
which Lardner demonstrates almost in a virtuoso manner his
mastery of vernacular speech, 'Some Like Them Cold', an exchange of letters between an aspiring popular songwriter from
the Middle West on the make in New York City and a girl he has
met by chance in the Lasalle Street railway station in Chicago. In
their letters, the two characters expose themselves. As Wilson
observed, Lardner understood the difference between the spoken
language of his characters and the language they used for writing, and demonstrated all the grossness of their complacency and
self-regard, all their pettiness and genteel affectations. No element of compassion for or of identification with them is allowed
to creep into their delineation, which suggests the difference between Lardner's art and Sinclair Lewis's on the one hand and
Sherwood Anderson's on the other.

I can do no better than transcribe the opening paragraphs of
the first two letters:

N. Y. Aug. 3

Dear Miss Gillespie: How about our bet now as you bet me I would
forget all about it the minute I hit the big town and would never write
you a letter. Well girlie it looks like you lose so pay me. Seriously we
will call all bets off as I am not the kind that bet on a sure thing and it
sure was a sure thing that I would not forget a girlie like you and all
that is worrying me is whether it may not be the other way round and
you are wondering who this fresh guy is that is writing you this letter. I
bet you are so will try and refreshen your memory.

Well girlie I am the handsome young man that was wandering round
Lasalle St. station Monday and 'happened' to sit down beside of a
mighty pretty girlie who was waiting to meet her sister from Toledo
and the train was late and I am glad of it because if it had not of been
that little girlie and I would never of met. So for once I am a lucky guy

but still I guess it was time I had some luck as it was certainly tough luck for you and I to both be living in Chi all that time and never got together till a half hour before I was leaving town for good. . . .

Tomorrow I expect to commence fighting the 'battle of Broadway' and will let you know how I come out that is if you answer this letter. In the meanwhile girlie au reservoir and don't do nothing I would not do.

Your new friend (?)
Chas. F. Lewis

Chicago, Ill., Aug. 6

My dear Mr Lewis: Well, that certainly was a 'surprise party' getting your letter and you are certainly a 'wonder man' to keep your word as I am afraid that most men of your sex are gay deceivers but maybe you are 'different'. Any way it sure was a surprise and will gladly pay the bet if you will just tell me what it was we bet. Hope it was not money as I am a 'working girl' but if it was not more than a dollar or two will try to dig it up even if I have to 'beg, borrow or steal'.

Suppose you will think me a 'case' to make a bet and then forget what it was, but you must remember, Mr Man, that I had just met you and was 'dazzled'. Joking aside I was rather 'fussed' and will tell you why. Well, Mr Lewis, I suppose you see lots of girls like the one you told me about that you saw on the train who tried to 'get acquainted' but I want to assure you that I am not one of those kind and sincerely hope you will believe me when I tell you that you was the first man I ever spoke to meeting them like that and my friends and the people who know me would simply faint if they knew I ever spoke to a man without a 'proper introduction'. . . .

Well, be sure to write soon and tell me what N.Y. is like and all about it and don't forget the little girlie who was 'bad' and spoke to a strange man in the station and have been blushing over it ever since.

Your friend (?)
Mabelle Gillespie.

In the dozen or so letters over a period of rather less than two months that are exchanged between them a whole ritual of courtship and display is gone through, until Chas. F. Lewis announces his engagement to Betsy Sears. His letter ends:

But just let me give you a word of advice before I close and that is don't never speak to strange men who you don't know nothing about as they may get you wrong and think you are trying to make them. It just happened that I knew better so you was lucky in my case but the luck might not last.

Which prompts the following reply from Miss Gillespie:

Chicago, Ill., Sept. 27

My Dear Mr Lewis: Thanks for your advice and also thank your fiancé for her generosity in allowing you to continue your correspondence with her 'rivals', but personally I have no desire to take advantage of that generosity as I have something better to do than read letters from a man like you, as specially as I have a man friend who is not so generous as Miss Sears and would strongly object to my continuing a correspondence with another man. It is at his request I am writing this note to tell you not to expect to hear from me again.

Even more uncompromising as an exposure of vulgarity, small-mindedness, and ineffable self-complacency is 'The Golden Honeymoon'. The narrator characterizes himself in his speech:

Yes, sir, we was married just fifty years ago the seventeenth day of last December and my daughter and son-in-law was over from Trenton to help us celebrate the Golden Wedding. My son-in-law is John H. Kramer, the real estate man. He made $12,000 one year and is pretty well thought of around Trenton; a good, steady, hard worker. The Rotarians was after him a long time to join, but he kept telling them his home was his club. But Edie finally made him join. That's my daughter.

Throughout, we are in the presence of a relentless bore, but we are anything but bored, so minute is the detail in which the character conducts his self-exposure. Wilson sums up the quality of the story admirably when he described Lardner's irony as 'both fresh and morose'.

Also for a time a sports reporter, no short-story writer could have been more different from Lardner than Conrad Aiken, whose first reputation was as a poet, though he was a fine novelist, autobiographer, and literary journalist. Reviewing Katherine Mansfield's stories, he wrote: ' . . . in Miss Mansfield's short stories, as in the poems of a lyric poet, it is always Miss Mansfield's voice that we hear, Miss Mansfield we see.' The generalization could be true for Aiken's work in all its forms. His subject was always himself in the sense that all his characters and situations were exhibited in the light of his own singular, highly idiosyncratic vision of man's life on earth, a glimpse of which may be caught in half a dozen lines from his early poem 'The Morning Song of Senlin':

It is morning, Senlin says, and in the morning,
When light drips through the shutters like the dew,
I arise, I face the sunrise,
And do the things my fathers learned to do.
Stars in the purple dust above the rooftops
Pale in a saffron mist and seem to die,
And I myself on a swiftly tilting planet
Stand before a glass and tie my tie.

Aiken and the typical Aiken character are men who are aware that even as they go about their daily business, standing before a glass and tying their ties, they are living poised between vast immensities between which they die too, as one sees in the extraordinary story of a man's death on the operating-table, 'Mr Arcularis'. The immensities are not of space and time alone; they are also of the interior world of dreams and the unconscious, a sometimes insidiously attractive world. As with the characters of Poe, with whom Aiken has affinities, one feels that Aiken's have only to take one step further to fall into the abyss of madness or death.

The least ambiguous dramatization of this is probably 'The Dark City', which describes the relief felt each evening by a commuter from New York as he goes back to the pleasure of family life in the suburbs. The story is kept deliberately light. Andrew's private terror of the Dark City is something he can joke about as a fantastic extravaganza with his wife, who does not take it seriously. The story ends:

'Really, Andrew, I think you're going mad.'
'Going? I'm gone! My brain is maggoty.'
They laughed, and rattled the chessmen into their wooden box. Then they began locking the doors and windows for the night.

The inference is clear. Andrew can hold his hysteria at arms' length, play it as a joke, so long as he is able to lock himself behind the doors of family life. But the terror is real, the Dark City a true symbol of evil: 'Its people are maggots – maggots perhaps the size of human children; their heads are small and wedge-shaped, and glow with a faint bluish light.' In this communication of the horror of life, Aiken was one of the first Anglo-Saxon writers to be influenced by Freud. No one has better suggested the precariousness of sanity and the mind's vulnerability to obsession, mania, and fugue. Here, his masterpiece is 'Silent Snow, Secret Snow', a story as terrifying as it is beautiful.

Aiken found Katherine Mansfield's stories characterized by a 'hallucinated vividness of style' and again the phrase could be applied to Aiken himself. Since every story he wrote bears his own unmistakable stamp, it might be thought that intensity would preclude variety and his range be narrow. This is not so. Besides the stories of incipient psychological breakdown, which in stories like 'The Disciple' merges into the macabre, there is a whole range of stories celebrating what we recognize as normal experience. Some of these take us back to the Boston and Cambridge, Mass. of Aiken's undergraduate days at Harvard, where he was a contemporary and friend of T. S. Eliot, some, like 'The Orange Moth', to his days as a young writer in New York City, others, like 'The Young Vikings', to his years in England at Rye, Sussex, between the wars.

The best of these stories have a Chekhovian quality of seeming to sum up in a single incident the significant experience of a lifetime. The masterpiece of these stories of normal experience is 'Round by Round', in which a sports reporter in a newspaper office is writing his report of a championship fight and simultaneously composing in his mind a letter to his unfaithful wife. The drama critic is with him and they type side by side, chatting, the sports reporter reliving the fight with only part of his mind.

'Well,' said Cush, to his typewriter, 'did Zabriski win, or who?'

'There is a new champion, and it was a swell fight, science defeats slug, but I didn't watch it. I was elsewhere.'

'All right, I'll bite, where were you?'

'I was picking flowers.'

'You mean Ann's given you the bum's rush again, or something. Who is it now?'

He didn't answer at once, he frowned over his notes. Cush turned the sheet of paper into his machine and began typing. Round even. ROUND TWO. . . . Zabriski scored a light left to jaw before clinch. Romero reached the champion with two good rights to jaw. The man behind him was saying, this fellow's good, this fellow is pretty good, watch him. Zabriski can't touch him, look at the way he ties him up. Oh, baby, and was that a sock.

'It isn't the same guy, it's two other fellows. If you know what I mean.'

We come to the core of the story, its central symbol to which everything has reference.

He paused in his typing, and straightened his back, and looked up at the dingy white-washed wall, on which hung a small photograph of the James family – Henry and William sitting in garden chairs beside a wicker table, Alice standing between them holding a sunshade, a cocker spaniel sprawled on the path. The garden was an English garden, an apricot or perhaps a peach tree was crucified flat on the brick wall, and the three faces looked forward at him with an extraordinary integrity. Integrity! Yes, that was it, it wasn't only the intelligence, the wisdom, it was the profound and simple honesty of all three faces – faces carved slowly out of some sort of benign marble. A book lay on the table – too large for *The Wings of the Dove*, too small for *Varieties of Religious Experience*. What would it be? And what were they thinking, what were they remembering together, as they thus faced the camera, or the world, with such triune simplicity and kindness? . . . Romero crossed a right to the jaw as Pat scored with a light left to face. The challenger neatly ducked Zabriski's right and left swings. Both landed light lefts to body.

The two reporters go on typing till they have finished their articles, and when Cush leaves the sports writer hands him his copy to take below, saying he wants to write a letter. And he begins his letter to the unfaithful Ann, trying to set out the nature of their problem and combat her belief that merely physical infidelity does not matter. The reader, finding the letter unsatisfactory, assumes the writer does also. He suddenly writes:

'Before me as I write is a photograph of three people. What I really want to tell you about is these three people. I would like to tell you what they mean to me, what art-shape they make of their lives, what it might mean to you or to anybody to *realize* what they are as they sit there –'

He dropped his hands from the machine in a sudden despair. It was impossible, it was a kind of absurd day-dream, it was unreal, he ought to have known better. It could not be done, never would be done. It could not be said. You felt these things or you didn't. . . . Instead, they would quarrel, and then quarrel again, they would quarrel day after day and night after night, there would be no end to it for ever.

'Round by Round' is one of the best stories ever written about either boxing or newspaper work, and obviously it transcends both. Technically, it is extremely daring, especially in the way it relates the loyalty of the defeated champion's fiancée, who is at the ring side, to the integrity, 'the profound and simple honesty of all three faces', apparent in the photograph of the Jameses. In seven pages Aiken sums up a relationship between a man and a woman.

The tone of Aiken's stories, dealing as they do with characters on the edge of disintegration or stricken with remorse for opportunities lost, might be expected to be depressing. This is not so; partly because of its style, which for all its subtlety has a curious quality of gaiety, but even more because of something of which the style seems a reflection. This is Aiken's acceptance of what seemed to him the nature and limitations of man's existence on a swiftly tilting planet. 'This is how it was': so Aiken described the effect of Chekhov's stories on the reader. 'This is how it was' is the feeling we have, too, when we read the best of Aiken.

IV

The titles of many of F. Scott Fitzgerald's books, novels, and collections of short stories alike, are exercises in romantic irony: *This Side of Paradise, Flappers and Philosophers, The Beautiful and the Damned, Tender is the Night, All the Sad Young Men.* It was Fitzgerald who invented what has become the stock label for the decade of the nineteen-twenties in America, the Jazz Age, 'the ten-year period', as he said, 'that, as if reluctant to die outmoded in its bed, leaped to a spectacular death in October 1929.' Fitzgerald was its chronicler and laureate, its celebrant, and in some ways its sternest critic.

In his short story 'The Rich Boy' he made his famous statement, 'Let me tell you about the very rich. They are different from you and me.' To which Hemingway retorted in 'The Snows of Kilimanjaro': 'Yes, they have more money.' But Fitzgerald was wiser; he goes on to say:

They possess and enjoy easily, and it does something to them, makes them soft where we are hard, and cynical where we are trustful, in a way that, unless you were born rich, it is very difficult to understand. They think, deep in their hearts, that they are better than we are because we had to discover the compensations and refuges of life for ourselves. Even when they enter deep in our world or sink below us, they still think they are better than we are. They are different.

This describes Fitzgerald's attitude to the world he made his own. It was a world in which by birth and background he was an outsider. He was from the Middle West but went to a preparatory school on the eastern seaboard and then to Princeton. If he had been an Englishman from the middle class he might have fallen in love with an ideal of aristocracy. As it was, he fell in love with the very rich of America, but was always conscious of being among foreigners whose values, fundamentally, were not his.

In his lifetime, Fitzgerald published 160 short stories, and their point of view scarcely changes. He is the poet of regret for opportunities lost and of remorse for action wrongly or unheedingly taken. In this respect, his masterpiece is probably the tragic

'Babylon Revisited', the story of Charlie Wales's return to Paris after the boom is over. He had 'lost a lot in the crash' but, even more, 'I lost everything I wanted in the boom' – his wife Helen, who had died partly as a result of his mindlessness, and his small daughter, who had been adopted by his wife's relations when he had been hospitalized for alcoholism. Now, some years later, a reformed character, he has come back to Babylon to claim his child and is defeated in the attempt by a chance encounter with a couple from his unregenerate past. The story ends:

> He would come back some day; they couldn't make him pay for ever. But he wanted his child, and nothing was much good now, beside that fact. He wasn't young any more, with a lot of nice thoughts and dreams to have to himself. He was absolutely sure Helen wouldn't have wanted him to be so alone.

It is an intolerably moving story, but no less remarkable is 'May Day', written ten years earlier, when Fitzgerald was just out of the army. Like most of his work, it is in many respects autobiographical; it is also long, complex, marvellously orchestrated, and in a sense prophetic. The day is May Day, 1919, the scene New York. We first meet a young man named Gordon Sterrett who has called on his college friend and ex-room-mate Philip Dean at the Biltmore Hotel. Both are recently back from the war; Dean is one of the very rich, while it is difficult not to see Sterrett as a representation of Fitzgerald himself in an all-too-possible avatar. He has lost his job, bled his family until he's ashamed to ask for another nickel, and must have three hundred dollars immediately because he's in trouble with a girl named Jewel Hudson. Dean gives him some money but is increasingly censorious; his comfort is being assaulted, and he feels Sterrett has betrayed the code.

> He took a five-dollar bill from his wallet and tossed it over to Gordon, who folded it carefully and put it in his pocket. There was an added spot of colour in his cheeks, an added glow that was not fever. For an instant before they turned to go out their eyes met, and in that instant each found something that made him lower his glance quickly. For in that instant they quite suddenly and definitely hated each other.

They lunch together at the Yale Club, and arrange to meet later in the evening at a fraternity ball at Delmonico's.

The story, which is in eleven parts, shifts to two very different characters, Carrol Key – Key, incidentally, was one of Fitzgerald's own names – and Gus Rose, private soldiers in a drafted division from New Jersey, landed in New York three days before.

They were ugly, ill-nourished, devoid of all except the very lowest form of intelligence, and without even that animal exuberance that in itself brings colour into life; they were lately vermin-ridden, cold, and hungry in a dirty town of a strange land; they were poor, friendless; tossed as driftwood from their births, they would be tossed as driftwood to their deaths.

They saunter down Sixth Avenue 'wielding toothpicks with great gusto and complete detachment'. Pathetic rather than sinister, they are all the same menacing in their mindlessness. All they know is that they have got to 'getta holda some liquor'. It is illegal for men in uniform to buy drink, but they set out to find Key's brother, who can get them some liquor since he is a waiter in a hash joint. On the way they join up with a gang of soldiers who are gathered round a Socialist orator. Having effectively beaten up the 'God damn Bolshevik', the mob sets out for Tenth Street in order to break up a Socialist meeting there, but Key and Rose break away in order to find the liquor-providing brother. The hash joint turns out to be Delmonico's, where preparations are in progress for the fraternity ball, so Rose steals a bottle and they have their first drink.

Peter Himmel, a drunken Yale student, arrives at the ball with Edith Bradin, whom in the past Gordon Sterrett has entertained at Yale.

So she came out of the dressing-room at Delmonico's and stood for a second in the doorway looking over the shoulders of a black dress in front of her at the Yale men who flitted like dignified black moths around the head of the stairs. From the room she had left drifted out the heavy fragrance left by the passage to and fro of many scented young beauties – rich perfumes and the fragile memory-laden dust of fragrant powders. This odour drifting out acquired the tang of cigarette smoke in the hall, and then settled sensuously down the stairs and permeated the ballroom where the Gamma Psi dance was to be held. It was an odour she knew well, exciting, stimulating, restlessly sweet – the odour of a fashionable dance. . . .

She thought of what she would say tonight at this revel faintly pre-saged already by the sounds of high and low laughter and slippered footsteps, and movements of couples up and down the stairs. She would talk the language she had talked for many years – her line – made up of the current expressions, bits of journalese and college slang strung together into an intrinsic whole, careless, faintly provocative, delicately sentimental. She smiled faintly as she heard a girl sitting on the stairs near her say: 'You don't know the half of it, dearie!'

She finds herself dancing with Sterrett. She thinks she loves him and then realizes something is wrong. They sit down and she listens to his self-pitying evasive talk.

As he talked she saw he had changed utterly. He wasn't at all light and gay and careless – a great lethargy and discouragement had come over him. Revulsion seized her, followed by a faint, surprising boredom. His voice seemed to come out of a great void. . . . Her distaste was growing. She barely nodded this time, waiting for her first possible cue to rise.

Suddenly Gordon's eyes filled with tears.

'Edith,' he said, turning to her with what was evidently a strong effort at self-control. 'I can't tell you what it means to me to know there's one person left who's interested in me.'

He reached out and patted her hand, and involuntarily she drew it away. . . .

– Love is fragile – she was thinking – but perhaps the pieces are saved, the things that hovered on her lips, that might have been said. The new love words, the tendernesses learned, are treasured up for the next lover.

At one o'clock she slips away from the dance and walks a few blocks to the office of her brother, also a Yale man, who is editor of a Socialist newspaper; Sterrett in the meantime has been confronted with and taken away by Jewel Hudson, the girl he has got into trouble, though the implication seems to be that she is a prostitute. While Edith is with her brother the news-paper office is suddenly invaded by the gang of drunken-soldier red-baiters. In the fracas, her brother's leg is broken and one of the soldiers falls through an open window to his death on the pavement below. It is Key.

At eight in the morning, the ball over, the revellers are having breakfast in one of a chain of popular restaurants. 'Within its pale but sanitary walls one finds a medley of chorus girls, college boys, debutantes, rakes, *filles de joie* – a not unrepresentative mixture of the gayest of Broadway and even of Fifth Avenue.' The soldier, Gus Rose, is there, though how he got there he does not know. So are Sterrett and Jewel; and Dean and Himmell; and Edith, with a new escort. Dean and Himmell, very drunk, are thrown out of the restaurant and, solemn and hysterical with laughter, they wander down Fifth Avenue masquerading as Mr In and Mr Out. In the Commodore Hotel, to the scandal of the other guests and the waiters, they breakfast on champagne and ham sandwiches. Then, trailed by Gus Rose, they leave for the Biltmore, where they have breakfast again.

They were torn between intermittent laughter and sudden spasmodic discussions of politics, college, and the sunny state of their dispositions. Their watches told them it was now nine o'clock, and a dim idea was born in them that they were on a memorable party, something that they would remember always. They lingered over the second bottle.

At the same time, in the bedroom of a small hotel just off Sixth Avenue, Gordon Sterrett wakes up 'with a pain in the back of his neck and a sick throbbing in all his veins'.

It must have been thirty seconds after he perceived the sunbeam with the dust on it and the rip of the large leather armchair that he had the sense of life close beside him, and it was another thirty seconds after that before he realized that he was irrevocably married to Jewel Hudson.

He went out half an hour later and bought a revolver at a sporting goods store. Then he took a taxi to the room where he had been living on East Twenty-Seventh Street, and, leaning across the table that held his drawing materials, fired a cartridge into his head just behind the temple.

Fitzgerald was twenty-four when he wrote 'May Day'. It is beautifully constructed; technically, it strikes one, at the lowest level, as a superb juggling feat. But it is much more than that. A brilliant piece of social history, it catches a memorable day and its mood. It was an actual day in what at the time of writing was very recent history but it was also the traditional May Day with all its associations of youth and merriment and young love. The irony of Fitzgerald's treatment of these is plainly evident, but all the same he writes of the day, the characters, and the events with delight, as witness his renderings of the sensuous and the frankly silly; they wear the quality of innocence.

From one point of view the story is a paean of youth and its accompaniments, love, tenderness, folly, and the illusion that youth lasts for ever, but that is not all. His attitude and the style that expresses it are romantic but the events he describes cast their shadows only too plainly before them. The two private soldiers, Key and Gus, weave in and out of the action like Shakespearian clowns. They are not presented with less sympathy than the college boys but they are without redeeming qualities, and in the end we see them as the college boys' *doppelgangers*, their shadows in the Jungian sense. They are Fitzgerald's comment on the rich young men whose behaviour and way of life he found so attractive and with whom he appeared to identify himself. They sound a note of foreboding, and we can realize now that Fitzgerald was writing the elegiac epitaph of the Jazz Age while the decade was still in its first years, and, even more than that, was prophesying symbolically the shapes of things to come. This was one of his great strengths as a writer. He was never taken in by the glitter; he was always aware of the presence of the Furies, even though others were not.

'The reputation of Ernest Hemingway, has, in a very short time,' wrote Edmund Wilson in *The Shores of Light* in 1927, when Hemingway had published three books only, 'assumed such proportions that it has already become fashionable to disparage him.' His reputation is still in the trough into which a highly successful author's almost inevitably falls immediately after his death, and at present it is difficult to see him either clearly or fairly. The case against him was put powerfully and persuasively by Frank O'Connor in *The Lonely Voice*:

> Nobody in Hemingway ever seems to have a job or a home. . . .
> Even the submerged population that Hemingway writes of is one that is associated with recreation rather than with labour – waiters, barmen, boxers, jockeys, bullfighters, and the like. . . . Even war is treated as recreation, an amusement for the leisured classes. In these stories practically no single virtue is discussed with the exception of physical courage, which from the point of view of people without an independent income is usually mainly a theoretical virtue. . . .
> In Hemingway the obsession with physical courage is clearly a per-

sonal problem . . . and it must be regarded and discounted as such if one is not to emerge from one's reading with a ludicrously distorted impression of human life.

Whether this is fair or not, the implications of O'Connor's charge against Hemingway, that his vision of life was too narrow and expressed in his own especial clichés of character and situation, in other words, in terms of self-parody, must be taken into account in any consideration of him. This is especially necessary since it is shared in some degree, however reluctantly, by many critics who grew up, as it were, in his shadow and at first responded to him with great enthusiasm.

The essential Hemingway story, inasmuch as it is an unambiguous clue to his values, is probably the relatively early 'A Clean, Well-Lighted Place'. Set in Spain, it begins:

It was late and everyone had left the café except an old man who sat in the shadow the leaves of the trees made against the electric light. In the daytime the street was dusty, but at night the dew settled the dust and the old man liked to sit late because he was deaf and now at night it was quiet and he felt the difference. The two waiters inside the café knew that the old man was a little drunk, and while he was a good client they knew that if he became too drunk he would leave without paying, so they kept watch on him.

The paragraph is a good example of Hemingway's deceptively simple style, with its short, mainly monosyllabic words through which a scene is created in intense focus.

The two waiters discuss the old man. One is young, impatient, and unsympathetic, eager for the café to close so that he can get home to his wife. The old man has recently attempted suicide. Why? The older waiter says, 'He was in despair.' Despair is something the young waiter understands. But why did he bungle his suicide? When the old man calls for another glass of brandy it is refused; the café is being closed. The difference between the two waiters, which perhaps is not one of age entirely, is revealed in a snatch of dialogue between them before they leave:

'We are of two different kinds,' the older waiter said. He was now dressed to go home. 'It is not only a question of youth and confidence although those things are very beautiful. Each night I am reluctant to close up because there may be some one who needs the café.'

'Hombre, there are bodegas open all night long.'

'You do not understand. This is a clean and pleasant café. It is well lighted. The light is very good and also, now, there are shadows of the leaves.'

The waiter continues the conversation with himself as he walks home:

It is the light of course but it is necessary that the place be clean and pleasant. You do not want music. . . . What did he fear? It was not fear or dread. It was a nothing that he knew too well. It was a nothing and a man was nothing too. It was only that and light was all it needed and a certain cleanness and order. Some lived in it and never felt it but he knew it all was nada y pues nada y nada y pues nada. Our nada who art in nada, nada by thy name thy kingdom nada thy will be nada in nada as it is in nada. Give us this nada our daily nada and nada us our nada as we nada our nadas and nada us not into nada but deliver us from nada; pues nada. Hail nothing full of nothing, nothing is with thee.

He pauses at a bar for coffee. He notes that though it is very bright and pleasant, the bar is unpolished.

Apart from the fact that he is old and alone, the story presents us with no detailed knowledge of the waiter at all; yet it is impossible not to think that he speaks for Hemingway and states his values. Life is meaningless, *nada*, a nothing. To survive in it, light is demanded. But light, though essential, is not enough. If the lot of man is to be more than to skulk by the fire then, in the waiter's imagery, the bar must be polished. In other words, a certain dignity is demanded in the way a man faces death. A 'good end', one might say, is everything, and since it is the good end that vindicates a man, there is an emphasis in Hemingway on the nature of a man's death.

From his earliest days, Hemingway was obsessed with violent death. We may speculate on the source of the obsession. His father, a Chicago doctor, who initiated him into hunting, committed suicide while Hemingway was still a boy. In the first world war, he was badly wounded on the Italian front; as a war correspondent he was present at later wars. Death was his theme. His aim as a writer, he said in his book on bullfighting *Death in the Afternoon*, was 'to know what you really felt, to put down purely what really happened, what the actual things were that produced the emotions you experienced'. He was not always successful and then he parodied himself; but, given his avowed ends, some at least of O'Connor's charges against him appear invalid.

In a sense, everything that is significant in Hemingway is contained in his first book of stories *In Our Time*, which is as fresh today as when it was first published in 1924. The stories relate the adventures of a boy called Nick Adams – the choice of names is surely significant – in the woods and lakes of Michigan and, as he grows to manhood, in the world beyond. They are interspersed with shorter stories, often not more than vignettes of paragraph length, of the First World War, the Turko–Greek War, and the bull fight. Hemingway described his method in *In Our Time* and its rationale in a letter to Edmund Wilson before the book was published:

Finished the book of 14 stories with a chapter of *In Our Time* between each story – that is the way they were meant to go – to give the picture of the whole between examining it in detail. Like looking with your eye at something, say a passing coast line, and then looking at with 15 × binoculars. Or rather, maybe, looking at it and then going in and living in it – and then coming out and looking at it again.

'Indian Camp' is characteristic. Nick Adams goes with his doctor father to an Indian camp where an Indian woman is 'very sick'. She is in childbirth, and Nick acts as assistant to his father at a caesarian operation performed with a jack-knife – 'one for the medical journal'. The dénouement is Nick's discovery that the squaw's husband, unable to bear his wife's pain, has cut his throat. The story ends:

'I'm terribly sorry I brought you along, Nickie,' said his father, all his post-operative exhilaration gone. 'It was an awful mess to put you through.'
'Do ladies always have such a hard time having babies?' Nick asked.
'No, that was very, very exceptional.'
'Why did he kill himself, Daddy?'
'I don't know, Nick. He couldn't stand things, I guess.'
'Do many men kill themselves, Daddy?'
'Not very many, Nick.'
'Do many women?'
'Hardly ever.'

'Don't they ever?'

'Oh, yes. They do sometimes.'

. . . 'Is dying hard, Daddy?'

'No, I think it's pretty easy, Nick. It all depends.'

They were seated in the boat, Nick in the stern, his father rowing. The sun was coming up over the hills. A bass jumped, making a circle in the water. Nick trailed his hand in the water. It felt warm in the sharp chill of the morning.

In the early morning on the lake sitting in the stern of the boat with his father rowing, he felt quite sure that he would never die.

The most remarkable story in the collection is the last, 'Big Two-Hearted River'. It is preceded by a vignette of death in the bull ring, and itself forms two parts, between them coming a vignette of a hanging in an American jail; and there is a short envoi, recounting a visit to the King of Greece, which ends: 'It was very jolly. Like all Greeks he wanted to go to America.' 'Big Two-Hearted River' presents something of a problem: having first read it in its context in *In Our Time*, it is not easy to be certain how we should have interpreted it if we had read it on its own, as a self-contained story, as it appears in many anthologies, though I think our conclusion would have been the same. It opens with Nick Adams, having returned from the wars, getting off a train at a wayside station in Michigan. The town has been burnt down in his absence. What happens after he gets down from the train? It is very simple, an account of two days in a man's life in which he goes fishing for trout. At the end of the first day he makes camp in a deserted countryside by a trout-stream and on the second he wades in the river and fishes. That is all but the detail is exact. The story ends:

> Nick stood up on the log, holding his rod, the landing net hanging heavy, then stepped into the water and splashed ashore. He climbed the bank and cut up into the woods, towards the high ground. He was going back to camp. He looked back. The river just showed through the trees. There were plenty of days coming when he could fish the swamp.

For all that it exists in a context, 'Big Two-Hearted River' seems to me completely self-contained. We recognize it as a story of rebirth, an extraordinarily successful attempt to create an objective correlative to Nick's state of mind. It describes Nick's –

and one thinks Hemingway's too at this stage of his life – idea of what Henry James called the Great Good Place. It is a place where a man can be alone because there are no other human beings there to violate his solitude.

Short of retreating into madness, it is exceedingly doubtful, of course, whether opting out of society is ever possible in any real sense. We can escape into the artificial world of holiday, and it is a criticism of Hemingway that so many of his stories depict men and women living the holiday lives of the irresponsible very rich. But at their finest, no matter how exotic the characters and their circumstances, Hemingway's stories can still be seen as para-digms of man's behaviour at the great moments of life. 'The Old Man and the Sea', the last and probably the least successful long short story, tells of an old Cuban fisherman who fights with a great fish. Few of us are Cuban fishermen, and our problems, even our extreme problems, are not like the fisherman's. Aiming at simplicity, Hemingway too often fell into the fake simplicity Matthew Arnold called *simplesse*. What he set out to do in 'The Old Man and the Sea' he had already done better twenty-five years earlier and in terms more germane to modern urban man in 'The Undefeated', 'The Killers', and 'Fifty Grand'. However remote from the experience of most of us the exoticism of these stories may be, the bull-fighting of 'The Undefeated', the gang-ster-feud of 'The Killers', and the rigged championship fight of 'Fifty Grand', it is central, it must be admitted, to the folklore of our times; indeed it might be said that at times the folklore becomes part of modern man's mythology.

'The Undefeated' is a story of Manuel, an old bull fighter who attempts, having just come out of hospital after an accident in the ring, to make a comeback. Knowing that the picadors provided by the management will be incompetent, he seeks to persuade Zurito, an experienced friend, to act as picador for him. Zurito is unwilling, but in the end he agrees to act on con-dition that Manuel quits the ring and cuts off his bull fighter's pigtail if he fails to 'go big' on the night of the fight. Manuel agrees.

Nothing happens in the story that we do not expect. The sus-pense comes from the narrative excitement of Hemingway's rendering of the fight between the bull and the old fighter, who before he finally kills the bull is pelted with cushions and bottles by the crowd. He has been so badly gored that he is carried to hospital. On the operating-table he thinks:

To hell with this operating-table. He'd been on plenty of operating tables before. He was not going to die. There would be a priest if he was going to die.

Zurito was saying something to him. Holding up the scissors.

That was it. They were going to cut off his coleta. They were going to cut off his pigtail.

Manuel sat up on the operating-table. The doctor stepped back, angry. Someone grabbed and held him.

'You couldn't do a thing like that, Manos,' he said.

'That's all right,' Zurito said. 'I won't do it. I was joking.'

'I was getting good,' Manuel said. 'I didn't have any luck. That was all.'

The story ends:

Manuel opened his eyes and looked at Zurito.

'Wasn't I going good, Manos?' he asked, for confirmation.

'Sure,' said Zurito. 'You were going great.'

The doctor's assistant put the cone over Manuel's face and he inhaled deeply. Zurito stood awkwardly, watching.

Our assent is won to the relentlessness of the tragedy by the spareness and sureness of the dialogue. Heroic feelings are never stated for the heroic is played down both by the economy with which the action is described and by the inconsequence, in bull-fighting terms, of the action. We are made conscious all the time of the incongruity between Manuel's desperate bid for survival and self-respect and the tawdriness of attendant circumstances.

In that 'The Undefeated' depicts a confrontation between man and bull it is a relatively simple story. 'The Killers' is complex by contrast, since it seems almost entirely a matter of circumstances, the central character in the action appearing only briefly and then very much as a dumb ox, which is Wyndham Lewis's name for Hemingway's heroes.

The action begins in Henry's lunch-room, a restaurant in a small Mid-West town. Two men come in and sit at the counter:

'What's yours?' George asked them.

'I don't know,' one of the men said. 'What do you want to eat, Al?'

'I don't know,' said Al. 'I don't know what I want to eat.'

Outside it was getting dark. The street-light came on outside the window. The two men at the counter read the menu. From the other end of the counter Nick Adams watched them. He had been talking to George when they came in.

'I'll have a roast pork tenderloin with apple sauce and mashed potatoes,' the first man said.

'It isn't ready yet.'

'What the hell do you put it on the card for?'

'That's the dinner,' George explained. 'You can get that at six o'clock.'

George looked at the clock on the wall behind the counter.

'It's five o'clock.'

'The clock says twenty minutes past five,' the second man said.

'It's twenty minutes fast.'

'Oh, to hell with the clock,' the first man said. 'What have you got to eat?'

'I can give you any kind of sandwiches,' George said. 'You can have ham and eggs, bacon and eggs, liver and bacon, or a steak.'

'Give me chicken croquettes with green peas and cream sauce and mashed potatoes.'

'That's the dinner.'

'Everything we want's the dinner, eh? That's the way you work it.'

'I can give you ham and eggs, bacon and eggs, liver—'

'I'll take ham and eggs,' the man called Al said. He wore a derby hat and a black overcoat buttoned across the chest. His face was small and white and he had tight lips. He wore a silk muffler and gloves.

'Give me bacon and eggs,' said the other man. He was about the same size as Al. Their faces were different, but they were dressed like twins. Both wore overcoats too tight for them. They sat leaning forward, their elbows on the counter.

'Got anything to drink?' Al asked.

'Silver beer, bevo, ginger-ale,' George said.

'I mean you got anything to *drink*?'

'Just those I said.'

'This is a hot town,' said the other. . . .

This is surely a brilliant opening for a story. The reader's attention is arrested immediately and rivetted. It seems significant that Nick Adams appears in the story. He is not characterized; he is merely a friend of George, the counter-hand, but from our knowledge of the other stories in *In Our Time* we will suspect him of being an aspect of Hemingway and likely to be the story's centre of consciousness.

The two strangers, Al and Max, take over the lunch-room. Al produces a shot-gun, goes into the kitchen, binds Nick and the Negro cook back to back, and watches over the lunch-room from the hatch. There is no resistance to them, partly because the two men are presented almost as instruments of destiny. George is ordered to serve short orders only and to tell any one who orders dinner that the cook has not shown up. Al and Max are awaiting the arrival of Ole Andreson, an old prize-fighter who habitually dines in the lunch-room.

'Talk to me, bright boy,' Max said. 'What do you think's going to happen?'

George did not say anything.

'I'll tell you,' Max said. 'We're going to kill a Swede. Do you know a big Swede named Ole Andreson?'

'Yes.'

'He comes here to eat every night, don't he?'

'Sometimes he comes here.'

'He comes here at six o'clock, don't he?'

'If he comes.'

'We know all that, bright boy,' Max said. 'Talk about something else. Ever go to the movies?'

'Once in a while.'

'You ought to go to the movies more. The movies are fine for a bright boy like you.'

The two gangsters wait for an hour, Andreson does not appear, and they go. George releases the Negro cook and Nick, who goes to Andreson's lodging to warn him.

Nick opened the door and went into the room. Ole Andreson was lying on the bed with all his clothes on. He had been a heavyweight prize-fighter and he was too long for the bed. He lay with his head on two pillows. He did not look at Nick.

'What was it?' he asked.

'I was up at Henry's,' Nick said, 'and two fellows came in and tied up me and the cook, and they said they were going to kill you.'

It sounded silly when he said it. Ole Andreson said nothing.

'They put us out in the kitchen,' Nick went on. 'They were going to shoot you when you came in to supper.'

Ole Andreson looked at the wall and did not say anything.

'George thought I better come and tell you about it.'

'There isn't anything I can do about it,' Ole Andreson said.

Ole Andreson accepts his fate as the bull fighter Manuel does not, but the shape the fate takes is not important. This is why the machinery of death in these short stories is irrelevant. Among other things, 'The Killers' is about the reactions of youth and age respectively to the fact of imminent death. When the boy Nick says: 'I'm going to get out of this town. I can't stand to think about him waiting in the room and knowing he's going to get it,' he is for opting out. But, like Ole Andreson, we know that in the face of the ultimate there is no opting out; and Andreson's passive acceptance of what is coming to him is as heroic as Manuel's refusal to do anything but fight back.

The strength of 'Fifty Grand', its theme apart, derives very considerably, like 'The Killers', from the brilliance with which a specific time in America and a specific mode of life are summed up. Jack Brennan has been a great welter-weight boxer, but now he is at the end of his career, about to fight his last fight, tired of it all and convinced he cannot win. He cannot sleep for worrying.

'What do you think about, Jack, when you can't sleep?' I said.

'Oh, I worry,' Jack says. 'I worry about property I got up in the Bronx, I worry about property I got in Florida. I worry about the kids. I worry about the wife. Sometimes I think about fights. I think about that kike Ted Lewis and I get sore. I got some stocks and I worry about them. What the hell don't I think about?'

'Well,' I said, 'tomorrow night it'll all be over.'

'Sure,' said Jack. 'That always helps a lot, don't it? That just fixes everything up, I suppose. Sure.'

Brennan's values are those of the conventional American business man of the time, the Prohibition era; shift the angle of view ever so slightly, and he could be a typical victim of Ring Lardner's deadpan satire. This is one of the strengths of the story, which is narrated in demotic American by his trainer. Through him, Brennan is shown to us in his meannesses, his anxieties, his narrowness and hardness. The day before the fight, he is visited by his manager and two gamblers and agrees to sell the fight; he tells his trainer that he is betting on Walcott, his opponent, to the tune of fifty thousand dollars.

The fight takes place.

Walcott was just getting into the ring. The crowd gave him a big hand. He climbed through between the ropes and put his two fists together and smiled, and shook them at the crowd, first at one side of the ring, then at the other, and then sat down. Jack got a good hand coming down through the crowd. Jack is Irish and the Irish always get a pretty good hand. An Irishman don't draw in New York like a Jew or an Italian but they always get a good hand. Jack climbed up and bent down to go through the ropes and Walcott came over from his corner and pushed the rope down for Jack to go through. The crowd thought that was wonderful. Walcott put his hand on Jack's shoulder and they stood there just for a second.

'So you're going to be one of these popular champions,' Jack says to him. 'Take your goddam hand off my shoulder.'

'Be yourself,' Walcott says.

This is all great for the crowd. How gentlemanly the boys are before the fight. How they wish each other luck.

Then, towards the end of the fight,

It was going just the way he thought it would. He knew he couldn't beat Walcott. He wasn't strong any more. He was all right though. His money was all right and now he wanted to finish it off right to please himself. He didn't want to be knocked out.

And Walcott deliberately fouls him. He goes down but rises before he can be counted out and steps forward to face Walcott. 'If he went down there went fifty thousand bucks. He walked as though all his insides were going to fall out.' He tells the referee that the foul was an accident and the blow wasn't low, and the fight is resumed. Brennan taunts Walcott and then fouls him as he himself has been fouled. Walcott goes down and is declared the winner on a foul. The story ends with Brennan in the dressing-room with his manager waiting for the doctor.

He lies there, his eyes are open now. His face has still got that awful drawn look.

'It's funny how fast you can think when it means that much money,' Jack says.

'You're some boy, Jack,' John says.

'No.' Jack says. 'It was nothing.'

'Fifty Grand', which seems to me the finest American story written in the vernacular, a story of cross and double-cross, is consciously unheroic. Yet, for all his surliness and meanness,

Brennan reveals himself as a man of standards and of resolute courage. Against all the odds, he makes what on his own terms is a 'good end'. What finally lingers in the mind after reading this story and 'The Undefeated' and 'The Killers' too is an echo of the last lines of the heroic Old English fragment 'The Battle of Maldon';

> Heart and head shall be keener, mood the more
> As our might lessens.

This is to say that at his best, in a handful of stories, Hemingway is an heroic writer, the supreme representative in our time of a very old tradition in writing in English.

ii

In the years between the wars and indeed for many years before, the most popular short-story writer in the English-speaking world was W. Somerset Maugham. Maugham himself said of the kind of story he wrote: 'One thing you will notice about it is that you can tell it over the dinner table or in a ship's smoking-room and it will hold the attention of the listener.' It is to this end that he seems to have adapted his prose style. As T. O. Beachcroft has noted in *The Modest Art*: '... he chooses a blunted kind of language ... and where Joyce aimed for "a scrupulous meanness" because it was integral to his characters, Somerset Maugham becomes the conscious artist of the cliché, because it suits the narrator.'

Maugham, then, set his sights low. The stories bear a superficial resemblance to Conrad's because he too dealt with the exotic scene, the Far East, and the islands of the Pacific. There is a resemblance in attitude to Maupassant, who was his master. In Maugham, however, observations of the spectacle of the human race with its pretensions to virtue and to logic and its proneness to rationalization seldom rise above the condition of weary truisms, for the writing is just not good enough to make the commonplace new. One sees this in his most famous story 'Sadie Thompson', which was even more famous in its day in the form of the play and the film 'Rain'.

The hazards of the weather force a missionary and his wife to take refuge for a while in a boarding house on a Samoan island. Narrow, self-righteous, the Davidsons possess all the unpleasing attributes credited to missionaries by the unsympathetic imagination; Mrs Davidson complains that it is 'so hard to give the natives a sense of sin'. Stranded, too, at the boarding house is Sadie Thompson, a prostitute, whose very existence is an affront to the Davidsons. The missionary sets out to get Miss Thompson expelled from Samoa and also aims to win her to a sense of sin, of *her* sins especially. He 'wrestles' with her night after night:

'All day I pray with her and when I leave her I pray again. I pray with all my might and main, so that Jesus may grant her this great mercy. I want to put in her heart the passionate desire to be punished so that at the end, if I offered to let her go, she would refuse.'

And he is successful. As Mrs Macphail, a fellow-boarder, says: 'I should never have thought it possible. It makes one feel humble.'

Then one morning Davidson's body is found in the lagoon. 'The throat was cut from ear to ear, and in the right hand was still the razor with which the deed was done.' As for Sadie Thompson,

she was standing at the door, chatting with a sailor. A sudden change had taken place in her. She was no longer the cowed drudge of the last days. She was dressed in all her finery, in her white dress, with the high shiny boots over which her fat legs bulged in their cotton stockings; her hair was elaborately arranged; and she wore that enormous hat covered with gaudy flowers. Her face was painted, her eyebrows were boldly black, and her lips were scarlet. She held herself erect. She was the flaunting queen that they had known at first. As they came in she broke into a loud, jeering laugh; and then, when Mrs Davidson involuntarily stopped, she collected the spittle in her mouth and spat. . . . She gathered herself together. No one could describe the scorn of her expression or the contemptuous hatred she put into her answer.

'You men! You filthy, dirty pigs! You're all the same, all of you. Pigs! Pigs!'

Dr Macphail gasped. He understood.

'Rain' now seems an infinitely predictable story. The crudity of the anecdote is in no way transcended nor is the coarseness with which missionary and prostitute alike are rendered. Both are stereotypes uninformed by insight. Melodrama and the melodramatic possibilities of the situation are all, and melodrama was always Maugham's fatal enemy.

Generally, his best stories are those set in the South Seas, and the best of these is probably 'Mackintosh'. It is a story of the relationship between the administrator of a Samoan island, Walker, and Mackintosh, his assistant. Mackintosh is consumed with an intense loathing for his superior. Walker is vulgar, grossly fat, uneducated, a bully though cordial in a crude way, living for the natives he loves and rules: Mackintosh by contrast is introverted and a 'highbrow' who despises detective novels and reads Burton and Gibbon. It is the story of two incompatibles forced to live in intimate contact with each other. In the end, Walker is shot by a native with Mackintosh's revolver, after which, Walker having died of his wounds, Mackintosh shoots himself with the revolver.

Walker is very well done, and through him Maugham dramatizes very vividly a phase of colonial government in the South Pacific. It is Mackintosh that makes one pause. The whole story, everything that happens, hinges on his loathing of Walker. His feeling is so intense that one finds oneself asking, as one should never be prompted to do in a short story: Why doesn't he go somewhere else, why doesn't he apply for a transfer? The situation strikes us, in other words, as fabricated in order to provide the motive for a sensational dénouement.

Maugham was at his best when least ambitious, as in 'The Verger', in which a man who has been verger of a fashionable London church for nineteen years is sacked when the new vicar discovers he can neither read nor write. He buys a tobacconist's shop, is successful, and buys a second and a third and so on until he owns a chain of such shops. When he has amassed thirty thousand pounds his bank manager suggests that he should invest it, which forces the man to admit his illiteracy:

> The manager stared at him as though he were a prehistoric monster.
> 'And you mean to say that you've built up this important business and amassed a fortune of thirty thousand without being able to read or write? Good God, man, what would you be now if you had been able to do so?'
> 'I can tell you that, sir,' said Mr Foreman. 'I'd be verger of St Peter's, Nevill Square.'

It is no more than an anecdote scarcely adorned, the story returning to its simplest form, the joke. But it is briskly told and the anecdote, though irreverent, is not pointless.

A short-story writer very highly thought of in the Twenties was Stacy Aumonier. He is now almost completely forgotten, for the same reason that accounts for his success in his lifetime: he was so completely of his period. He was an exceedingly careful craftsman, a truly professional writer, and very obviously a man of humane values, but for the most part his stories seem as remote from us now as those of O. Henry. 'He is not tricky. He follows no fashion and no school. He is always himself. . . . He will outlive nearly all the writers of his day.' That was Galsworthy, introducing a collected edition of Aumonier's stories in 1929. All one can say is that, reading him now, it is difficult to believe that he was writing at the same time as D. H. Lawrence and James Joyce.

Two of his most ardently admired stories, 'Them Others' and 'The Great Unimpressionable', deal with the Great War. The first is set in a seedy working-class street in Dalston which is presented in such a way as to suggest that the street may be taken as representative. It is seen from an attitude of *de haut en bas*, and it is a Mrs Ward who particularly interests Aumonier. Ernie, her son, is a soldier at the front, and she wonders about 'them others', the Germans, who for her are symbolized by the Stellings, her erstwhile next door neighbours who, when war was declared, returned to Germany. When Ernie is reported missing she becomes a model of stoic hope. And one evening, months having passed, while the narrator is visiting the Wards, Ernie does return. He has escaped from a German prisoner-of-war camp and made his way back to England. Mrs Ward remembers her old next door neighbour Mrs Stelling:

'She used to make a very good puddin',' Mrs Ward said suddenly, at random. 'Dried fruit inside, and that. My Ernie liked it very much. . . .'

'In that great hour of her happiness,' the narrator thinks, 'her mind was assailed by strange and tremulous thoughts', thoughts of fellow-feeling for 'them others', and he goes on his way 'for I knew that she was wiser than I'.

'The Great Unimpressionable' is the story of Ned Picklekin, the village postman. As a private soldier he passes through the most hair-raising experiences unperturbed, for all the time he is thinking of home and his dog. Almost miraculously, Ned does return home unscathed, only to break down on finding that his dog is dead.

These stories are not in the least chauvinistic or overtly sentimental and they are told with tact. But they are also guilty of a false simplicity. The images of a German woman's skill at pudding-making and Ned Picklekin's grief for the death of his dog are inadequate to convey the quality of emotion the author wishes to express. These stories are the counterparts, in that they share similar weakness, of the Georgian poetry of the time.

Aumonier's talents are seen at their finest in 'The Two Friends', which is a very impressive story, a revelation of emptiness and misapprehension. Though it appeared in 1924, the world described is very much of the pre-war period. In the purlieus of the furniture trade in the Tottenham Court Road the friendship between White and Mapleson is legendary. Theirs is a friendship 'quickened by the curious coincidence of their mental vision when stimulated by alcoholic fumes'.

Their day follows its regular ritual. It begins in the saloon bar at the Monitor; they go on to Polati's in Oxford Street for lunch, where they choose a mixed grill as 'something English that you could get your teeth into, followed by a Welsh rabbit or a savoury, and during the course of the meal they would drink two gin-and-bitters, a tankard of ale or, more often, whisky and soda and finish off with coffee, a cigar, and a couple of liqueurs'. All this takes two and half hours to consume, after which they return to their respective shops to do some work. Often they have tea together and invariably they meet in the Monitor between six-thirty and seven, play billiards for an hour or so, adjourn to the dining-room where they regale themselves with chops, cheese, and ale, 'by which time Mapleson would arrive at the conclusion that it wasn't worth while going home; so an adjournment would be made once more to the bar, and the business of the evening would begin.'

They would sit very often till nearly twelve o'clock, when the Monitor shut, drinking whisky and talking. . . .

Mapleson was very fond of talking about 'his principles'. In conversation it seemed that his actions must be hedged in by these iron-bound conventions. In effect they were virtually as follows: business comes first always; never fail to keep a business appointment; never mix port and whisky; never give anything to a stranger that you might give to a pal.

Just after midnight, 'thoroughly exhausted with the day's business', Mapleson takes a cab to Baker Street to catch his last train, 'having spent during the day a sum varying between twenty and thirty shillings, which was precisely the amount he allowed his wife every week to keep house for a family of five, and to include food, clothing, and washing'.

Fifteen months later, White falls down in the street and is taken to hospital. It is rumoured that he is dead. Mapleson cracks up. 'He was not aware of an affection for White, or of any sentiment other than a vast fear and a strange absorbing depression.' When six weeks later White is discharged from hospital he is warned that if he touches alcohol in any shape or form again, he might as well put a bullet through his head. With ginger-beer taking the place of whisky, he resumes the pattern of his days with Mapleson. He seems quite content but 'ginger-ale got on Mapleson's nerves' and a settled gloom and depression takes hold of him that leads White to say one evening that he'll have a whisky and soda with him.

This was one of the happiest evenings of Mapleson's life. As soon as his friend began to drink, some chord in his own nature responded; his eyes glowed, he became garrulous and entertaining.

They go to a music hall, by the end of the evening White has drunk eleven whisky and sodas and Mapleson is 'cheerfully and gloriously drunk'. They part and do not meet again, because by four next afternoon White is dead.

At the funeral, Mapleson discovers that White's house is in a near-slum and that his family are living in poverty. White had never taken out life insurance and for the four years before his death it was his wife, a milliner 'clever with her fingers', who paid the rent. Mapleson discovers too that White had been a bird fancier; in the house there are two canaries, a bullfinch, and a small, highly coloured 'Orstrylian' bird. It is a discovery that peculiarly affects him. 'The breach of confidence on White's part of never telling him that he kept birds upset Mapleson even more than his breach of confidence in not talking about his wife.'

This story seems to have been almost entirely forgotten. The only critical comment on it that I have come across is in Beachcroft's *The Modest Art*: 'The story moves through agonies of farce, although heightened, yet convincing: it is reminiscent of Gogol rather than Chekhov, and not unlike some of the scenes created by William Sansom thirty years later.' This is very perceptive and though for me 'The Two Friends' is one of the most truly Chekhovian stories in English, I do not for a moment imagine that Aumonier was consciously under Chekhov's influence. Much of the story's power comes from the quality Henry James called 'density of specification'. There is nothing, we feel, that Aumonier does not know about the furniture trade of Tottenham Court Road or of the manners and quality of life of those employed there in the first decade of the century. To this material Aumonier subjects himself self-abnegatingly and in doing so catches, one would think permanently, an image of life at that time.

iii

Katherine Mansfield – her real name was Kathleen Mansfield
Beauchamp – was born near Wellington, New Zealand, in 1888.
As a child she was sent to London to be educated, returned to
New Zealand in 1907, and came back to England two years later
with a small allowance from her father and began to write, publishing her first book of stories, *In a German Pension*, in 1911.
She married the literary critic John Middleton Murry and died
of tuberculosis at Fontainebleau at the age of thirty-four, leaving
behind eighty-eight stories, twenty-six of which are unfinished.
She remains difficult to judge, for she died before she had ful-
filled her talent. She is as easily underpraised as overpraised and
judgement is made the more difficult by the sad circumstances
of her life and death and by the legend, as something like a saint
of women's liberation, that has been woven about her. Beyond
that, her stature will obviously differ in accordance with the
point of view from which she is seen.

'She left us,' Elizabeth Bowen wrote, in her introduction to
the Vintage Books edition, 'with no "typical" Katherine Mansfield story to anatomize.' Nevertheless, it is generally agreed that
a considerable part of her talent is foreshadowed in 'The
Tiredness of Rosabel', which she wrote when she was nineteen
and before she had read anything by Chekhov, who is usually
seen as the formative influence on her art. It begins:

At the corner of Oxford Circus Rosabel bought a bunch of violets, and
that was practically the reason why she had so little tea – for a scone
and a boiled egg and a cup of cocoa at Lyons are not ample sufficiency
after a hard day's work at a millinery establishment. As she swung on
to the step of the Atlas bus, grabbed her skirt with one hand and clung
to the railing with the other, Rosabel thought she would have sacrificed
her soul for a good dinner – roast duck and green peas, chestnut stuff-
ing, pudding with brandy sauce – something hot and strong and filling.

Thence, the story becomes one of day-dreaming as the involuntary protest against inescapable conditions of living. Rosabel

thinks of the young woman who came into the shop to buy a hat and of the young man who accompanied her. She imagines herself engaged to him:

'I'll call for you at nine,' he said as he left her. The fire had been lighted in her boudoir, the curtains drawn, there was a great pile of letters awaiting her – invitations for the Opera, dinners, balls, a weekend on the river, a motor tour – she glanced through them listlessly as she went upstairs to dress. A fire in her bedroom, too, and her beautiful, shining shoes, silver scarf, a little silver fan. . . .

She dreams of her marriage to the young man at St George's, Hanover Square; and then:

The real Rosabel got up from the floor and undressed slowly, folding her clothes over the back of a chair. She slipped over her head her coarse, calico nightdress, and took the pins out of her hair – the soft, brown flood of it fell round her, warmly. Then she blew out the candle and groped her way into bed, pulling the blankets and grimy 'honeycomb' quilt closely round her neck, cuddling down into the darkness. . . .

'The Tiredness of Rosabel' would be a remarkable story for any girl of nineteen to write and what is most remarkable about it is the way Katherine Mansfield identifies herself with, becomes, Rosabel. That, at any rate, is one's first impression, but as one reads more of her stories one begins to wonder. The truth is, Katherine Mansfield can be the most subjective of writers, subjective to the point of solipsism, and this causes problems. They come to a head in her 'Life of Ma Parker', which begins:

When the literary gentleman, whose flat old Ma Parker cleaned every Tuesday, opened the door to her that morning, he asked after her grandson. Ma Parker stood on the doormat inside the little dark hall, and she stretched out her hand to help her gentleman shut the door before she replied. 'We buried 'im yesterday, sir,' she said quietly.
  'Oh, dear me! I'm sorry to hear that,' said the literary gentleman in a shocked tone. He was in the middle of his breakfast. He wore a shabby dressing-gown and carried a crumpled newspaper in one hand. But he felt awkward. He could hardly go back to the warm sitting-room without saying something – something more. Then because these people set

such store by funerals he said kindly, 'I hope the funeral went off all right.'

'Beg parding, sir?' said old Ma Parker huskily.

Poor old bird! She did look dashed. 'I hope the funeral was a – a – success,' said he. Ma Parker gave no answer. She bent her head and hobbled off to the kitchen, clasping the old fish bag that held her cleaning things and an apron and a pair of felt shoes. The literary gentlemen raised his eyebrows and went back to his breakfast.

'Overcome, I suppose,' he said aloud, helping himself to the marmalade.

The story is obviously meant to be intensely moving in its depiction of the loneliness of the woman and her fervent, but checked desire to cry and so express her grief, and it has been much admired. It seems to me little more than an exercise in tear-jerking. Ma Parker is at once sentimentalized and patronized, which cannot have been intended. But how else is one to interpret a passage like this?

At sixteen she'd left Stratford to come up to London as kitchen-maid. Yes, she was born in Stratford-on-Avon. Shakespeare, sir? No, people were always asking her about him. But she'd never heard his name until she saw it on the theatre. . . .

That was a dreadful place – her first place. She was never allowed out. She never went upstairs except for prayers morning and evening. It was a fair cellar. And the cook was a cruel woman. She used to snatch away her letters from her before she'd read them, and throw them in the range because they made her dreamy . . . And the beedles! Would you believe it? – until she came to London she'd never seen a black beedle. Here Ma always gave a little laugh, as though – not to have seen a black beedle! Well! It was as if to say you'd never seen your own feet.

It does not necessarily diminish the dignity of an illiterate woman to render her in terms of her own illiteracy, as Kipling's old women in 'The Wish-House' show. By comparison with Kipling, Katherine Mansfield is crude.

As it happens, there is a Chekhov story, 'Misery', with which one can compare 'The Life of Ma Parker', which may indeed be a conscious imitation of 'Misery'. Chekhov's story is about an old cab-driver whose son has died. He tries to tell his passengers about his loss: in vain, for they are concerned with their own

affairs. They have no time to listen to him, and the story ends
with his telling his grief at night in the stable to his old horse.

The cabby's customers in Chekhov's story however, strike us
as representative figures from a real world whereas those in 'The
Life of Ma Parker' do not. In her story, Katherine Mansfield's
gift of empathy failed her, mainly because she did not know her
character well enough. She was insulated from the common
people by virtue of the fact that those among whom she lived,
people like Murry and the Lawrences and the Woolfs were
writers and intellectuals, people who, whatever else they may be,
are scarcely ever representative. It is among such people that the
equally famous 'Bliss' is set. In some measure it seems an incur-
sion into territory that a year or two later would be thought of as
peculiarly Aldous Huxley's. It is, or so it seems to me, a very
difficult story.

Its theme, as the first two paragraphs make plain, is the state
of bliss:

Although Bertha Young was thirty she still had moments like this when
she wanted to run instead of walk, to take dancing steps on and off the
pavement, to bowl a hoop, to throw something up in the air and catch it
again, or to stand still and laugh at – nothing – at nothing, simply.

What can you do if you are thirty and, turning the corner of your
own street, you are overcome, suddenly, by a feeling of bliss – absolute
bliss! – as though you'd suddenly swallowed a bright piece of that late
afternoon and it burned in your bosom, sending out a little shower of
sparks into every particle, into every finger and toe? . . .

Bertha Young, happily married with a small daughter, conscious
that she has everything, gives a small dinner-party that evening
for a theatre director and his wife, a young poet, and a woman
she has recently met and for whom she feels an elective affinity.
The party is a success and she looks forward to making love with
her husband when it is over. The mood of bliss is wonderfully
well evoked and sustained and for Bertha it seems symbolized by
the pear tree in blossom in the garden:

The windows of the drawing-room opened on to a balcony overlooking
the garden. At the far end, against the wall, there was a tall, slender
pear tree in fullest, richest bloom; it stood perfect, as though becalmed
against the jade-green sky. Bertha couldn't help feeling, even from this
distance, that it had not a single bud or a faded petal.

One is reminded of Pater's famous sentence in *The Renaissance*: 'Every moment some form grows more perfect in hand or face; some tone on the hills or the sea is choicer than the rest; some mood or passion or intellectual excitement is irresistibly real and attractive – for that moment only.' Never, except perhaps in comparable passages in Virginia Woolf, has Pater's intuition been more magically ensnared than in 'Bliss'.

Or almost so. When reviewing the story in 1922, Conrad Aiken in *A Reviewer's ABC* noted that there were times when 'Miss Mansfield resorts to cleverness, esurient humour, or even, as in the termination of "Bliss", to the trickery of surprise: the story should have ended indecisively.' As it is, it ends with Bertha, the guests departing, seeing Harry her husband, passionately kissing her new friend Miss Fulton. The surprise ending is not quite trickery, as Aiken suggests, for it has been foreshadowed. The paragraph, quoted above, describing the pear tree, ends:

Down below, in the garden beds, the red and yellow tulips, heavy with flowers, seemed to lean upon the dusk. A grey cat, dragging its belly, crept across the lawn, and a black one, its shadow, trailed after. The sight of them, so intent and so quick, gave Bertha a curious shiver.

Yet the last lines of the story seem to show another trick:

Miss Fulton held out her hand a moment longer. 'Your lovely pear tree!' she murmured.

And then she was gone, with Eddie following, like the black cat following the grey cat.

'I'll shut up shop,' said Harry, extravagantly cool and collected.

Bertha simply ran over to the long windows.

'Oh, what is going to happen now?' she cried.

But the pear tree was as lovely as ever and as full of flower and as still.

But has the state of bliss, which the pear tree has symbolized, been shown to be illusion or delusion? Are we to take it merely, to quote Aiken on Katherine Mansfield's heroines, as 'a description of the feverish hyperaesthesia of a neurotic young woman'? In that case, it seems to me we have been cheated into taking seriously something that does not call to be taken seriously. Or does the story ask us to accept that sex is the great wrecker and that men and women can meet only at the level of copulating cats? There are other possibilities. Since Bertha and Miss Fulton appear to have shared a similar intuition into the nature of the pear tree, why not share a similar love for Harry? The point is, none of these questions is answerable, because all the information from which an answer could be derived is given us by Bertha, who is discredited in the last paragraph of the story.

We can only decide that 'Bliss' is a profoundly unsatisfactory story, and generally, with the bulk of Katherine Mansfield's work we are in the realm of the tentative. Yet, paradoxically, she had begun her career as a writer with great sureness, with the collection *In a German Pension*, which was published in 1911 when she was twenty-three. It was successful and went into three impressions though later Katherine Mansfield disowned it and refused to allow republication. In many ways it is a terrifying collection of stories, savagely funny and unnervingly perceptive. The story 'The Modern Soul' may be taken as representative. It begins:

'Good evening,' said the Herr Professor, squeezing my hand; 'wonderful weather! I returned from a party in the wood. I have been making music for them on my trombone. . . .'

He sat down, tugging at a white-paper package in the tail pocket of his coat.

'Cherries,' he said, nodding and smiling. 'There is nothing like cherries for producing free saliva after trombone playing, especially after Grieg's "Ich Liebe Dich". Those sustained blasts of "liebe" make my throat as dry as a railway tunnel. Have some?' He shook his bag at me.

'I prefer watching you eat them.'

'See what a fat one!' cried the Herr Professor. 'That is almost a mouthful in itself; it is beautiful enough to hang from a watch-chain.' He chewed it up and spat the stone an incredible distance – over the garden path into the flower bed. He was proud of this feat. I saw it. 'The quantity of fruit I have eaten on this bench,' he sighed; 'apricots, peaches, and cherries. One day that garden bed will become an orchard grove, and I shall allow you to pick as you please, without paying me anything.'

I was grateful, without showing undue excitement.

The stories in *In a German Pension* were seen initially as satire on the national characteristics of the Germans but what startles now is, first, the virulence of Katherine Mansfield's satire on the male of the species, who is shown as complacently gross and brutal, as by right of superiority, in his treatment of women, and after that the cruel and contemptuous exposure of the pliant, adoring, masochistic female. One can, especially in the light of biographical information, understand and appreciate Katherine Mansfield's revulsion against these stories: they spring from the time when she had gone to Germany to have an illegitimate child, which miscarried. It was some six or seven years afterwards when she rediscovered her New Zealand infancy that she began to write those stories, 'Prelude' and 'At the Bay' in particular, on which her reputation finally rests.

They are rediscoveries, re-creations, of her childhood and her family. She appears in them as the little girl Kezia, but she has rigorously subordinated herself to the family story she is telling; either that or she has transcended herself. We do not see the action only through Kezia's eyes and mind; her two sisters, her parents, her grandmother, her aunt Beryl, Pat the Irish gardener, and Alice the servant-girl are all as important as she and are rendered in the same balance of vision.

The action of 'Prelude' covers rather less than forty-eight hours, in which the Burnells and their servants move house from the town to the not-too-distant country. We are conscious all the time of felicitous penetration into character, though the felicities are always subject to the major felicity which is the story itself. We see Kezia alone in the house she is about to leave:

Upstairs in her father's and mother's room she found a pill-box black and shiny outside and red in, holding a blob of cotton wool.
'I could keep a bird's egg in that,' she decided.

There is the scene in the new house just before bedtime:

The grandmother brought the children bread and milk and they sat up to the table, flushed and sleepy behind the wavy steam.
'I had meat for my supper,' said Isabel, still combing gently.
'I had a whole chop for my supper, the bone and all and Worcester sauce. Didn't I, father?'
'Oh, don't boast, Isabel,' said Aunt Beryl. Isabel looked astounded.
'I wasn't boasting, was I, Mummy? I never thought of boasting. I thought they would like to know. I only meant to tell them.'

There is the vignette of Mr Burnell dressing next morning:

'Oh, damn! Oh, blast!' said Stanley, who had butted into a crisp

white shirt only to find that some idiot had fastened the neckband and
he was caught. He stalked over to Linda waving his arms.

'You look like a big fat turkey,' said she.

'Fat. I like that,' said Stanley. 'I haven't a square inch of fat on me.
Feel that. . . .'

'My dear, don't worry. You'll never be fat. You are far too energetic.'

'Yes, yes, I suppose that's true,' said he, comforted for the hun-
dredth time.

There is the truly remarkable scene in which Pat the gardener
decapitates a duck in order to amuse the children, for Pat 'loved
little children', a scene in which the horrifying and obscene are
made delightful. As O'Connor commented in *The Lonely Voice*:
'This is the garden of Eden before shame and guilt came into the
world.'

There was an old stump beside the door of the fowl-house. Pat
grabbed the duck by the legs, laid it flat across the stump, and almost
at the same moment down came the little tomahawk and the duck's
head flew off the stump. Up the blood spurted over the white feathers
and over his hand.

When the children saw the blood they were frightened no longer.
They crowded round him and began to scream. Even Isabel leaped
about crying: 'The blood! The blood!' Pip forgot all about his duck. He
simply threw it away from him and shouted, 'I saw it. I saw it,' and
jumped round the wood block.

Rags, with cheeks as white as paper, ran up to the little head, put out
a finger as if he wanted to touch it, shrank back again and then again
put out a finger. He was shivering all over.

Even Lottie, frightened little Lottie, began to laugh and pointed at
the duck and shrieked: 'Look, Kezia, look.'

'Watch it!' shouted Pat. He put down the body and it began to
waddle – with only a long spurt of blood where the head had been; it
began to pad away without a sound towards the steep bank that led to
the stream. . . . That was the crowning wonder.

'Do you see that? Do you see that?' yelled Pip. He ran among the
little girls tugging at their pinafores.

'It's like a little engine. It's like a funny little railway engine,'
squealed Isabel. . . .

These passages may seem to be what the eighteenth century
called 'beauties', yet they rise naturally from what gives the story

its great authority, which is its authenticity as a picture of a family at once closely knit and yet in which all the members think their own thoughts, go their separate ways, and are caught by the author as it were off guard.

After more than half a century, 'Prelude' remains one of the most advanced stories ever written in English, along with Kipling's 'Mrs Bathurst', Joyce's 'The Dead', and Fitzgerald's 'May Day'. Each of these stories is a cross-section of a number of lives that come together at a certain point in a natural, unforced yet significant relationship one with the others. Story in anything like the usual sense has all but disappeared.

'Prelude' seems to have grown out of a work Katherine Mansfield called *The Aloe* and referred to as a 'book', which suggests that it was conceived if not as a novel certainly as a lengthy piece of fiction. When it had reached thirty thousand words she revised it, cut it by a third, and gave it its present title. It had been more than two years in the writing. 'What,' asks C. K. Stead, in his essay 'Katherine Mansfield and the Art of Fiction', 'had that prolonged exercise taught Katherine Mansfield?'

First I think it had taught her that fiction did not have to be shaped towards a conclusion, a climax, a dénouement; or . . . that a fiction is not quite the same thing as a story. A fiction survives, not by leading us anywhere, but by being at every point authentic, a recreation of life, so that we experience it and remember it as we experience and remember actual life itself. Immediacy is of the utmost importance. The writer must imagine, not invent. She must efface herself. She must see and become the characters or the objects she wishes to represent.

That is excellent and of first importance, but it is clear that the word fiction is being used in a special sense which is at the opposite pole to its ordinary meaning. Once again we are faced with the paradox of the fictitious as a means to truth.

Stead makes another important point when he writes:

The items of 'Prelude' and 'At the Bay' cohere without narrative linking. And individually they are most successful when they are not forced to make a point.

He links this to the great Modernist discovery as we see it, for example, in *The Waste Land* and Pound's *Cantos*, that poetry is not a form but a quality which 'will naturally cohere, without structural linking'. In 'Prelude' and 'At the Bay' we see how Katherine Mansfield is related to the great Modern masters from Kipling onward.

There is also another connection which is hinted at by Elizabeth Bowen when she says in the introduction to her edition of the New Zealand stories, 'The day-to-day receives the full charge of poetry.' As we see often in the stories of Chekhov, in 'The Lady with the Little Dog', for instance, poetry is the great distancer. This is especially apparent in 'At the Bay', written four years later than 'Prelude', though conceived of as a sequel to it and, like it, written in a sequence of numbered parts or movements. It is, again, a day in the life of the Burnells, who are now, since it is summer, living at the seaside. They do not, nor indeed does any human being enter the story until the beginning of the second part, the first being given over to a quite lengthy description of morning:

Very early morning. The sun was not yet risen, and the whole of Crescent Bay was hidden under a white sea-mist. The big bush-covered hills at the back were smothered. You could not see where they ended and the paddocks and bungalows began. The sandy road was gone and the paddocks and bungalows the other side of it; there were no white dunes covered with reddish grass beyond them; there was nothing to mark which was beach and where was the sea. A heavy dew had fallen. The grass was blue. Big drops hung on the bushes and just did not fall; the silvery, fluffy toi-toi was limp on its long stalks, and all the marigolds and the pinks in the bungalow gardens were bowed to the earth with wetness. Drenched were the cold fuchsias, round pearls of dew lay on the flat nasturtium leaves. It looked as though the sea had beaten up softly in the darkness, as though one immense wave had come rippling, rippling – how far? Perhaps if you had waked up in the middle of the night you might have seen a big fish flicking in at the window and gone again. . . .

Ah-Aah! sounded the sea. And from the bush there came the sound of little streams flowing, quickly, lightly, slipping between the smooth stones, gushing into ferny basins and out again; and something else – what was it? – a faint stirring and shaking, the snapping of a twig and then such silence that it seemed someone was listening.

Then there follows the marvellous description of the sheep as they wander, with attendant shepherd and sheepdog, through the summer colony and the village to their destination as the sun rises. In the penultimate paragraph of this first part or movement 'the first inhabitant appeared'. It is the Burnell's cat Florrie. The part ends: 'Then pushing, nudging, hurrying, the sheep rounded the bend and the shepherd followed after out of sight.' It is only then, in the first paragraph of the second movement that the first human being appears, Stanley Burnell in his bathing suit going down for his early-morning swim. The story proper begins.

That of course is wrong, for the description of early morning and the sheep is essential, establishing the Burnells in the context of nature and time. It is not until our reading is over that we realize that we have been present at a profound rendering in mimetic form of the cycle of the relations between the sexes.

Somerset Maugham and T. F. Powys were born within a year of each other but so different is the manner and content of their stories that centuries and continents might have separated them. Powys is at his best when he is at his furthest remove from the world as normally observed and experienced, when he is writing what he calls, explicitly, fables, the most famous of which is probably 'Mr Pim and the Holy Crumb'. Mr Pim, a former rabbit-trapper and ploughman, is the church clerk. It is Christmas morning and holy communion is to be celebrated, a fact of importance to Mr Pim only because he has to get up earlier than he likes in order to light the church fire. But on this particular Christmas morning Mr Pim has been greatly excited because the clergyman Mr Thomas Tucker has explained the meaning of the sacrament to him.

Pim was not a man to keep anything to himself. If he heard any surprising news he would always tell it to the first person he met, whether the news was of a maiden ill-treated, a nest of eggs stolen from Farmer Todd, or a fire in London. 'Mr Tucker do tell I', said Pim, addressing himself to Miss Jarrett, 'that the Lord God, the Creator of the world, who be named Christ by drunken folk when pubs do close, do change 'Isself into they skrimpy bites of Mr Johnson's bread that thee do take and eat up at church railings.'

Pim takes the sacrament. After he has eaten God he wonders what God is like. He sees a crumb he has dropped on the floor and thinks: "''tis likely 'E won't be best pleased wi' Pim for dropping 'E upon church carpet so carelessly. 'Tain't proper for a Holy Crumb to be so fallen.''' He thereupon apologizes to the crumb, which replies, and so a conversation between God and Mr Pim follows, ending with God saying: '"When I consider the trouble I have caused I almost wish I had entered into a mouse instead of a man."' And the tale ends:

'Hist! Hist!' whispered Pim, 'Thee may do thik now, for a mouse do live under altar table who do creep out when all's quiet.'

Pim moved to the front pew, winked at the crumb and remained silent. A little mouse, with a pert prying look, crept out from under the altar and devoured the Holy Crumb.

Thus by eating the Holy Crumb, the mouse is shown to contain everything that is miraculous, 'to be', as Whitman said in 'Leaves of Grass', 'miracle enough to stagger sextillions of infidels'. The story, which is humorous and devout at the same time, is also a delineation of a simple man, which makes it possible for us to accept 'Mr Pim and the Holy Crumb' as a true short story.

It reveals clearly Powys's affinities and the influences upon him. We are aware of the language of the King James Bible, the Prayer Book, and *A Pilgrim's Progress*, and of the presence too of two contrasted seventeenth-century poets and clergymen, Herbert and Herrick. One feels that at his best Powys has tapped a very ancient source of life; there is a deep sense, as John Holloway has said in his essay, 'The Literary Scene', in *The Modern Age*, 'of the total round rich fertility and sour brutality of rural life, and a command over both fable and symbol as fictional vehicles'.

A. E. Coppard was one of Powys's most admired contemporaries. Indeed, the three short-story writers who have also written on the art and history of the form, O'Connor, Bates, and Beachcroft, are agreed in seeing him as an innovator in the English story, a form he made his own, totally ignoring the novel.

A late starter as a writer, Coppard did not publish his first collection of tales until he was forty-five. He was entirely self-educated, having been apprenticed to a tailor in Whitechapel at the age of nine. When he was thirty he became a clerk at an ironworks in Oxford, where he cultivated and was cultivated by a number of dons and undergraduates and began to write. For a time he made his home in a caravan, and in his best work one can feel the sense of freedom, the exposure to nature and country life, that must have been his on escaping into a gipsy-like existence. Some of his best stories seem to come out of this, as for example 'The Higgler', probably his best-known story.

The higgler, Harvey Witlow, is a young man just back from the war, and wondering what to do about Sophie Daws, who expects him to marry her. Prospecting for trade, he is exploring part of the moor new to him when he comes across a little farm:

It had a small rickyard with a few small stacks in it; everything here seemed on a small scale, but snug, very snug; and in the field were hundreds of fowls, hundreds, of good breed, and mostly white. Leaving his horse to sniff the greensward, the higgler entered a white wicket gateway and passed to the back of the house, noting as he did so a yellow wagon inscribed ELIZABETH SADGROVE. PRATTLE CORNER.

Efficient yet unfussy and unbuttoned, easy and well-mannered, that is a good example of Coppard's prose; behind it there is a personality and a human voice speaking.

Witlow calls on Mrs Sadgrove, who is a widow with a daughter.

Beautiful she was: red hair, a complexion like the inside of a nut, blue eyes, and the hands of a lady. He saw it all at once, jacket of bright green wool, black dress, grey stockings and shoes, and forgot his errand, his mother, his fifty pounds, Sophy – momentarily he forgot everything.

He is recalled to himself when Mrs Sadgrove sells him fifteen score of eggs, two dozen pullets, and a young goose. He drives home rejoicing.

He begins a regular trade with Mrs Sadgrove. Soon, when he calls, he is given a cup of tea. He helps when the bees swarm. He buys the cherry crop. But he can get nowhere with the girl.

Harvey would try a lot of talk, blarneying talk or sensible talk, or talk about events in the world that was neither the one nor the other. No good. The girl's responses were ever brief and confused. Why was this? Again and again he asked himself that question. Was there anything the matter with her? Nothing that you could see; she was a bright and beautiful being. And it was not contempt, either, for despite her fright, her voicelessness, her timid eyes, he divined her friendly feeling for himself.

He is invited to Sunday dinner and after dinner strolls round the farm with Mrs Sadgrove. She asks him if he will marry her daughter, telling him that Mary will inherit the farm and five hundred pounds when she is twenty-five. Yet she puts no pressure on him. The outcome of each visit is the same; he wonders about the mystery, suspecting a dodge on the part of Mrs Sadgrove which Mary does not know about. Suddenly he marries Sophy and gives up calling at Prattle Corner. His luck changes. Sophy and his mother quarrel endlessly; he can find nowhere that will take the place of Mrs Sadgrove's farm as a source of the goods he must buy for trade; his horse dies. As a last resort he decides to call on Mrs Sadgrove and see if she will lend him some money. But when he arrives at Prattle Corner he finds Mary alone. Her mother has died the night before and the girl, unaided, has been trying without success to lay her out. Witlow takes over; the account of the laying out is a most memorable piece of writing.

As they are leaving the corpse he asks her whether she knew that her mother had suggested he should marry her.

'I've often wondered why,' he murmured, 'why she wanted that.'

'She didn't,' said the girl. . . . The girl bowed her head, lovely in grief and modesty. 'She was against it, but I made her ask you. . . . Mother tried to persuade me against it, but I was fond of you – then.'

The story ends:

He drove away into deep darkness, the wind howling, his thoughts strange and bitter. He had thrown away a love, a love that was dumb and hid itself. By God, he had thrown away a fortune, too! And he had forgotten all about the loan! Well, let it go; give it up. He would give up higgling; he would take on some other job; a bailiff, a working bailiff, that was the job that would suit him, a working bailiff. Of course there was Sophy; but still – Sophy!

What happens in 'The Higgler' is unpredictable; the story is as wayward as life itself. Nothing seems to have been arranged or contrived by the author. Coppard is at his best when writing about women. He responds to their moods, and whether or not he understands them does not matter for the response is all. There is 'Dusky Ruth', which appeared in 1921 and was a piece, according to Bates, such as the English short story had not seen before. In a Cotswold town a walker meets an attractive barmaid. He makes an assignation with her, and she duly comes to his room at night but 'she was crying there, crying silently with great tears, her strange sorrow stifling his desire', so that he spends the night comforting her. When he leaves the inn next morning to go on his way she greets him 'with a curious gaze, but merrily enough', and her 'shining glances follow him to the door, and from the window as far as they could view him'. Again, in relation to the heroine, reader and central character are in similar positions.

Of all Coppard's stories of women the finest is probably 'The Field of Mustard', in which two country women, 'sere and dis-virgined women', come together after an afternoon gathering kindling in their common memory of a gamekeeper they loved years ago, '. . . a pretty man. Black as coal and bold as a fox.'

I find in Coppard at his best, as in these stories, something very close to Hardy. They are as it were natural and apparently effortless equivalents to lyric poems and are not marred at all by the faults that beset Coppard when he is not at his best, faults that Bates, in *The Modern Short Story*, sums up as 'a certain literary dandiness, pretty play of words, elaborate metaphorical crochet-work, a love of subtle conceits for their own sake'.

For good historic reasons the literature of the South, roughly the states that comprised the Confederacy of the Civil War, has always been significantly different from that of the rest of the country. The founding of the first American colony, Virginia, was rooted in an ideology markedly different from that which brought Massachusetts and New England into existence, and this difference was accentuated by the introduction into the South of Negro slavery, the 'peculiar institution', which led ultimately to the secession of the South and the war between the states. The Confederacy was beaten. For three generations after, the South lived through a trauma the effects of which are clearly evident in the Southern writing of this century and which may be summed up in what Allen Tate has called 'the pervasive Southern subject of our time', 'the image of the past in the present'.

In our time, the great exponent of the subject in fiction has been William Faulkner, especially in his novels and stories set in and dramatizing the history of the imaginary Yoknapatawpha County of Mississippi. He was a highly conscious artist, yet one sometimes has the impression that what he has done he has done 'by guess and by God'. As with Conrad, one is likely to find that a short story becomes in the process of time a novel.

The Hamlet, the first of his novels of the Snopes family, seems to have grown out of five uncollected stories published in the *Saturday Evening Post*. Similarly, what is often considered his greatest novel, *Absalom, Absalom!*, seems to have its genesis in the story 'Wash'. Again, there is the problem of *Go Down, Moses*. It was first published in 1942 as *Go Down, Moses and Other Stories* and the English edition still retains the title. The seven parts that compose it were all published originally as separate stories in magazines. The stories are subordinated to a single developing theme, gradually revealing the history of the McCaslin family, and Faulkner himself saw the whole work as a novel. One of the seven parts is 'The Bear', which has probably been the most discussed of Faulkner's shorter works. Faulkner himself said 'The Bear' was 'part of the novel', and should be read 'just as a chapter in the novel'.

Even so, 'The Bear' itself presents its own problem of definition. In five sections and dealing with Ike McCaslin's initiation into manhood, it is as complex and as difficult a piece of writing as exists in American literature. We meet Ike first as a boy of ten. He is a member of Major de Spain's annual hunting party the aim of which is to kill the legendary great bear. Ike has never known his father; he has, instead, several spiritual fathers, the most important of whom is Sam Fathers. The son of an Indian chief and a mulatto woman, Fathers is a slave, but his innate dignity and his gifts as a hunter prevent him from being treated as inferior. He is, one feels, the human counterpart of Old Ben, the great bear, and like the bear is identified with the wilderness.

In the third section, Old Ben is killed, by Boon Hogganbeck, another of Ike's spiritual fathers, also part Indian but regarded as white. He kills Old Ben by stabbing him with his knife in defence of his dog, Lion. When Ben is killed Sam Fathers decides to die too.

In the fifth and last section of the story Ike, now eighteen, goes again to the scene of the killing of Old Ben to hunt with Boon. The wilderness is now on the point of being wilderness no longer; commerce has taken over. Near the graves of Sam Fathers and Old Ben Ike is confronted by an enormous rattlesnake, which he greets as he might have done the bear. He finds Boon almost demented and trying to mend his gun in a grove of squirrels. Boon screams at him: 'Get out of here! Don't touch them! Don't touch a one of them! They're mine!'

These last words of Boon's are an ironic comment on Faulkner's theme, which is expounded in the fourth section of the story. Significantly, when 'The Bear' was published as a story before it became part of *Go Down, Moses*, this fourth section was omitted. The omission makes the story much more obviously a short story, makes it a story of initiation into natural piety almost in a Wordsworthian sense. But equally obviously, with the fourth section omitted, much is lost which is dear to Faulkner and essential to his vision of man's life on earth. The section is chronologically out of order in the story. Ike is now a man.

He is staying with Cass Edmonds, a second cousin older than himself. Going through his father's papers, he learns the history of his family, learns of his Negro kinsmen who are equally the offspring of his grandfather Lucius Quintus Carothers McCaslin. He renounces the plantation to which he is heir, thereby losing his wife, and, a carpenter by trade, spends most of his time hunting. It is as though Sam Fathers has prevailed.

Faulkner wrote much outside the Yoknapatawpha canon, short stories which are indisputably short stories, and in which he often seems to become the anonymous story-teller, the mouthpiece as it were of the community. He is so in the first story he published in a national magazine, 'A Rose for Emily'.

Miss Emily has survived as an honoured figure in town, the last of a distinguished family. When she was a young woman her father had prevented her from marrying but just before his death she had been courted by a working-man, a Northerner. He had disappeared and Miss Emily had become more and more a hermit. When she dies in her seventies and the townsfolk flock to her house, they find one bedroom arranged as a bridal suite and on the bed the remains of Homer Barron, her working-class lover. As Faulkner tells it:

Already we knew that there was one room in that region above stairs which no one had seen in forty years, and which would have to be forced. They waited until Miss Emily was decently in the ground before they opened it.

The violence of breaking down the door seemed to fill the room with pervading dust. A thin, acrid pall as of the tomb seemed to lie everywhere upon this room decked and furnished as for a bridal: upon the valance curtains of faded rose colour, upon the rose-shaded lights, upon the dressing table, upon the delicate array of crystal and the man's toilet things backed with tarnished silver, silver so tarnished that the monogram was obscured. Among them lay a collar and tie, as if they had just been removed, which, lifted, left upon the surface a pale crescent in the dust. Upon a chair hung the suit, carefully folded; beneath it the two mute shoes and the discarded socks.

The man himself lay in the bed.

For a long while we just stood there, looking down at the profound and flashless grin. . . .

We are reminded of Miss Havisham's bridal suite in *Great Expectations*, not simply because of the similarity of scene but also because of the authority with which the scene is executed, the acclimatization as it were of the horrific to the normal world. We are in the presence of the Gothic and we shall be further reminded of Poe. There is the final touch of horror in the last paragraph:

Then we noticed that in the second pillow was the indentation of a head. One of us lifted something from it, and leaning forward, that faint and invisible dust dry and acrid in the nostrils, we saw a long strand of iron-gray hair.

The suggestion of necrophilia is unmistakable; but – and this is the difference from Poe – in Faulkner the corruption and degeneracy portrayed are not there for their own sake, to provide a *frisson* of horror, but exist rather as an exceedingly powerful metaphor for the lost, bewildered, ruined, post-war South. And, as in Dickens, the metaphor is executed with absolute authority. Faulkner's South is violent and lurid, obscure in both senses of the word, but his scenes and characters are caught in intense flashes of lightning, and what G. H. Lewes said of Dickens in his essay, 'Dickens in Relation to Criticism', is equally applicable to him:

He was a seer of visions; and his visions were of objects at once familiar and potent. . . . What seems preposterous, impossible to us, seemed to him simple fact of observation. When he imagined a street, a house, a room, a figure, he saw it not in the vague schematic way of ordinary imagination, but in the sharp definition of actual perception, all the salient details obtruding themselves on his attention. He, seeing it thus vividly, made us also see it; and believing in its reality however fantastic, he communicated something of his belief to us.

This seems to be bound up with what Professor Norman Holmes Pearson means when he says in his essay 'Faulkner's Three Evening Suns', 'Faulkner came to understand that what is created by presentation need not be repeated by statement', though at first sight this may seem to run counter to the impression we have of Faulkner as an unusually prolix writer – the adjective is not used pejoratively but merely to imply density, repetition, involution, and convolution, devices used to render the scene or character in its full complexity, as in the opening paragraph of the fine story 'Dry September', which is set in Jefferson, Yoknapatawpha County:

Through the bloody September twilight, aftermath of sixty-two rain-less days, it had gone like a fire in dry grass – the rumour, the story, whatever it was. Something about Miss Minnie Cooper and a Negro. Attacked, insulted, frightened: none of them, gathered in the barber shop on that Saturday evening where the ceiling fan stirred, without freshening it, the vitiated air, sending back upoh them, in recurrent surges of stale pomade and lotion, their own stale breath and odours, knew exactly what had happened.

'Except it wasn't Will Mayes', a barber said. He was a man of middle age; a thin sand-coloured man with a mild face, who was shaving a client. 'I know Will Mayes. He's a good nigger. And I know Minnie Cooper, too.'

The barber, Hawkshaw, is the voice of reason and sanity but he is powerless to quell the hysteria aroused by the alleged rape. A lynch-ing party is rapidly organized, led by an ex-soldier named McLan-don, and when all is over he returns home. The last paragraph runs:

He went through the house, ripping off his shirt, and on the dark screened porch at the rear he stood and mopped his head and shoulders with the shirt and flung it away. He took the pistol from his hip and laid it on the table beside the bed, and sat on the bed and removed his shoes, and rose and slipped his trousers off. He was sweating again already, and he stooped and hunted furiously for the shirt. At last he found it and wiped his body again, and, with his body pressed against the dusty screen, he stood panting. There was no movement, no sound, not even an insect. The dark world seemed to lie stricken beneath the cold moon and the lidless stars.

Prose could scarcely be simpler. It is a description of physical action; but the description, the presentation, carries its own com-ment.

Another instance from the story of presentation making its own comment on what is being presented is the description of the behaviour of Miss Cooper after the alleged rape. On the Saturday evening she goes into the town with some women friends, and is commented upon:

'That's the one, see? The one in pink in the middle.' 'Is that her? What did they do with the nigger? Did they —?' 'Sure. He's all right.' 'All right, is he?' 'Sure. He went on a little trip.' Then the drug store, where even the young men lounging in the doorway tipped their hats and followed with their eyes the motion of her hips and legs when she passed. . . .

They reached the picture show. It was like a miniature fairyland with its lighted lobby and coloured lithographs of life caught in its terrible and beautiful mutations. Her lips began to tingle. In the dark, when the picture began, it would be all right; she could hold back the laughing so it would not waste away so fast and so soon. So she hurried on before the turning faces, the undertones of low astonishment, and they took their accustomed places where she could see the aisle against the silver glare and the young men and girls coming in two and two against it.

The lights flicked away; the screen glowed silver, and soon life began to unfold, beautiful and passionate and sad, while still the young men and girls entered, scented and sibilant in the half dark, their backs paired in silhouette delicate and sleek, their slim, quick bodies awkward, divinely young, while beyond them the silver dream accumulated, inevitably on and on. She began to laugh. In trying to suppress it, it made more noise than ever; heads began to turn. Still laughing, her friends raised her and led her out, and she stood at the curb, laughing on a high sustained note, until the taxi came up and they helped her in.

The passage shows among other things Faulkner's mastery of American colloquial speech, with its laconic irony that is constantly about to emerge as a wisecrack. Indeed, in this respect he is the equal of Hemingway.

But, as the passage also indicates, 'Dry September' is a splendid instance of Faulkner the anonymous story-teller of the folk at work. The story is told in not more than 5,000 words and in that space Faulkner describes a number of specific characters; yet beyond them we feel the presence of a whole community. In this ability to present a whole community Faulkner is unsurpassed among short-story writers. He is an anonymous voice, the recorder, historian, dramatist of the community, his role that of the writer of the medieval ballad. And he brings the community triumphantly to life as it erupts into racial violence and death at the end of the hot, dry summer.

'That Evening Sun' may be seen as an appendage; almost a footnote, to the events narrated in *The Sound and the Fury* and *Absalom, Absalom!* which make up the saga of the Compson family. For all that, 'That Evening Sun' is entirely self-contained. It is told by Quentin Compson and begins:

... we have a city laundry which makes the rounds on Monday morning, gathering the bundles of clothes into bright-coloured, specially-made motor cars; the soiled wearing of a whole week now flees apparitionlike behind alert and irritable electric horns, with a long diminishing noise of rubber and asphalt like tearing silk, and even the Negro women who still take in white people's washing after the old custom, fetch and deliver it in automobiles.

But fifteen years ago, on Monday morning the quiet, dusty, shady streets would be full of Negro women with, balanced on their steady, turbaned heads, bundles of clothes tied up in sheets, almost as large as cotton bales, carried so without touch of hand between the kitchen door of the white house and the blackened washpot beside a cabin door in Negro Hollow.

From the point of view of the small boy he was fifteen years ago – he cannot have been more than five or six – Quentin tells the story of one of these Negro washerwomen, Nancy, who lives in a cabin on the Compson property. When the Compson's cook, Dilsey, is ill, Nancy cooks for them. She is a prostitute and she is terrified of Jesus, the husband who has deserted her, believing he is trying to kill her, for she is pregnant by another man. She is allowed to sleep in the Compson's kitchen, but when Dilsey comes back Mrs Compson, the neurotic mother, refuses to let her stay.

'I can't have Negroes sleeping in the bedrooms,' mother said. Jason cried. He cried until mother said he couldn't have any dessert for three days if he didn't stop. Then Jason said he would stop if Dilsey would make a chocolate cake. Father was there.

'Why don't you do something about it?' mother said. 'What do we have officers for?'

'Why is Nancy afraid of Jesus?' Caddy said. 'Are you afraid of father, mother?'

'What could the officers do?' father said. 'If Nancy hasn't seen him, how could the officers find him?'

'Then why is she afraid?' mother said.

'She says he is there. She says she knows he is there tonight.'

'Yet we pay taxes,' mother said. 'I must wait here alone in this big house while you take a Negro woman home.'

'You know that I am not lying outside with a razor,' father said.

'I'll stop if Dilsey will make a chocolate cake,' Jason said. Mother told us to go out and father said he didn't know if Jason would get a chocolate cake or not, but he knew what Jason was going to get in about a minute. We went back to the kitchen and told Nancy.

'Father said for you to go home and lock the door, and you'll be all right,' Caddy said. 'All right from what, Nancy? Is Jesus mad at you?' Nancy was holding the coffee cup in her hands again, her elbows on her knees and her hands holding the cup between her knees. She was looking into the cup. 'What have you done that made Jesus mad?' Caddy said. Nancy let the cup go. It didn't break on the floor, but the coffee spilled out, and Nancy sat there with her hands still making the shape of the cup. She began to make the sound again, not loud. Not singing and not unsinging. We watched her.

Nancy is not to be shaken in her conviction or persuaded. She is passively awaiting the death she assumes will be hers; and when Mr Compson and the children eventually leave her in her own cabin she does not even bother to bar the door.

Everything in the story is recorded through the eyes and feelings of the children, and there is much that they do not know or understand; for them, Nancy is merely behaving oddly, and their incomprehension is summed up in Quentin's question to his father: 'Who will do our washing now, Father?' We are not told so, but I think we assume that the threat of death is real and that before the day is out she will be killed, though if that is so, Faulkner brings her to life again in his novel, *Requiem for a Nun*, published twenty years after the appearance of the story.

That in itself throws light on the way in which Faulkner's mind worked in creation. He was seized by his characters and by his tragic vision of the South which he dramatized through them. He was constantly adding to that vision, revising it, making it richer, more detailed, more compelling and authoritative as imaginative history, making it more true. In the reader's mind his opus constitutes a whole world, to which the short stories contribute. They will always be overshadowed by the novels, but they express with comparable hallucinatory power, the same vision of a society shaped by tragic experience.

Older than Faulkner by three years, Katherine Anne Porter has some affinity with him in subject, though by contrast her attitudes towards the South and their expression appear classical and controlled rather than romantic and extravagant. No American writer of the century has been more admired by American critics, though her published fiction comprises no more than three volumes of short stories, five longer short stories, and a single novel. One reason for this admiration is probably what can only be called her Americanness. Like Hawthorne, Willa Cather, and Faulkner, she seems to encapsulate in herself and her family history a whole significant part of the American story. She was born in Texas in 1890 of a family prominent in the development of Kentucky – she is a great-great-great-granddaughter of Daniel Boone – and educated at convent schools in Texas and Louisiana. This family background, which may be thought of as typical of that of the established upper-class Anglo-Saxon South-erner, she has drawn upon in a number of her stories, in which she appears as Miranda.

One of these is 'Old Mortality', written in three parts, the first covering the years 1885–1903, the second 1904, and the third 1912, and takes in events that happened years before Miranda was born and that she knows of only through family legend and tradition, which affect her as powerfully as poetry and fairy stories. Through her – she appears at times indeed as the consciousness of the family – we receive an impression of aristocratic Southern life that is largely conventional in its attributes but also richly detailed and evocative. To this extent it is faithful to the pattern of Southern fiction, to Faulkner and Allen Tate, even, though the events described postdate those of *Gone with the Wind*, to Margaret Mitchell. Yet the final outcome at which Miranda – and, by inference, Kath-erine Anne Porter – arrives is almost a direct opposite of Faulkner's.

The first part of 'Old Mortality' had at its centre the beautiful, magical, capricious, adored, romantic Aunt Amy who had died young, and whom Uncle Gabriel, who had loved her so desperately, had waited five years to marry. In the last part of the story Miranda is in a railway train; she is now eighteen and travelling home for Uncle Gabriel's funeral. On the train she meets her elderly Cousin Eva, who has appeared briefly in the first part of the story:

Eva, shy and chinless, straining her upper lip over two enormous teeth, would sit in corners watching her mother. She looked hungry, her eyes were strained and tired. She wore her mother's old clothes, made over, and taught Latin in a Female Seminary. She believed in votes for women and travelled about, making speeches.

It is impossible not to see Cousin Eva, ugly, eccentric by Parrington standards, something of a figure of fun, as a counterpart to Miranda, who in the course of the train journey gathers an entirely different version of Aunt Amy's life and character from that presented to her in her father's reminiscences.

'She had a lovely complexion,' said Cousin Eva, 'perfectly transparent with a flush on each cheekbone. But it was tuberculosis, and is disease beautiful? And she brought it on herself by drinking lemon and salt to stop her periods when she wanted to go to dances. There was a superstition among girls about that. They fancied that young men could tell what ailed them by touching their hands, or even by looking at them. As if it mattered? But they were terribly self-conscious and they had immense respect for man's worldly wisdom in those days. My own notion is that a man couldn't – but anyway, the whole thing was stupid.'

'I should have thought they'd have stayed at home if they couldn't manage better than that,' said Miranda, feeling very knowledgeable and modern.

'They didn't dare. Those parties and dances were their market, a girl couldn't afford to miss out, there were always rivals waiting to cut the ground from under her. The rivalry –' said Cousin Eva, and her head lifted, she arched like a cavalry horse getting a whiff of the battle-field – 'you can't imagine what the rivalry was like. The way those girls treated each other – nothing was too mean, nothing too false. . . .'

Cousin Eva wrung her hands. 'It was just sex,' she said in despair; 'their minds dwelt on nothing else. They didn't call it that, it was smothered under pretty names, but that's all it was, sex. . . .'

So much, then, for romantic notions of the South and its chivalry. It is impossible to read 'Old Mortality' today without being conscious of the strong undercurrent in it of a sense of the need for what we now call women's liberation. For the core of the story is Cousin Eva's cry: 'I thank God every day of my life that I have a small income. It's a Rock of Ages. What would have become of me if I hadn't a cent of my own?'

While she is on the train we gather that Miranda has already married, has eloped from school. She and Cousin Eva are met at the station by her father and she hears that the house will be full of cousins. 'Her blood rebelled against the ties of blood', and she realizes now why she ran away to marriage and why she will run away from marriage. The last lines of the story are:

I can't live in their world any longer, she told herself, listening to the voices back of her. Let them tell their stories to each other. Let them go on explaining how things happened. I don't care. At least I can know the truth about what happens to me, she assured herself silently, making a promise to herself, in her hopefulness, her ignorance.

So, with these words, Miranda disengages herself from the stifling family of the South; and with her, Katherine Anne Porter. The South, of course remains a subject of her stories but only one of several.

Miranda reappears in the sequence of seven stories called 'The Old Order'. Every summer, at Grandmother's behest, the family returns to the plantation in the country, to a way of life that seems to belong to the days before the Fall or at least before the Civil War. At Grandmother's death, part of the family land is sold, among it the grave in which Grandfather lies buried, so his body is moved. Miranda, aged nine, and her brother Paul, three years older, are playing in the empty grave, scrabbling with their hands in the dry soil, when she finds in it 'a silver dove no larger than a hazel nut, with spread wings and a neat fan-shaped tail', while Paul finds a thin white gold ring carved with flowers and leaves. Paul explains that the silver dove is the screw head for a coffin, and since each fancies what the other has found they make an exchange. Then Paul shoots a rabbit, which he skins while Miranda looks on admiringly.

The flayed flesh emerged dark scarlet, sleek, firm; Miranda with thumb and finger felt the long fine muscles with the silvery flat strips binding them to the joints. Brother Paul lifted the oddly bloated belly. 'Look,' he said, in a low amazed voice. 'It was going to have young ones.'

Very carefully he slit the thin flesh from the centre ribs to the flanks, and a scarlet bag appeared. He slit again and pulled the bag open, and there lay a bundle of tiny rabbits, each wrapped in a thin scarlet veil. The brother pulled these off and there they were, dark grey, their sleek wet down lying in minute even ripples, like a baby's head just washed, their unbelievably small delicate ears folded close, their little blind faces almost featureless.

Miranda said, 'Oh, I want to *see*,' under her breath. She looked and looked – excited but not frightened, for she was accustomed to the sight of animals killed in hunting – filled with pity and astonishment and a kind of shocked delight in the wonderful little creatures for their own sakes, they were so pretty.

Urgently, Paul makes her promise never to tell anyone what she has seen, for their father would be very angry with him. Miranda never does tell and, indeed, forgets the incident entirely until, as we are told in the last paragraph, nearly twenty years later:

One day she was picking her path through the puddles and crushed refuse of a market street in a strange city of a strange country, when without warning, plain and clear in its true colours as if she looked through a frame upon a scene that had not stirred nor changed since the moment it happened, the episode of that far-off day leaped from its buried place before her mind's eye. She was so reasonlessly horrified she halted suddenly staring, the scene before her eye dimmed by the vision back of them. An Indian vendor had held up before her a tray of dyed sugar sweets, in the shapes of all kinds of small creatures: birds, baby chicks, baby rabbits, lambs, baby pigs. They were in gay colours and smelled of vanilla, maybe. . . . It was a very hot day and the smell in the market, with its piles of raw flesh and wilting flowers, was like the mingled sweetness and corruption she had smelled that other day in the empty cemetery at home: the day she had remembered always until now vaguely as the time she and her brother had found treasure in the opened graves. Instantly upon this thought the dreadful vision faded, and she saw clearly her brother, whose childhood face she had forgotten, standing again in the blazing sunshine, again twelve years old, a pleased sober smile in his eyes, turning the silver dove over and over in his hands.

In 'Pale Horse, Pale Rider', the romantic past might not exist at all, it is very much a story of the feverish present, the present of November 1918. We meet an older Miranda, a Miranda in her middle-twenties waking to find herself in bed in the County hospital, aware of the presence of a 'lank, greenish stranger' who is somehow familiar to her. He rides a grey horse and she on her horse outstrips him in a race. Awake, as she steps back into yesterday, all becomes clear. It is wartime, the last weeks indeed of the First World War, and an influenza epidemic is sweeping the world. Miranda is oppressed by her inability to afford Liberty Bonds, and is therefore fearful of being judged unpatriotic – among other things, the story is a notable presentation of war-hysteria in the United States of the period. At the same time, she is in love with Adam, a young officer stationed in the town and waiting to be sent to the front. Both of them are conscious that his death may be imminent but where she is cynical in a way that anticipates the immediately post-war mood of disillusionment, he is much more fatalistic:

'If I didn't go,' said Adam, in a matter-of-fact voice, 'I couldn't look myself in the face.'

So that's all settled. With her fingers flattened on his arm, Miranda was silent, thinking about Adam. No, there was no resentment of revolt in him. Pure, she thought, all the way through, flawless, complete, as the sacrificial lamb must be. The sacrificial lamb strode along casually, accommodating his long pace to hers, keeping her on the inside of the walk in the good American style, helping her across street corners as if she were a cripple – 'I hope we don't come to a mud puddle, he'll carry me over it' – giving off whiffs of tobacco smoke, a manly smell of scentless soap, freshly cleaned leather, and freshly washed skin, breathing through his nose and carrying his chest easily. He threw back his head and smiled into the sky which still misted, promising rain.

Next day, influenza has hit Miranda. More than a month passes before she recovers and can face the world. The war is over, but Adam has died from the same influenza. As for Miranda:

No more war, no more plague, only the dazed silence that follows the ceasing of the heavy guns; noiseless houses with the shades drawn, empty streets, the dead cold light of tomorrow. Now there would be time for everything.

The Miranda of 'Pale Horse, Pale Rider', one feels, has broken free of the past and of the ties of place. Equating Miranda with her creator, one can see how Katherine Anne Porter could develop into being the leading twentieth-century exponent of James's International Subject, stories of which throughout her career are mingled with stories of the old South. All of them are distinguished, two of them, 'A Day's Work' and 'The Leaning Tower', especially so. Indeed, as Beachcroft has said in *The Modest Art*, 'A Day's Work' seems almost an extension of Joyce's art; it is the story of the efforts of an Irish immigrant in New York, who feels himself handicapped by the nagging pieties and Irish Catholic puritanism of his hard-working washerwoman wife, to find a seedy political job, efforts which entail the consumption of much alcohol. So, after a visit to his patron, Mr

Halloran has to be brought back to his apartment and his wife by Officer Maginnis.

When the door was shut and locked, Mrs Halloran went and dipped a large bath towel under the kitchen tap. She wrung it out and tied several good hard knots in one end and tried it out with a whack on the edge of the table. She walked in and stood over the bed and brought the knotted towel down on Mr Halloran's face with all her might. He stirred and muttered, ill at ease. 'That's for the flatiron, Halloran,' she told him, in a cautious voice as if she were talking to herself, and whack, down came the towel again. 'That's for the half-dollar,' she said, and whack, 'that's for your drunkenness. . . .'

She stood back breathless, the lump on her forehead burning in its furious colours. When Mr Halloran attempted to rise, shielding his head with his arms, she gave him a push and he fell back again. 'Stay there and don't give me a word,' said Mrs Halloran. He pulled the pillow over his face and subsided again, this time for good.

Later, she telephones her daughter:

'It's late to be calling, but there's news about your father. No, no, nothing of that kind, he's got a job. I said a *job*. Yes, at last, after all my urging him onwards. . . . It's clean enough work, with good pay; if it's not just what I prayed for, still it beats nothing, Maggie. After all my trying . . . it's like a miracle. You see what can be done with patience and doing your duty, Maggie. Now mind you do as well by your own husband.'

Among other things, 'A Day's Work' shows what can still be done by a writer not normally associated with situations of low comedy, for the story is at once an illuminating study of the Irish immigrant, vying in this respect with the work of James T. Farrell, a revealing insight into New York City politics, and one of the best stories of the economic depression of the Thirties.

When 'The Leaning Tower' is set beside it one gets some notion of Katherine Anne Porter's range of scene and of her power to subordinate herself to her theme. Charles Upton is a poor art student from Texas, in the Berlin of 1931. The currency has depreciated on an unprecedented scale and unemployed men stand on the kerbs with placards hanging round their necks, saying: 'I will take any work you can offer.' All this is heightened by the spectacle all around of conspicuous consumption. She tells of one of the young man's peregrinations through the city;

He had watched a group of middle-aged men and women who were gathered in silence before two adjoining windows, gazing silently at displays of toy pigs and sugar pigs. These persons were all strangely of a kind, and strangely the most prevalent type. The streets were full of them – enormous waddling women with short legs and ill-humoured faces, and round-headed men with great rolls of fat across the backs of their necks, who seemed to support their swollen bellies with an effort that drew their shoulders forward. Nearly all of them were leading their slender, overbred, short-legged dogs in pairs on fancy leashes. The dogs wore their winter clothes: wool sweaters, fur ruffs, and fleece-lined rubber boots. The creatures whined and complained and shivered, and their owners lifted them up tenderly to show them the pigs.

In one window there were sausages, hams, bacon, small pink chops; all pig, real pig, fresh, smoked, salted, baked, roasted, pickled, spiced and jellied. In the other were dainty artificial pigs, almond paste pigs, pink sugar pigs, chocolate sausages, tiny hams and bacons of melting cream streaked and coloured to the very life. . . .

With their nervous dogs wailing in their arms, the people, shameless mounds of fat, stood in a trance of pig worship, gazing with eyes damp with admiration and appetite. They resembled the most unkind caricatures of themselves, but they were the very kind of people that Holbein and Dürer and Urs Graf had drawn too. . . .

To that list of painters Katherine Anne Porter might have added the name of the most famous of twentieth-century German satirical draughtsmen, George Grosz, for it is through Grosz's Berlin that, standing half-concealed in shop doorways to sketch the types, Charles Upton wanders.

Later he takes a room in a pension and becomes friendly with the other guests. He celebrates New Year's Eve with them in a cabaret, and though the evening is successful he realizes how fragile is the harmony between them, how easily it can dissolve into national antagonisms. When he gets back to his room, he sees that the small plaster replica of the Leaning Tower of Pisa which had crumbled at his touch when he engaged the room has been repaired and restored. It stands there again 'in its bold little frailness'.

Leaning, suspended, perpetually ready to fall but never falling quite, the venturesome little object – a mistake in the first place, a whimsical pain in the neck, really towers shouldn't lean in the first place; a curiosity, like those cupids falling off the roof – yet had some kind of meaning in Charles's mind. Well, what? He tousled his hair and rubbed his eyes and then his whole head and yawned himself almost inside out. What had the silly little thing reminded him of before? There was an answer if he could think what it was, but this was not the time. But just the same, there was something terribly urgent at work, in or around him, he could not tell which. There was something perishable but threatening, uneasy, hanging over his head or stirring angrily, dangerously at his back.

He goes to bed with a feeling he has never known before, 'an infernal desolation of the spirit, the chill and the knowledge of death in him'. The whole edifice of the city seems to be on the point of crumbling. The Tower stands, too, for Charles's own stance as he feels himself threatened in the city by everything that is alien to his American sensibilities. The latter is perhaps the more important, for the story is a noteworthy expression of the expansion of the American sensibility in the presence of Europe analogous in its way, despite the vast difference in the scales of the two works, to James's *The Ambassadors*.

A Southern short-story writer almost aggressively different from Katherine Anne Porter and coming out of a quite different region of the South and of quite other traditions is Erskine Caldwell. In a writing career that has spanned more than forty-five years and is not yet ended he has written twenty-six novels, some fifteen volumes of short stories, and fifteen other books. Because of his characteristic material, he seems best approached historically.

In 1728, on the King's orders, William Byrd, the Virginia gentleman who was later to develop the capital city of Richmond, led an expedition to the backwoods of the colony and of North Carolina. He records in his journal his discovery on the frontier of 'indolent wretches' with 'custard complexions' who lived in a 'dirty state of nature' subject to 'gross humours' and a 'lazy, creeping habit' that made them content to exist on the edge of the world. They lived on what the land provided and on milk stolen from their more vigorous and virtuous neighbours. The climate was enervating, the conditions in which they lived were swampy, and their diet was inadequate. This 'haven for the innately idle', Byrd discovered, was kept permanently populated by the official policy of increasing the citizenry by taking in debtors, criminals, and fugitives from justice. 'To speak the truth,' wrote Byrd, ''tis a thorough aversion to labour that makes people file off to North Carolina, where plenty and a warm sun confirm them in their disposition to laziness for their whole lives.' There was probably much inbreeding too.

The point of this historical excursion, the information for which I am indebted to Sylvia Jenkins Cook's *From Tobacco Road to Route 66: The Southern Poor White in Fiction*, is that Byrd was describing for the first time what is probably the oldest American stereotype, the poor white. He is characteristically a Southern product and is the foil to that other stereotype the Southern gentleman. Indeed, in Jungian terms he is the Southern gentleman's shadow. The poor white is seen as feckless, immoral, superstitious, and lazy, though whether these are qualities due to environment and genetics or to innate depravity are questions that can be argued endlessly. One thing is certain, however. Throughout his history he has been the great comic figure in Southern writing.

Sometimes he is sinister, too, as in Faulkner's depiction of him in the various members of the Snopes family, where he is seen as the despoiler of traditional Southern values. Later, in the fiction of Flannery O'Connor, he seems to become a paradigm of original sin. In our time, however, his great celebrant has been Erskine Caldwell, who has celebrated not only him but on occasion the rural Negro.

Caldwell has always been a swift, economical writer and his stories tend to be very short. He has a number of modes. In the Thirties, when he seemed to be writing as a propagandist exposing man's inhumanity to man and equating the poor white with the downtrodden proletariat, his besetting sin was sensationalism, as in 'Knife to Cut the Cornbread With'. Roy, a young sharecropper, lies hopelessly paralysed after an accident in the fields for which he has received no compensation. He and his wife are now dependent entirely on her work in the fields. It is mid-week, they have only dry bread, and the landlord refuses to let them have their allowance of fat bacon until the weekend.

Roy lay still for a while. He was hungry, hungry as he could be. He could smell the coffee boiling, and he could hear Nora taking the pan of hot corn bread from the oven, but he was so hungry for a little piece of meat he felt as though he would be willing to cut a slice out of his numb legs if he dared. He had never thought of that before, and he wondered what would happen to him if he did. . . .

Later, having had a vision of his landlord Mr Gene entertaining the preacher to Sunday dinner at a 'table piled high with chicken and pork and sweet potatoes and white bread', he asks Nora if she has brought a knife to cut the corn bread with. His question puzzles her.

He was thinking that he could keep the knife beside him in bed until the next day, when she would be away chopping cotton in the field.
    'You never wanted a knife before, Roy. Do you want me to get one now?'
    'The sharpest knife,' he said, 'the sharpest knife to cut the corn bread with.'
    The moment she took her hand from his forehead he could remember nothing. He closed his eyes and lay there waiting for her to come back. He did not know how he would ever again be able to let her leave him, even for so short a time as a second or two.

Caldwell's particular brand of black humour seems to have its roots very deep in the past. In 'Blue Boy', a farmer keeps a deaf-and-dumb Negro imbecile with whom to entertain his guests at the turkey-and-hog dinner on New Year's Day. In 'The Negro in the Well', which is set on a night when the whole of Georgia is given over to fox-hunting, a white farmer finds that a Negro has fallen into his well and sets the price of his freedom (and of his life too, one suspects), at two of his most precious fox-hounds. The trouble with Caldwell's stories, outweighing their virtues of economy, narrative speed, and comic invention, is that the characters in them tend to be so dehumanized as scarcely to be human at all, and this finally robs them of their interest.

V

In 1867, a British government brought the Dominion of Canada into being. It did not thereby necessarily transform a geographical expression into a nation or give Canadians a sense of national identity. No doubt, the sheer immensity of the country and the variety of the ethnic groups that make up its population work against this. In *O Canada*, published in 1967 and a pioneer work since it marked the first time a major critic of the English-speaking world beyond Canada had taken a look at Canadian literature, Edmund Wilson narrowed down the problem facing Canadians when he wrote of the novelist Hugh MacLennon: 'The problem for this type of independent mind is, on the one hand, to shake off the traditional ties that have in the past bound the Canadian to old England and, on the other, to survive the pressures that have been driving him towards the new United States.' In the short story, the exemplar of this type of independent mind is Morley Callaghan, who may be said to have solved the problem triumphantly.

A native of Toronto and a graduate of its university, Callaghan was a colleague of Hemingway on the *Toronto Star* and a friend of Hemingway and Fitzgerald in Paris. He spent some years in New York and since his stories were published in the Thirties in American magazines, he was generally believed in England to be an American. His stories are set indifferently in Canada, generally in Toronto or on the nearby shores of Lake Ontario, and in the United States, in New York City below Fourteenth Street; the localities are quite precisely described but rarely named specifically. In the final paragraph of his 1960 review, Wilson wonders 'whether the primary reason for the current under-estimation of Morley Callaghan may not be simply a general incapacity – apparently shared by his compatriots – for believing that a writer whose work may be mentioned without absurdity in association with Chekhov's and Turgenev's can possibly be functioning in Toronto'.

Certainly no other Canadian short-story writer could be

mentioned without absurdity in association with Chekhov and Turgenev, and their evocation by Wilson provides us with a clue to Callaghan, for he could have profited little from his Canadian forbears. The best of them seems to have been Duncan Campbell Scott, who lived from 1862 to 1947, was born in Ottawa, brought up and educated there and in eastern Quebec, where his father was a minister, and worked as a civil servant in the department of Indian affairs in Ottawa. He was rare among Canadian writers of his time in being aware of continental European writing; the influence of Flaubert and Maupassant can be seen in his first book of stories, published in 1896, *The Village of Viger*, stories about the inhabitants of a French-Canadian village.

There is nothing in the least sensational in these stories, or rather there is nothing that is presented sensationally. Throughout, there is a complete absence of emphasis, and sometimes this lack of stress means that one must re-read the story in order to take in its meaning. And the stories are very short, generally not more than half a dozen pages long; they are little vignettes of characters and families. 'My French-Canadian critics here,' said Scott, 'who are well acquainted with the book have accepted the atmosphere as "particular"; in fact, one thought I was dealing with the village where she was born and brought up.' Modern Canadian critics seem to find Viger more a 'literary' than an actual village. To me, ignorant of French Canada, Scott's achievement seems comparable to his American contemporary Sarah Orne Jewett's in *The Country of the Pointed Firs*. He has a similar honesty and fidelity.

One of the best stories is 'The Desjardins', which deals with two brothers and a sister, prosperous farmers who lead a secluded life, for it is believed there is insanity in the family. Charles, the elder brother, is a bookish man who has had ambitions of studying the law. The others respect his studious habits:

He only worked in the mornings; in the afternoons he read, history principally. His favourite study was the 'Life of Napoleon Buonaparte', which seemed to absorb him completely. He was growing more retired and preoccupied every day – lost in deep reveries, swallowed in ambitious dreams.

There comes the evening at harvest-time when he announces to his brother and sister: 'I am the Great Napoleon.' The others accept this as though it is a visitation they have been waiting for and resign themselves to a life apart as the last of their race. With intervals of sanity, Charles lives the life of the Emperor. 'During the summer he is engaged, with no very definite operations, in the field, but when winter comes he always prepares for the invasion of Russia.' His younger brother Philip humours him, enacting a role in the fantasy. Half-frightened village boys hide in the long grass to hear him go muttering by. The story ends:

Only once has a gleam of light pierced these mists. It was in the year when, as Adele said, he had had two Waterloos and had taken to his bed in consequence. One evening Adele brought him a bowl of gruel. He stared like a child awakened from sleep when she carried in the lamp. She approached the bed, and he started up.

'Adele!' he said, hoarsely, and pulling her face down, kissed her lips. For a moment she had hope, but with the next week came winter; and he commenced his annual preparations for the invasion of Russia.

Some Canadian critics complain that in this story Scott gave in to 'the temptations of sentimentalism or melodrama'. On the contrary, he seems to handle the theme of hereditary madness with great austerity, and the Poe who may have influenced him there, as I suspect he did in other of the Viger stories, is a severely domesticated and as it were chastened Poe.

Besides *In the Village of Viger*, he wrote two other collections of stories. Dealing with traditional Canadian material, stories of the Northern wastes at the beginning of the nineteenth century and of Indian life, they are comparatively undistinguished and could certainly have had little to say to the young Morley Callaghan.

Callaghan's first volume of stories appeared in 1929, and over the years his style and art have scarcely changed, so that it is difficult to speak of his development. Almost uniformly, the stories are short, 'clipped' to no more than two or three thousand words. Reading the two volumes of collected stories, one is struck by the very ordinariness of his characters: no fiction-writer has more closely hugged to himself Flaubert's counsel that 'art is not made to paint exceptions'. And then one must be struck by the scrupulous fidelity with which Callaghan seems to subordinate himself to his characters. Short stories could go no further in terms of Naturalism. There is, however, something else, which Wyndham Lewis noted in them when he observed: 'There is good and evil, not merely good luck and bad luck.' Callaghan was brought up a Roman Catholic, and reading his short stories, one senses what Edmund Wilson found in Callaghan's novels:

> . . . in order to describe these books properly, one must explain that the central element in them, the spirit that preserves the whole, is deeply if undogmatically Christian. Though they depend on no scaffolding of theology, though they embody no original vision, they have evidently somewhere behind them the tradition of the Catholic Church . . . One is scarcely aware of doctrine; what one finds is, rather, an intuitive sense of the meaning of Christianity.

Callaghan has written a number of stories about Roman Catholic priests, and perhaps a good way of approaching his art would be to look at one or two of these. There is 'The Young Priest', which tells of Father Vincent Sullivan:

> At the seminary, four years ago, he had been lazy, goodnatured, and very fond of telling long funny stories, and then laughing easily, showing his white teeth. He had full red lips and straight black hair. But as soon as he was ordained he became solemn, yet energetic. He never told stories. He tried to believe that he had some of the sanctity that a young priest ought to have. At his first mass, in the ordination sermon, an old priest had shouted eloquently that a very young priest was greater and holier and more worthy of respect than anyone else on earth. Father Vincent Sullivan, hearing this, couldn't believe it entirely, but it gave him courage even if it did make him more solemn and serious.

The parishioner Father Sullivan particularly wishes to cultivate is Mrs Gibbons.

> She was a large, plump, well-kept woman walking erectly and slowly to the street. Her clothes were elegant. Her skin had been pink and fine. It was very satisfactory to think that such a well-groomed, dignified, and competent woman should appreciate the necessity of strict religious practice in her daily life.

There have been rumours about her 'laxity' but:

> Insinuations against the good name of Mrs Gibbons, who, they knew,

was one of the finest women of the parish, were in a measure an insinuation against the Church. Father Sullivan had decided some time ago that Mrs Gibbons was really a splendid woman and a credit to any community.

One evening, he is called to the telephone. It is Mrs Gibbons's sister-in-law asking for a priest for Mrs Gibbons. '"There's really nothing wrong with her, but if you've got any influence you ought to use it on her. She's a terrible woman. Come over and talk to her."' He is received by Mrs Gibbons, dressed in a kimono that scarcely conceals her body. She looks depressed and unhappy but then, watching him staring at the bottle of beer beside her, 'she started to laugh a little, her whole body shaking'. He feels humiliated and ashamed by the spectacle before him, embarrassed and bewildered.

Some words did actually come into his head, but Mrs Gibbons, sitting up suddenly, stared at him and said flatly: 'Oh, he's too young. How do you expect me to talk to him?'

He leaves:

He was still breathing irregularly and feeling that he had been close to something immensely ugly and evil that had nearly overwhelmed him. He shook his head a little because he still wanted to go on thinking that Mrs Gibbons was one of the finest women in the parish, for his notion of what was good in the life in the parish seemed to depend upon such a belief. And as he walked slowly he felt, with a kind of desperate clarity, that really he had been always unimportant in the life around the Cathedral. He was still ashamed and had no joy at all now in being a young priest.

Beside this story may be set another, 'A Sick Call', about a priest summoned to a dying woman. This time, the priest is old.

... young girls who were in trouble, and wild but at times repentant young men, always wanted to tell their confessions to Father Macdowell, because nothing seemed to shock or excite him, or make him really angry, and he was even tender with those who thought they were most guilty.

The girl who comes to fetch him explains that the dying woman's husband is not a Catholic and will not want Father Macdowell to see his wife. And indeed the young man, who is not a believer and is hostile to the Church, is extremely unwilling that the priest should hear her confession.

'You don't understand, sir! We've been very happy together. Neither you nor her people came near her when she was in good health, so why should you bother her now? I don't want anything to separate us now; neither does she. She came with me. You see you'd be separating us, don't you?' He was trying to talk like a reasonable man who had no prejudices.

Father Macdowell got up clumsily. His knee hurt him, for the floor was hard. He said to Mrs Williams in quite a loud voice, 'Did you really intend to give up everything for this young fellow?' and he bent down close to her so he could hear.

'Yes, Father,' she whispered.

'In Heaven's name, child, you couldn't have known what you were doing.'

'We loved each other, Father. We've been very happy.'

'All right. Supposing you were. What now? What about all eternity, child?'

'Oh, Father, I'm very sick and I'm afraid.' She looked up to try to show him how scared she was, and how much she wanted him to give her peace.

He gets the young husband out of the room by pleading tiredness and asking for a glass of water. Then quickly he gives the young woman absolution. The young man comes back as he is making the sign of the cross over her. As he goes down the stairs to the street he wonders whether he has played fair with the young husband and whether he has come between them.

He shuffled along, feeling very tired, but he couldn't help thinking, 'What beauty there was to his staunch love for her!' Then he added quickly, 'But it was just a pagan beauty of course.'

As he began to wonder about the nature of this beauty, for some reason he felt inexpressibly sad.

'A Sick Call' is a beautiful example of Callaghan's art. His theme, one might say, is the responsive conscience, which is seen to be an instrument of extraordinary sensitivity and subtlety as it oscillates, before reaching a point of rest, between the bewildering discrepancies of life. The characters who possess these consciences seem to live in a kind of freedom that one realizes, since it is the essential condition of their being, is in fact the compassionate charity of Callaghan's mind.

Only relatively few of his stories, of course, deal with priests, but these stories are fundamentally different from those, for instance, by the American short-story writer J. F. Powers, who writes almost solely of priests. Powers writes of priests as of a special kind of man, as indeed they are. But what, whether deliberately or not, is emphasized in his stories are the secondary factors that distinguish priests from other men; he writes of priests, in other words, as he might write of soldiers, or firemen, or lighthouse-keepers, of men moulded to a special pattern by a life set apart by circumstances from ordinary life. This is the great value of Powers's stories; but it makes them quite unlike Callaghan's, in which the priestly conscience and the layman's function in identical ways, as one sees in examining the fine – perhaps his finest – story, 'A Cap for Steve', which begins with Callaghan's customary terseness and swiftness:

Dave Diamond, a poor man, a carpenter's assistant, was a small, wiry, quick-tempered individual who had learned how to make every dollar count in his home. His wife, Anna, had been sick a lot, and his twelve-year-old son, Steve, had to be kept in school. Steve, a big-eyed, shy kid, ought to have known the value of money as well as Dave did.

But the boy was crazy about baseball . . .

Callaghan is describing one of the oldest and most universal of situations, father and son at loggerheads because of the sense of responsibility engendered in the man by his experience and the boy's twelve-year-oldness. When a famous baseball team visits the town, Dave allows himself to be won over and, fighting his resentment, accompanies Steve to the ball-park.

As the game went on, Dave had to listen to Steve's recitation of the batting average of every Philly that stepped up to the plate; the time the boy must have wasted learning these averages began to appal him. He showed it so plainly that Steve felt guilty again, and was silent.

Then, when the game is over, Dave is dragged on to the field to keep the boy company while he tries to get autographs from the Philly players. A famous player drops his cap and when Steve gets possession of it and is unwilling to return it, he lets the boy keep it.

On the way home Dave couldn't get him to talk about the game; he couldn't get him to take his eyes off the cap. Steve could hardly believe in his own happiness. 'See,' he said suddenly, and he showed Dave that Eddie Condon's name was printed on the sweat-band. Then he went on dreaming. Finally he put the cap on his head and turned to Dave with a slow, proud smile. The cap was away too big for him; it fell down over his ears. 'Never mind,' Dave said. 'You can get your mother to take a tuck in the back.'

Boy and cap are inseparable, and over the days Dave's ex-asperation increases. Then one night Steve returns having lost it; for the past three hours he has been going round the houses of the boys on the park trying to find it. Dave is even more angry.

Two weeks later, while out with his father, Steve spots a boy wearing the cap he has lost. They challenge and accompany him to his house in a wealthy apartment block. The boy's father, a lawyer, is polite and affable but Dave feels at a disadvantage. The boy says he bought the cap for two dollars. Dave's pride is hurt because he senses that the father and son have decided that he is broke. He looks at Steve.

What he saw in Steve's face was more powerful than the hurt to his pride: it was the memory of how difficult it had been to get an extra nickel, the talk he heard about the cost of food, the worry in his mother's face as she tried to make ends meet, and the bewildering embarrassment that he was here in a rich man's home, forcing his father to confess that he could not afford to spend two dollars. Then Dave grew angry and reckless. 'I'll give you the two dollars', he said.

In the end, the lawyer offers Steve twenty dollars for the cap and Steve takes the money. Dave is overjoyed; the boy will be able to have a new windbreaker, and there'll still be ten dollars over for his bank. But outside, the boy repulses him and tries to walk home on the other side of the road. Once they are at home he goes into Steve's room and stumblingly apologizes to his son, admits his failure in understanding.

Steve, who had never heard his father talk like this, was shy and wondering . . . He said, 'I guess you do know how important that cap was.' His hand went out to his father's arm. 'With that man the cap was – well, it was just something he could buy, eh Dad?' Dave gripped his son's hand hard. The wonderful generosity of childhood – the price a boy was willing to pay to be able to count on his father's admiration and approval – made him feel humble, then strangely exalted.

This ending is an excellent example of what Wyndham Lewis meant when he wrote: 'Every one, or almost all, of these discrete miniature dramas ends softly and gently. At the end of some anguish there is peace; at the end of some bitter dispute there is reconciliation.' Callaghan's case is an object lesson on how a new literature may come into being. Canadian writing that went before him, concerned as it was with life in the wilds or with pastoral studies of life in Quebec or the maritime provinces, could offer little to a boy brought up in an urban spread like Toronto. As Wilson suggests, Chekhov is the source of Callaghan's art. By putting himself to school with the great Russian, he made himself a short-story writer belonging both to Canada and the world.

Moore and Joyce established part of the tradition of the Irish story, the most significant part, but still only a part. The provincial, indeed the parochial – and the words are used in no pejorative sense – always existed side by side with it. An instance is Daniel Corkery's story 'The Awakening'. Corkery was older than Joyce and survived him by more than twenty years. 'The Awakening' is the story of a young man coming into his own, assuming command of the family fishing boat. He goes down at night to look at the boat that is now his:

> With slow lingering steps, with stoppings and turnings, at last he too began to make towards his home. His head was flung up, almost flung back. More than once he told himself that he didn't ever remember the sky to have been so full of stars. Somehow he felt like raising his hand towards them.

The parochial can be the universal, and this is what makes Corkery's story admirable. It focuses on a single situation, a young man's solemn exhilaration in being accepted as a man, a special man at that, a skipper. Corkery's story is rooted deeply in an Irish community, yet the story cannot be compared with Moore's or Joyce's: it exists in a different world from theirs.

This quality of admirable parochialism, in which the limits of the parish suffice for the writer, may be found conspicuously in a later Irish writer, born thirty years after Corkery and comparable with him in no way except that they share a common honesty, a common accuracy in the rendering of what they have seen. Michael McLaverty is from the North of Ireland: his settings are County Antrim, Rathlin Island, and working-class, Catholic Belfast. His stories are very close to the grain of common experience and observation, and this is reflected in the texture of his prose, which is always concrete in its detail; as in the first paragraphs of the story 'The Prophet', in which a small boy persuades himself he can predict the weather:

> Brendan stood on the big stone near the byre, letting the rain splash

on his bare head and dribble down his face. It was cold standing bare-footed on the stone, but he didn't seem to mind, for now and again he'd stick out his tongue and catch the trickling drops. The byre door was open and the dark entrance showed the rain falling in grey streaks; it stuttered in the causeway, and trickled in a puddle around the stone carrying with it bits of straw and hens' feathers. Beside him was a steaming manure heap with a pitchfork sticking in the top, its handle varnished with the rain. Under a heeled-up cart stood hens, humped and bedraggled, their grey eyelids blinking slowly with sleep.

Brendan shouted at them and laughed at the way they stretched their necks and shook the rain off their feathers. He waited until they hunched again to sleep and then he let out another yell followed by louder laughs. A white duck clattering from behind the byre caught his attention. It stopped, looking from side to side, then it flapped its wings and quacked loudly. Brendan thought this was a sign for the rain to stop and he clodded the duck with a few lumps of turf. He looked up at the sky and out to sea. The sky was grey; the Mull of Kintyre was smothered in fog; and turning round he saw a tonsure of mist on Knocklayde. He smiled at the prospect of more rain.

That is excellent writing. It is the prose of a man who has *looked* at things; and reading McLaverty, one is struck by the freshness of observation and the consequent freshness of imagery. The least pretentious of writers, his exactness is such as to enable him to capture the particularity of experience. This serves him especially well when he is writing from the point of view of a child, as in 'The Prophet' or 'A Game Cock'.

But the most clear example of the provincial, the parochial, in the Irish story is Liam O'Flaherty. In his introduction to his anthology *Modern Irish Short Stories*, Frank O'Connor makes a comparison between Moore's 'Home-Sickness' and O'Flaherty's 'Going into Exile', in which he says: 'O'Flaherty ignores everything but the nature of exile itself: a state of things like love and death that all men must in some way endure.' This is true. Whatever else he may have been, Moore was not an Irish peasant, and in a sense 'Home-Sickness' is a dramatization of a theory of Irish exile, which, examined objectively, scarcely stands up. Was clerical authoritarianism a serious cause of Irish exile? It may have been for Moore himself, if he is seen as an exile and not merely an absentee landlord. But, for the peasant it seems doubtful, whereas there can be no doubt about the effect of poverty and landlessness.

With O'Flaherty's story, the question does not arise at all: O'Flaherty simply describes a fact of life. Michael Feeney and his sister Mary are going into exile, going to the United States, and the eve of their departure is the occasion of a dance, a dance which could be thought of as a wake.

> Towards dawn, when the floor was crowded with couples, arranged in fours, stamping on the floor and going to and fro, dancing the 'Walls of Limerick', Feeney was going out to the gable when his son Michael followed him out. The two of them walked side by side about the yard over the grey sea pebbles that had been strewn there the previous day. They walked in silence and yawned without need, pretending to be taking the air. But each one of them was very excited. Michael was taller than his father and not so thickly built, but the shabby blue serge suit that he had bought for going to America was too narrow for his broad shoulders and the coat was too wide around the waist. He moved clumsily in it and his hands were altogether too bony and big and red, and he didn't know what to do with them. During his twenty-five years of life he had never worn anything other than the homespun clothes of Inverara, and the shop-made clothes appeared as strange to him and as uncomfortable as a dress suit worn by a man working in a sewer. His face was flushed a bright red and his blue eyes shone with excitement. Now and again he wiped the perspiration from his forehead with the lining of a grey tweed cap.

'Going into Exile' is a moving story precisely for what it does not say. Michael scarcely knows the meaning of exile. For him, it is an exciting event, an initiation into manhood even though his blue serge suit is shabby and does not fit. As for Mary, she keeps

> thinking feverishly of the United States, at one moment with fear and loathing, at the next with desire and longing. Unlike her brother she did not think of the work she was going to do or the money she was going to earn. Other things troubled her, things of which she was half ashamed, half afraid, thoughts of love and of foreign men and of clothes and of houses where there were more than three rooms and where people ate meat every day.

For the parents, it is different: they know they may never see their children again.

What O'Flaherty does is to dramatize the experience of the moment of departure into exile. There is no comment, either direct or implied. 'Going into Exile' is a much more highly organized story than, say, O'Flaherty's 'The Cow's Death' but, apart from this, there is little significant difference between his stories of animals and those of human beings. 'The Cow's Death' describes, again without comment of any kind, how a cow that has delivered a dead calf, the body of which has been tossed over the cliff, plunges over it herself in pursuit of her offspring. O'Flaherty's animals are not anthropomorphized; rather, men and animals seem to exist in the same context of nature where differentiation is comparatively rudimentary. At times, O'Flaherty achieves stories of great lyrical intensity: one admires them individually but finds oneself in the end asking: Yes, but where is the interest, what the significance? Something is missing, the interpretive mind.

This cannot be said at all of the stories of O'Flaherty's younger contemporaries Sean O'Faolain and Frank O'Connor. They belong to the immediately post-Joyce generation in Ireland and write, often, in reaction against Joyce. Both, as very young men, were soldiers in the Irish Republican Army in the wars against the British and the Free State alike, both, afterwards, changed their political positions. In their different fields, they were scholars of distinction who taught in American universities. Between them they have done more than any other writers since Joyce to interpret Ireland to the outside world.

All this is to make the point that O'Faolain and O'Connor were men who maintained what Matthew Arnold called the tone of the centre. They knew London, Paris, and New York and what was going on there as well as they knew Dublin. This means that though their work is deeply rooted in the Irish experience of this century it is not provincial or parochial in any sense at all. As short-story writers, they were very conscious that they belonged to a company that included Chekhov and Maupassant and Kipling. In other words, they belonged to modern literature, which is world literature.

There is an interesting passage in O'Faolain's introduction to the 1958 edition of his collected stories. Having noted that when he began to write he was a very romantic young man – and, incidentally, his early work contains some fascinating stories of the Civil War in Ireland written in a tone of romantic disillusionment – he says:

... by the time I had more or less adjusted myself to the life about me, it suddenly broke in on me that Ireland had not adjusted herself to the life about her in the least little bit. Irishmen in general were still thinking about themselves, or rather, in their usual way, double-thinking or squint-thinking about themselves, in terms of *dawns*, and *ands*, and *buts*, and *onwards*, and *dew*, and *dusk*, while at the same time making a lot of good, hard cash to the evocative vocabulary of *tariff*, *tax*, *protection*, *quota*, *levy*, *duties*, or *subsidies*, meanwhile carefully compiling a third and wholly different literary style (*pious*, *holy*, *prudent*, *sterling*, *gorsoons*, *lassie*, *maids*, *sacred*, *traditional*, *forefathers*, *mothers*, *grandmothers*, *ancestors*, *deep-rooted*, *olden*, *venerable*, *traditions*, *Gaelic*, *timeworn*, and *immemorial*) to dodge more awkward social, moral, and political problems than any country might, with considerable courage, hope to solve in a century of ruthless thinking. This ambivalence, once perceived, demanded a totally new approach. I have been trying to define it ever since.

At the same time as helping to define O'Faolain's own attitude towards writing and its results, this passage obviously carries a tone of criticism of Ireland and the Irish that is echoed in the stories. But it is not an uncompromising or hostile criticism. There are stories, 'Unholy Living and Half Dying' and 'Childybaun', for example, which in many ways are reminiscent of some of the stories in *Dubliners*, but always in the end O'Faolain flinches from Joyce's style of scrupulous meanness. This humour, or lingering sentimentality appears particularly in his stories of priests and nuns, but poking fun at priests is a traditional Irish pastime, and these stories strike one as doing little more than falling into the convention. In the end, O'Faolain's attitude is very much that of the curate in 'The Man Who Invented Sin'. Censorious and stern as a young priest, the curate is met several years later by the narrator:

When I spoke to him and he turned, the sunlight struck his rosy face and lit the sides of his hat so that they glowed and shone. With difficulty I brought his mind back to those years, but when I did he greeted me as heartily as if I was his best friend, and laughed so merrily at the memory of those old days that I almost expected him to clap me on the back.

'Of course, you know,' he confided with wide eyes, 'they were only children. Such innocents!' He laughed at the thought of the innocents. 'Of course, I *had* to frighten them!' And he laughed again, and then threw up his head and said 'Heigh-ho' in a big sigh. Then he shook my hand, and beamed at me, told me I was looking grand, and went his cheerful way. He bowed benevolently to every respectful salute along the glowing street, and, when he did, his elongated shadow waved behind him like a tail.

'The Man Who Invented Sin' is a highly successful and delightful story. It makes its criticism much less intransigently than the stories of Moore or Joyce.

In O'Faolain's stories, in the scenes, situations, and characters involved in them, there is constant ambivalence; his critical stance is always shifting under pressure of nostalgia and regret. This is a source of strength to him as a short-story writer. It gives his best stories a quality of mystery that is disturbing. This comes out particularly in the story 'Lovers at the Lake', which is a love story and also a story about religion.

In it, the lovers are Flannery, a distinguished Dublin surgeon, a lapsed Catholic, a scientist, a free-thinker, and his mistress, Jenny, a middle-class married woman, childless, who still keeps up minimum religious duties. They are 'modern', worldly people; and the genuineness of their love for each other is beautifully conveyed throughout the story. She asks him to drive her to Lough Derg, in the west of Ireland, which is depicted as a place of forbidding pilgrimage, barbarous in its medieval masochism. Flannery reacts to it in this way. He expostulates:

'But what I can't get over is that this thing you're doing is so utterly extravagant. To go off to an island, in the middle of a lake, in the mountains, with a lot of Crawthumpers of every age and sex, and peel off your stockings and your shoes, and go limping about on your bare feet on a lot of sharp stones, and kneel in the mud, psalming and beating your breast like a criminal, and drink nothing for three days but salt water. . . .'

Nevertheless, he drives her to the island. Their relationship, the recognition each one has of the limits of his claims on the other, is finely and scrupulously rendered.

At the end of the first night, in the pouring rain,

She completed the second circle. Her prayers were become dumb by now. She stumbled, muttering them, up and down the third steeply sloped cell, or bed. She was a drenched cat, and one knee was bleeding. At the fourth cell she saw him.

Flannery too, almost it seems in ironical sympathy with her, is making the pilgrimage, which is a trial by endurance.

After their three days, Flannery and Jenny drive to a hotel and to their separate rooms. We know, though it is not explicitly stated, that their ten years love-affair is over, though not their love for each other.

'Lovers at the Lake' is mysterious and disturbing, but the details of the ordeal are vivid enough to overcome the reader's intellectual disbelief. The story is convincing in a way that the fiction, when explicitly Catholic, of Graham Greene for instance, is not.

O'Faolain is a romantic writer: Frank O'Connor is very much less so. The difference between them is clear when one compares their stories of the Civil War. O'Faolain's stories are about the sensibility of a lone young man oppressed by his disillusionment, striving to salvage something from it, oppressed too by his feeling that the Republican cause has failed and has in some sense been betrayed, along with his idealism. O'Connor's stories are much more of men living in a community, the community of the military life. In 'Guests of the Nations', two British soldiers, held prisoner by the I.R.A., establish human relations with their captors and are later shot as hostages. In 'Freedom', a young I.R.A. man held by the Free State forces revolts against the conditions of military life; and at the end his friend, the narrator, reflects:

Choice was an illusion. Seeing that a man can never really get out of jail, the great thing is to ensure that he gets into the biggest possible one with the largest possible range of modern amenities.

The attitude is one of realistic acceptance of actual conditions, whatever the nature of a man's political ideals; and these Civil War stories of O'Connor's are illumined with a large humanity. Although the stories are of the military life, beyond that they are metaphors for the condition of life itself.

O'Connor's stories about children, such as 'My Oedipus Complex', 'My Da', and 'Old Fellows' have been greatly admired but seem to me less satisfactory. One assumes they are autobiographical, but they would be better if they were less indulgent. O'Connor has often been compared to Chekhov, and the comparison seems to have been first made by Yeats, though he was probably merely applying to O'Connor the name of the first famous short-story writer that came into his head. All the same, what is often considered O'Connor's finest story, 'The Holy Door', is also the most Chekhovian.

It could be construed as a story critical of Irish life and in part it is: a dramatized comment of priest-induced sexual repression. It begins with a delightfully funny conversation between two provincial middle-class girls, Polly Donegan and Nora Lawlor, after eight o'clock Mass.

Now Nora ... had a knack which Polly found very disconcerting of bringing the conversation round to the facts of life. To Nora the facts of life were the ultimate invitation; acceptance meant never-ending embarrassment, refusal a curiosity unsatisfied till death. While she struggled to put her complex in words, Polly adopted a blank and polite air, retreated into her own thoughts of what they should have for dinner ...

Nora could see that Polly wasn't even interested in the facts of life. She wondered a lot about that. Was Polly natural? Was it possible not to be curious? Was she only acting sly like all the Donegans? Nora had thought so long about God's inscrutable purpose in creating mankind in two sexes that she could hardly see the statue of a saint without wondering what he'd be like without clothes. That was no joke in our church, where there are statues inside the door and in each of the side chapels and along the columns of the arcade. It made the church quite gay, but it was a terrible temptation to Nora, who found it hard not to see them all like Greek statues, and whatever it was about their gestures they seemed worse like that than any Greek divinities. To the truly pious mind there is something appalling in the idea of St Aloysius Gonzaga without his clothes.

That particular notion struck Polly as the height of nonsense.

The ensuing conversation centres on the subject of what happens on the wedding night and it ends with the girls promising each other that if she is married first she will divulge the mysterious secret. '"Oh, I will to be sure, girl," said Polly in the tone of one promising to let her know when the coalman came.'

Nora finds herself courted by Charlie Cashman, who was her father's commanding officer in the Volunteers during The Troubles. He is what is called a good catch but Nora decides he is 'sensual, flighty'. He asks her if she has read *Romeo and Juliet*:

'As a matter of fact, I have,' she said steadily.

'What did you think of it?' he asked.

'I thought it contained a striking moral lesson,' said Nora.

'Go on!' Charlie exclaimed with a grin. 'What was that, Nora?'

'It shows where unrestrained passion can carry people,' said Nora.

'Ah, I wouldn't notice that,' said Charlie. 'Your father and myself were a bit wild, too, in our time.'

Rejected by Nora, Charlie marries Polly, who, of course, refuses to tell Nora what happened on the wedding night: 'I don't think it can ever be right to talk about things like that.' She dislikes sex but wants a child. When there are no signs of that appearing she and Charlie go to Rome to walk through the Holy Door, which is opened one day in seven years and is very efficacious in the promotion of pregnancy. But all that Polly brings back from Rome is 'her astonishment at the way the men in St. Peter's pinched her bottom'.

Charlie, who throughout is presented as a perfectly decent man, solaces himself with the servant girl, who is immediately pregnant. He is then in total disgrace. Polly dies; and with the aid of the parish priest, Charlie once again proposes to Nora, and this time he will be accepted.   'The Holy Door' is a wonderfully rich and warm story. If it is critical of Irish morality, the criticism is affectionate. A possible sub-title for it might be that of *Madame Bovary*, 'Moeurs de Province'. By implication, 'The Holy Door' presents in detail and sums up life in a provincial Irish town from the point of view of a singularly humane mind that is both of it and outside it.

The Welsh language possesses one of the longest literary traditions in Europe, and its literature still flourishes. But writing in
what is called Anglo-Welsh, the English of Welshmen, is now a
recognized sub-division of literature in English, like Anglo-Irish.
According to Gwyn Jones in his introduction to *Welsh Short
Stories*, later Anglo-Welsh writers have found it difficult to
fight clear of the shape and style that became characteristic of
the Welsh short story in English in the nineteen-twenties and
thirties. If this is so, it is due in all likelihood to the enormous
influence of the founding father of the Anglo-Welsh story,
Caradoc Evans, whose collection of stories *My People* appeared
in 1915.

Its effect in Wales was astonishing. It must have come as
something like a declaration of war. It was much misunderstood.

Among the more notable and lasting errors were the assumption of the
city-bred that Caradoc was a realistic portrayer of the countryside; the
belief of all to whom Wales is more remote and less understood than
Tibet that he was a realistic portrayer of the Welsh; the suspicion of
many Welshmen that he was a malignant, blasphemous, and obscure
person holding up his fellow-countrymen to the derision of the English; and the curious notion that he was an illiterate buffoon who had
murdered the English and Welsh languages because he knew no better.
All these errors were the more deadly for their tincture of truth, and
Caradoc's reaction to them was uniformly mischievous.

I quote from Professor Gwyn Jones. The English may find
Evans a difficult writer and certainly not an immediately attractive one, for he describes a people who, in Gwyn Jones's words,
'are elementals, stripped to the very fork, and at one with the soil
and the beasts. The mainsprings of their actions are greed, hypocrisy, and lust.' They were in fact the Welsh-speaking peasantry
of West Wales, and Evans found the medium through which he
narrated their actions in a combination of the Book of Genesis in
the Authorized Version and the narrative art of the music hall
actress Marie Lloyd, who, he said, 'tells a story not by what she

says but by what she says not'. It is in his characteristic practice
of compression and ellipsis that difficulties begin to arise; but
there are also the constant and 'perversely literal translations
(which are therefore mistranslations) of Welsh idiom' which,
according to Jones, 'are exactly designed to lay bare the mental
processes of the spiritual troglodytes who inhabit the stories and
give them a savour all their own'. Altogether, the style through
which we see his characters is an exceedingly powerful element
of refraction which produces the effect of the grotesque at the
same time as it formalizes.

Evans's work is of a piece and any one story of his will
represent him as well as another. I have chosen 'Joseph's House',
from the volume *My Neighbours*. A widow named Madlen, who
lives at Penlan, is worried about the future of her son Joseph.
She thinks it 'unbecoming to his Nuncle Essec that he follows
low tasks'. She therefore takes Joseph to the chapel at Mount
Moriah, where her husband's brother Essec is minister.

'Your help I seek,' she said.

'Poor is the reward of the Big Preacher's son in this part,' Essec
announced. 'A lot of atheists they are.'

'Not pleading I have not the rent am I', said Madlen. 'How if I
prentice Joseph to a shop draper. Has he any odds?'

'Proper that you seek,' replied Essec. 'Seekers we all are. Sit you. No
room there is for Joseph now that I am selling Penlan.'

'Like that is the plan of your head?' Madlen murmered, concealing
her dread.

'Seven pounds of rent is small. Sell at eighty I must.'

'Wait for Joseph to prosper. Buy then he will. Buy for your mam
you will, Joseph?'

'Sorry I cannot change my think,' Essec declared.

'Hard is my lot; no male have I to ease my burden.'

'A weighty responsibility my brother put on me,' said Essec.
'"Dying with old decline I am"', the brother mouthed. "Fruitful is the
soil. Watch Madlen keeps her fruitful." But I am generous. Eight shall
be the rent. Are you not the wife of my flesh?'

After that she had wiped away her tears. 'Be kind,' said Madlen, 'and
wisdom it to Joseph.'

When he is fourteen Joseph goes to the drapery shop of Rees
Jones in Carmarthan. He does well and moves on to a 'very busy
emporium' in Swansea for twenty pounds a year. 'Pounds with-

out number he is earning,' boasts Madlen. To which Essec retorts: 'Gifts from the tip of my tongue fell on him. Religious were my gifts,' and raises the rent of Penlan to nine pounds. Joseph begins to save in order to buy Penlan and, deciding that 'footling is he that is content with Zwanssee', gets a job in Cardiff.

Pleading the necessity of poverty, Essec puts the price of Penlan up again. Madlen writes to Joseph. 'Horrid,' she says, 'that your mam must go to the House of the Poor.' Joseph sends her ten pounds, which leaves him three shillings. 'Give Nuncle the ten as earnest of my attentions.'

Nine years after the day he had gone to Carmarthen he says to himself, 'London shops for experience,' and gets a job in a shop in the West End at thirty pounds a year. As he reports to Madlen:

'Fashionable this shop is, and I have to be smart and wear a coat like preachers, and mustn't take more than three swap lines a day or you have the sack. Two white shirts per week; and the dresses of the show-room young ladies are a treat. Five pounds enclosed for Nuncle.'

His mind is wholly on Penlan and his mother's welfare; he neglects himself, becomes tubercular, and begins to steal money daily from his employers. Every night he makes his peace with God: 'Don't let me be found out, Big Man bach. Will you strike mam into her grave? And disgrace Respected Essec Pugh Capel Moriah?' Frightened that his customers may complain because of his sickness, he increases his pilfering, and when he has five pounds more than the sum needed to buy the house, 'he heaved a deep sigh and said: "Thank you for your favour, God bach. I will now go home and heal myself."'

He goes home and Madlen takes the money to Nuncle. She comes back with the news that it is enough only for the land and that Essec is selling the house. Joseph is too weak to go to Moriah and advises her to go instead, to try to soften Nuncle's heart by telling him that his nephew's funeral is near. Madlen puts on her mourning clothes and tarries in a field as long as it would take her to have travelled to Moriah. She returns laughing, telling Joseph that she had made a mistake and that the house was theirs. 'Cross was your Nuncle. "Terrible if Joseph is

bad with me," he said. "Man religious and tidy is Essec."' And
she prays that Joseph will die before her fault is found out.

The story ends:

> Joseph did not know what to do for his joy. 'Well – well, there's better
> I am already,' he said. He walked over the land and coveted the land of
> his neighbours. 'Dwell here for ever I shall,' he cried to Madlen. 'A
> grand house I'll build – almost as grand as the houses of the preachers.'
>
> On the fifth night he died, and before she began to weep, Madlen
> lifted her voice: 'There's silly, dear people, to covet houses! Only a
> smallish bit of house we want.'

This is a more genial story than those of *My People* and harks
back to a theme that transcends the merely local. And it is more
obviously humorous. All the same, this does not prevent the
story being a chilling exposure of overweening greed and hypocrisy, in which all the characters, widowed mother, tubercular
son, and holy man uncle, are caught.

Rhys Davies was born in the Rhondda Valley twenty-five
years after Evans and was therefore a boy when *My People* was
published. Its influence on him is obvious, though he is plainly
warmer and a much less intransigent hater than Evans; he is
aware of the eccentricity of his characters rather than of their
vices. He has a very revealing generalization, which is also psychologically brilliant, in his story 'The Dilemma of Catherine
Fuchsias':

> A bad shock can work wonders with a person's sensibility. Buried ta-
> lents can be whisked up into activity, a primitive cunning reign again in
> its shady empire of old instincts. Or such a shock can create – women
> especially being given to escape into this – a fantasy of bellicose truth,
> a performance of the imagination that has nothing to do with hypocrisy
> but is the terrified soul backing away from reality.

Such a shock assails Catherine Fuchsias. The story begins:

> Puffed up by his success as a ship-chandler in the port forty miles
> away, where he had gone from the village of Banog when the new town
> was rising to its heyday as the commercial capital of Wales, Lewis had
> retired to the old place heavy with gold and fat. With him was the
> bitter English wife he had married for her money, and he built the
> pink-washed villa overlooking Banog's pretty trout stream. And later he
> had set up a secret association with an unmarried woman who was

usually called Catherine Fuchsias, this affair – she receiving him most
Sunday evenings after chapel in her outlying cottage – eluding public
notice for two years. Until on one of these evenings, Lewis, who for
some weeks had been complaining of a 'feeling of fullness', expired in
her arms on the bed.

This opening, incidentally, is an excellent example of what
Davies means when he writes, in the preface of his collected
stories: 'That instinct to *dive*, swift and agile, into the opening of
a story holds, for me, half the technical art; one must not on any
account loiter or brood in the first paragraph; be deep in the
story's elements in a few seconds.' It is an excellent example,
too, of the amount of information he can pack into a single
paragraph and yet keep it light.

When her paramour died on her bed she at first refused to believe it, so
pertinacious and active was he and so unlike her idea of a man of sixty-
four. Nevertheless, she ran howling downstairs. There she madly poked
the fire, flung the night cloth over the canary's cage, ran into the kitchen and swilled a plate or two in a bowl, straightened a mat, and tidied
her hair.

She fills the kettle and lights the cooker. She goes to the stairs
and calls: 'Mr Lewis . . . Mr Lewis, here I am! Just put the kettle
on. Time's going on. Come down straight away.' When he
doesn't, she shouts: 'I'll go for a walk, that's what I'll do. And
don't you be here when I'm back.' She goes out and slams the
door behind her, deciding to go mushrooming. When she does
get back,

'Well, Mr Lewis,' she exclaimed loudly, 'better you are after the
rest?' She went close to the bed and peered down at the stout dusky
figure lying on the patchwork quilt. 'Well now, I am not liking the look
of you at all,' she addressed it, half scoldingly. 'What have you taken
your jacket off for? Hot you were? Dear me, quite bad you look. Best
for me to fetch your wife and the doctor. But you mustn't lie there
with your coat off or a cold you will be catching.' Volubly tut-tutting,
she lit a candle and set about the task.

With great effort she gets his jacket on, drops his umbrella
beside the bed, places his hat on the bedside table, and lays his
hymn-book on the quilt as though it has dropped from his
hand. And all the while she utters 'clamorous remarks of distress
at this condition':

'Oh, Mr Lewis, you didn't ought to have taken a walk, unwell like you are. Climbing! Lucky I saw you leaning over my gate. Dropped dead in the road you might have, and stayed there all night and got buried by the stoats! You rest quiet now, and I won't be long.'

She places a glass of water by the bedside, dashes out and in half an hour is banging on the door of the pink villa, calling excitedly; 'Mrs Lewis, come to your husband . . . Put you hat on quick, Mrs Lewis, and tell Milly Jones to go to Dr Watkins.' They arrived at the cottage:

'You ought to have left a light for him,' remarked Mrs Lewis on the landing.

'What if he had tumbled and set the bed on fire!' said Catherine indignantly. In the heavily silent room she struck a match and lit the candle. 'Oh!' she shrieked.

Mrs Lewis stood staring through her glasses. And then, in a strangely fallen voice, said, 'John! . . . John!' Catherine covered her face with her hands, crying in a dramatic woe. 'Hush, *woman* . . . hush,' said Mrs Lewis sternly.

Catherine moved her hands from her face and glared. *Woman*, indeed! But all she said was: 'Well, Mrs Lewis, enough it is to upset anyone with a soft heart when a stranger dies in her house. . . . Why,' she began insidiously, 'was he wandering in the lanes all by himself in his bad state? Poor man, why is it he didn't go home after chapel? Wandering lost outside my gate like a lonely orphan child!'

So the story goes on, with Catherine developing her fantasy of justification, innocence, and persecution. She develops pains in her back, 'so heavy was poor Mr Lewis to take up my stairs'. And when Mr Lewis's will is read it is found that he has left her three hundred pounds, because, as Vaughan Solicitor says, 'your cleaning wage was so small and you were a good worker'. She decides to live in Aberystwyth and invest it in a boarding house there. But she is ostracized by the ladies of Banog, and the story ends with an unpleasant encounter in the post office.

'Two stamps.' The postmistress flung them down grudgingly at last, and took up Catherine's coin as if she was picking up a rotten mouse by the tail. 'Wishing you'd buy your stamps somewhere else.'

Catherine, after licking and sticking them, seemed to regain strength as she walked to the door, remarked haughtily:

'There's wicked jealousy when a person is left money! Jealous you are not in my shoes, now *and* before.'

But, rightly, the postmistress had the last word: 'A cousin I have in Aberystwyth. Wife of a busy minister that is knowing everybody there. A letter I must write to Aberystwyth too.'

'The Dilemma of Catherine Fuchsias' is a brilliant psychological comedy in which puritanism is set against the sensual. The relatively complex and highly-wrought nature of the language suggests that not far behind the story lies a powerful oral tradition. The 'perversely literal translations' of Welsh idiom however, like 'Mrs Lewis is a nasty', strike us after a first meeting as too easy and self-conscious. This exploitation of the local for a London audience is a temptation that regional writers traditionally have found difficult to resist. One remembers Arnold Bennett with 'The Matador of the Five Towns' and 'The Death of Simon Fuge'. But one remembers also that one of the great strengths of *The Old Wives' Tale* and *Clayhanger* is the sense we have that in them the folk memory of the region is being tapped. It is as though a whole community has become articulate in the author. We feel this, too, in Rhys Davies's stories, in 'The Dilemma of Catherine Fuchsias', and in what is perhaps his best-known story, 'Canute', in which we can watch a new folk tale coming into being.

'Canute' among other things is a celebration of the South Wales man's passionate enthusiasm for Rugby football and his passionate partisanship at the annual matches between Wales and England. Rowland is one of the contingent going up to London that Friday midnight from Pleasant Row, 'a respectable road of houses leading up to a three-shafted coal-mine'. He leaves his house in Twlldu:

'Now be careful you don't lose your head, Rowland!' fretted his wife on their doorstep. 'You take things quiet and behave yourself. Remember your trouble.' The 'trouble' was a hernia, the result of Rowland rescuing his neighbour, Dicky Corner House, from a fall of roof in the pit.

Rowland travels on the crowded excursion train with Dicky. They reach Paddington at 4 a.m. and wander the streets waiting for opening-time, though Rowland says austerely: 'We have come to see the International, not to drink. Plenty of beer in Wales.' Seeing that admission was free, they go into the National Gallery.

It was the Velasquez 'Venus' that arrested their full attention. 'The artist', observed Emlyn Chrysanthemums – he was called that because he was a prize-winner of them in a home-made glasshouse – 'was clever to make her turn her back to us. A bloke that knew what was tidy.'

'Still,' said Rowland, 'he ought to have thrown a towel or something across her, just by her –'

'Looking so alive it is,' Ivor breathed in admiration, 'you could smack it, just by here –'

An attendant said: 'Do not touch the paintings.'

'What's the time?' Dicky Corner House asked the attendant. 'Are the pubs open yet?'

'A disgrace he is,' said Rowland sharply as the contingent went out. 'He ought to have stayed at home.'

The game itself is disposed of in a paragraph, and in the paragraph that follows we are back in Paddington Station at a quarter to midnight; the big clock's face stares over the station 'like an amazed moon'. The trains that left were like ambulance trains. But men still kept pouring into the station.

Elsewhere, an entwined group of young men sang *Mochyn Du* with an orderly sweetness in striking contrast to their mien; a flavour of pure green hills and neat little farm-houses was in their song about a black pig. On adjacent platforms other groups in the victorious concourse sang *Sospan Fach* and even a hymn. As someone said, if you shut your eyes you could fancy yourself in an eisteddfod.

In the gentlemen's lavatory on No. 1 platform, however, the drains have clogged; men going down the steps find the floor at the bottom covered by water to a depth of several inches.

. . . within the deserted convenience one man was marooned over that sheet of water. He sat on the shoe-shine throne which, resting on its dais, was raised safely – up to the present – above water. With head lolling on his shoulder he sat fast asleep, at peace, comfortable in the full-sized armchair . . .

'Who does he think he is,' someone else exclaimed in an English voice – 'King Canute?'

The man goes on sleeping, and his fame spreads along the plat-

forms. Sam Recitations, the smoking concert elocutionist from
Twlldu, recognizes him and makes his way to the Pleasant Row
contingent.

'I've seen him!' he yelled. 'Your Rowland! He isn't lost – he's down
in the men's place under Number 1, and they can't budge him. People
calling him King Canute — ... He's down in the Gents under Number
1,' Sam howled despairingly. 'English strangers poking fun at him and
water rising up! He'll be drowned same as when the Cambrian pit was
flooded.' He beat his chest as if he was giving a ballad in a concert.
'Ten minutes and the train will be in! And poor Rowland sitting helpless and the water rising round him like on the sands of Dee!'

A deputation from the Pleasant Row contingent goes to the convenience to wake him up. But in vain. It falls to Dicky Corner
House to pay his debt. With a sudden dramatic cry he leaps into
the water, plunges across to the throne, and bears Rowland
across his shoulders to safety.

Some weeks later, Rowland's wife finds out from a neighbour
why people now call him Canute. She is outraged. She 'pursed
her lips like a pale tulip, opening them hours later to shout as
Rowland tramped in from the pit':

'Ah, *Canute*, is it! ... Sitting there in the London place', she
screamed, 'and all those men —' She whipped about like a hailstorm.
'You think I'm going to stay in Twlldu to be called Mrs Rowland
Canute, do you? We'll have to move from here – you begin looking for
work in one of the other valleys at once.'

A couple of months later, they move to the Powell pit in the
Cwm Mardy valley over the mountains, and almost the first man
Rowland meets in the bar-room in Cwm Mardy is Sam Recitations, come to give selections from his repertoire at a smoking
concert.

'Why, now,' his voice rolled in delight, 'if it isn't Rowland Canute! Ha,
ha —' And not noticing Rowland's dropped jaw of dismay, he turned
and told all the clustering men what had happened under Paddington
platform that time after the famous International – just as the history
of the rescue had been told in all the clubs in the valley away over the
mountains.

Davies's first books, a novel and a volume of short stories,
appeared as long ago as 1927, and since then he has published

thirteen other novels and almost as many collections of stories. In many stories, one cannot but be aware that Davies is attempting too much and he falls into romantic excesses of language and situation. In the end, his finest story is probably 'Nightgown', which, though its background is that of the Welsh pits, is not a humorous story. It is a fable, and, better than anything else he has written, it shows what he learned from D. H. Lawrence, who was, apart from Caradoc Evans, the greatest single influence on him.

It begins:

> She had married Walt after a summer courtship during which they had walked together in a silence like aversion.
> Coming of a family of colliers, too, the smell of the hulking young man tramping to her when she stepped out of an evening was the sole smell of men. He would have the faintly scowling look which presently she, too, acquired. He half resented having to go about this business, but still his feet impelled him to her street corner and made him wait until, close-faced and glancing sideways threateningly, she came out of her father's house. They walked wordless on the grit beside the railway track, his mouth open as though in a perpetual yawn.

With the fourth paragraph we are in the heart of the story:

> The big sons had arrived with unchanging regularity, each of the same heavy poundage. When the sex of the fifth was told her, she turned her face sullenly to the wall and did not look at him for some time. And he was her last. She was to have no companionable daughter after all, to dote on when the men were in the pit. As the sons grew, the house became so obstreperously male that she began to lose nearly all feminine attributes and was apt to wear a man's cap and her sons' shoes, socks, and mufflers to run out to the shop. Her expression became tight as a fist, her jaw jutted out like her men's, and like them she only used her voice when it was necessary, though sometimes she would clang out at them with a criticism they did not understand. They would only scowl the family scowl.

It seems right that we never learn the woman's Christian name, though we know her husband's and that of at least one of her sons, for we are concerned with the fate of woman in a wholly male world, of woman oppressed by maleness.

> Gathered in their pit-dirt for the important four o'clock meal, with bath pans and hot food steaming in the fireplace, the little kitchen was

crowded as the Black Hole of Calcutta. None of the sons, not even the eldest, looked like marrying, though sometimes, like a shoving parent bird, she would try to push them out of the nest. One or two of them set up brief associations with girls which never seemed to come properly to anything. They were of the kind that never marry until the entertainments of youth, such as football, whippet-racing, and beer, have palled at last. She would complain to her next-door-up neighbour that she had no room to put down even a thimble.

Her one pleasure is to stop for a moment at the draper's on the corner of the main road and peer into the window

where two wax women, one fair and one dark, stood dressed in all the latest and smiling a pink, healthy smile. . . . They had no big men to feed and, poised in their eternal shade, smiled leisurely above their furs and silk blouses.

She is fifty when she has her revelation. One morning, looking in the draper's window,

she was startled to find the fair wax lady attired in a wonderful white silk nightgown, flowing down over the legs most richly and trimmed with lace at bosom and cuffs. That anyone could wear such luxuriance in bed struck her at first like a blow in the face. Besides, it was a shock to see the grand lady standing there undressed, as you might say, in public. But, staring into the window, she was suddenly thrilled.

She went home feeling this new luxury round her like a sweet, clean silence. Where no men were.

She overcomes the reluctance of the draper to let her buy the nightgown by instalments and manages to pay for it in a year. She hides it in a parcel in a drawer which the men never use. The following Easter she is taken ill, and her neighbour Mrs Lewis, who has been given her instructions weeks before, takes over. She calls the husband and sons up to the bedroom:

They slunk up in procession, six big men, with their heads ducked, disturbed out of the rhythm of their daily life of work, food, and pub. And entering the room for the last view, they stared in surprise.

A stranger lay on the bed ready for the coffin. A splendid, shiny, white silk nightgown flowing down over her feet, with rich lace frilling bosom and hands, she lay like a lady taking a rest, clean and comfortable. So much they stared, it might have been an angel shining there. But her face jutted stern, bidding no approach to the contented peace she had found.

The father said, cocking his head respectfully: 'There's a fine 'ooman she looks. Better than when I married her!'

The father tells the sons that 'the grand nightshirt . . . in with the medical benefits it is. Don't they dock us enough every week from our wages?' They file downstairs, where Mrs Lewis is waiting for them.

The father shakes his head, scowling in effort to concentrate on a new problem. Big, black-curled, and still vigorous, he sits among his five strapping sons who, like him, smell of the warm, dark energy of life. He said:

'A new missus I shall have to be looking for. Who is there about, Mrs Lewis, that is respectable and can cook for us and see to our washings? My boys I got to think about. A nice little widow or something you know of that would marry a steady working chap? A good home is waiting for her by here, though a long day it'll be before I find one that can feed and clean us like the one above; *she* worked regular as a clock, fair play to her.'

'I don't know as I would recommend any 'ooman,' said Mrs Lewis with rising colour.

'Pity you're not a widow! Ah well, I must ask the landlady of the Miskin if she knows of one,' he said, concentrated.

During the last half-century it has become increasingly difficult in writing in English to assign writers categorically to specific literatures. William Plomer wrote in his autobiography *Double Lives*: 'I should be no more justified in pretending to be a South African than in declaring myself a Bantu', for all that he was born in North Transvaal. Coming from what he called 'the stranded gentry', he was sent back to England to go to school at Rugby and then returned to South Africa at the age of sixteen to become first a farmer and then keeper of a native store in Zululand. After five years he came back to England by way of Japan. He had begun to write – poetry, novels, and short stories – and had founded and edited with Roy Campbell the literary magazine *Voorslag*. He remained in England for the rest of his life, a professional writer of great distinction.

Yet throughout his life he remained in some sense an amateur. In the introduction to his selected volume of short stories, *Four Countries*, he wrote: 'I cannot pretend that when I began writing fiction I had any cut-and-dried theory about the nature and art of the short story', and this is apparent in his work. Often, he does not seem quite to know what he is doing or trying to do. 'When the Sardines Came' is a case in point.

Mrs Reymond is the wife of an ex-officer, equable, and popular with the natives because she treats them fairly and kindly. Childless 'but obviously very happy', the Reymonds live in a sequestered retreat on the south coast of Natal. Indeed, they seem a model couple, 'until a slight restlessness in Mrs Reymond's behaviour becomes noticeable'. For his knowledge of this the narrator is indebted to a character called Edwards, a medical student, a kinsman of the Reymonds, with whom he is staying while studying for an examination.

Mrs Reymond's restlessness comes to a head with the coming of the sardines. Annually, immense shoals pass slowly up the coast, pursued by flocks of seabirds and predatory fish. Everyone for miles around comes to the beach to try and catch the sardines.

The excitement of the hour had already worked an extraordinary, an almost magical effect upon the minds of all these people – an effect as violent and as magical as upon the fish. Divided at all times by a thousand barriers, of race, of money, of caste, of class, of language, of pride and fear, but especially by various kinds of colour-bar – the Indians and natives living in mutual contempt, the 'coloured' people looking down on their darker neighbours, the whites and near-whites looking down on everybody else, and being, in consequence, for the most part mistrusted in their turn – divided like this at all times, they were now, quite surprisingly, all brought to a level. Just as enemies will unite in a common fear of a common danger, so they will sometimes be united by something which makes an appeal to any emotion as primitive as fear – by a promise, for example, of something for nothing. In this case, one rather heavy touch of nature had made the whole world kin.

It is in these circumstances that Edwards watches Mrs Reymond fall in love with a twenty-year-old White Russian boy who is fishing with the others. He has a fish on his line that seemed to the heightened imaginations of the onlookers as big as a dolphin, and, the better to fight it, he leaps on to a high rock. He tumbles off it into the sea and is picked up with a badly cut leg and a fractured foot. Put to bed at the Reymonds', he is nursed back to health by Mrs Reymond. Edwards cannot avoid being the observer and indeed the eavesdropper on the woman's passion. The story ends:

> When Edwards left the South Coast his mind was quickly filled with his own affairs, but whenever he thought of the Reymonds he was haunted by that woman's voice saying 'I shall never forget . . .' and again he seemed to see her trying to hurry forward, her high heels sinking into the sand at every step, towards the last passion of her life.

'When the Sardines Came' raises questions whose nature indicates that something is wrong with the telling of the story. There is the relation between the narrator and Edwards, who duplicates his function. There is the relation between the coming of the sardines, the natural phenomenon, and Mrs Reymond's falling in love, the psychological state. Is the depiction of the shoal of sardines meant to be something more than coincidental or merely a backdrop to Mrs Reymond's passion? If we follow Lawrence's advice to trust the tale not the teller we may conclude that what above all else interested Plomer was describing the invasion of the sardines and its effect on the local community.

One of the impulses moving him to write was that which produces good travel-writing. Another, behind his Japanese and Greek stories particularly, was the impulse to sketch national types and illustrate national characteristics. An example of this is 'Nausicaa', a modern story, which takes place on Corfu, the island where Ulysses swam ashore and was received by Nausicaa. Reading it, one has the pleasure of contact with an eminently civilized mind which delights in the contemplation of the past and is fascinated by the spectacle of the present. Yet one is bound to feel that these qualities could have been as well shown in an unequivocal travel sketch, for what is valuable in the story lies in its incidentals.

The story which is the great exception to these and similar criticisms is 'Ula Masonda', Plomer's finest and the one in which his sympathies for the black African are most completely engaged. It is the more effective because he never voices overt indignation at the white man's treatment of the black man. We have an account without comment of the effect of going to work in the gold mines of the Rand upon an unsophisticated young native.

In the first phase of the story Ula Masonda is seen at home, a boy on the tribal reservation, and we glimpse him first through the eyes of the white trader from whom, before breakfast, he has bought a blanket:

'Yes,' he said musingly to his wife, 'those Masondas. That young Ula was in this morning for a twenty-five bob blanket. At this time of the morning! And what does he want with that, I should like to know? What I like about that family is, they're not afraid to spend a bit of money, and they're so united. It's the old mother who keeps them all together, a fine old girl she is! Five strapping sons and four handsome daughters, and the old man not dead yet! The sons go out to work, and the daughters get married, but they all keep in touch with the old people. And so they'll go on, generation after generation. Ula's life will be just like his father's. What is there to change? Except that the natives are getting to want more and more every year, and by and by little Freddy will be able to start another Harrods here in Lembuland. Yes, they always come back to the old people, and you'll come back too when you're big, won't you, Freddy?'

And he patted the curly head of a child on his knee, a little blue-eyed boy with a bib under his chin.

The next phase of the story, which recounts the response of his family to Ula's purchase, reinforces the impression we have gained from the storekeeper of the pastoral quality of tribal life in Lembuland. For the purchase becomes an occasion for dance and celebration. And the pastoral, indeed idyllic, impression of tribal life intensifies in the next, very brief, phase of the story, which presents the old father, the warrior now in retirement, watching the spontaneous dance from a distance and coming down to examine the blanket.

The following phase begins: 'The train was crowded, and it took two days and two nights to get to Johannesburg from Lembuland.' Ula is on his way to his life on the Rand, to work in a mine and to live in a compound. The great day is Sunday, when the natives are allowed to 'put off the blanket and wear clothes instead: and the wearing of clothes was a permanent adventure for one who had been naked for the first decade of his life'. Ula acquires a friend, Vilakazi, who believes that since Sunday occurs only once a week, 'it should be spent in going restlessly from one debauch to another'. They share the same women, Vilakazi exploits his illiteracy, and when Ula has a letter from his mother Vilakazi reads it to him. His mother is writing to ask for money since the crops have failed, but in Vilakazi's rendering it becomes a report that all is well at home, that he must stay in the mine and earn money for himself. Which is tantamount to saying for Vilakazi, who looks after the money for both of them.

Through Vilakazi Ula makes more friends; Emma, a pretty prostitute who lives with a white man; Stefan, who has served three terms in gaol; and Smile, a psychopath who appears to his white employers as a cheerful houseboy. Ula is 'fascinated by the daring and sinister insouciance of Stefan, obsessed with the Christian dandyism of Smile, and infatuated with the over-ripe charms of Emma'. They plan a robbery of Smile's masters which Ula helps them to carry out.

In the mine next day Ula is buried under a fall of rock. The terror he feels and his delirium is brilliantly rendered in the form of a poem which could, one feels, have been translated from a Lembu tongue. His delirium ending with delightful dreams of possession of Emma, he is dug out by a search-party and taken to hospital.

Ten days later he walked out of the hospital with his hat cocked over one eye, and the other blinking in the sun. Although he moved with something of the natural style of his race, and although he was trying now to walk jauntily in the manner he most admired, an injury still obliged him to limp: it had been caused by an almost crushing weight that had lain on his leg while he was walled up in the mine.

In the hospital records he is judged 'a bit queer', but it is thought he will get over it, since it was probably the result of shock and of having been half-suffocated. He goes to join Emma, who is pregnant, by whom she does not know, and they set out to return to Lembuland. 'News', we are told, 'travels quickly in Lembuland, and though Ula Masondo had sent no word to his relations they all knew of his return.'

His mother, 'clapping her hands excitedly against her scrawny thighs', is waiting for him at the station. He refuses to recognize her and turns to Emma, and when she clutches at his coat he shakes himself free, saying: 'Who are you? Leave me alone, you bloody heathen.'

The last words are the white storekeeper's as he tells his wife at supper that Ula's mother has hanged herself:

'Hanged herself! Mind you, it's only the second time I've ever heard of a native committed suicide. By Jove, there's an example for you, of a boy going away all right, and coming back with all this Christian dandy business that I can't stand at any price. Give me the raw nigger any day, is what I've always maintained.'

'Oh, go on, Fred, you're the one that's always talking about increasing their wants, and getting the trade built up for little Freddy —'

'Yes, that's all very well, but if that Ula Masonda ever comes here again, won't I give him a piece of my mind.'

According to Laurens van der Post, Plomer's 'was the first imagination to allow the black man to enter it in his own right. . . . He was the first to accept him without qualification or reserve as a human being.' As a study of the corruption of a primitive by the forces of colonial exploitation 'Ula Masonda' has never been bettered. Plomer wrote of it and of his first novel twenty years later: 'Both these productions have influenced or been imitated by other writers.' In fact, it is clear after more than half a century has passed since his early stories and novels appeared that Plomer set the pattern for a great part of the

South African imaginative prose in English that was to come. He had left South Africa by the time he was twenty-five and he was never again to meet scenes that moved him to the controlled response, which was half savage indignation and half aesthetic appreciation, with which he faced the colonial South African experience.

James Stern, a near-contemporary of Plomer, could also be described as belonging to the stranded gentry. Born in Ireland, after Eton and Sandhurst at the age of twenty he went out to Rhodesia to farm. He does not seem to have been there for much more than a year, after which he was briefly in Germany and then lived for many years in the United States. His fiction has been confined to short stories, of Africa, of a wealthy childhood in the English and Irish countrysides, of Germany and America, a variety that makes it impossible not to compare him with Plomer. He strikes one as a writer at once more powerful and less subtle. The best of his African stories, though flawed, is probably 'The Man Who Was Loved', which through the portrait of a settler, Major Carter, catches Rhodesia at a relatively early stage in its history, just after the First World War.

Major Carter sat at the wheel as if he had spent all his life in that position – his left leg thrust straight out before him, the other bent so that the foot rested on the rusty throttle. Not a muscle of the Major moved; he might have been made of clay. The skin of his face was the colour of the earth beneath the long-scorched grasses, which was also the colour of the houses in the town. Worn and lined it was, parched by the thin air and the sun. I looked at the plaster-like cheeks and wondered had they ever been kissed; it would be like kissing the walls of a house, I thought. His hands gripping the thin steering wheel were much the same, gnarled, huge and misshapen, like chucks of wood hewn from a pale tree . . .

This is plainly muscular prose of great power eminently suited to express physical sensation and physical nature.

Professionally, the Major is a trader in livestock, but what above all else he likes to do is to kill snakes.

He would creep up behind them, grab them by the tail-end, swing them round and round till he cracked their heads off in the air, as a huntsman cracks a riding whip. It may sound improbable, but this and the fact that he had pleasing manners with mothers and their manless daughters, could tell good stories and drink much whisky with men, account for his having earned the love and admiration of the people of every colour in the town.

One day, in the course of the narrator's and the Major's drive over the veldt in the Major's old Ford, they are forced to stop because of a stationary wagon and a span of oxen. 'In the middle of the road, its sharp and venomous head pointing towards the terrified oxen, lay the shining coils of the longest snake I had ever seen.'

There follows a brilliant description of the Major's sleight-of-hand with the snake at the end of which the narrator 'watched it soar into the sky and then, though obviously headless, saw it coil itself and fall yards away into the depths of the bush'. Then he hears a howl and sees the Major clutch his stomach and fall to the ground. He has been bitten, they have no serum, and by the time they get him to the town he is dead.

Next day, the town's activities cease, and at noon all file to the Town Hall, where the Major lies in state.

The dense crowd confronting us on all sides was impenetrable . . . The fact that the white people among the mass of Negroes were draped in black made the spectacle even darker than perhaps, had everyone come naked, it would then have appeared. Nevertheless, as I pushed my way through the thick odour of human beings and the more solid resistance of their bodies, I don't think I passed more than a dozen white faces in the silent crowd. To some extent, this was explained when, approaching the steps to the Hall, a notice in large black letters above the entrance caught my eye:

NATIVES NOT ADMITTED

Setting out ten minutes late for the service at the Protestant church, the narrator is astonished to see long lines of cars already being driven away and none of them turning down the road to the cemetery. Yet he finds the hearse and its two black horses still waiting at the gate of the church surrounded by a multitude of Negroes. He sees the coffin being borne down the steps on the shoulders of four young Africans 'dressed alike, from neck to naked feet in pure white linen', and he notices that their faces, strangely brown, all bore a definite resemblance one with the other, and that each face shone with tears'. They are followed by a dozen very dark Negro women, some middle-aged, others young and beautiful, and behind these trotted 'a crowd of brown-faced boys, girls, and tiny piccaninnies, all holding hands'.

It is as though the Negroes have claimed Major Carter as their own and the whites have accepted this by giving his body over to them. 'The Man Who was Loved' is an exceedingly powerful story, the celebration of a man who because of his quite exceptional bravery becomes a folk hero to the inhabitants of the Colony regardless of colour and race. Nevertheless, our reponse to the story is bound to be mixed, for it is very ambiguous, though whether the ambiguity is intentional or, as at times it seems, the consequence of a failure in literary tact, is not clear. The ambiguity is apparent in the title. In what way was the Major loved? Do the whites reject him because the Negroes hero-worship him, or is there a suggestion of a saintly man who is suddenly discovered to have feet of clay? Has he been found guilty of miscegenation? Are the bearers of the hearse, who strongly resemble one another and have complexions 'strangely brown', his sons and are the women, middle-aged and young, following the hearse, his wives and mistresses? If this is the case, and Stern is attempting simultaneously to do two entirely different things, to celebrate a real hero for his courage and prowess with the snakes and to expose the hypocrisy of a colonial order by means of a sensationally ironical ending, then the question of literary tact must arise.

It may be that I have grievously misread 'The Man Who Was Loved'. If that is so, then something seems badly wrong with the telling of the story as compared with that of 'The Force', a story about George Newman, an officer in the British South African Police running what is called a One-Man Station, 'a two-roomed, one-storey house made of sun-baked brick, with a corrugated-iron roof. And it was one hundred and fifty miles from a town and seventy miles from a railway.' It is nine months, during which time he had not seen a white man or spoken a word of English, before he is given two weeks' leave. In his mind, the town, which has about a thousand whites, has become 'some fantastic city with glaring lights revealing the delirious night-life of a Western European capital'. It takes him four days' riding to reach it.

When he had ordered a room he left the hotel. But at the end of two hours he had walked through every street in the town and he had seen no one to whom he even wished to say a word. He went to the Club, where he signed in for a week's membership: he sat down to read the papers, but it was so long since he had heard any news of the world that the word-covered sheets failed to interest him. And the Club was empty. He returned to the hotel, hating the town, hating the Police Force, hating Africa, despising himself.

He strikes up a kind of friendship with Bright, the local police-man, who tells him how wonderful it is to be married and invites him to go to a dance at the hotel on the Saturday night, the last night of his leave, though, as Bright warns him, 'there are never many there, because there are so few unmarried girls in the town'. At the dance he meets Elsa Bright, whom he finds sym-pathetic, perhaps because he senses that she is unhappy. He buys a bottle of champagne and Elsa persuades him to dance with her while Bright conducts a busy social life of his own among the other diners and dancers.

Then to his consternation it is all over. Bright says jovially, 'All good things must come to an end', and Newman goes up to his room to relive his dances with Elsa and the communication he has imagined between them. In his mind he sees the one-man station he will be returning to. He rings the bell and orders a whisky of the black chambermaid. He smiles 'involuntarily' at her friendliness, and when she returns with the drink they sleep together. 'The Force' is a chilling study of loneliness.

Of Stern's non-African stories the best is probably 'The Broken Leg'. It is certainly the most powerful. It begins:

Neither Donald nor Hilda Archer had ever been aware that they spent rather more time and money on their animals than they did on their children. There exist a number of English homes where parental atten-tion is divided, equally and unequally, between offspring and animals.

That gives us the theme, the fate of children among that section of the English upper class which lives for horses. Hilda Archer 'loathed physical cowardice and she adored fox-hunting', but she has a fall and breaks her leg in such a way that she is left lame and unable to ride. One morning, she feels recovered enough emotionally to go with her husband to see their sons ride their ponies.

Max loved horses, loved all animals, loved to look at them, watch them, play with them; but riding he hated with that deep hatred prompted by fear. And in England, as Max already knew so well, there are homes where to hate riding is to sin, to be oneself despised, even hated.

That morning, his pony bolts with him. Thrown, he bursts into tears and when he sees his mother's deformity, her huge mis-shapen leg, 'his body gives one convulsive shudder, he again burst into sobs'.

He is ordered home in disgrace and he leaves the field feeling that he will never be able to atone for having committed the two great sins: he has shown fear on a horse and has cried before he was hurt.

He goes with Elliott, his younger brother, to their first meet. Hilda Archer is in attendance in a trap, thinking 'on a wave of love' of Elliott, who is a born horseman. Max fights with and masters his panic, behaves well and wins golden opinions from his father, who sends him back to his mother with commendations. When he finds his mother she is in the middle of a group of people kneeling over Elliott, who, Max realizes, has had a fall and broken a leg.

I think it must be admitted that 'The Broken Leg' is flawed by melodrama: two broken legs seem one too many. Yet for all that it reads at times like propaganda against blood sports for the sake, not of the animals, but of the human beings, 'The Broken Leg' is a fine story. Stern himself passes no judgement, but implicitly a whole code of behaviour is being arraigned, a code of behaviour as strange and as barbarous as anything out of Africa.

In 1949 William Plomer wrote a preface to a reprint of Pauline Smith's first collection of short stories, *The Little Karoo*, which was first published with an introduction by Arnold Bennett in 1925, the year in which Plomer's first novel had appeared. Bennett's introduction was a eulogy, which Plomer's preface echoes. No stories of Africa could be more different from Plomer's for all that both writers had lived in the same part of Africa only a dozen years apart. As we know from Bennett, Pauline Smith was the daughter of an English doctor who had settled in the Little Karoo region of Cape Province, a district of intense droughts sparsely populated by Boer farmers. These, rather than the natives, are her subject.

She left the region when she was twelve to return to England to go to school, and in effect her stories are based on her childhood reminiscences and impressions of the scene. She writes of poor whites. The phrase is her own, and her characters have nothing in common with the poor whites of the American Deep South as depicted by Faulkner, Caldwell, and Flannery O'Connor, nothing, that is, except their poverty, and even that is not in the forefront of the picture of them painted by Pauline Smith. They appear almost as primitive Christians living in a patriarchal and pastoral society. They are, to quote Bennett, 'simple, astute, stern, tenacious, obstinate, unsubduable, strongly prejudiced, with the most rigid standards of conduct – from which standards the human nature in them is continually falling away, with fantastic, terrific, tragic, or quaintly comic consequences. They are very religious and very dogmatically so.' In English fiction puritans of the kind Bennett is describing are commonly presented as comic figures or, at least, are treated ironically, for puritanism invites irony by its very nature, but Pauline Smith's puritan Boers are not comic, and there is little irony in her rendering of them; this is especially obvious in her story, 'The Father':

Piet Pienaar of Volharding was a harsh, grasping, hard-working, bitter-minded man of sixty, whose wife Aantje had been reduced in the first months of their marriage to complete submission to his will, and whose son Klaas was still, at twenty-seven, an unknown labourer on his father's lands. His farm, which he had bought morgen by morgen through years of labour and scrimping and saving, and which he himself had named 'Perseverance', was one of the poorest and one of the smallest in the Magerplatz region of the Plotkops district. It lay like a narrow wedge driven towards the river between the farms of richer men, and the homestead – a low, mud-walled building which time seemed never to draw into the surrounding landscape – stood bare and harsh in the bare grey veldt.

Such authority is carried by the writing, much of it stemming from the sense of physical impact conveyed by monosyllabic words based on monosyllabic roots, that we are ready to take everything following the paragraph as gospel truth.

Piet is a poor white, an illiterate who has 'risked friendship with no man' and kept his mind a closed book to his wife and son. Above all, 'for the poverty of her womb Piet had never forgiven his wife – and never forgiven his God. Against God he had harboured – and still harboured – the resentment of a victim with no direct means of redress.' His son Klaas, we are told, was born a slave, and yet it was just this quality of acquiescence to his will that Piet most resented and feared, for Klaas's acquiescence denied him battle, and for Piet battle was the natural means of intercourse with his fellows.

He finds satisfaction only in the acquisition of land:

Coming to the Magerplatz as a young man with nothing but the clothes he wore he had, by labour and saving, by foresight and scheming, and by the ungrudged toil of his wife and son, raised himself slowly above the station of the poor white and made this portion of the earth his own. And dreary as the Magerplatz was – its very name meant 'meagre' – all the beauty of the world for Piet lay in his own Volharding.

His consuming aim is to obtain possession of the lands that are adjacent to his, farmed for the wealthy landowner, Mijnheer Andries van Reenan by a poor relation known as Oom Phanse. Piet believes that the land would grow tobacco profitably but he says nothing of this to Oom Phanse, encouraging him instead to complain of the land's poverty to van Reenan. When drought strikes, Piet harnesses his donkey-wagon and drives to van Reenan's farm. There he explains that he has come to make an offer for the land farmed by Oom Phanse, who has decided to retire and live with his daughter.

Piet named the sum which had been quoted in the Platkops market, and added that what with the continued drought and old Oom Phanse's neglect of the lands this must surely be more than Mijnheer could now expect. His offer, therefore, was thirty pounds less. Two hundred and seventy pounds would he give, and he had the money with him here, in gold and silver, in his wagon-box.

Van Reenan treats his offer with contempt, telling him that there will not always be drought in the Magerplatz and that his new tenant will plant the tobacco that Klaas has told him could be grown there with profit.

Pauline Smith describes the effect of this on Piet as follows:

... there came upon him suddenly, with that icy touch of an enemy tapping his spine, a sense of unbearable loneliness. The cold crept from his spine into the back of his head filling him with unreasonable terror. At that moment he would have cried out for help and friendship even to the grim, ironic, determined and powerful man before him. No sign could he give of his agony.

Van Reenan's new tenant, a middle-aged widower whose seven children are tended by his niece Dientje, moves into the neighbouring farm. He treats Klaas as an equal, a man whose judgement as a farmer is respected by van Reenan, and Klaas falls in love with Dientje, a 'quiet, large-hearted woman of thirty', whose smile brings to his vision 'a radiance that lay light as the breath and dew of heaven upon all this drought-parched world'.

Engrossed with bitter thoughts about him and knowing that before his marriage his wife knew van Reenan, Piet decides that Klaas is not his but Mijnheer's son. He tries to shoot the boy but as he is about to fire, he hears a voice calling his name; he swings suddenly round 'in uncontrollable terror', jerks his elbow, and, lurching forward, falls to the shattering report of the gun.

When Klaas runs up he finds Dientje on her knees beside Piet:

The stricken man looked up at the son who had thus, to the last, eluded him – but speech was beyond him. So, too, perhaps, was hatred. So, too, perhaps, were bitterness and unjust suspicion. But none who watched him could tell what passed through his mind. In life his thoughts had been secret from them, and so now they were on the threshold of death. All that was known and could afterwards be told was that, with his last conscious movement, it was towards Dientje and away from his son that he turned – and under her compassionate gaze that he closed his eyes upon the world.

As moving is 'Ludovitje' and a miracle of literary tact too, for the subject could scarcely be more difficult. The story of Ludovic is that he was born weak and was believed weak in mind, also. Illness prevented him from going often to school, but he learned to read from the Bible. When he planted a garden for his grandfather his father got in a gang of Kaffirs to build a dam for him, and watching them, the boy would sing the 114th psalm, 'The mountains skipped like rams and the little hills like young sheep.' The Kaffirs, who were heathens, began to sing the psalm too, and the head of the gang, Maqwasi, would ask him questions about it, such as, 'Who is this King Jacob? Where runs now this

River of Water of Life?' When Ludovic is too ill to visit the dam Maqwasi begs to be allowed to see him.

Gently he came, but Ludovitje heard him, and sitting up in his bed he held out his arms and cried: 'Maqwasi! Maqwasi! Clear as crystal is the River of the Water of Life and close by the throne of God and of the Lamb it runs. Can you not yet believe, Maqwasi?'

And Maqwasi, standing there with tears in his eyes, answered him: 'Master, now I believe.'

Hearing of the seeming miracle of the conversion, neighbours from all the farms around flock in to witness the Kaffir nurse, as it were, the child to his death.

Presented thus, 'Ludovitje' must seem the most naive and artless of sentimental Evangelical tracts. When it is seen as what it really is, a dramatic poem in prose, it appears quite otherwise and in today's terms something of a literary miracle: the expression of a simple, literal, and unflawed faith recorded without patronage or sentimentality. Plainly, the true subject of the story is the grandmother, the woman who narrates it. It is very unlikely that it was an expression of Pauline Smith's own faith but rather the fruit of her self-abnegating art. Her work is in the tradition of Flaubertian realism, and she was aided in her art by the place and time in which she passed her childhood. Plomer wrote:

I do not know how commonly it is still possible in South Africa to maintain such isolation. . . . I imagine that there are still families of farmers and *bijwoners* with elbow-room and wonderfully restricted interests, still 'poor whites' as remote from flashy Johannesburg in their poverty and simple-mindedness as the veldt-flower is from the stock-jobber: but the way of the world is against them because it is against isolation.

Pauline Smith was in time to catch that vanishing life, which seems now to belong to a world before the Fall, a world unaffected by the modern. Her stories, to quote Plomer again, 'are a reminder that a life "narrow in its setting, harsh in its poverty" may allow, as it did Dientje Mostert, dignity and grace'.

Better known as a novelist, John O'Hara wrote a great many
short stories in his thirty years' life as a writer. There is little
apparent development in his work. He continued as he began,
and he began as a naturalist with sharp incisive stories of several
different aspects of contemporary American life in the Prohibition era. He wrote of his own background of upper middle-class
life in Pennsylvania, and more specifically of the town of Potts-
ville, which he called Gibbsville, and which he observed with a
sociologist's eye for distinctions of class and ethnic types and for
the relationships between professional men and policemen,
miners, saloon-keepers, and gangsters of recent immigrant stock,
Irish, Italian, German, Hungarian. In these stories, the worlds of
the Ivy League and the country club exist cheek by jowl with the
criminal underworld. But he wrote, too, of life on Broadway and
in Hollywood, of the lives of film-stars, small-part players,
extras, agents, and script-writers; and always, whatever his scene,
he observed with an unabashed, seemingly cynical gaze.

His ear for American speech was as accurate as his eye. He
had some kinship, in his attitude towards riches and the rich,
with Fitzgerald, though he had none of his romanticism; and in
his hard-boiledness he followed after Hemingway. His expertise
and professional accomplishment, allied to a somewhat intimi-
dating air of worldliness, often suggest an American Maugham,
though his prose is less tired than Maugham's, more obviously
efficient.

Just as his finest novel, *Appointment in Samarra*, published in
1934, was his first, so he wrote nothing better in the short story
than 'The Doctor's Son', of much the same date. It is set in the
time of the influenza epidemic of 1918, and the doctor is exhausted. He sends to Philadelphia for a graduating medical student to assist him in his practice until the epidemic has run its
course. His duties are to tend the sick miners and their families,
and James, the doctor's son, is deputed to act as his chauffeur.
James watches a love affair spring up between the student,

Myers, and Mrs Evans, the wife of the district superintendent of one of the mining corporations and mother of the girl James is in love with. Essentially, however, the story is an account of doctoring in rural America during the influenza epidemic. It is a description of life under strain in a little-known enclave of the United States.

In the afternoon Dr Myers decided he would like to go to one of the patches where the practice of medicine was wholesale, so I suggested Kelly's. Kelly's was the only saloon in a patch of about one hundred families, mostly Irish, and all except one family were Catholics. . . .
Most of the people were Irish, but there were a few Hunkies in the patch, although not enough to warrant Mr Kelly's learning any of their languages as the Irish had had to do in certain other patches. It was easy enough to deal with the Irish: a woman would come to the table and describe for Dr Myers the symptoms of her sick man and kids in language that was painfully polite. My father had trained them to use terms like 'bowel movement' instead of those that came more quickly to the mind. After a few such encounters and wasting a lot of time, Dr Myers more or less got the swing of prescribing for absent patients. I stood leaning against the bar, taking down the names of patients I didn't know by sight, and wishing I could have a cigarette, but that was out of the question because Mr Kelly did not approve of cigarettes and might have told my father. I was standing there when the first of the Hunkie women had her turn. She was a worried-looking woman who even I could see was pregnant and had been many times before, judging by her breasts. She had on a white knitted cap and a black silk shirtwaist – nothing underneath – and a nondescript skirt. She was wearing a man's overcoat and a pair of Pacs, which are short rubber boots that men wear in the mine. When Dr Myers spoke to her she became voluble in her own tongue. Mr Kelly interrupted: 'Wait a minute, wait a minute,' he said. 'You sick?'
'No, no. No me sick. Man sick.' She lapsed again into her own language.

A fragment of American social history is captured and set down in precise detail, and presented within it is a moment of importance in a boy's life, for what is described is the initiation of the doctor's son into an awareness of the facts of adult life, one of which is responsibility and another sexual passion. O'Hara is not a writer one would normally link with Chekhov, but in this story he is Chekhovian in his fine objectivity. He is, too, in a story he wrote twenty years later, 'Pat Collins', a story set in Gibbsville during the Prohibition years. It opens:

Now they are both getting close to seventy, and when they see each other on the street Whit Hofman and Pat Collins bid each other the time of day and pass on without stopping for conversation. It may be that in Whit Hofman's greeting there is a little more hearty cordiality than in Pat Collins's greeting to him; it may be that in Pat Collins's words and smile there is a wistfulness that is all he has left of thirty years of a dwindling hope.

Hofman is a very wealthy man, the quintessence one might say of Ivy League and country club; Collins has his own garage, 'hardly more than a filling station and tyre repair business on the edge of town'. Years before, despite the difference in their social positions and wealth, Hofman and Collins had been fast friends, intimates. The story traces the reason for their estrangement.

Collins had been a commercial traveller in men's hats, but had come to Gibbsville in order to break into the garage business. Having done so, he meets Hofman, who is instrumental in getting him elected to the country club. Appointed local Chrysler agent, he prospers. At first, his wife Madge is against the rise in the social scale which is the concomitant and condition of his growing prosperity. But, disastrously, she falls in love with Hofman, whose own marriage is in the process of breaking down, and their liaison is carried on behind Collins's back until Madge is so consumed with guilt that she confesses to him. The friendship between him and Hofman ends; he neglects his business, sitting in speakeasies all day, until it has all but disappeared.

He is rescued from his troubles by a gentle drunk in the speakeasy, a wealthy man who has spent all his life writing a book, which will never be finished, and who says to him about jobs:

'Isn't there something in the automobile-line? A man ought to work on the job he likes best. We have only one life, Pat. The one in this vale of tears.'

'Right now the automobile business is a vale of tears. I heard Walt Michaels isn't having it too easy, and I could only move four new Cadillacs in fourteen months.'

'Suppose you had your own garage today. Could you make money, knowing as much as you do?'

'Well, they say prosperity is just round the corner.'

'I don't believe it for a minute.'

'I don't either, not in the coal regions. A man to make a living in the automobile business today, in this part of the country, he'd be better off without a dealer's franchise. Second-hand cars and service and repairs. New rubber. Accessories. Batteries. All that. The people that own cars have to get them serviced, but the people that need cars in their jobs, they're not buying new cars. Who is?'

The kindly drunk asks him how much his dream would cost to realize. He replies, '. . . anywhere between five and ten thousand'. 'Tomorrow,' says George, 'sometime before three o'clock, I'll deposit ten thousand dollars in your name, and you can begin to draw on it immediately.'

There are many sides of life that O'Hara neglects: he is concerned entirely with the materialistic; but he was an exact observer of his times and their manners and he wrote, as much as any American short-story writer, as though special correspondent to posterity.

VI

Sylvia Townsend Warner's *Kingdoms of Elfin* bears as epigraph the following quotation from Peacock's *Gryll Grange*:

THE REVD DR OPIMIAN: You are determined to connect the immaterial with the material world, as far as you can.
MR FALCONER: I like the immaterial world. I like to live among thoughts and images of the past and the possible, now and then.

In the light of Miss Townsend Warner's fiction over the past fifty years it is clear that Mr Falconer echoes her own feelings. When her first novel appeared in 1926 she was called a fantasist. It is not as simple as that, even though the short stories of *Kingdoms of Elfin* explore in depth the life and manners of assorted fairylands during the last two thousand years. If the world she creates is flanked on the one side by fairyland, the frontier on the opposite side runs along the territory of Jane Austen. Typical of her work is the story 'A View of Exmoor', which might be called an exercise in civilized frivolity.

The action takes place in 1936 when, according to Miss Townsend Warner, 'weddings could be garish'. The Finches, who are staying in Bath, drive into Devon to attend the wedding of Mrs Finch's niece, Arminella Blount.

The Finches made a very creditable family contribution – Mrs Finch in green moire, Cordelia and Clara in their bridesmaids' dresses copied from the Gainsborough portrait of an earlier Arminella Blount in the Character of Flora, Mr Finch in, his wife said, his black-and-grey, Arden Finch in an Eton suit would have looked like any normal twelve-year-old in an Eton suit if measles had not left him prematurely thin, pale, and owl-eyed.

After the wedding, they are returning to Bath with a picnic case and 'Arminella's piping bullfinch and the music box that was needed to continue its education'. They stop the car on Exmoor and get out to eat their cucumber sandwiches. The bullfinch in its cage is brought out, too, to have a little fresh air. Arden tries to play 'Rule Britannia' on the wires of the birdcage, when suddenly a glissando passage on the birdcage was broken by a light twang, a flutter of wings, a cry from Arden. The cage door had flipped open and the bullfinch had flown out. Everybody said 'Oh!' and grabbed at it. The bullfinch flew to the gate, balanced there, flirted its tail, and flew into the lane.

The family follows after it, Mrs Finch bidding her husband bring the music box. 'If it hears the music box, it will be reminded of its home and remember it's a tame bullfinch.' While he is sitting at the side of the lane playing the music box Mr Finch hears a voice behind him say, 'somewhat diffidently . . . "Can I be of any help?"' It is a young man 'with bare ruined legs' on a walking tour. Mr Finch thanks him dismissively. Then 'around the bend of the lane came two replicas, in rather bad condition, of Gainsborough's well-known portrait of Arminella Blount in the Character of Flora', followed by Arden and Mrs Finch. The young man on a walking tour skirts round them and hurries on.

'Why the deuce couldn't you *explain* to that young man?' asked Mr Finch. 'Elinor, why couldn't you explain?' 'But why should I?' Mrs Finch asked. 'He looked so hot and careworn, and I expect he only gets a fortnight's holiday all the year through. Why should I spoil it for him? Why shouldn't he have something to look back on in his old age?'

So the story ends, and since it is one that lingers in the mind with the resonance of a lyric poem, it seems worthwhile examining why this should be so. There are, for instance, the parallels on which the story seems to be based. Is it by chance that a family named Finch is conveying and then chasing a captive bullfinch? The bullfinch is a garish bird, the Finches are resplendent in their wedding finery. The birdcage is in some sense also a music box. The young man on the walking tour escapes *his* birdcage for only two weeks in the year. And will not the spectacle of the Finches chasing a finch on Exmoor with Mr Finch playing a music box become in the young man's memory a wonderfully mysterious, inexplicable, and romantic event?

Beside it we may set, as showing a different facet of Miss Townsend Warner's talent, 'But at the Stroke of Midnight', which is a story of innocence and madness written with a glancing satirical wit.

One Monday morning Mrs Barker, the charwoman, lets herself as usual into the flat belonging to Mr and Mrs Ridpath.

The flat was empty. The Aga Cooker was stone-cold, the kitchen was all anyhow; the milk bottles hadn't been rinsed, let alone put out. The telephone rang, and it was Mr Ridpath, saying that Mrs Ridpath was away for the week-end . . .

For naturally, when he got home from his office on Saturday (the alternate Saturday when he worked during the afternoon), he expected to find Lucy in the flat, probably in the kitchen. There was no Lucy. There was no smell of cooking. In the refrigerator there was a ham loaf, some potato salad, and the remains of the apple mousse they had on Friday. It was unlike Lucy not to be there. He turned on the wireless for the six o'clock news and sat down to wait. By degrees an uneasiness and then a slight sense of guilt stole into his mind. Had Lucy told him she would not be back till after six? He had had a busy day; it might well have slipped his memory. It was even possible that she had told him and that he had not attended. It was easy not to attend to Lucy. She had a soft voice, and a habit of speaking as if she did not expect to be attended to. Probably she had told him she was going out to tea, or something of that sort. She sometimes went to picture galleries. . . .

Next morning he thinks she must be spending a weekend in the country. 'He was glad of that. It would do her good.' He remembers that when Lucy visited her cousin Aurelia in Suffolk, she always left quantities of soup. Since she hasn't done so this time, he knows that she cannot be with Aurelia; which relieves him. 'Family affection is all very well, but it was absurd that visits to a country cousin – a withered virgin and impecunious at that – should be so intoxicating that Lucy returned from them as from an assignation. . . .'

On the Monday morning 'the reality of Lucy's absence was stronger than the ideality of her breakfast tray floating somewhere in the Home Counties', and that evening he telephones his widowed sister Vera, who tells him: 'If Lucy doesn't reappear and you haven't told the police, you'll probably be suspected of murder.'

At this point, we switch back to Saturday and another scene, to Aurelia walking towards the Tate Gallery. She notices that she is wearing a wedding ring, and decides that it would be practical to sell it at a nearby second-hand jeweller's. At the Tate she looks at the Turners.

When she left the gallery, Joseph Mallord William Turner had got there before her. The rain had stopped. A glittering light thrust from beneath the arch of cloud and painted the river with slashing strokes of primrose and violet. The tide was at the full, and a procession of Thames shipping rode on it in blackness and majesty.

In her excitement she seizes the elbow of a man beside her, who offers her a lift in his taxi. 'Where can I take you?' he asks. She replies: 'Whither will I not go with gentle Ithamore?', adding: 'Marlowe, not me. I'm afraid it may have sounded rather forward.'

So it was in London that she breakfasted in bed, that Sunday morning, wearing white silk pyjamas with black froggings. . . . In all his life he had never been called Ithamore. In all his life he had never met anything like Aurelia. She was middle-aged, plain, badly kept, un-travelled – and she had the aplomb of a *poule de luxe*. Till quite recently she must have worn a wedding ring, for the dent was on her finger; but she bore no other mark of matrimony. She knew how to look at pictures, and from her ease in nakedness he might have supposed her a model – but her movements never set into a pose. He could only account for her by supposing she had escaped from a lunatic asylum.

He takes her into the country for the day and finds her 'as frank as a nymph . . . or a kinkajou . . . totally devoid of calculation or self-consciousness'. He decides to take her to Provence and next morning, before going briefly to the bank, he telephones for a passport application form to be sent round. When he gets back to his flat he finds it empty. The application form is on the table. It was filled in without a waver.

But at the Signature of Applicant something must have happened. She had begun to write – it seemed to be a name beginning with 'L' – and had violently, scrawlingly erased it.

She had packed her few miserable belongings and was gone. For several weeks he haunted the Tate Gallery and waited to read an unimportant paragraph saying that the body of a woman, aged about forty-five, had been recovered from the Thames.

Meanwhile, Vera has telephoned the police station to demand a police officer to come round and interview Ridpath about the missing Lucy. Aurelia has spent the day wandering round London, going in the evening to a free lecture in Clerkenwell about town and country planning and spending the night in the ladies' waiting room at King's Cross. In the morning she visits Highgate Cemetery, and seeing a gravestone there that says 'I will dwell in the house of the Lord for ever', she thinks of hostels; a passing clergyman gives her the name of a guest-house in Bedfordshire.

Thinking about her afterwards – and she was to haunt his mind for the rest of his life – Lancelot Fogg acknowledged a saving mercy. His Maker, whom he had come to despair of, an ear that never heard, a name that he was incessantly obliged to take in vain, had done a marvel and shown him a spiritual woman. His life was full of women: good women, energetic women, forceful women, blighted women, women abounding in good works, women learned in liturgies, women with tragedies, scruples, fallen arches – not to mention women he was compelled to classify as bad women: bullies, slanderers, backbiters, schemers, organizers, women abounding in wrath; there were even a few kind women. But never a spiritual woman till now. So tall and so thin, so innocently frank, it was as if she had come down from the west front of Chartres into a world where she was a stranger.

Aurelia goes to the guest-house and there she finds a cat, injured, hungry, and verminous. It is a tomcat but she calls it Lucy. 'The cat was exactly like her cousin Lucy.' In the meantime, money is getting short, but she contrives to extract money from her husband and sister-in-law by a sort of bribery.

She then takes a train with Lucy for nowhere in particular, trusting she will know her destination when she reaches it. A man in the compartment has a bungalow to let and she decides to move in immediately.

Happiness is an immunity. In a matter of days Aurelia was unaffected by the flight of blue pottery birds, sat in armchairs so massive she could not move them, slept deliciously between pink nylon sheets. With immunity she watched Lucy sharpening his claws on the massive armchairs. She had a naturally happy disposition and preferred to live in the present. Happiness immunized her from the past – for why look back for what has slipped from one's possession? – and from the future, which may never even be possessed. Perhaps never in the past, perhaps never in the future, had she been, could she be, so happy as she was now. The cuckoo woke her; she fell asleep to Lucy's purr. In the mornings he had usually left a dent beside her and gone out for his sunrising. Whatever one may say about bungalows they are ideal for cats. She hunted his fleas on Sundays and Thursdays. He was so strong and splendid that for the rest of the week he could perfectly well deal with them himself. She lived with carefree economy, seldom more than a single plate, drinking water to save rinsing the teapot, and as far as possible eating raw food, which entailed a minimum of washing up. Every Saturday she bought seven new-laid eggs, hard-boiled them, and spaced them out during the week – a trick she had learned from Vasari's *Lives of the Artists*. It was not an adequate diet for anyone leading an active life, but her life was calculatedly inactive – as though she were convalescing from some forgotten illness.

One foggy November evening the cat fails to return. At last she hears a dragging sound approaching the door, but when she pulls the door open she sees nothing but rain, 'a curtain of flashing arrows lit by her lighted room'. Lucy appears, a 'sodden shapeless thing'. One side of his head had been smashed in; his front leg is broken. She watches him die.

When it is light she gets into her mackintosh and carries the cat outside. 'The level landscape was gone.' She is faced with a flood. She follows the track, and when she reaches the road 'the water was halfway to her knees'. She crosses the footbridge over the roadside ditch, and the water is up to her thighs:

When a twig was carried bobbing past her, she felt a wild impulse to clutch it. But her arms were closed about the cat's body, and she pressed it more closely to her and staggered on. All sense of direction was gone; sometimes she saw light, sometimes she saw darkness . . . The ground rose above her feet; the level of water had fallen to her knees. Tricked and impatient, she waded faster, took longer strides. The last stride plunged her forward. She was out of her depth, face down in the channel of a stream. She rose to the surface. The current bowed her, cracked her skull against the concrete buttress of a revetment, whirled the cat out of her grasp.

'But at the Stroke of Midnight' is a story in which all Sylvia Townsend Warner's diverse talents are held in perfect balance.

Elizabeth Bowen was like Sylvia Townsend Warner in that in her art she too lived simultaneously in two disparate worlds. These came together in the short stories and novels she wrote during the Second World War. By that time, she had been writing for twenty-five years, for her first book, the collection of stories called *Encounters*, was published in 1923, the stories having been written between the ages of twenty and twenty-two. They remind one a little of Katherine Mansfield's early stories in the sharpness of their satirical eye.

The best of *Encounters* is perhaps 'Daffodils', which has for its theme the efforts of a young schoolteacher to persuade her charges to feel a response towards the freshly blossoming daffodils similar to her own. She invites some of the girls into her house after school; the essays she has been correcting lie in front of her:

> 'It was a beastly subject,' said someone, heavily.
> 'Beastly? Oh, Mill – Rosemary, have you never seen a daffodil?'
> They giggled.
> 'No, but looked at one?' Her earnestness swept aside her embarrassment. 'Not just heard about them – "Oh yes, daffodils: yellow flowers; spring, mother's vases, borders, flashing past flower-shop windows" – but taken one up in your hands and felt it?'
> 'It's very difficult to be clever about things one's *used* to,' said Millicent. 'That's why history essays are so much easier. You tell us about things, and we just write them down.'

The story ends:

> The three, released, eyed one another with a common understanding.
> 'Miss Murcheson has never really *lived*,' said Doris.
> They linked arms again and sauntered down the road.

'Daffodils' captures perfectly the earnestness, the flounderings, of Miss Murcheson, the young teacher, and the gaucheness of the girls, with whose embarrassment before Miss Murcheson's enthusiasm one is bound to feel some sympathy. It is a parable, executed in unmalicious irony, of the artist's endeavour to make you see.

Encounters looks forward to Miss Bowen the writer of social comedy, the heir both to Jane Austen and Henry James. 'I claim for *Encounters*', Miss Bowen writes in her 1949 preface, 'one other virtue – susceptibility, rendered articulate, to places, moments, objects, and times of year.' It is this quality that makes her uniquely distinguished, a quality seen at its best in her novel, *The Death of the Heart*, and in the collection of short stories written during the second war, *The Demon Lover*, which is one of the enduring literary monuments in English to that war.

Miss Bowen wrote of these stories, in her postscript to the volume in the uniform edition of her works:

They were sparks from experience – an experience not necessarily my own. . . . These are all war-time, none of them *war*, stories. . . . These are, more, studies of climate, war-climate, and of the strange growths it raised. I see war (or should I say feel war?) more as a territory than as a page of history: of its impersonal active historic side I have, I find, not written. Arguably, writers are always slightly abnormal people: certainly, in so-called 'normal' times my sense of the abnormal has been very acute. In war, this feeling of slight differentiation was suspended: I felt one with, and just like, everyone else. Sometimes I hardly knew where I stopped and somebody else began. The violent destruction of solid things, the explosion of the illusion that prestige, power, and permanence attach to bulk and weight, left all of us, equally, heady and disembodied. Walls went down; and we felt, if not knew, each other. We all lived in a state of lucid abnormality.

They are not, or very rarely, ghost stories. Typical of them and one of the best is 'Mysterious Kor', the first paragraph of which is:

Full moonlight drenched the city and searched it; there was not a niche left to stand in. The effect was remorseless: London looked like the moon's capital – shallow, cratered, extinct. It was late, but not yet midnight; now the buses had stopped the polished roads and streets in this region sent for minutes together a ghostly unbroken reflection up. The soaring new flats and the crouching old shops and houses looked equally brittle under the moon, which blazed in windows that looked its way. The futility of the black-out became laughable; from the sky, presumably, you could see every slate in the roofs, every whited kerb, every contour of the naked winter flowerbeds in the park; and the lake, with its shining twists and tree-darkened islands, would be a landmark for miles, yes, miles, overhead.

However, the sky, in whose glassiness floated no clouds but only opaque balloons, remained glassy-silent. The Germans no longer came by the full moon. . . .

This is surely a very remarkable evocation of the full moon over London, the great city blanched and seemingly deserted in a lunar landscape. But the purpose of the evocation goes beyond the merely sinister, though indeed the season of the full moon was sinister enough in wartime London. It is the symbolic landscape—

> Mysterious Kor thy walls forsaken stand,
> Thy lonely towers beneath a lovely moon—

of one of the two lovers in the story, which is concerned with a soldier on leave and his girl, Pepita, who are homeless wanderers: for the girl, the city is the place where they can be alone, but a place that can be realized only in dreams.

> She still lay, as she had lain, in an avid dream, of which Arthur had been the source, of which Arthur was not the end. With him she looked this way, that way, down the wide, void, pure streets, between statues, pillars, and shadows, through archways and colonnades. With him she went up the stairs down which nothing but moon came; with him trod the ermine dust of the endless halls, stood on terraces, mounted the extreme tower, looked down on the statued squares, the wide, void, pure streets. He was the password, but not the answer: it was to Kor's finality that she turned.

'Mysterious Kor' is not in any strict sense a story of the supernatural, much less a ghost story. Elizabeth Bowen sees in the light of the full moon an epiphany in the Joycean sense: it bodies forth, especially powerfully, a state of mind. The stories that can be truly called ghost stories are the weakest in the collection. The best, 'Pink May', is relatively slight, an exchange of dialogue between two unnamed people, one of whom has been haunted by a ghost. Elizabeth Bowen, in her postscript to the volume, provides her own gloss on the story when she writes: 'The worthless little speaker in "Pink May" found the war made a moratorium for her married conscience.' The 'foolish wanton', as Miss Bowen calls her, has betrayed her husband with a lover, and the ghost may best be explained as the objectification of the woman's guilty conscience.

The finest of the stories are those in which cracks appear in the present through which a character falls into the past. Sometimes these cracks have a perfectly rational explanation, as in 'Ivy Gripped the Steps', a story I find reminiscent of Henry James. It opens:

Ivy gripped and sucked at the flight of steps, down which with such a deceptive wildness it seemed to be flowing like a cascade. Ivy matted the door at the top and amassed in bushes above and below the porch. More, it had covered, or one might feel consumed, one entire half of the high, double-fronted house, from the basement up to a spiked gable: it had attained about half-way up to the girth and more than the density of a tree, and was sagging outward under its own weight. One was left to guess at the size and the number of windows hidden by looking at those in the other side. But these, though in sight, had been made effectively sightless: sheets of some dark composition that looked like metal were sealed closely into their frames. The house, not old, was of dull red brick with stone trimmings.

The description vaguely suggests Poe, the first paragraphs of 'The Fall of the House of Usher' perhaps. Yet, in the setting of its place and time – the date is September 1944, the place Southstone, a holiday resort on the south coast facing France – it is not extraordinary. Gavin Doddington is discovered looking at the ivy-covered house, which in 1912 belonged to Mrs Nicholson, his mother's friend, whom he loved, and with whom as a small boy he stayed in school holidays. Miss Bowen again provides a gloss on her story when she writes in her postscript: '. . . in "Ivy Gripped the Steps", a man in his early forties peers through the rusted fortifications and down the dusty empty perspectives of a seaside town at the Edwardian episode that has crippled his faculty for love.' The story, in other words, tells of a man's re-discovery of his childhood past, the full meaning of which seems to be summed up at the end of it when he attempts to pick up an ATS girl:

'I've got nobody to talk to,' Gavin said, suddenly standing still in the dark. A leaf flittered past. She was woman enough to halt, to listen, because this had not been said to her. If her 'Oh yes, we girls have heard that before' was automatic, it was, still more, wavering . . . She had seen the face of somebody dead who was still there – 'old' because of the presence, under an icy screen, of a whole stopped mechanism for feeling. Those features had been framed, long ago, for hope. The dints above the nostrils, the lines extending the eyes, the lips' grimacing grip on the cigarette – all completed the picture of someone wolfish. A preyer. But who had said, preyers are preyed upon?

His lower lip came out, thrusting the cigarette up at a debonair angle towards his eyes. 'Not a soul,' he added – this time with calculation, and to her.

'Anyway,' she said sharply, 'I've got a date. Anyway, what made you pick on this dead place? Why not pick on some place where you know someone?'

That is a beautiful example of Elizabeth Bowen's grave and ruthless analysis, catching her characters at unexpected angles and posing them in unexpected settings in time and place.

In 'The Happy Autumn Fields' we are presented with an experience of simultaneous two-way communication between two people separated by a century. It begins:

> The family walking party, though it comprised so many, did not deploy or struggle over the stubble but kept in a procession of threes and twos. Papa, who carried his Alpine stick, led, flanked by Constance and little Arthur. Robert and Cousin Theodore, locked in studious talk, had Emily attached but not quite abreast. Next came Digby and Lucius, taking, to left and right, imaginary aim at rooks. Henrietta and Sarah brought up the rear.

They are joined by Fitzgeorge, 'Papa's heir', an Army officer, and his friend Eugene, the neighbouring squire, who is in love with Sarah. They are on horseback. The vignette of upper-class Victorian family life is followed by a scene of family life in London during the war: the explosion of a flying-bomb brings down the ceiling, and Mary discovers she has had a 'sister' named Henrietta. From the records unearthed later, it is found that Eugene was killed when he was thrown from his horse, which shied because of an explosion a century ahead.

'The Happy Autumn Fields' is Miss Bowen's most subtle, complex story. It brings to mind something that Pepita says in 'Mysterious Kor': 'If you can blow whole places out of existence, you can blow whole places into it. I don't see why not.'

ii

It was probably due to the dominance of Coppard that during the Twenties the short story in England often appeared as a specifically bucolic form registering a scene and ways of life that had scarcely changed since those depicted in Hardy. Parallels with Georgian poetry abound. At his best, Coppard himself rose above these criticisms and, at his best, his true successor was H. E. Bates. He never, as Coppard does from time to time, surprises with a fine excess but he was an exceedingly careful craftsman who kept up a consistent excellence. In his book, *The Modern Short Story*, he described Stephen Crane's method as that

by which a story is told not by the carefully engineered plot but by the implication of certain isolated incidents, by the capture and arrangement of casual episodic movements. It is the method by which the surface, however seemingly trivial or unimportant, is recorded in such a way as to interpret the individual emotional life below.

He was describing his own practice, which he had learned from Chekhov. And this careful craftsmanship was infused with a sensitivity to beauty and character that led David Garnett to write that 'his best stories have the extreme delicacy and tenderness of Renoir's paint'. Having been read once, some of his stories exist in the mind as pictures, often as still life, as does 'The Gleaner', probably the most famous of his early stories. Movement in it seems arrested almost to the point of having been frozen.

Her fingers were rustling like quick mice over the stubble, and the red wheat ears were rustling together in her hands before she had taken another step forward. There was no time for looking or listening or resting. To glean, to fill her sack, to travel over that field before the light is lost; she has no other purpose than that and could understand none. . . .

But later, in the heat of the afternoon, with her sack filling up, and the sun-heat and the bright light playing unbrokenly upon her, she begins unconsciously to move more slowly, a little tired, like a child that has played too long. She will not cover the field, she moves there,

always solitary, up and down the stubble, empty except for herself and
a rook or two, she begins to look smaller and the field larger and larger
about her. . . .

At last she straightens her back. It is her first conscious sign of
weariness. She justifies it by looking into the sky and over the autumn-
coloured land sloping away to the town; she takes in the whole soft-
lighted world, the effulgence of the wine-yellow light on the trees and
the dove-coloured roofs below and a straggling of rooks lifting off the
stubble and settling further on again.

The impression he creates of stillness, of stasis, seems at times
akin to the rendering of a state of trance, as in the late long short
story 'Death of a Huntsman', published in 1957, almost a quarter of a century after 'The Gleaner'. 'Death of a Huntsman'
shows admirably, by the way, Bates's range of social types and
scenes, which is considerably wider than one at first thinks. It
begins:

Every week-day evening, watches ready, black umbrellas neatly rolled
and put away with neat black homburgs on carriage racks, attaché cases
laid aside, newspaper poised, the fellow-travellers of Harry Barnfield,
the city gentlemen, waited for him to catch – or rather miss – the five-
ten train. . . .
'Running it pretty fine tonight.'
'Doomed. Never make it.'
'Oh! Harry'll make it. Trust Harry. Never fluked it yet. Trust
Harry.'
All Harry's friends, like himself, lived in the country, kept farms at a
heavy loss and came to London for business every day. J. B. (Punch)
Warburton, who was in shipping and every other day or so brought up
from his farm little perforated boxes and fresh eggs for less fortunate
friends in the city, would get ready, in mockery, to hold open the
carriage door.

Barnfield lives for his life in the country and his riding. His
wife is gin-soaked, and he falls in love with a girl who habitually
rides across his land. She proves to be the daughter of a neighbour, a woman of his own age who was one of the circle he
mixed with as a young man. They are sitting, he and the woman,
in his stationary car after a hunt ball.

'I think she has to be told,' she said, 'that you and I were lovers. Of
course it was some time ago. But wouldn't you think that that was only fair?'

He could not speak. He simply made one of his habitual groping gestures with his hands, up towards his face, as if his spectacles had suddenly become completely opaque with the white sickening smoke of her cigarette and he could not see.

'Not once,' she said, 'but many times. Oh! yes, I think she has to be told. I think so.'

He is so much beside himself at the woman's attempt at blackmail that he loses control of himself and blindly hits out at her. Then he begins furiously to drive away and as she screams and prepares to jump out of the car she has a moment of memory:

Out of the darkness sprang a remembered figure of a Harry Barnfield in a white straw hat, white flannel trousers and a college blazer, a rather soft Harry Barnfield, simple, easy-going, good-time-loving, defenceless and laughing; one of the vacuous poor fish of her youth, in the days when she kept a tabulation of conquests in a little book, heading it *In Memoriam; to those who fell*, her prettiness enamelled and calculated and as smart as the strip-poker or the midnight swimming parties she went to, with other, even younger lovers, at long weekends.

It is a good example of Bates's ability to dramatize vital information about the past of a character in such a way that the progress of the story is not held up but indeed furthered.

The woman jumps out of the car, having struck out at Barnfield and knocked off his spectacles. Reduced to near-blindness he crashes the car into a telegraph pole and is killed. At his funeral, with which the story ends, everyone joins in to pay tribute to 'a good huntsman, a good sport, a great horse-lover, and a man in whom there was no harm at all'.

'Death of a Huntsman' has a grave and subtle beauty. The relation between Valerie and her mother, who treats her as though she were still a schoolgirl, is very well conveyed and that between her and the business man twenty-five years older than herself is admirably rendered. In the following passage of what I have called stasis, the middle-aged man and young girl appear somehow transfigured:

'I think I know every path here now. There's a wonderful one goes down past the holly-trees. You come to a little lake at the bottom with quince trees on an island – at least I think they're quince trees.'

If he had time, she went on, she wanted him to walk down there. Would he? Did he mind?

He tethered his horse to a fence and they started to walk along a path that wound down, steeply in places, through crackling curtains of bracken, old holly trees thick with pink-brown knots of berry and more clumps of birch trees sowing in absolute silence little pennies of leaves.

At the bottom there was, as she had said, a small perfectly circular lake enclosed by rings of elder, willow, and hazel trees. In the still air its surface was thick with floating shoals of leaves. In absolute silence two quince trees, half-bare branches full of ungathered golden lamps of fruit, shone with apparent permanence on a little island in the glow of noon.

'This is it,' she said.

Neither then, nor later, nor in fact at any other time, did they say a word about her mother. They stood for a long time without a word about anything, simply watching the little lake soundlessly embalmed in October sunlight, the quince-lamps setting the little island on fire.

'I don't think you should go away,' he said.

He answered her in the quiet, totally uncomplex way that, as everyone remarked, was so much part of him, so much the typical Harry Barnfield.

Generally, prose-poetry is a pejorative phrase: that Bates's prose has a genuine relation to poetry is shown by the frequency with which his rendering of nature in its minute particulars especially, as in the description of the quince-trees on the tiny island, reminds us of poets, of Tennyson for example. At the same time, he wrote some splendid heroic stories. This was a development in his talent brought to fruition during the war, when as 'Flying Officer X' he was commissioned in the Royal Air Force to write stories of the war in the air. The finest of these is perhaps 'The Cruise of *The Breadwinner*', which appeared over his own name in 1946. *The Breadwinner* is a characteristic British wartime improvisation. A small lugsail fishing boat, she patrols the Channel looking for the pilots and crews of shot-down aeroplanes. Her skipper is Gregson who appears to Snowy, the cabin-boy as a 'man of unappeasable frenzy', and Jimmy is the engine-man.

When the story opens, Snowy is still a boy, pining for a pair of binoculars (for he is also the plane-spotter), but when he returns from the day's cruise he is a boy no longer. They have picked up a wounded RAF pilot, who replies to Gregson's 'Summat go wrong?':

'One of those low-level sods. . . . Chased him across the Marsh at nought feet. Gave him two squirts and then he started playing tricks. Glycol and muck, pouring out everywhere. Never had a bloody clue and yet kept on, right down the deck, bouncing up and down, foxing like hell. He must have known he'd had it.' The young man paused to look round at the sea. 'He was a brave sod, the bravest sod I ever saw.'

'Don't you believe it,' Gregson said. 'Coming in and machine-gunning kids at low-level. That ain't brave.'

'This was brave,' the young man said.

He spoke with the tempered air of the man who has seen the battle, his words transcending for the first time the comedy of the moustache. He carried suddenly an air of cautious defined authority, using words that there was no contesting.

At his behest, *The Breadwinner* turns about to look for the German pilot and in the end finds him and picks him up very badly wounded. 'In a moment of painful and speechless joy' Snowy notices that he carries binoculars. The boy is back in his galley about his never-ending job of brewing tea when *The Breadwinner* is shot up by an enemy fighter, which sheers off, having put the engines out of action and killed Jimmy the engine-man. Engines are a mystery both to Gregson and the boy, and they strive in vain to get her going. A storm gets up rapidly and Gregson unfurls the sail. He orders the boy to go below in order to look after the two wounded men, and Snowy watches them die.

In the late afternoon *The Breadwinner* comes in under the shelter of the dunes. She is safe. Snowy grasps the binoculars in his hands and presses them against his stomach. He goes over his talks with the RAF pilot. He remembers the German pilot in the end mainly as the man who carried the binoculars, 'the only things that had come out of the day that were not sick with the ghastliness of foul and indelible dreams'. Standing beside Gregson, the dead pilots 'became for him, at that moment, all the pilots, all the dead pilots, all over the world'.

Gregson continued tenderly to hold him by the shoulder, not speaking, and the boy once more looked up at him, seeing the old tired face as if bathed in tears. He did not speak, there rose in him a grave exultation.

He had been out with men to War and had seen the dead. He was alive and *The Breadwinner* had come home.

'The Cruise of *The Breadwinner*' is an austere work in which there are no heroics and no sentimentality. Among other things, it is a story of initiation into manhood. The characters are drawn boldly and simply, and this gives them a representative quality. The British officer partakes of the stereotype of the RAF pilot of the day, and Bates allows for this. He sees the pathos and the paradox of the stereotype: '. . . his words transcending for the first time the comedy of the moustache'. Gregson is beautifully rendered and Snowy is the epitome of boy at that moment in national history: he is defined completely in terms of one or two simple symbols, his prowess as a plane-spotter, his lust after the binoculars, his awe of Gregson. 'The Cruise of *The Breadwinner*' is among the masterpieces of the years it celebrates.

Since the death of D. H. Lawrence, the outstanding English short-story writer has been V. S. Pritchett. Besides his short stories, he has written novels, literary criticism of great distinction, and two volumes of autobiography that are among the best of our time. In whatever genre he writes, he is always *sui generis*, marked by an unfailing curiosity about and a constant delight in the oddities and vagaries of human nature and by an exceedingly close observation of the human scene, all of which are expressed in a darting, idiosyncratic prose compounded of unexpected images and of brilliant, fresh generalization. It is a prose uncannily close to the speaking voice. The great influence on it is Dickens, though the Dickens that emerges in Pritchett's short stories is a Dickens who has absorbed the lessons of Dostoevsky and of Freud.

If there is one thing that Pritchett has made his own it is puritanism. He is, so to say, the connoisseur of puritanism in its characteristically English manifestations, which, in social terms, have generally been lower-middle class. Writing on puritanism in an essay on Gosse's *Father and Son*, he describes the territory of much of his own fiction:

Extreme puritanism gives purpose, drama, and intensity to private life. . . . Outwardly, the extreme puritan appears narrow, crabbed, fanatical, gloomy, and dull; but from the inside – what a series of dramatic climaxes his life is, what a fascinating casuistry beguiles him, how he is bemused by the comedies of duplicity, sharpened by the ingenious puzzles of the conscience, and carried away by the eloquence of hypocrisy.

In that passage, Pritchett defines exactly the comedy of such short stories as 'It May Never Happen', 'The Saint', 'The Sailor', and 'Aunt Gertrude'.

In these stories, which date from the late Thirties and the war years, an adolescent boy very much like the young Pritchett often appears as the centre of consciousness of the story. 'The Saint' is the obvious way of entry into Pritchett's world.

At seventeen, the boy is introduced to and joins a sect which 'regarded it as "Error" – our name for Evil – to believe the evidence of our senses and if we had influenza or consumption, or had lost our money or were unemployed, we denied the reality of these things, saying that since God could not have made them they therefore did not exist.' His family is visited one Sunday for lunch by a man from the headquarters of the sect, Mr Hubert Timberlake.

'This is my son,' my father said introducing me. 'He thinks, he thinks, Mr Timberlake, but I tell him he only thinks he does ha, ha.' My father was a humorous man. 'He's always on the river,' my father continued. 'I tell him he's got water on the brain. I've been telling Mr Timberlake about you, my boy.'

A hand as soft as the best quality chamois leather took mine. I saw a wide upright man in a double-breasted navy blue suit. He had a pink square head with very small ears and one of those torpid, enamelled smiles which are so common in our sex.

'Why, isn't that just fine?' said Mr Timberlake dryly. Owing to his contacts with Toronto he spoke with an American accent. 'What say we tell your father it's funny he thinks he's funny.'

The eyes of Mr Timberlake were direct and colourless. He had the look of a retired merchant captain who had become decontaminated from the sea and had reformed and made money. His defence of me had made me his at once. My doubts vanished. Whatever Mr Timberlake believed must be true and as I listened to him at lunch I thought there could be no finer life than his.

After lunch, at Mr Timberlake's request, the boy takes him on the river.

'Now I want you to paddle us over to the far bank', he said, 'and then I'll show you how to punt.'

Everything that Mr Timberlake said still seemed unreal to me. The fact that he was sitting in a punt of all commonplace material things was incredible, that he should propose to pole us up the river was terrifying. Suppose he fell into the river? At once I checked the thought. A leader of our church under the direct guidance of God could not possibly fall into the river.

But he does so all the same. He ignores the accident and its possible consequences, saying, 'If God made water it would be ridiculous to suggest He made it capable of harming his other creatures.' After a time they draw in and lie on the buttercups in the sun. At last, they rise to go.

We both stood up and I let him pass in front of me. When I looked at him again I stopped dead. Mr Timberlake was no longer a man in a navy blue suit. He was blue no longer. He was transfigured. He was yellow. He was covered with buttercup pollen, a fine yellow paste of it made by the damp, from head to foot.

'Your suit,' I said.

He looked at it. He raised his thin eyebrows a little, but he did not smile, or make any comment.

The man is a saint, I thought. As saintly as any of those gold leaf figures in the churches of Sicily. Golden he sat in the punt, golden he sat for the next hour as I paddled him down the river. Golden and bored. Golden as we landed at the town and as we walked up the street back to my parent's house. There he refused to change his clothes or to sit by a fire. He kept his eye on the time for his train back to London. By no word did he acknowledge the disasters or the beauties of the world. If they were printed upon him it was as upon a husk.

The story ends sixteen years later when the narrator hears of Timberlake's death:

I thought of our afternoon on the river. I thought of him hanging from the tree. I thought of him indifferent and golden, in the meadow. I understood why he had made for himself a protective, sedentary blandness, an automatic smile, a collection of phrases. He kept them on like the coat after his ducking. And I understood why – though I had feared it all the time we were on the river – I understood why he did not talk to me about the origin of evil. He was honest. The ape was with us. The ape that merely followed me was already inside Mr Timberlake eating at his heart.

Though relatively early, 'The Saint' is probably the best-known of Pritchett's stories. It is indeed very fine and a complete success. But, for Pritchett, it is a comparatively simple work. It could be reduced in précis to an anecdote something like Johnson's comment on Berkeley, 'I refute him thus.' Richer in its amplitude and more searching into the crannies and recesses of the Puritan mind in its worldly manifestations, is 'It May Never Happen'.

It is an exploration of the lower-middle class world of small business men in the home counties; one thinks inevitably of Dickens and Wells. It begins:

I shall not forget the fingers that fastened me into the stiff collar. Or how I was clamped down under the bowler hat which spread my rather large ears outwards, and how, my nose full of the shop smell of a new suit, I went off for the first time to earn my living.

'You are beginning life,' they said.

'You have your foot on the first rung of the ladder,' they said.

'Excelsior!' my new Uncle Belton said. I was going to work in the office of one of my uncles, a new uncle, the second of my mother's sister, who had just married into the family.

So the theme is announced, a boy's initiation into what is called real life, and the way in which the announcement is made illustrates the high spirits with which Pritchett writes. The name of the firm the boy is entering is Belton and Phillimore. 'The push of Mr Belton, the designing of Mr Phillimore, his partner, made it irresistible.' Mr Belton, the new uncle, the first employer, is presented as follows:

A new business, a new marriage, a new outlook on life – my brand new uncle looked as though he had come straight out of a shop window. He had been hardly more than a quarter of an hour in our house before we thought our paint looked shabby and the rooms small. The very curtains seemed to shrink like the poor as he talked largely of exports, imports, agencies, overheads, discounts, rebates, cut prices, and debentures. And when he had done with these, he was getting at what we paid for our meat, where we got our coal and how much at a time, telling us, too, where to buy carpets and clothes, gas fires, art pottery, and electric irons. He even gave us the name of a new furniture polish. It sounded like one of the books of the Old Testament. He walked around the house touching things, fingering picture-frames, turning chairs round, looking under tables, tapping his toes thoughtfully on the linoleum. Then he sat down and, lifting his foot restfully to his knees and exposing the striking pattern of his socks, he seemed to be working out how much we would get if we sold up house and home. The message, 'Sell up and begin again', flashed on and off in the smiles of his shining new face like morse.

The passage is typical of Pritchett and his way of building up a story, which is through the character-sketch, as in Dickens.

On his first morning of employment the boy Vincent travels to the office by train with his uncle. Again, the account of it is a masterly piece of comic writing.

When he and I sat in the train that morning I thought Mr Belton looked larger.

'I don't want you to think I'm lecturing you, boy,' he said, 'but there are many boys who would give their right hand to walk straight into this business as you are doing.'

'Yes, uncle,' I said.

'A little thing – you must call me "Sir".'

'Yes, uncle,' I said. 'Sir.'

'And you must call Mr Phillimore "Sir".'

I had forgotten all about Mr Belton's partner.

'But for Mr Phillimore you would not have had this chance,' Mr Belton said, detecting at once that I had forgotten. 'It's a very remarkable thing, it's really wonderful, some people would think more than wonderful, that Mr Phillimore agreed to it. He's a very busy man. A man with a great deal on his mind. There are people in the trade who would be glad to pay for the privilege of consulting Mr Phillimore. His word is law in the firm, and I want you to be most respectful to him. Don't forget to say "Good morning, sir" to him when you see him, and if he should offer to shake hands you must, of course, shake hands with him. I think he may offer to shake hands, but he may not. If he rings his bell or asks you to do anything you must do it at once. Be quick and mind your manners. Open the door for him when he leaves the room. Mr Phillimore notices everything.'

Naturally, Mr Belton had seemed all-powerful to me, and it awed me to hear that behind this god was yet another god to whom even he deferred. . . .

'I'll give you a little tip, boy,' he said, putting his hand on my knee, a touch that sent an uncomfortable thrill through my body and flushed me with all the shyness of my age. 'Do you mind if I give you a little piece of advice, something helpful?'

'No, uncle,' I murmured. 'Sir.'

'You needn't call me sir now,' he said, relaxing. 'If Mr Phillimore should ring for you,' he said, 'just remember the infant Samuel. You remember how when Our Lord called Samuel the boy said, "Speak Lord. Thy servant heareth." Well, just pause and say that, just quietly to yourself, before you go and see what Mr Phillimore wants. Don't hang around, of course. Sharp's the word. But say it.'

My throat pinched, my mouth went dry. I should have said that Mr Belton was a religious man. His expression became dreamy.

'I think there'd be no harm in your saying it if I ring, too,' he said. Even he looked surprised after making this suggestion.

Mr Phillimore proves to be quite other than Vincent had expected. 'He was young, not more than thirty-five, and my first sight of Mr Phillimore suggested the frantic, yelping, disorganized expression of a copulating dog.' What we observe through Vernon's eyes is something very much like the break-up of a marriage between Belton and Phillimore, a break-up marked by jealousy, intrigue, flirtations and worse with business competitors, until the split is made final when Mr Phillimore actually joins one of the firm's rivals.

'It May Never Happen' is one of the most brilliant of Pritchett's early stories. In his stories of the Sixties and Seventies, behaviour that was once seen as special to puritanism is now presented as human nature *tout court*. Obsession, eccentricity, the passion to conform or dissent are now fundamental to all Pritchett's characters. And with this has gone a broadening of his canvas, so that now only part of his gallery of characters is recruited from the lower-middle class.

An excellent example of a late Pritchett story is 'The Camberwell Beauty' which appeared in the collection of the same title published in 1974. It is a story about the antique trade as seen through the eyes of one who has been fascinated by it, dabbled in it, and failed in it. It is shown as a tight, self-contained world governed by fantasy:

It is a trade that feeds illusions. If you go after Georgian silver you catch the illusion, while you are bidding, that you are related to the rich families who owned it. You acquire imaginary ancestors. Or, like Pliny with a piece of Meissen he was said to keep hidden somewhere – you drift into German history and become a secret curator of the Victoria and Albert Museum – a place he often visited. August's lust for the 'ivories' gave to his horse-racing mind a private oriental side; he dreamed of rajahs, sultans, harems, and lavish gamblers which, in a man as vulgar as he was, came out, in sad reality, as a taste for country girls and the company of bookies. Illusions lead to furtiveness in everyday life and to sudden temptations; the trade is close to larceny, to situations where you don't ask where something has come from, especially for a man like August whose dreams had landed him in low company. He had started at the bottom and very early he 'received' and got twelve months for it.

The generalizations in that passage on the antique business and antique dealers are felt to be the fruits of fresh perception, shrewd and enlightening; we are presented with the psychology of a trade. And the character who makes the generalizations, the narrator, is noticeably quite different from the narrators of the stories of puritanism. There they are obviously personae for the young Pritchett himself, whereas in 'The Camberwell Beauty' the narrator's analyses and descriptions of the trade are ways by which he is differentiated from his creator.

Pritchett has been publishing short stories for fifty years and during that time his art has continued to expand in scope and to deepen in penetration. One could instance 'Blind Love' in the volume of that title published in 1969. It tells how a blind lawyer falls in love with his secretary-housekeeper, a woman whose emotional life has been ruined by a physical blemish. As a study of blindness and its effects on character one has to go back to Lawrence to find anything comparable. Witness this account of the secretary Mrs Johnson's first insights into her employer, Armitage:

Mrs Johnson could not herself describe what keyed her up; perhaps, being on the watch? Her mind was stretched. She found herself trans- lating the world to him and it took her time to realize that it did not matter that she was not 'educated up to it'. He obviously liked her version of the world, but it was a strain having versions. In the morn- ings she had to read his letters. This bothered her. She was very moral about privacy. She had to invent an impersonal, uninterested voice. His lack of privacy irked her; she liked gossip and news as much as any woman, but here it lacked the salt of the secret, the whispered, the found out. It was all information and statement. Armitage's life was an abstraction for him. He had to know what he could not see. What she liked best was reading legal documents to him. . . . When visitors came she noticed he stood in a fixed spot: he did not turn his head when people spoke to him and among all the head-turning and gestur- ing he was the still figure, the law-giver. But he was very cunning. If someone described a film they had seen, he was soon talking as if he had been there. Mrs Johnson, who had duties when he had visitors, would smile to herself at the surprise on the faces of people who had not noticed the quickness with which he collected every image or scene or character described.

'Blind Love' is a triumph of empathy and perception but as remarkable in an utterly different way is 'When My Girl Comes Home', which appeared in the collection of that name in 1961 and which I am tempted to think Pritchett's finest story. Cer- tainly it is his finest and funniest evocation of working-class life. It is set in South London and describes, through the eyes of a young borough librarian, the dismay and bewilderment set up in her family when thirteen years after the war and imprisonment in a camp in Japan, Hilda, who had been married to an Indian named Singh, finally returns home.

It captures with great sympathy and without snobbishness English working-class manners, meaning by manners Lionel Trilling's 'a culture's hum and buzz of implication . . . the whole evanescent context in which its explicit statements are made . . . that part of a culture which is made up of half-uttered or un-utterable expressions of value'.

The talent of Leslie Halward came to a brief fruition in the last years of the nineteen-thirties. His first collection of stories, *To Tea on Sunday*, appeared in 1936 and his only other volume, *The Money's All Right*, before the decade was over. The nature of his work is partly defined by the traditional image of the decade, for he was a writer from the working class, coming from the small shopkeeping section of it, working as a toolmaker and then, as a result of the depression, as a builder's labourer and a plasterer; his hobby was boxing. Mysteriously, he suddenly conceived an ambition to write short stories and taught himself to do so by reading Chekhov, taking to heart, as he tells us in his autobiography *Let Me Tell You*, Chekhov's precepts: 'If you want to touch your reader's heart you must be cold'; 'I don't want to know how *you* feel about the matter, I want to know how *your characters* feel'; and 'Why belabour your readers with a long-winded, detailed description of a scene by moonlight when a sharper impression is given by the statement that the light of the moon was reflected by a bottle lying by the roadside?' It was under Chekhov's tutelage that he wrote what he considered his first 'real story', 'To Tea on Sunday', an account of a youth's first visit to his girl's home.

Halward made himself the most objective of writers and the most economical; his stories are stripped; his prose is admirably direct and terse; no opinions are expressed. He has nothing of Chekhov's pity and his habitual stance is sardonic. He was dealing with characters who were deprived and largely dispossessed, and they do not necessarily arouse his sympathy; they interest him.

So the basis of his art is the character sketch, as in 'Belcher's Hod'. It is very short. Belcher is a good workman, and his speciality, which symbolizes him, is his hod.

For Belcher's hod was unique. It was an immense size. He had made it himself and had painted the outside a brilliant green. He was very proud of his hod. 'It takes a man', he would say, 'to carry that.' He would let nobody else use his hod or even touch it. Every night before he knocked off he washed it and dried it with rags as carefully as if it had been made of gold.

One morning, after a night of hard drinking, Belcher is told by the foreman to go home and get some sleep. Truculently, he refuses to go. The plasterers ignore him, and smoulderingly Belcher observes the labourer who is serving them.

Belcher watched Curly climb the first ladder. Then he had an idea. He'd show him how to load and carry a hod. By Christ, he would! He fetched his hod and with difficulty set it right way up. He held the shaft in his left hand just under the box. Curly's shovel was standing upright in the cement. Belcher stretched out his right hand and leaned forward, but he couldn't reach it. He leaned forward more, and almost overbalanced. He stood still for a moment, staring at the shovel. Then he loosed his hod, stepped forward, and pulled the shovel out of the cement. The hod fell to the ground and the shaft broke off just under the box.

Curly puts the broken hod in his arms and he staggers off down the road. The story ends:

When he got home he went into the kitchen.
'Look,' he said to his wife. Tears ran down his cheeks. 'Look, mother. I broke me hod.'

'Belcher's Hod' is a subtle story enshrined in the form of an anecdote. A considerably longer character story, 'Arch Anderson' seems to encapsulate a whole working-class lifetime. One Saturday night, Anderson is on his way home when, turning a street corner, 'something came hurtling along and hit him with such a smack that it knocked all the wind out of him'. A girl has bumped into him.

She stood upright, tossing the hair out of her eyes, giving Arch his first chance to see her properly. She was only a kid – eighteen or nineteen, perhaps. Not bad-looking neither. Nice bit of stuff, Arch thought. *Very* nice bit of stuff.
'In a bit of a rush, wasn't you?' he said.
She nodded. 'I was hurrying home. I'm late. There'll be a row if the old man's in first.'
'Where'd you live?'

'Price Street.'

'Better let me come with you, in case there's a rumpus.' Arch hoped he sounded gallant.

'No, thanks.' She said hastily.

Arch tried again. 'It ain't safe, you know, walking the streets by yourself this time o' night.'

She laughed again. 'I shall be all right, don't you bother about that. Nobody'll run off with me.' She slapped the back of her coat, knocking the dust off it. 'Sorry if I give you a shock.'

'It's all right,' said Arch. She was beginning to walk away. 'Whereabouts in Price Street d'you live?' he asks quickly.

'About half-way up.' She took three or four steps. 'Good night,' she called, over her shoulder.

'What's your name?' cried Arch.

She didn't answer. And in another moment she was out of hearing.

In such snatches of dialogue, and 'Arch Anderson' is written mainly in dialogue graphic, laconic, steeped in its background of Birmingham, Halward tells his story of a courtship of the streets.

As far as Arch was concerned, Saturday was a wash-out. The pictures went down all right and Lil liked the sweets. It was a fine night, so she agreed that it would be nice to go for a walk. They wandered about for some time, and then, as they were passing a pub, he said, casually, 'I could do with a wet. Coming in?'

'No thanks,' said Lil.

'Come on,' he urged. 'Have a drop of port. Do you good.'

'No thanks.'

He kept on trying to persuade her, but she refused to go into the place.

'You go in and have yours,' she said. 'I'll wait outside.'

'It doesn't matter,' he said. 'I can do without.'

'Please yourself,' said Lil.

They wandered about for an hour or so longer, not saying much to each other, and then Lil said she'd better think about getting towards home.

That's cased it, thought Arch.

As they walked towards Price Street he kept his eyes open for a quiet gateway or entry where he could take her for a quarter of an hour, but before he knew where he was they had halted on the corner and Lil was saying that she'd had a good time and that she'd better go in now.

The portrait emerges of a working-class Lothario, selfish perhaps but not more than is usual among young men, the portrait of *l'homme moyen sensuel* as urban factory worker. The courtship follows its usual course:

> Going out with Lil so regularly, Arch found that he was dropping all his old pals. It didn't worry him much. One night it occurred to him that he hadn't had a drink for a week. He hadn't missed it, he was forced to admit to himself.

After several months, Lil finds herself pregnant. Arch is not particularly surprised and he indulges in no recriminations. They are married within six weeks and set up house in two rooms. The baby is born and they are very happy. Then one Sunday morning Arch is caught by a rain-storm and goes into the pub to shelter. A crowd of his old friends comes in. He has to drink with them, and they chaff him about his changed status and his tutelage to his wife. He is on the defensive and drinks more than he should. They chaff him about the milkman, which is the oldest and most familiar gag in such circumstances. Arch finishes his drink and without a word walks out of the pub.

> He walked unsteadily along the street. A pack of bloody fools, that's what they were. Wanted something to do, he should think. Thought they were funny. He ought to have thumped a couple of them under the chin. Learn 'em to keep their traps shut, that would. What did they think he was, anyway? A muggins? They could think what they liked. *They* were the mugginses, not him. They didn't know what they were missing. Trying to get a laugh out of him, were they? Well, let 'em laugh. Let 'em laugh their bloody heads off. The joke was on them. He knew who was best off—

But he is still brooding on what his old pals have told him about the milkman when he turns into his street and sees the milkman's cart outside his house. The milkman has called for his weekly payment. Arch beats him up, is sentenced to a month's hard labour for assault, loses his job, and has to turn to labouring.

> As time went on he was out of work more than he was employed. He hadn't any decent clothes. He began to hang about on street corners, waiting for someone to take him into a pub and buy him a pint. Once in a while he went home drunk.
> Lil grew pale and thin. She never reproached him, for it seemed to her that, somehow or other, she was to blame.

The success of 'Arch Anderson' depends on Halward's power to persuade us that Arch is a representative figure. It is, it seems to me, an almost perfect Naturalistic short story but when Halward feels the need to go beyond this Naturalism he fails. An example of this is the story 'No Use Blaming Him'. It is the story of a selfish small-time shyster. But this is not how Halward wants us to take him, as the title indicates. In his autobiography, *Let Me Tell You*, Halward writes of his own experience of unemployment:

I began to get used to it. In that seven months I learned that nothing makes you so idle as enforced idleness. In the first few weeks I must have ridden hundreds of miles on my bicycle, going, full of hope, from job to job. Then I began covering shorter distances, telling myself that there was little or no hope but at least I would try. Finally arguing to myself that to go out at all was a sheer waste of energy and time, I stayed at home. My sympathies are with all those poor devils who, after, say, two years of unemployment, are told that they do not *want* work. After two years of fruitless tramping or bicycling from place to place not many men can be as keen as those in comfortable jobs would like them to be.

It was plainly some such feeling as that that was behind the writing of 'No Use Blaming Him'. Alan, the young protagonist, is an unemployed clerk whose parents keep a shop. One evening, he steals from the till, lets his mother give him treat money, and allows his girl friend to pay for their cinema tickets. When he gets home he helps himself to his mother's bottle of whisky, which she keeps for medicinal purposes ('she wouldn't miss that drop – had never missed it yet, anyway'), and settles down with the evening paper. He stumbles on an advertisement for a job for which he is suited:

In his excitement he got to his feet and began to pace up and down the room. He kept stopping first to have a sip of whisky and then to re-read the advertisement. Gosh! A job! After two years! He hadn't got it yet, of course, but it was almost a certainty . . .

Then, as if he heard a startling sound, he stood still, his head cocked on one side. A cunning look came to his eyes . . . quickly, he tore out the half-column containing the advertisement, rolled it into a spill, and lit a cigarette with it. He took the paper into the scullery and put it half-way down a pile of others that were waiting to be burnt.

'No Use Blaming Him' is an extremely effective character-sketch of a scrounger and petty pilferer, and this was surely the opposite of Halward's intentions here. He had no way of indicating how we should take his protagonist except by giving his story a title which invites a sentimental gloss upon the young man's behaviour. He was, it is clear, imprisoned in the strait-jacket of his technique of Naturalism.

Halward published two collections of stories before he was thirty-five and, though he lived for another thirty-five years, nothing afterwards. For two or three years he was greatly admired. Then there was the war, and the magazines that had published him disappeared. After the war, his kind of writing was no longer fashionable. He seems to have been powerless to change it. His was a trapped talent. For all that, his achievement within that talent was unrivalled in England at the time.

In the thirty-five years of his writing life William Sansom's short stories were his initial success and remained the backbone of his later reputation. He could, one feels, have made a story out of any experience, however slight. Indeed, Sansom wrote of himself: 'A writer of my sort lives in a state of continual wonder at life. Even if the subject or episode is sordid, or plain humdrum, that amazement is still there. It is the sense of this which I want to convey to others. Much of it is visual, I am a painter *manqué*.' And, as Elizabeth Bowen said, his stories induce 'sympathetic suspense – will they come off?' Miss Bowen answers her own question. 'It is staggering how they do. Their doing so is anything but a matter of fortuity.'

'Gliding Gulls and Going People', which is about a cruise on a steamer off the north-west coast of Scotland, begins:

Two girls in high shorts, their plump thighs redly raw in the blue cold; a blood-filled man in black broadcloth, his big stomach carrying him like a sail along; a queer-eyed girl in a transparent white mackintosh; an old gentleman and an old lady eyeing each other, strangers yet; a young man, curly-haired and hard-fleshed, whose frank grey eyes bristled with sneaking contempt; two wives with soldier-peaked caps, navy and nigger, cheery and cake-loving; a small lean man in blue serge and a woolly chequered cap whose friends and family, at his expense, flowed round him only to exclaim and demand.

Such were some of the six hundred lined up raggedly along the quayside waiting for several strolling ample officers to give them permission to embark. . . .

Sansom presents his characters with the precise descriptive adjective or phrase, provocative, paradoxical, or challenging, that will spark off our curiosity in them. Dwarfed, as we are, by 'this formidable and dismaying world' of sea and mountains, the characters exist to divert us for the moment and not beyond. As such, 'Gliding Gulls and Going People' is the quintessential experience of being a passenger on an excursion steamer.

In these stories Sansom is concerned with the superficies of things, the master, as T. O. Beachcroft has written in *The Modest Art*, 'of sensuous and atmospheric effects, an artist in working up the sounds, the scents, and the colours which surround his characters'. This is an integral part of his talent, but still only part of it, for in his finest stories it is accompanied by the frightening or even the terrible, which is so because unaccountable and unpreventable. This is graphically expressed in what is almost a story within a story, the old man's dream in the late story 'Old Man Alone'.

Several hours later, at about four in the morning, he awoke struggling for breath. He had had a terrible dream. An old and true story had echoed into his sleeping mind; shadowed in sleep, he had become the central figure.

Once, within living memory, before anaesthetics were properly developed, dentists had pinioned their patients to the chair. They could not otherwise work on a painful tooth with the necessary precision. And there had been a man so pinioned in a surgery one Friday evening, after the dentist's nurse had been dismissed. The dentist had placed in the man's mouth the hooked metal tube that sucks the mouth dry of saliva. The dentist had turned the suction on – and had collapsed – dead of a heart attack heavy across his patient's jaw, but not disturbing its dreadful action. Nobody was due to come to the surgery until Monday morning. And there the patient had to sit with the little tube sucking his mouth dry until, light-headed and swollen, he was discovered by a cleaner on the Monday morning. But in the old man's dream the cleaner had not come, and he sat staring at the dentist's glass window stained with a purple and yellow pattern and his mouth had got drier and drier as he struggled with his numb, bound arms . . .

What is being recounted is obviously the stuff of nightmares, and Sansom is most successful in embodying it when he faces up to it full on, as 'Old Man Alone' shows. We know that the story was sparked off by Sansom's reading Hemingway's 'The Old Man and the Sea' and his consequent ambition to depict comparable heroism in much less exotic circumstances. Sansom's setting is central London on the eve of August Bank Holiday, a season when it can be guaranteed that town will be deserted except for tourists and trippers. On the Friday before, Charles Dowson, an ex-soldier in his eighties, goes to the butcher's to buy the wherewithal for his weekend treat, steak-and-kidney pudding. Back in his rooms, he prepares his repast 'with the precision and love of an expert', then drops off to sleep.

He wakes an hour and a half later, gets up, and takes the cooked pudding from the gas. In doing so, he slips on a sliver of melted suet, and the pudding is sent slithering across the linoleum to the other end of the room.

He lay for a moment stunned. He saw himself comic and fallen over and his mouth opened to smile when he remembered the pudding and was struck with anxiety. He started to raise himself, feeling in his muscles and hands the moving intention of prising himself up. But he found he was not moving at all. He seemed to have gone dead. His body seemed no longer to be part of himself. He waited a minute and tried again. He could move his arms, no more. His pale eyes sharpened as he looked from the linoleumed floor about the room – the gas stove still on, the heat dancing, the pudding steaming, the bird singing, everywhere a small life of movement except for himself, dead as lead. Then his propped head fell back to the floor with no more than a little thump, like a single knuckle on a door, as he fainted deep away.

When he comes to more than three hours later he realizes that he is paralysed; we assume he has had a stroke. It is Friday evening; no one will possibly call until Monday. If he could get to the pudding on the other side of the floor, he thinks, he could sustain himself and then try to open the door and get on to the stairs outside. He makes the attempt. Each movement is painful, and he finds that after three moves he must rest, and he is moving only by inches. Outside, night is falling; he hears the theatre traffic in the streets and the clattering of plates in the kitchen of the hotel nearby.

He felt less abandoned than helpless. It gritted him with exasperation. The soldiering days were long past, but old habits of discipline and responsibility were engrained in him. He had a hard ability to expect little and manage for himself without complaint.

He falls asleep, and it is during this sleep that he has the dream already reported. It is about four in the morning when the dream wakes him up. He sees the familiar walls of his room with immense relief, but 'then the full realization came back, and with it reality worse than the dream; no relief from reality, except in dream, from which there is no relief'.

Sansom has an uncanny facility for showing the passage of time as it were in slow motion, for rendering a scene or an action as a sequence of minute particulars; so that, reading 'Old Man Alone' we seem to be very close to the cutting edge of Charles Dowson's experience as he lives through his dreadful two days. For he is, of course, discovered, and we leave him sitting up in his hospital bed days later. But he has had, for example, to suffer seeing the stray cat he has been caring for eat the steak-and-kidney pudding he is striving so painfully to reach.

'Old Man Alone' is a considerable feat of imaginative writing, in which terror akin to that transmitted by Poe and Bierce is domesticated in a Defoe-esque way. It is possible that Dowson suffers from being too much the stereotype of the long-service private soldier with his years of campaigns on the North-west frontier and in South Africa behind him; and the criticisms that Arnold brought against passive suffering as a subject for poetry and that Yeats brought against the poetry of Wilfred Owen could probably be brought against this story.

Sansom's finest stories remain those with which he made his reputation in the war-years, when he served in the Auxiliary Fire Service in London. 'The Wall' is perhaps the most famous. It is impossible, describing it, to avoid the word *tour de force*, for it recounts, recreates, 'the agonizing seconds', to use Beachcroft's phrase, when the wall of a blazing five-storey building falls towards a team of firemen. Again we have the uncanny sense of seeing something in slow motion or as through the eyes of an observer paralysed by the encroachment of irresistible force.

Six yards in front stood the blazing building. A minute before I would never have distinguished it from any other drab Victorian building happily on fire. Now I was immediately certain of every minute detail. The building was five stories high. The top four stories were fiercely alight. The rooms inside were alive with red fire. The black outside walls remained untouched. And thus, like the lighted carriages of a night express, there appeared alternating rectangles of black and red that emphasized vividly the extreme symmetry of the window spacing: each oblong window shape posed as a vermilion panel set in perfect order upon the dark face of the wall. There were ten windows to each floor, making forty windows in all. In rigid rows of ten, one row placed precisely above the other, with strong contrasts of black and red, the blazing windows stood to attention in strict formation. The oblong building, the oblong windows, the oblong spacing. Orange-red colour seemed to *bulge* from the black framework, assumed tactile values, like boiling jelly that expanded inside a thick black squared grill.

One has the impression of almost unnatural formality, rigidity. The paragraphs that follow exist in counterpoint to it, as the great mass crumbles down. 'We dropped the hose and crouched. Afterwards Verno said that I knelt slowly on one knee with bowed head, like a man about to be knighted.' And how does the story end?

Lofty, away by the pump, was killed. Len, Verno, and myself, they dug out. There was very little brick on top of us. We had been lucky. We had been framed by one of those symmetrical, oblong window spaces.

'The Wall' is magisterial in its authority. It appeared in Sansom's first collection, *Fireman Flower*, published in 1944. The title-story, which is much longer, is very different in manner, a fireman's fantasia partaking of dream and nightmare.

It begins with a paragraph consisting of a single sentence:

It was not fear, but rather an oppresive sense of expectancy that made the fireman study his belt buckle with such nervous energy.

In the second paragraph we discover the fireman is on his way to a fire with the trailer pump attached to his van. The third paragraph runs:

The fireman scrutinized the buckling of his belt and thought: 'Now I can see quite plainly, perhaps for the first time, that this is me, that this is Fireman Flower, that I am riding my pump to a most important fire, that inevitably I shall soon be engaged upon my most important task. I knew the nature of that task as soon as I heard the call to this particular fire. My task is succinctly – to discover the kernel of the fire. I must disregard the fire's offshoots, I must pass over the fire's deceptive encroachments, and I must proceed most determinedly in search of the fire's kernel. Only in that way can I assess efficiently the whole nature of the fire. . . .'

It might be the K of *The Trial* speaking or thinking and it was this story in particular that led the critics of the day to find parallels between Kafka and Sansom. Sansom goes on in this

way, the way of the Kafka hero's obsession with bureaucratic
minutiae, for three or four pages until a warehouse, the scene of
the fire, is reached. Through this enormous warehouse Fireman
Flower chases the kernel of the fire, the source, and as he chases
along the corridors and up stairs fire is everywhere, its sources
endlessly duplicated, until the warehouse itself seems as vast as
the universe and man's life dedicated to fighting fire. Warehouse, fire, and fire-fighting take on metaphysical implications,
the more so since in the course of his quest Flower meets old
friends, is conscious of the girl he loves. Life, Sansom almost
persuades us, is conflagration.

And there is 'How Claeys Died', in which, to quote Elizabeth
Bowen, portrayal of the terrible, or the nature of terror, reaches
one of its highest levels. It begins:

In Germany, two months after the capitulation, tall green grass and
corn had grown up round every remnant of battle, so that the war
seemed to have happened many years ago. A tank, nosing up from the
corn like a pale grey toad, would already be rusted, ancient: the underside of an overturned carrier exposed intricacies red-brown and clogged
like an agricultural machine abandoned for years. Such objects were no
longer the contemporary traffic, they were exceptional carcasses; one
expected their armour to melt like the armour of crushed beetles, to
enter the earth and help fertilize further the green growth in which
they were already drowned.

The paragraph sets the tone for the imaginative level the story
will occupy throughout its length. Claeys, who is a Belgian engaged on relief measures, 'perhaps a sort of half-brother-of-
mercy as during the occupation he had been a sort of half-killer',
drives with his party of two officers to a cathedral town:

Now as they entered the main street, where already the white tram-
trains were hooting, where the pale walls were chipped and bullet-
chopped, where nevertheless there had never been the broad damage of
heavy bombs and where therefore the pavements and shop fronts were
already washed and civil – as they entered these streets decked with
summer dresses and flecked with leaf patterns, Claeys looked in vain
for the town of big letters, and smelled only perfume; they seemed to
have entered a scent-burg, a sissy-burg, a town of female essences,
Grasse – but it was only that this town happened to be planted with
lime-trees, lime-trees everywhere, and these limes were all in flower,

their shaded greenery alive with the golden powdery flower whose essence drifted down to the streets and filled them. The blood was gone, the effort of blood had evaporated. Only scent, flowers, sunlight, trams, white dresses.

They press on towards their destination, a camp where forced labourers from all over Europe are waiting for shipment home. They are told there is trouble there; there has been fighting between the expatriates and returning German prisoners-of-war. As they near the camp they encounter a crowd of the expatriates on the road and Claeys jumps down from the car, which moves on, to greet them. He speaks to them in English, French, Dutch, and then German.

... as he repeated this word 'friend' he realized what his tongue had been quicker to understand – that none of his listeners knew the meaning of these German words. They knew only that he was speaking German, they knew the intonation well.

He stopped. For a moment, as the men nudged each other nearer, as the Slav words grew into accusation and imprecation, Claeys's mind fogged up appalled by this muddle, helplessly overwhelmed by such absurdity, such disorder and misunderstanding.

Raising his hand in an attempt to call for silence, he is immediately cut down by a scythe. He screams, shots ring out from soldiers, and two of the expatriates fall.

An officer bends over him. Claeys manages to grasp the officer's hand and shake it. And then he points at the foreign workers. The officer understands.

Instinctively, for this hand of his was wet with blood, he wiped it on his tunic as he walked forward. Without knowing this, he raised his hand into its gesture of greeting. There was a distasteful expression on his face, for he hardly liked such a duty.

So that when he shook hands with the first of the men, proffering to them, in fact, Claeys's handshake, none of these expatriates knew whether the officer was giving them Claeys's hand or whether he had wiped Claeys's gesture away in distaste and was now offering them his congratulation for killing such a common enemy as Claeys.

Thus ambiguously 'How Claeys Died' ends. It is the index of Sansom's achievement here, as in 'The Wall' and 'Fireman

Flower', that the works it consorts with in our minds are Piper's and Sutherland's wartime paintings and, especially, Henry Moore's drawings of sleeping bodies in the London tube-shelters.

V

Angus Wilson first appeared, in the last months of the war, as a short-story writer whose work, in Stephen Wall's words was characterized by a 'novel aggressiveness' marked by 'a continuous exhibition of those contemporary manners which set our teeth on edge ... cultural snobbery, food snobbery, travel snobbery; middle-class philistinism and nordic fey-ness; left-wing wishful thinking and the bogus sincerity of popular political commentators; academic crankiness and mind-less proletarian violence; theatrical bitchiness and homosexual malice'.

A simple but typical story is the very short 'Higher Stan-dards'. Elsie Corfe is a young school teacher who because of the intellectual pretensions of herself and her mother is cut off from the ordinary contacts available to a village girl. It is Elsie's fate to teach Standard IV, and 'that famous undisciplined class' has become the symbol of everything that the Corfes disapprove of. After tea, Elsie goes to the pillar-box to post a letter. The box is surrounded by youths who nightly hang around the village streets to call after girls. 'Our Standard IV' is the Corfes' name for these youths. Among them Elsie notices Jim Stoker and Bill Daly with whom she went to school.

Bill Daly addresses her in 'the usual imitation American'.

The retort came easily to Elsie's lips, 'Does teacher know you're out of school, Bill Daly?' she said; but the words came strangely – not in her customary schoolmarm tone, but with a long-buried, common, cheeky giggle. She even smiled and waved, and her walk as she left them was almost tarty in its jauntiness. She was tempted to look back, but another wolf whistle recalled her to her superior taste, her isolated social position in the village.

When she gets back her mother says of Bill Daley's behaviour: 'It's lucky there are folks with higher standards' and, faithful to her precept of self-conscious rectitude, prepares to go and sit with a sick neighbour, saying: 'I don't like leaving your father though. . . .'

Through the flat acceptance of their life implied in her mother's tone came once more the wolf whistles and guffaws, and mingled with them now the high giggles of the village girls. Elsie's laugh was hard and hysterical. 'Oh! don't fuss so, mother,' she cried, 'I'll sit up with father. You haven't got a monopoly of higher standards, you know.'

So the story ends, and so much, one may think, for educational aspirations and the widening of cultural horizons. Nor can one fail to note the intellectual snobbery with which the story is written or the writing down of working-class pretensions. All the same, one knows that these are diametrically opposed to Wilson's beliefs. He is a liberal humanist who has said, when comparing himself with E. M. Forster in *Contemporary Novelists*: 'It seems to me that I am at once a more impulsive, a more bitchy, and a more compassionate author . . . that my humanism has less high hope for the future but more acceptance of liking human beings as they are.' If this is true, it is so largely because of the ambiguity of his position, which is reflected in the tension apparent in his stories. The ambiguity and the ability equally to identify with and to expose opposed characters allow him to write stories that are dramatized social criticism, reminiscent in amplitude and range of the great Victorians.

One instance is 'A Bit off the Map'. Very much a story of the nineteen-fifties, the central figure is a young man named Kennie Martin, and the story begins with his addressing us: 'See, some people go about like it doesn't matter why we're here or what it's all for, but I'm not like that.' Through his own words we learn what he is:

I've got the figure and legs that could make a dancer and I could sing, if only I could stop smoking. There's Elvis Presley's got all those cars and Tommy Steele started just in a skiffle group like in one of the coffee bars that I spend most time in.

He has also been to an approved school where he was diagnosed as a psychopath, and is now in the process of finding salvation through Huggett and the Crowd. Huggett 'believes in Power and Leadership for the Regenerations (*sic*) of the World'. Kennie, one might say, is fodder for fascism.

After some pages of Kennie's interior monologue the method of narration switches to that of omniscient third-person narration, for Kennie has to be placed in his context as mascot of the Crowd.

Amid the uniformity of elaborate male hair styles and female horsehair tails, the jeans and fishermen's sweaters, the dilapidated grammar school heartiness of the Crowd's male attire, the dead but fussy gen-teelness of their women might have suggested a sort of inverted exhibi-tionism. But the clothes of the Crowd – the tired suits, the stained flannels and grubby corduroys; the jumpers and skirts, the pathetically dim brooches and ear-rings – were no conscious protests, only the ends of inherited and accepted taste, the necessities of penurious earnings. Even Harold's was just what he had always worn. They were as un-conscious of the bejeaned world about them as they were of the rubber plant, the Chinese chequer players, or the guitar of the skiffle group. They always met at the Italian coffee house and they drank Cona. They were always talking; or rather the men were talking and the women were seeming to listen. Clothes were the last thing that either sex would have noticed in the other. The young women, except for Susan, were plain, and, except for Rose, without makeup; but Rose alone had a bad skin. The young men had strong faces with weak chins. . . .

The writing is obviously the result of close observation and the period is accurately caught. The Crowd is composed of lower-middle class aspirants to intellectuality and advanced thinking. By contrast:

Kennie's appearance, when as this evening he let his self-admiration have rein, caused comment even in the most extravagant world of jeans and hair does. Among the Crowd he seemed flagrant. His jeans were tighter than seemed altogether likely, and they were striped. His belt was bigger and more decked with brass studs. His sweater (the famous model) was unlikely ever to be repeated in its zebra-like weave. Beneath his swirling, sweeping mass of black hair, luxuriant with the strong-scented 'Pour les hommes', his pale face was embarrassingly foolish and beautiful. His huge eyes stared vacantly, his wide sensual lips fell apart in a weak smile. Kennie always breathed through his mouth. He wore one small brass ear-ring. Above all, he was too short for so ex-travagant an attire. . . .

Here, Wilson comes dangerously near to destroying at a single blow any claims his story may make for significance. His talent for contemptuous and malignant caricature seems to have taken over. And yet Wilson retrieves the situation with the sheer energy of his story. After yet another party, Kennie, having drunk too much, sets out to walk on Hampstead Heath.

At this point there is another switch in the story and a new character enters to occupy the centre of the picture. 'Colonel Lambourn looked at his watch and noted 'with annoyance that it was already half-past midnight.' He has fallen asleep after dinner and is late for his night walk. He walks erectly and briskly for a man of seventy-four and is still handsome and smartly dressed. He carries his dispatch-case with him – 'in fairness to the community'. He has had frustrating interviews at the central offices of the Prudential, the Royal Geographical Society, the Treasury, the Board of Trade, Peter Jones, the Bolivian Embassy, the Wallace Collection, and Church House. Passing 'some young fellow in distress apparently', he asks

'Is there anything I can do to help?'

The boy turned enormous eyes upon him. 'Look,' he said, 'I'm not interested.'

Colonel Lambourn was familiar with these words. 'I'm not surprised,' he said, 'few people are interested to find out the truth.' To his amazement, however, the boy took him up on those words.

'Who says I'm not interested in the Truth. That's what I'm searching for, see.'

Whereupon the Colonel unlocks his dispatch-case and opens his maps for Kennie's inspection, maps of old bridle paths of the eighteenth and nineteenth centuries, of Government defence zones, atomic power stations and gun sites, of treasure trove as issued by the Office of Works, and, finally, 'a diagram of the intersections of the three maps when superimposed'.

'You see what they show?' he asks Kennie, who stares open-mouthed.

He sat back with a look of triumph. And the boy leaned forward excitedly.

'I think,' Colonel Lambourn said, 'that if the intersections of these pentacles themselves were to be fully explored, indeed I have no doubt, that humanity would be in possession of what I may call the putative treasure and, if that were to happen, I have no doubt that our enemies would be, to put it mildly, seriously discomforted.' He began to fold up the maps and replace them in the dispatch-case.

'What's it mean?' cried the boy. 'What's it tell you?'

. . . The despair of his screams made the Colonel turn towards him. Kennie banged his fist on the old man's face. Blood poured from the

Colonel's nose and he fell backwards, hitting his head on the bench corner. Kennie got up and ran across the grass.

The last paragraph, which follows, is Kennie's, in his own voice:

'See, it's like I said, when I see red I don't know my own strength. And it's all, all of it, a bloody cheat and I don't know what I shall do. But if there's questions, I'll be all right, see, because what's an old bloke like that want talking to me on Hampstead Heath at one o'clock in the morning. That's what they'll want to know.'

'A Bit off the Map' has been called an 'allegory of post-war England trying to find itself amidst the din of discordant, prophetic voices and conflicting loyalties'. This may be doubted. The Colonel has been in a lunatic asylum, Kennie has been diagnosed as a psychopath, Huggett appears to be a neo-Nazi. The story is a vision of unreason triumphing in circles where unreason may be expected to triumph.

A carefully calculated and more successful allegory is the story 'Ten Minutes to Twelve'. Again, it opens with a monologue. Lord Peacehaven is sitting at his great walnut desk on the late winter afternoon of a New Year's Eve, writing:

MEMORANDUM TO THE BOARD OF DIRECTORS OF HENRY BIGGS AND SON, he wrote at the top of his folio sheet of paper. And then, after a pause, when he chuckled slightly – FROM THEIR CHAIRMAN. Then at the side of the paper he wrote in even larger letters TEN MINUTES TO TWELVE.

We read the old man's paper, an expression of intransigent authoritarianism that cannot have been practised in British industry for at least a century. The old man, we feel, must be indulging in a mad dream of early-Victorian *laissez-faire* sanctioned by approved theology and moral principles alike.

Downstairs, a little later, Nurse Carver tells old Lady Peacehaven that His Lordship will be ready for bed when he has had his supper and that she will give him a sedative; she then hands Lady Peacehaven the report, explaining that the doctor has asked that all Lord Peacehaven's writings are to be kept so that they can be shown to the new specialist. This precipitates a quarrel within the family: Walter, the elder son, who is now running the

business, accuses the doctors of using his father as a guinea-pig;
Roland, the younger son, a bio-chemist, says his brother 'knows
nothing about anything'. The bickering goes on until Walter
picks up Lord Peacehaven's memorandum and begins to read it
to himself. Exclaiming that the old man really did run the firm
almost as autocratically as he writes in the memorandum, he
begins suddenly to read it aloud from the beginning.

When he had finished, Walter said, 'I don't know. Nobody seems to
realize the scope and the complication of business today. In father's
day they could bludgeon their way through things. Nowadays it's like a
sensitive precision instrument – the least faulty handling in one department and the effects may be felt right through the whole Trust. And
the nation depends on it for survival,' he added, in what should surely
have been a proud manner, but came out in the same grumbling, whining voice as the rest.

In contradistinction to Walter, Roland stresses the note of
anxiety and fear that runs through the paper; 'their certainty was
limited. In fact it wasn't there. There was only a bottomless pit
beneath their strength of will.' Geoffrey and Patience, Walter's
children, also disagree violently, so that Lady Peacehaven says,
'Perhaps it wasn't a very good thing to read poor Henry's letter
really. But I don't know. He always liked to raise an argument.'
And she tells her grandchildren of his energy and of how hard
he worked and of how anxious he always was. And she remembers how she realized that he was ill.

'He got so angry sometimes that I could hardly recognize him and
moody too. His face seemed different. Like someone changing in a
dream. One minute it's them and the next minute it's someone else. I
think the first time I really realized how ill he was came about through
that. It was New Year's Eve 1935.' She stopped and then said, 'Perhaps
I shouldn't tell it now, but there's no sense in superstition. Henry was
sent out into the garden before midnight. You know – the darkest man
must come in with something green. Although Henry was already turning. very grey. But when he came in again, I didn't recognize him for
the moment. It seemed as though someone else had been substituted
for him when he was outside. And soon after that he had that terrible
scene at the "office". . . .'

It is ten minutes to twelve and Nurse Carver suggests that
since Geoffrey is the darkest man present he should go outside

to bring the New Year luck in. In the silence after the boy has left them Nurse Carver says, 'He's the spit image of Lord Peacehaven, isn't he?' and then, 'Perhaps he'll grow up to be quite a great man.'

The New Year being celebrated is 1956, the year of the Suez crisis, a date of special and sinister significance in recent British history. This fact alone might make us smell out allegory in the story, but lightly sketched though they are, the characters are adequate both as characters and as figures in the allegory and they are given a greater dignity than Wilson normally concedes his *dramatis personae*. Altogether, 'Ten Minutes to Twelve' shows as much as any short story he has written Wilson's claims to distinction in the form. It shows, too, how unusual in a short-story writer is his range of reference.

VII

Dylan Thomas's first volume of poems, which brought him an almost instant reputation, was published in 1934, when he was nineteen. He had been writing verse throughout his boyhood, and stories too, and though his fame is primarily that of a poet he continued to write stories for the rest of his short life. They fall into two kinds, which may be differentiated fairly sharply. The first are those in the style of the contents of his first prose book, *A Portrait of the Artist as a Young Dog*, the second those in the manner of the stories in *The Map of Love*, which are more akin to the poems written on surrealist principles. Typical of them is 'The Mouse and the Woman', the central character of which is a patient in a lunatic asylum who dreams of men with nests of mice in their beards.

These stories are of controlled hallucination, obviously the work of 'good old three-adjectives-a-penny belly-churning Thomas, the Rimbaud of Cwmdonkin Drive', as he called himself in *A Portrait of the Artist as a Young Dog*. By contrast, the stories in that volume are just as obviously the work of the brilliant young man who had self-knowledge and humour enough to denigrate himself mercilessly. They remind us that though he may have been a poet of tragic vision Thomas was also, as his friend the poet Vernon Watkins said, 'a born clown, always falling naturally into situations which became ludicrous'. These stories are exercises in humorous and affectionate self-derision which illustrate moments in Thomas's life in Swansea from infancy until, and shortly after, the time when 'Young Mr Thomas was at the moment without employment, but it was understood that he would soon be leaving for London to make a career in Chelsea as a freelance journalist; he was penniless, and hoped, in a vague way, to live on women'.

A good example of these stories is 'The Fight', which depicts Thomas at the age of fourteen and three-quarters. It begins:

I was standing at the end of the lower playground and annoying Mr Samuels, who lived in the house just below the high railings. Mr Samuels complained once a week that boys from the school threw apples and stones and balls through his bedroom window. He sat in a deck chair in a small square of trim garden and tried to read the newspaper. I was only a few yards from him. I was staring him out. He pretended not to notice me, but I knew he knew I was standing there rudely and quietly. Every now and then he peeped at me from behind his newspaper, saw me still and serious and alone, with my eyes on his. As soon as he lost his temper I was going to go home. Already I was late for dinner. I had almost beaten him, the newspaper was trembling, he was breathing heavily, when a strange boy, whom I had not heard approach, pushed me down the bank.

I threw a stone at his face. He took off his spectacles, put them in his coat pocket, took off his coat, hung it neatly on the railings, and attacked. Turning round as we wrestled on the top of the bank, I saw that Mr Samuels had folded his newspaper on the deck chair and was standing up to watch us. . . .

The two boys turn and combine against him. They pelt him with gravel. Then they walk home together, admiring each other's bloody nose and black eye. They become firm friends, and in the evening Dylan goes round to the other boy's home for supper. They play the piano together. Dylan reads him an exercise-book full of poems. At supper Dylan meets the boy's parents and the other guests, the Reverend Bevan and Mrs Bevan. The Reverend Bevan is a poet too, the author of a volume called *Proserpine, Psyche, and Orpheus* and he asks Dylan to recite to him the latest poem he has written. Explaining that he does not think the minister will like his latest, Dylan obliges.

Dan kicked my shins in the silence before Mr Bevan said: 'The influence is obvious, of course. "Break, break, break, on the cold, grey stones, O sea." '

'Hubert knows Tennyson backwards,' said Mrs Bevan, 'backwards.'

What seems important about the story is the glimpse it gives us of culture in Swansea at the end of the nineteen-twenties, that and the impression of a youth obviously about to conquer the world, for the prose in which the story is written pulses with almost maniacal high spirits. The thing most astonishing in it is perhaps that it reminds us of the prose of a poet with whom, one feels, Thomas had nothing in common, Rudyard Kipling in *Stalky & Co*.

Caradoc Evans and Rhys Davies, the major figures in the Welsh short story in English, discovered a way of looking at and expressing their race which seemed to be characteristic of the race itself. To the non-Welsh eye the Welsh story-writers who followed after them may often seem too much of a kind, so strong is the family resemblance of one writer to another. There is a strong suspicion of literary inbreeding. No doubt this is to exaggerate, though Gwyn Jones seems plainly to feel it in the introduction to his anthology *Twenty-Five Welsh Short Stories*. In fact, his own story in the anthology, 'The Pit', is itself a refutation of the generalization. An exceedingly powerful story, it recreates the wanderings of a man lost in ancient pit workings.

Location apart, there is nothing exclusively Welsh about the story. It belongs essentially to modern writing, particularly to that epitomized by Kafka, and thus avoids parochialism. The same was true for Dylan Thomas. Ignorance of the language prevented him from being a Welsh poet and the fact that he became an English one necessarily gave him something of an outsider's view of Wales and the Welsh. He was also, of course, influenced by Surrealism, which was nothing if not an international movement. His Welshness can in no way be denied but it always existed in a larger context, and in *A Portrait of the Artist as a Young Dog* he tended to present his youth and his Welshness alike in terms of parody.

The case of Alun Lewis is rather different. A South Wales man, he was killed in an accident while on active service in India in 1943. He was then a lieutenant in the South Wales Borderers. Lewis's primary reputation was and remains that of a poet, but he left behind a handful of stories of great promise which suggest also that he might have become a novelist of stature. It would be easy to believe that it was the experience of war that wrenched Lewis out of a narrow, parochial tradition of English writing in Welsh. That this was not so is shown conspicuously by 'The Wanderers', one of the five stories in his volume *The Last Inspection* that do not deal with the war. It is perhaps the finest story he ever wrote; in its suggestion of a kinship with the young Lawrence it indicates the nature of his talent and his affinities.

The opening sets its scene and ambience:

The heat inside the caravan was too much for her. The wooden wall-boards were warped and the paint bubbled and flaked by the burning hot noon. She fell asleep in the middle of stitching a corner of the red quilt in the boy's trousers. Running up the steps in nothing but his rough green jersey, the boy found her lolling open-mouthed in the chair, beads of sweat on her pale face. He twined his grubby fingers in the fall of her black hair and pulled gently.

'Wake up, mam,' he said, 'Dad's coming across the fields.'

She woke with a start, surprised to find herself sleeping.

'Jewks!' she muttered, rubbing her eyes. 'I'm that sleepy. Where is he, Micah?'

'Just crossing the river,' Micah replied. 'He's got two rabbits.'

'We'll have a change from bread and dripping, then,' she said, yawning.

She – we never know her name – is a farmer's daughter who has run away with and married a gipsy. From the beginning of the story we are conscious of tension and lack of trust between them. She discovers that he has been unfaithful to her and she has her own back by being unfaithful with Johnny Onions, an itinerant Breton onion-seller. She begs him to stay with her but he refuses, and next day she runs away intending to join him. At sunset there are still fifteen miles to go.

She took her shoes off and bathed her swollen feet in a little brook. The water prattled like ice over her toes. She moved them up and down and her body sighed with relief. She took a handful of cress, broke off the roots, washed it and put it in her mouth. It was cool on her tongue, and yet it burnt her like a remorse. Ever since she had seen the gipsy come out of the cowshed, dusting his knees, she had been helpless in the whirlpool of her mind and body. She saw it clearly, looking down upon herself. She must go back to the caravan. If he had stayed in town overnight, he would never know. And Micah there alone – God! She pulled her sandals on, fingers trembling with haste, and started back along the lane.

She reaches the caravan at first light. Her husband is waiting for her, drunk; they trade insults and recriminations and then they fight. They fight each other into reconciliation. And the story ends:

After an hour lying in the deepest part of the wood, Micah came back slowly and fearfully to the clearing. Slowly he tiptoed up the steps of the caravan, apprehensive of the silence, and found them lying together under the red blanket, face to face and fast asleep.

The child did not wake them. Instead he sat quietly on the steps and carved a whistle out of a sycamore branch, knowing that when they woke everything would be the way he liked it.

What is impressive in this story of sexual passion is the sense of being in the presence of a young writer who is ready to confront unflinchingly the great subjects of literature. He sees his action from a great height, and this allows us more than one point of view. We find ourselves, for instance, identifying with the small boy as well as with his mother; and this without strain.

The qualities conspicuous in 'The Wanderers' similarly distinguish the stories of Army life. Among the best, and characteristic of them all, is 'Cold Spell', which narrates the course of the love of a Naafi counterhand, Gracie, for a flight sergeant in the Royal Air Force. The first paragraph sets the tone of the story:

Gracie worked in the Naffy on the aerodrome and it had begun with him buying coffee from her during the morning break, or before taking off of a winter morning on practice, or after dark on a raid. She always saw to it that his coffee was piping hot; the very first time she served him a cup she had heated it up for him.

We are told next to nothing about their antecedents and backgrounds and we never learn the flight sergeant's name, but both spring to life under Lewis's pen. The course of their love flows smoothly enough, though always checked by the constraints of their situation, by the knowledge, particularly for Gracie, that it may have no future.

And gradually, by herself, she made terms with life, figuring out just how it was. He had never said a word about the future. Marriage wasn't in his mind. And how could it be when he didn't expect to live? She wasn't blaming him for that. Their whole life was limited in a way, limited to the aerodrome, its routine and conventions and personnel and operations ... They were just part of the aerodrome, that was all, a little corner of the war. And he was more a part of it than she. He belonged to his kite, and was part of its crew. He talked of her engines and controls and guns with the intimate quietness of a lover ... She meant more to him than Gracie did. And she wasn't blaming him for that, either.

With its strong yet unemphatic rhythms, its colloquial ease, this is surely a beautiful piece of unstudied prose, which again may recall early Lawrence. Then in mid-December the ground freezes up, and one afternoon he takes Gracie to the neighbouring town. They walk by the lake in the public park.

'Look, Gracie,' he said, stopping and turning to her and kicking a stump of gorse with his toe, 'I've been thinking it out this week. Shall I tell you what I think?'

'Yes,' she said, her whole life suddenly pausing. If after all it was just this Saturday afternoon beside the lake for which she had been waiting with such fixed frightened endurance?

'Well, I've been thinking about the kite and the boys,' he said.

Something flared up in her, blind anger, like a heath fire half-stamped-out that breaks again into flame with a gust of wind.

'Yes?' she said. 'That's not unusual, is it?'

And he tells her that Micky, the rear-gunner, who had been wounded on the flight back from the last trip, had died that day.

After kicking the stump of gorse for a long time he said, 'I can't forget the stink of blood, and the clots of black flesh congealed in his clothes and the mess on the floor his face was sprawled on – I can't get it out of my mouth, Gracie, the filthy mess it was, and the stink.'

Then he proposes marriage to her; and the story ends with a beautiful image that seems the perfect resolution of everything that has gone before:

'Oh, look!' he said. 'Look at those two swans.'

A brace of swans, swift and white, cut like arrows slantwise through the lemon clouds of misty sunlight over the pines, wings firm-spread and glittering white in their downrushing and furling, scarcely disturbing the surface of the lake.

'Perfect landing!' he said. 'Wasn't it? Couldn't have done it better myself.'

Lewis left behind him half a dozen further stories, which are published together with letters from India to his wife and parents. They show the direction he might have gone, had he survived the war. The best of them is probably the best-known,

'Ward "O" 3 (b)', which focuses on the fortunes of the four officers in the officers' convalescent ward of a British military hospital in southern India in the autumn of 1942. There is no plot in any usual sense; rather, it is as though the occupants of the ward and the ward-sister exist in the spotlight of Lewis's totally objective and unsentimental compassion. The ease with which Lewis passes from one to another of them and builds up relationships between them suggests that he would have gone on to writing novels; we know that he was planning a work on much the same theme as *A Passage to India*. He did not live to begin it, but enough of his writing survives, the two volumes of verse and the score and a half of short stories, to indicate how great a loss to English literature his death was.

Younger by a decade than O'Faolain and O'Connor, Mary Lavin was born in the United States and did not see Ireland until she was ten years old, by which time independence had been achieved. Her stories make it clear that she takes for granted Ireland and the nature of Irish life, the most important feature of which is probably the part played by the Roman Catholic Church, as Moore, Joyce, O'Faolain, and O'Connor never did. O'Connor observes that an Irishman reading her stories for the first time might, for the shock he would take from them, be reading Turgenev or Leskov; which is tantamount to saying that Ireland is a predominantly masculine society in which women writers are rare, for the shock could come only from the realization that he was reading the work of a woman.

Nevertheless, O'Connor has a point, which can be supported by a passage he cogently quotes from one of Miss Lavin's best stories, 'The Nun's Mother':

Women had a curious streak of chastity in them, no matter how long they were married, or ardently they loved. And so, for most women, when they heard that a young girl was entering a convent, there was a strange triumph in their hearts at once; and during the day, as they moved round the house, they felt a temporary hostility to their husbands, to the things of his household, towards his tables and chairs; yes, indeed, down to his dishes and dishcloths.

Generally, her theme is the role of women, as mothers, wives, daughters, and sisters, in a specifically Irish context. Without effort and always convincingly, she can shift her scene from the countryside to the market-town and thence to the city, treat of the lives of tradespeople's families who live over their business premises in provincial centres as impartially as she does those of professional men in Dublin. And what she writes is always very close to the grain of common experience. Her work is distinguished by the sober realism that George Eliot called Dutch realism. Indeed, Mary Lavin has a sense of fairness, dispassion-

ateness, and discrimination in judgement similar to George
Eliot's; and she seems the more akin because her prose tends to
move slowly for a modern short-story writer.

'The Will', which is perhaps her best story, is typical of the
way her stories move and work, exposing facet after facet of the
situation being dramatized. Here, in a provincial town, a middle-
class matriarch has just died among her children.

The Conroys are horrified by the shock of discovering that
Lally, the youngest of them, has not only been left out of their
mother's will but has remained unforgiven. It is recalled that the
last time their mother had spoken of Lally she had murmured
something about blue feathers. 'Her mind was astray for the
time being, I suppose,' says Kate, but Lally understands and
explains:

'I had two little blue feathers in my hat the morning I went into her
room to tell her I was getting married. I had nothing new to put on me.
I was wearing my old green silk costume, and my old green hat, but I
bought two little pale feathers and pinned them on the front of the hat.
I think the feathers upset her more than going against her wishes with
the marriage. She kept staring at them all the time I was in the room,
and even when she ordered me out of her sight it was at the feathers in
my hat she was staring and not me.'

Their mother's behaviour has shocked Lally's brothers and
sisters into generous feelings and they each decide to contribute
a share of the inheritance to her. Lally refuses the offer as going
against her mother's wishes, which sparks off Kate to say: 'It's
late in the day to let thought of going against her wishes trouble
you.' It becomes increasingly plain that their generous feelings
serve only to mask their mother's attitude towards her. And
when they advise Lally against the propriety of keeping lodgers
it appears that generosity is not so dominant in them as the wish
to bribe her into conformity; the shock they have felt at their
mother's behaviour begins to seem nothing more than distaste at
the socially awkward or inconvenient.

'You may think you are behaving unselfishly,' said Kate, 'but let me
tell you it's not a nice thing for children to feel that their first cousins
are going to free schools in the city and mixing with the lowest of the
low, and running errands for your dirty lodgers. And as if that isn't

enough, I suppose you'll be putting them behind the counter in some greengrocer's, one of these days!'

Lally then insists that she must leave and catch her train. When she refuses Matthew's offer to drive her in his car to the station, they expostulate again. What will people think, Lally leaving for the city so soon after her mother's funeral? People will say there was a quarrel over the will. But Lally is not to be persuaded and she runs through the rain to the station. She has just time enough before catching her train to slip into the priest's house.

'I'm sorry to disturb you. I only wanted to ask a question.' Her short phrases leaped uncontrollably as the leaping flames in the grate. 'I want to know if you will say a mass for my mother first thing in the morning? My name is Lally Conroy. I'll send you the offering money the minute I get back to the city. I'll post it tonight. Will you do that, Father? Will you?'

The priest's curiosity is aroused to such a degree that she has to explain.

'I'm afraid,' said Lally. 'I'm afraid she might suffer. I'm afraid for her soul.' The eyes that stared into the flaming heart of the fire were indeed filled with fear, and as a coal fell, revealing a gaping abyss of fire, those eyes filled with absolute horror. The reflection of the flames leaped in them. 'She was very bitter,' Lally Conroy sobbed for the first time since she had news of her mother's death. 'She was very bitter against me all the time, and she died without forgiving me. I'm afraid for her soul.' She looked up at the priest. 'You'll say them as soon as ever you can, Father?'

He consents, and in the train driving through the night she feverishly works out ways of skimping and pinching on the house-keeping in order to pay for the masses. The story ends:

She tried to comfort herself by these calculations, but as the train rushed through the darkness she sat more upright on the red-carpeted seats that smelled of dust, and clenched her hands tightly as she thought of the torments of Purgatory. Bright red sparks from the engine flew past the carriage window, and she began to pray with rapid unformed words that jostled themselves in her mind like sheafs of burning sparks.

'The Will' must be one of the most compelling stories against the bourgeoisie ever written. It seems to me on the level of Maupassant at his best. It is Lally alone who sees what the consequences of her mother's behaviour may be, and the prospect of her mother in Purgatory, if not damned, is a spur to generous action. Mary Lavin's values are proclaimed in this story: she is on the side of love and disinterestedness, for the more spontaneous rather than the less.

This is clear, too, in 'Frail Vessels', which Frank O'Connor thought her best story:

... the story of two sisters, one of whom marries for convenience, the other for love. The prudent marriage turns out well, the love marriage turns out disastrously, and the frail vessel, Liddy, has to beg from her well-to-do sister, who is pregnant. By an exquisite touch of irony Bedelia, the hard woman, can still in feminine terms regard herself as the more successful of the two, but the moment Liddy reveals that she, too, is pregnant, Bedelia's whole façade of success collapses. Even penniless, homeless, abandoned by her ineffectual husband, Liddy carrying the child of someone she has loved is still the dominant figure, and nothing Bedelia can ever do now will alter the relationship between them.

That is excellent but it says nothing about the admirable balance of fairness between the characters Mary Lavin maintains. Liddy, the younger sister, is the one who claims our sympathies as the sister moved by love and not prudence. Yet in the end it is Bedelia who appeals to our instincts of fair play, for she appears as a Martha figure. She has married partly to provide for her motherless younger sister and has then found, as a bride, that it is Liddy she has to compete with. She has freely accepted responsibility, and responsibility is not an immediately attractive quality. Yet, however difficult the task, she has tried to be a loving sister. It is one of Mary Lavin's excellences that she compels us through her stories to contemplate the difficulties of the moral life. As she shows us time and again, our good intentions are equalled only by our weaknesses. The theme implicit in her stories is the need for charity.

'The Southern school,' wrote Flannery O'Connor, conjures up 'an image of Gothic monstrosities and the idea of preoccupation with everything deformed and grotesque.' She added, somewhat ruefully: 'Most of us are considered, I believe, to be unhappy combinations of Poe and Erskine Caldwell.' It cannot be denied that there is a strong family resemblance between Southern writers and that the family face, as Thomas Hardy defined it in a famous poem, has persisted through more than a century of Southern writing. There are times, for instance, when Eudora Welty, plainly a writer of great sophistication and, one guesses, of considerable literary learning, is unmistakably kin to Caldwell. To pinpoint differences of manner, theme, and content however, one need only pick out Eudora Welty's story 'First Love', which is indeed remarkable. It is set in the river-town of Natchez, Mississippi, in 1807, ten years before Mississippi became a state, and presents an oblique glance at an episode in the life of Aaron Burr, who, having been Vice President of the United States, killed Alexander Hamilton in a duel and then went down to the old Southwest to found a new settlement, was arrested, tried, and acquitted on a charge of treason.

The action of 'First Love' takes place in a January in which the winter is unusually severe. The third paragraph will give some indication of Miss Welty's artistry as a prose-writer:

The coated moss hung in blue and shining garlands over the trees along the changed streets in the morning. The town of little galleries was all laden roofs and silence. In the fastness of Natchez it began to seem then that the whole world, like itself, must be in transfiguration. The only clamour came from the animals that suffered in their stalls, or from the wildcats that howled in closer rings each night from the frozen cane. The Indians could be heard from greater distances and in greater numbers than had been guessed, sending up placating but proud messages to the sun in continual ceremonies of dancing. The red percussion of their fires could be seen night and day by those waiting in the dark trance of the frozen town. Men were caught by the cold, they dropped into its snare-like silence. Bands of travellers moved closer together, with intenser caution, through the glassy tunnels of the Trace, for all proportion went away, and they followed one another like insects at dawn through heavy grass. Natchez people turned silently to look when a solitary man that no one had ever seen before was found and carried in through the streets, frozen the way he had crouched in a hollow tree, grey and huddled like a squirrel, with a little bundle of goods clasped to him.

This evocation of winter is obviously the work of an unusual romantic imagination of a strongly visual cast. There are suggestions in it of Keats and also, in its slightly macabre, quasi-surrealist vein, of Poe. The scene seems to be depicted from an angle slightly at odds with the normal and this is borne out when we read the story, for its centre of consciousness, through which the events narrated are filtered, is a deaf and dumb boy of twelve, an orphan who is the boots at the hotel in Natchez. He too is quite remarkably imagined:

Joel Mayes, a deaf boy twelve years old, saw the man brought in and knew it was a dead man, but his eyes were for something else, something wonderful. He saw the breaths coming out of people's mouths, and his dark face, losing just now a little of its softness, showed its secret desire. It was marvellous to him when the infinite designs of speech became visible in formations on the air, and he watched with awe that changed to tenderness whenever people met and passed in the road with an exchange of words. He walked alone, slowly through the silence, with the sturdy and yet dreamlike walk of the orphan, and let his own breath out through his lips, pushed it into the air, and whatever word it was it took the shape of a tower. He was as pleased as if he had a little conversation with someone.

Yet in 'The Wide Net' which follows 'First Love' we are very evidently in Caldwell country. In her obsession with her pregnancy William Wallace Jamieson's wife ignores him to such an extent that he goes out one evening and stays out all night. When he returns in the morning Hazel has disappeared and left a note saying that she will not put up with him any longer and has gone to the river to drown herself. William Wallace calls for his friend Virgil Thomas to come and help him find her.

Within a page or two, however, it is clear that there is a great difference between Miss Welty's art and Caldwell's and in the nature of their comedy. In his rendering of poor whites Caldwell seems to be moved mainly by indignation at their condition and the way they are exploited. His comedy, therefore, is always close to satire. Eudora Welty, on the other hand, seems to revel in the spectacle of oddity for its own sake. Caldwell, one feels, has designs on us; Eudora Welty, none.

This, indeed, is borne out by 'The Wide Net', which becomes a celebration of what unwittingly is a holiday. If William Wallace and Virgil are to find Hazel, it will mean dragging the river, and for that they will need further help. 'The six Doyles and their dogs, and you and me, and two little nigger boys is enough, with just a few Malones,' says William Wallace, and the two little Rippen boys are allowed to come as well, for since their papa was drowned in the river William Wallace argues that 'those little-old boys' will particularly appreciate it. Old Doc joins the party too, for it is his net they borrow. They drag the river, and later, on a sandbar, they build a fire 'and for a long time among clouds of odours and smoke, all half-naked except Doc, they cooked and ate catfish'. Lying on the sand, 'There is nothing in the world as good as ... fish. The fish of Pearl River,' says William Wallace as, smiling, he falls asleep. 'The excursion,' as Doc says, 'is the same when you go looking for your sorrow as when you go looking for your joy.' Then, each with his string of fish, they march into town. People stare out of the post office and the store at them.

All the bird dogs woke to see the Doyle dogs and such a large number of men and boys materialize suddenly with such a big catch of fish, and they ran out barking. The Doyle dogs joyously barked back. The bluejays flashed up and screeched above the town, whipping through their tunnels in the chinaberry trees. In the cafe a nickel clattered inside a music box and a love song began to play. The whole town of Dover began to throb in its wood and tin, like an old tired heart, when the men walked through once more, coming round again and going down the street carrying the fish, so drenched, exhausted, and muddy that no one could help but admire them.

It is evening when William Wallace gets back to his home. It has not rained there, but to his surprise, curved over the roof is a rainbow, a rainbow at night. Hazel is in the house and they indulge in an amorous scuffle.

She lay smiling in the crook of his arm. It was the same as any other chase in the end.

'I will do it again if I get ready,' she said. 'Next time it will be different, too.'

Then she was ready to go in, and rose up and looked out from the top step, out across their yard where the China tree was and beyond, into the dark fields where the lightning-bugs flickered away. He climbed to his feet and stood beside her, with the frown on his face, trying to look where she looked. After a few minutes she took him by the hand and led him into the house, smiling as if she were smiling down on him.

As Sylvia Jenkins Cook has shown in *From Tobacco Road to Route 66*, the poor white has always been seen as incorrigibly ignoble. It is Eudora Welty's great achievement in 'The Wide Net' to have begun the process of the poor white's redemption by making him a figure in comedy uncontaminated by satire. The qualities that distinguish 'The Wide Net', lyrical happiness and a pervading sense of innocence, are almost certainly the rarest in modern literature anywhere in the world and to be able to express them through so old a stereotype as the poor white is well-nigh miraculous. If one ranks 'The Wide Net' higher than 'Petrified Man', for example, which is probably her most famous story, and which tells of poor white women in beauty-parlours, it is because satire has traditionally been seen as a lower form than pure comedy. It seems, perhaps, significant that even when Eudora Welty writes of Americans in Europe, or of Italian-Americans on a liner bound for Naples, she does not see them in any way different from the way in which she sees her poor whites of Mississippi.

Erskine Caldwell's Georgia mill towns are also part of Carson McCullers' territory, whose inhabitants also bear a family resemblance to his. Her extremely idiosyncratic view of human beings seems most successfully expressed in her long short-story, 'The Ballad of the Sad Café'.

If you walk along the main street on an August afternoon there is nothing whatsoever to do. The largest building, the very centre of the town, is boarded up completely and leans so far to the right that it seems bound to collapse at any minute. The house is very old. There is about it a curious, cracked look that is very puzzling, until you suddenly realize that at one time, and long ago, the right side of the front porch had been painted, and part of the wall – but the painting was left unfinished, and one portion of the house is darker and dingier than the other. The building looks completely deserted. Nevertheless, on the second floor there is one window which is not boarded; sometimes in the late afternoon when the heat is at its worst a hand will slowly open the shutter and a face will look down on the town. It is a face like the terrible dim faces known in dreams – sexless and white, with two grey crossed eyes which are turned inward so sharply that they seem to be exchanging with each other one long and secret gaze of grief. The face lingers at the window for an hour or so, then the shutters are closed once more, and as likely as not there will not be another soul to be seen along the main street. These August afternoons – when your shift is finished there is absolutely nothing to do; you might as well walk down to the Fork Falls Road and listen to the chain gang.

If one is reminded of the opening of 'The Fall of the House of Usher' it is appropriate, for Carson McCullers is one of the most remarkable writers of the South to emerge since Poe.

The story tells how the woman at the window came to be how she is and the house to be boarded up. It had once been a store and a café but at the centre of it was always the woman, known to the town as Miss Amelia. She was a rich woman and over six-foot tall, with bones and muscles like a man's. Since her father died she had been a solitary, except for ten days during which she was married to Marvin Macy, a handsome mill-hand and a sadist whom the whole town feared. After ten days she had had him turned off her premises and he had left town, leaving behind 'a wild love letter' in which he swore that one day he would get even with her. He became a criminal and perhaps a murderer and in the end was sent to the penitentiary near Atlanta. 'Miss Amelia was deeply gratified.'

All this took place ten years before the events narrated in the body of the story. On a soft quiet night in April something, someone, is seen approaching.

The man was a stranger, and it is rare that a stranger enters the town on foot at that hour. Besides, the man was a hunchback. He was scarcely more than four feet high and he wore a ragged, dusty coat that reached only to his knees. His crooked little legs seemed too thin to carry the weight of his great warped chest and the hump that sat on his shoulders. He had a very large head, with deep-set blue eyes and a sharp little mouth. His face was both soft and sassy – at the moment his pale skin was yellowed by dust and there were lavender shadows beneath his eyes. He carried a lopsided old suitcase which was tied with a rope.

The dwarf, whose name is Lymon Willis, claims to be a relation of Miss Amelia's, and she seems to accept him, although other people have, in the past tried, with absolutely no success, to prove kinship with her. Next day, Miss Amelia does not open the store, and throughout the whole town it is rumoured that Miss Amelia has murdered the hunchback for the contents of his suitcase. On the following day the store is open again and in the evening a group of men is waiting on her porch for her. What they intend to do we are not told, but it is plainly sinister. It does not happen because the hunchback appears. He came down the stairs

slowly with the proudness of one who owns every plank on the floor beneath his feet. In the past days he had greatly changed. For one thing he was clean beyond words. He still wore his little coat, but it was brushed and neatly mended.

Lymon has the art of making immediate contact with people. Because of him, the whole atmosphere of the group changes. Things wear the air of a party, at any rate of a 'vague festivity'. We are told who are present: Hasty Malone, Robert Calvert Hale, Merlie Ryan, Reverend T. M. Willin, Rosser Cline, Rip Wellborne, Henry Ford Crimp, and Horace Wells.

Except for Reverend Willin, they are all alike in many ways as has been said – all having taken pleasure from something or other, all having wept and suffered in some way, most of them tractable unless exasperated. Each of them worked in the mill, and lived with others in a two- or three-room house for which the rent was ten dollars or twelve dollars a month. All had been paid that afternoon, for it was Saturday. So, for the present, think of them as a whole.

Their presence in the story is important. They are hardly differentiated one from another, they precipitate no action, but all the action in the story takes place before their eyes. They scarcely speak and yet they function as a kind of chorus. They note the fuss Miss Amelia makes of the hunchback and to their surprise, for the first time in their lives, they are allowed to drink in the store itself. They see, in other words, the hunchback bringing a café into being, and it is something that changes their lives:

Recall that the night was gloomy as in wintertime, and to have sat around the property outside would have made a sorry celebration. But inside there was company and a genial warmth. Someone had rattled up the stove in the rear, and those who bought bottles shared their liquor with friends. Several women were there and they had twists of licorice, a Nehi, or even a swallow of whisky. The hunchback was still a novelty and his presence amused everyone. . . . Nor did the opening of liquor on the premises cause any rambunctiousness, indecent giggles, or misbehaviour whatsoever. On the contrary the company was polite even to the point of a certain timidity. For people in this town were then unused to gathering together for the sake of pleasure. They met to work at the mill. Or on Sunday there would be an all-day camp meeting – and though that is a pleasure the intention of the whole affair is to sharpen your view of Hell and put into you a keen fear of the Lord Almighty. But the spirit of a café is altogether different. Even the richest, greediest old rascal will behave himself, insulting no one in a proper café. And poor people look about them gratefully and pinch the salt in a dainty and modest manner. For the atmosphere of a proper café implies these qualities: fellowship, the satisfaction of the belly, and a certain gaiety and grace of behaviour.

So the café comes into being as the centre of the town's life. Cousin Lymon, the hunchback, is firmly established. He has Miss Amelia's confidence in all things except the knowledge of her ten-day marriage. Six years pass and then they hear that Miss Amelia's husband has been released on parole from the penitentiary. Months go by and it is the beginning of winter, but still when Miss Amelia speaks Cousin Lymon's name there lingers in her voice 'the undertone of love'. She is away on business in Cheehaw when the man drops off a van passing the café.

The first person in the town to see this newcomer was Cousin Lymon, who had heard the shifting of gears and come round to investigate. . . . He and the man stared at each other, and it was not the look of two strangers meeting for the first time and swiftly summing up each other. It was a peculiar stare they exchanged between them, like the look of two criminals who recognize each other. Then the man in the red shirt shrugged his left shoulder and turned away. The face of the hunchback was very pale as he watched the man go down the road, and after a few moments he began to follow along carefully, keeping many paces away.

It is immediately known throughout the town that Marvin
Macy is back. Almost without effort he imposes on it a reign of
terror but it is on Cousin Lymon that he has the profoundest
effect. The hunchback is as it were infatuated with him. It is he
who brings Marvin to the café for his meals and later installs
him on the premises. Because Lymon, who has a cold and is
believed consumptive, has given him his own bed, Miss Amelia
gives up hers to the hunchback and sleeps herself on the sofa,
which is much too short for her. The tension between them is
unbearable and the whole town waits for the fight that will take
place between Miss Amelia and Marvin.

It takes place on Ground Hog Day, the second of February.
Early in the morning Miss Amelia cuts down her punching bag,
Marvin greases himself with hog fat, and they both eat four
helpings of roast for dinner and lie down in the afternoon to
store up strength. The café is cleared of its furniture in readi-
ness for the fight. By seven o'clock the room is crowded with
spectators, Cousin Lymon standing on the counter raised above
them all.

He had his hands on his hips, his big head thrust forward, his little legs
bent so that the knees jutted forward. The excitement made him break
out in a rash, and his pale mouth shivered.

On the stroke of seven Miss Amelia walks down the stairs and
Marvin enters from the porch. Both strike out simultaneously.
After half an hour the boxing changes to wrestling, and gradually Miss Amelia forces Marvin to the floor, straddles him,
and has her big strong hands on his throat. Then, just as she is
winning, Cousin Lymon leaps from the counter, lands on her
strong broad back, and clutches 'at her neck with his clawed little
fingers'.

Before the crowd can come to its senses the fight had been
won by Marvin. Someone pours water over Miss Amelia, and
after a time she drags herself into her office. Before daylight
Marvin and the hunchback have disappeared, having, among
other things, placed temptingly on the counter a dish of Miss
Amelia's favourite food, grits with sausage, seaoned with enough
poison to kill off the county. For three years Miss Amelia sits
every night on the porch steps, waiting for the hunchback to

come back. But he never does. Report says that Marvin has sold him to a side-show. In the fourth year she has the premises boarded up and ever since has remained in closed rooms. 'There is absolutely nothing to do in the town . . . The soul rots with boredom.' You might as well go to Fork Falls Road and listen to the chain gang.

The gang is made up of twelve men, all wearing black and white striped prison suits, and chained at the ankles . . . The music will swell until at least it seems that the sound does not come from the twelve men on the gang, but from the earth itself, or the wide sky. It is music that causes the heart to broaden and the listener to grow cold with ecstasy and fright. Then slowly the music will sink down until there remains one lonely voice, then a great hoarse breath, the sun, the sounds of the picks in the silence.

And what kind of gang is this that can make such music? Just twelve mortal men, seven of them black and five of them white boys from this county. Just twelve mortal men who are together.

'The Ballad of the Sad Café' has the timelessness and remoteness precisely of a ballad. It describes a kind of ritual dance in which the loved one always turns away from the lover to love another one who also turns away. 'Only connect . . .' was Forster's cry in *Howards End*. That, in Carson McCullers' world, is impossible, and the impossibility is symbolized by the physical abnormality of the characters: Miss Amelia is grotesquely tall, Cousin Lymon a misshapen dwarf. One can see Carson McCullers turning the common properties of Southern writing to Expressionist ends: the stereotype of the poor white becomes a source of strength. The story has, curiously, an anonymous quality, as through the utterance of a folk-voice in the form of a prose of singular purity which transmits the ambience of the town and its inhabitants and the timeless quality that broods over the action.

The great contemporary exception to Flannery O'Connor's generalization about the Southern school and the image it conjures up of Gothic monstrosities and preoccupation 'with everything deformed and grotesque' is Peter Taylor. His characters are lawyers, judges, university professors, members of state legislatures, even state governors and their wives, in other words, members of the upper class, the class that rules. A native of

Tennessee, Taylor is closely related in origins and upbringing to the poets, novelists, and critics – John Crowe Ransom, Allen Tate, Cleanth Brooks, Robert Penn Warren and others – who are associated with such manifestations of the Southern Renaissance as *The Fugitives* magazine of the nineteen-twenties and the important New Criticism that grew out of it. The dominant theme of his stories is time, continuity, and change, 'the image of the past in the present', as Allen Tate has called it, 'the pervasive Southern subject of our time'. Taylor, however, is twenty years younger than Tate and the world he lives in exists no longer wholly in the shadow of the Civil War.

His stories are concerned very often with sensitive, gentle people whose ways and allegiances have been shaped by the past and who find themselves being betrayed by the present. In one of the most effective, 'What You Hear from 'Em?', he speaks through an old coloured woman, Old Aunt Munsie, who is a famous and privileged person in the small, decaying town of Thornton.

Aunt Munsie's skin was the colour of a faded tow sack. She was hardly four feet tall. She was generally believed to be totally bald, and on her head she always wore a white dust cap with an elastic band. She wore an apron, too, while making her rounds with her slop wagon. Even when the weather got bad and she tied a wool scarf over her head and wore an overcoat, she put on an apron over her coat. Her hands and feet were delicately small, which made the old-timers sure she was of Guinea stock that had come to Tennessee out of South Carolina. What most touched the hearts of old ladies on Jackson and Jefferson streets were her little feet. The sight of her feet 'took them back to the old days', they said, because Aunt Munsie still wore flat-heeled, high button shoes. Where did Munsie find such shoes any more?

'What You Hear from 'Em?' is the question Aunt Munsie calls to her patrons as she pushes her slop-wagon round Thornton collecting the garbage on which she feeds her pigs. By ' 'em' she means the Tollivers, Mr Thad and Mr Will. Periodically, one or the other visits her for twenty minutes from Nashville or Memphis. She always asks them, 'Now, look-a-here. When you comin' back?' She had brought them up as children in Thornton when old Dr Tolliver was alive, had been a second mother to them. That was before the Great World War. Now everything has changed and one day Aunt Munsie puts her question to old Miss Lucille Satterfield, who has brothers and sons who are lawyers in Memphis. Miss Lucille answers:

'Goodness knows when any of them are coming back to stay. . . . They're prospering so, Munsie', she said, throwing her chin up and smiling proudly. . . . 'They're *all* prospering so, Munsie. Mine *and* yours. You ought to go down to Memphis now and then, the way I do. Or go up to Nashville to see Mr Will. I understand he's got an even finer establishment than Thad. They've done well, Munsie – yours *and* mine – and we can be proud of them. . . .'

In the meantime, the old patrician ladies worry that Aunt Munsie, who is old, deaf, and almost blind, will be killed if she persists in pulling her slop-wagon along the middle of the road. The only way to prevent this is for a town ordinance to be passed forbidding the keeping of swine within the city limits. This is done: Aunt Munsie must get rid of her pigs. Even Mr Thad and Mr Will visit her and then call on the Mayor to set the wheels of conspiracy in motion.

Aunt Munsie does not exchange a word with anyone about the ordinance or the conspiracy but Crecie, her daughter, who lives next door to her, sees and overhears her when she is preparing to drive the pigs to their new owner. She swings the axe over her head and the animals scatter in all directions. She then addresses herself to the collie pup:

'You want to know what's the commotion about? I reckoned you would', she said with profound contempt, as though the collie were a more reasonable soul than the other animals, and as though there were nothing she held in such thorough disrespect as reason. 'I tell you what the commotion's about', she said. 'They *ain't* comin' back. They ain't never comin' back. They ain't never had no notion of comin' back. . . . Why don't I go down to Memphis or up to Nashville, like *you* does?' Aunt Munsie asked the collie. 'I tell you why. Becaz I ain't nothin' to 'em in Memphis, and they ain't nothin' to me in Nashville. *You* can, go!' she said, advancing and shaking the big axe at the dog. 'A collie dog's a collie dog anywhar. But Aunt Munsie, she's just their Aunt Munsie here in Thornton. I got mind enough to see *that*.'

Aunt Munsie lived for another twenty years; Mr Thad and Mr Will and their families continued to visit her but she never again asked when they were coming back and she, who had once been someone of status, took to tying a bandanna about her head and 'talking old-nigger foolishness'.

Auden has a line in an early poem which he later called 'Venus Will Now Say a Few Words', that well sums up the characters about whom Taylor has written some of his best and most characteristic stories: 'Holders of one position, wrong for years' – wrong because out of date, betrayed by history or simply the passing of time. Aunt Munsie is one of them, Miss Leonora, in 'Miss Leonora When Last Seen', is another. The story begins:

Here in Thomasville we are all concerned over the whereabouts of Miss Leonora Logan. She had been missed for two weeks, and though half a dozen postcards have been received from her, stating that she is in good health and that no anxiety should be felt for her safety, still the whole town can talk of nothing else. She was last seen in Thomasville heading south on Logan Lane, which is a narrow little street that runs alongside her family property. At four-thirty on Wednesday afternoon – Wednesday before last, that is to say – she turned out of the dirt driveway that comes down from her house and drove south on the lane toward its intersection with the by-pass of the Memphis–Chattanooga highway. She has not been seen since. Officially, she is away from home on a little trip. Unofficially, in the minds of the townspeople, she is a missing person, and because of events leading up to her departure none of us will rest easy until we know that the old lady is safe at home again.

The speaker is an anonymous citizen of Thomasville who was Miss Leonora's favourite pupil when she was English teacher in the high school. He is also, it may be, the spokesman of the town's guilty conscience towards Miss Leonora, for though such motor trips have been a common feature of the years of her retirement, this one follows on a decisive event:

The cause of our present tribulation is this: the Logan property, which Miss Leonora inherited from one of her paternal grand-uncles and which normally upon her death would have gone to distant relatives of hers in Chicago, has been chosen as the site of our county's new consolidated high school. A year and a half ago, Miss Leonora was offered a fair price for the three-acre tract and the old house, and she refused it. This summer, condemnation proceedings were begun, and two weeks ago the county court granted the writ. This will seem to you a bad thing for the town to have done, especially in view of the fact that Miss Leonora has given long years of service to our school system. She retired ten years ago after teaching for twenty-five years in the old high school.

As the narrator reminisces, even rambles on, an impression of Miss Leonora Logan emerges. She is the last member of the family that founded the town. It was unpopular, for as the narrator tells us, it was 'a family that for a hundred years and more did all it could to impede the growth and progress of our town. . . . Their one idea was always to keep the town unspoiled, unspoiled by railroads or factories or even local politics.' Of Miss Leonora the narrator says:

She cannot bear to think of us away from Thomasville. She thinks this is where we all belong. I remember one day at school when some boy said to her that he wished he lived in a place like Memphis or Chattanooga. She gave him the look she usually reserved for the people she caught cheating. I was seated in the first row of the class that day, and I saw the angry patches of red appear on her broad, flat cheeks and on her forehead. She paused a moment to rearrange the combs in her hair and to give the stern yank to her corset that was a sure sign she was awfully mad. (We used to say that, with her spare figure, she only wore a corset for the sake of that expressive gesture.) The class was silent, waiting. Miss Leonora looked out of the window for a moment, squinting up her eyes as if she could actually make out the Memphis or even the Chatanooga skyline on the horizon. Then, turning back to the unfortunate boy, she said, grinding out her words to him through clenched teeth, 'I wish I could *throw* you there!'

Having been told the news of her dispossession, Miss Leonora leaves on her trip, dressed as the narrator has never seen her before, looking like one of those blue-rinsed old women from Memphis 'who tell you how delighted they are to find a Southern town that is truly unchanged'; normally on her trips she wears either dungarees or a lace choker, appropriate costumes for her 'escapes into a reality that is scattered in bits and pieces along the highways and back roads of the country she travels'.

Equally memorable stories of people's inability to come to terms with the present are 'Venus, Cupid, Folly, and Time' and 'Their Losses'. These stories are ambiguous; Taylor, one feels, admires his characters reluctantly but does not necessarily approve; he is not in any ordinary sense a *laudator temporis acti*.

Indeed, irony and ambivalence constantly attend him. A beautiful instance of this is the story 'Dean of Men', in which a university professor tells his son, a student of the late Sixties, one would guess, an exemplary story from his own otherwise highly successful life to buttress his remark, 'I must try to warn you that I don't think even your wonderful generation will succeed in going very far along the road you are on.' It is a wise and authoritative story; the academic life is admirably realized, the professor is a vehicle of truth, yet even as one recognizes this one realizes that he is pompous and stuffy, 'a man of measured merriment', to borrow a memorable phrase from Sinclair Lewis's *Martin Arrowsmith*.

Taylor's stories are very close to the kinds of poem admired by the New Critics at whose feet he must have sat as an undergraduate at Vanderbilt University and Kenyon College; they succeed in the way such poems succeed, 'in the balance of reconcilement of opposite or discordant qualities: of sameness, with difference; of the general, with the concrete; ... a more than usual state of emotion, with more than usual order. ...' Taylor's art as a short-story writer is an art of paradox.

An admirer of Flannery O'Connor and a co-religionist has written of her stories:

What they contain is an astonishing and often appalling assortment of murderers, wild-eyed preachers, psychologically warped youngsters, charlatans, adulterers, perverts, ignorant rednecks, and generally wretched heroes. Brutality, violence, mayhem, deceit, sardonic twists, and the deaths of innocents are among the staples of her fiction. Her stories are seldom pleasant reading and, to the uninitiate, the sin and gore might seem pointless, nothing more than naturalism of the basest variety run utterly amok.

On the face of it, then, Flannery O'Connor might seem of the South, Southern, to the point of parody. Born in Georgia in 1925, she spent nearly all her life there, on the family farm, for she was crippled by incurable disease. She died at thirty-eight, the author of two novels and two books of short stories, *A Good Man is Hard to Find* and *Everything that Rises Must Converge*. Yet even though she was of the South, she was not entirely representative of it. In a region defined, almost, by Protestant Fundamentalism she was a Roman Catholic and it was as a Roman Catholic that she wrote. In her fiction the human race is shown as 'implicated', in Newman's words, 'in some terrible aboriginal calamity. It is out of joint with the purposes of its Creator.' She herself described her work as

literal in the same sense that a child's drawing is literal. When a child draws he doesn't try to be grotesque but to set down exactly what he sees, and as his gaze is direct, he sees the lines that create motion. I am interested in the lines that create spiritual motion.

Flannery O'Connor's stories are so absolutely of their own kind that any one of them will lead directly into the world and values she creates, and 'Good Country People' is as good an example as any. As every turn of her cliché-ridden speech shows, Mrs Hopewell is a widow who clings desperately to the normal. She has a daughter named Joy, though she calls herself Hulga, a name she has coined herself as the epitome of all that is ugly. In her thirties, Hulga has a wooden leg, a heart condition, and a doctorate in philosophy; she dresses like a teen-age girl and, an avowed atheist at utter odds with her mother's optimism, has retreated into a world of abstraction and re-created herself in the image of her deformity.

When the young Bible salesman, Manley Pointer, calls at the farm Mrs Hopewell takes to him because he seems so obviously what she calls 'good country people'. However, he arranges secretly to see Hulga, who is pretending to be seventeen, that evening. He makes tentative love to her and she tells him that she does not even believe in God, at which he whistles as if too astonished to say anything. Still carrying the suitcase which holds his Bibles, he leads her into a barn, tells her he loves her, and pleads with her to say that she loves him, challenging her to prove her love by letting him take off her wooden leg. She agrees; 'It was like surrendering to him completely.' He moves the leg out of her reach and opens the suitcase, which contains two Bibles. One proves to be a box containing a hip-flask of whisky, a pack of playing cards with dirty pictures on the back, and a packet of contraceptives.

Her voice when she spoke had an almost pleading sound. 'Aren't you,' she murmured, 'aren't you just good country people?'

The boy cocked his head. He looked as if he were just beginning to understand that she might be trying to insult him. 'Yeah,' he said, curling his lip slightly, 'but it ain't held me back none. I'm as good as you any day in the week.'

'Give me my leg,' she said.

He pushed it farther away with his foot. 'Come on now, let's begin to have a good time,' he said coaxingly. 'We ain't got to know one another good yet.'

'Give me my leg,' she screamed and tried to lunge for it but he pushed her down easily.

'What's the matter with you all of a sudden?' he asked, frowning as he screwed the top of the flask and put it quickly back inside the Bible. 'You just said a while ago you didn't believe in nothing. I thought you was some girl!'

Her face was almost purple. 'You're a Christian!' she hissed. 'You're a fine Christian! You're just like them all – say one thing and do another. You're a perfect Christian, you're. . . .'

The boy's mouth was set angrily. 'I hope you don't think', he said in a lofty indignant tone, 'that I believe in that crap! I may sell Bibles but I know which end is up and I wasn't born yesterday and I know where I'm going!'

He grabs the leg, packs it in the suitcase with the Bibles and runs out of the barn with it. At the top of the ladder, he taunts her, telling her that once he got a glass eye of a woman in the same way.

A little later, Mrs Hopewell and Mrs Freeman, who are digging up onions, see him emerge from the walk towards the road.

'Why, that looks like that nice dull young man that tried to sell me a Bible yesterday', Mrs Hopewell said, squinting, 'He must have been selling them to the Negroes back in there. He was so simple', she said, 'but I guess the world would be better off if we were all that simple.'

Mrs Freeman's gaze drove forward and just touched him before he disappeared under the hill. Then she returned her attention to the evil-smelling onion shoot she was lifting from the ground. 'Some can't be that simple,' she said. 'I know I never could.'

Stripped down to the naked anecdote – boy makes love to girl in order to steal her wooden leg – it might be an Erskine Caldwell story; for that matter, had there been wooden legs at the time, we might meet something like it among the medieval *fabliaux*. We recognize kinship with the primitive story, but the implications are no longer the same. If the characters were Caldwell's poor whites we should be in the presence of the all-but-mindless; but neither Hulga nor Pointer is mindless. In a curious way, they are as much in revolt against the mindless as they are contemptuous of the values of Mrs Hopewell and Mrs Freeman. Of the four characters in the story it is with Hulga and Pointer, if anywhere, that Miss O'Connor's sympathies lie. We are made to feel that Pointer's obsession with women's glass eyes and wooden legs is something more than the symptom of a merely psychological disability or neurotic disorder. We are not in the world of Naturalism at all. The obsession is the dramatic expression in symbolic form of a disability, an incongruity, a *grotesquerie*, at the heart of things. Like Carson McCullers, Flannery O'Connor is an Expressionist in a strict sense. As she wrote: 'You have to make your vision apparent by shock – to the hard of hearing you shout, and for the almost blind you draw large startling figures.'

In her essentials, Flannery O'Connor is probably nearer to Dostoevsky than to any Southern writer. Hulga and Pointer, who have withdrawn themselves from or rejected God, are all the same nearer to God and Salvation than are the respectable and unctuous who allow themselves to be committed to nothing.

This comes out very plainly in 'A Good Man Is Hard to Find', in which a family – mother and father, small son and daughter and grandmother – go on a trip to Florida. The grandmother, however, really wants to go to Tennessee and she tries to change her son Bailey's mind by showing him a paragraph in the local newspaper:

'Now look here, Bailey, see here, read this. . . . Here this fellow that calls himself The Misfit is aloose from the Federal Pen and headed towards Florida and you read what it says he did to those people. Just you read it. I wouldn't take my children in any direction with a criminal like that aloose in it. I couldn't answer to my conscience if I did.'

Bailey is adamant: they're going to Florida. With a bad grace the grandmother gets into the car, surreptitiously taking her cat with her. She is a typical O'Connor matron, sentimentally pious and censorious. Telling him that 'people are certainly not nice like they used to be' and that nowadays a good man is hard to find, she commiserates with a filling-station proprietor.

The old lady said that in her opinion Europe was entirely to blame for the way things were now. She said the way Europe acted you would think we were made of money and Red Sam said it was no use talking about it, she was exactly right.

Resuming their journey, on a whim of the grandmother they turn off on to a dirt road and the cat, disturbed, leaps off the old lady's lap on to Bailey's shoulder, which causes him to lose control of the car. It 'turned over once and landed right-side-up in a gulch off the side of the road'. A car approaches them along the road, with three men in it, and stops.

The driver got out of the car and stood by the side of it, looking down at them. He was an older man than the other two. His hair was just beginning to grey and he wore silver-rimmed spectacles that gave him a scholarly look. He had a long creased face and didn't have on shirt or undershirt. He had on blue jeans that were too tight for him and was holding a black hat and a gun. The two boys also had guns.

The grandmother recognizes him as The Misfit.

'Yes'm,' the man said, smiling slightly as if he were pleased in spite of himself to be known, 'but it would have been better for all of you, lady, if you hadn't of reckernised me.'

He is polite and respectful, and the grandmother says that she knows he must come from nice people. He agrees but all the same he invites Bailey and the boy to follow the two younger convicts into the wood. He is telling the grandmother about his parents when the shots ring out. The mother and daughter are then taken into the wood and there are two more shots. The Misfit goes on talking, almost indeed philosophizing. 'Jesus was the only One that ever raised the dead,' he says, 'and He shouldn't have done it. He threw everything off balance.'

'Maybe He didn't raise the dead,' the old lady mumbled, not knowing what she was saying and feeling so dizzy that she sank down in the ditch with her legs twisted under her.

She sees his face close to her as if he were going to cry, and murmuring, 'Why you're one of my babies. You're one of my own children,' leans forward to touch him.

The Misfit sprang back as if a snake had bitten him and shot her three times through the chest. Then he put his gun down on the ground and took off his glasses and began to clean them.

At the heart of the story, making it much more than a merely sensational tale of violence, is the Misfit's relation to Christ and his conviction that 'Jesus thrown everything off balance'. Flannery O'Connor had great gifts. She was a remarkable comic writer and a master of the vernacular speech of her community, who used black comedy to illustrate what Ignazio Silone meant when he wrote in his preface to *And He Did Hide Himself*, 'In the sacred history of man on earth, it is still, alas, Good Friday.'

VIII

In his own country, it seems generally agreed among other writers, the finest writer of fiction that New Zealand has produced since Katherine Mansfield is Frank Sargeson. He has said of himself '. . . as a schoolboy I became much aware that I was a European born in a country very remote from Europe: in the form of fiction I have *had* to say what in my view it means to be a New Zealander.' Appropriately, the influences and affinities – affinities more often than positive influences – one spots in his work are American rather than English.

Born in 1903, he began as a short-story writer, and though he has written novels it is on his short stories that his reputation mainly rests. The typical Sargeson story is truly short – generally no more than three or four pages in length – and characterized by an apparently complete absence of artifice. They are given the greater appearance of authenticity by being written in the first person, so that they seem to be transcripts of experience salvaged from memory.

One of the best of them and characteristic except for the fact that it is fully nine pages long, is 'A Man of Good Will', which tells of a tomato-grower, David Williams, who is generally thought to be eccentric. One day, he realizes that he is behind with his work and that it has become too much for him alone. Accordingly, he asks the narrator's father if the boy would like a job. 'I think my father was a bit doubtful. He wasn't the sort of man to approve of queer fish.' But since the boy has just left school and hasn't found other work, permission is given. Working beside the man, he learns more about him. He was against the use of quick manures and expensive and complicated spraying. He had begun life in a draper's shop and become an expert window-dresser. He earned good money but he wasn't happy and he wasn't satisfied.

He'd begun to feel it was wrong of people to shut themselves away from the sun and fresh air by working in such places, except that when you went home at night it was as though you'd been put in gaol. As for people who worked inside cages behind the counters of banks, or sat all day going up and down in lifts – well, you might just as well live in a cage out at the zoo. And such ideas had kept coming into his head, until he decided he'd cut out all his pleasure and save hard so that he could set himself up in a new way of life. . . . Then later on when he'd got started he found out the life meant much harder work than he'd ever imagined. Yet he liked it all right, he said. He'd feel prouder over the sight of a good bunch of tomatoes, with the top ones just beginning to colour, than he'd ever felt over any window he'd dressed.

Unconsciously, the boy begins to absorb Williams's ideas. He utters them at home, and they make his father, a man who 'gets upset if people say things that aren't like what the newspapers say', restive. It is a scorching summer and the work never stops, cannot be caught up with, until it is clear that the tomato crop everywhere is so good that a 'season of blight couldn't have been a worse blow'. The local tomato-growers' association decides that each man must dig in half his crop. Instead, Williams makes a huge heap of those he has grown.

Not just an ordinary heap though, he'd built them up into a sort of pyramid, the way you see them in the shop windows, only this one was a monster. He asked me if they looked nice, and I thought they certainly did. And it wasn't just because they made a pretty picture, each one a perfect specimen that showed a wonderful red polish in the sun. It was something more than that. I'd helped him do the work, and just to stand and look at the result gave me a wonderful feeling of being satisfied.

The growing heap of tomatoes attracts attention which reaches the proportion of scandal, but is forgotten when a terrific gale blows up and saves the growers by destroying the crop and so sending up the price of tomatoes.

Yet once things had been got straight my boss left me to work on my own again, while he went back to his chair, taking time off only to put more and more on the heap. Though by this time it had gone properly rotten inside, and was getting smaller if anything. Also it was smelling bad and bringing the flies around, and the sanitary inspector came and said it would have to be shifted into a hole and buried. And he didn't like it when my boss laughed and said it was a good smell, it meant that the earth was getting her own back again.

In manner and feeling the closest thing to this story is probably Sherwood Anderson's work. Williams is obviously a grotesque, but the stories are akin not only to those of Winesburg but to later stories of Anderson's like 'I'm a Fool', 'The Egg', and 'I Want to Know Why'. One sees how Sargeson has been a liberator for the New Zealand writers who followed after him as Anderson was for the younger Americans. He takes greater liberties with the language than Anderson did, but fundamentally Sargeson's is a prose of great limpidity. His first-person narrators can seldom give adequate or sophisticated expression to their thoughts and feelings, and it is an index of the success of his prose that the limitations of their articulateness are clearly seen. The sympathy between the narrator, whom we may take to be a persona of Sargeson, and his subject is always apparent; they share a belief in what E. M. Forster, commenting on Sargeson, called the 'unsmart, the unregulated, and the affectionate'. This comes out movingly and beautifully in 'The Old Man's Story', which begins with the narrator's seeing a frail old man sitting on the waterfront. The second paragraph continues:

It was good to be sitting there on the waterfront. Besides the old man there were ships alongside the wharves to look at, and the sea, and the seagulls. The seagulls were making their horrid squabbling noises. It was because of a slice of buttered bread lying close to our seat, the butter gone soft and yellow in the sun. The seagulls wanted it, but didn't dare to come so close to us, and I watched them, wanting to see if they'd have the courage. Then the old man frightened the birds away by saying the word, 'Terrible!' I looked at him, and his cheeks had turned red, and I understood it was because of something he'd read in the newspaper.

Old man and narrator exchange words about the newspaper item, a report of a court case about an adult man and a young girl:

Terrible! the old man said.
Yes? I said. Maybe you're right. Anyhow, I said, five years in gaol is terrible.
Yes, the old man said, five years in gaol.
Terrible!
Oh, I said, I get you. I don't go much on putting people away, I said.
No, the old man said, it's terrible.

But people say, I said, what can you do?

I don't know, the old man said. But I knew of a case once. It didn't get into the newspapers.

As a young boy on his uncle's farm, the old man had noticed the effect Myrtle, the girl who did the housework, had on the rough hired man, Bandy. Picking fruit in the orchard, he'd say, 'We'll keep that one for Myrtle.' And to the boy's surprise, Myrtle seemed to respond; he sensed a 'sort of situation between them'. At the same time, the boy found Bandy wasn't the company he'd been before.

If the boy tried to get him to talk on the old subject he wouldn't bite, or else he'd tell him he'd better behave himself or he'd grow up with a dirty mind. He couldn't make it out, the old man said. The idea he'd got of Bandy right from the beginning made it just impossible for him to make it out. And you only had to look at him and look at Myrtle. So far as they were concerned, one and one didn't make two at all. . . . Myrtle wouldn't eat her meals and Bandy did his work worse and worse. You felt something was going to happen, the old man said, things were absolutely ripe so to speak.

Late one night, walking across the garden, the boy surprises Bandy and the girl on the seat, holding hands and kissing.

And the whole time the boy stood there watching he never heard them say a thing.

It was a tremendous experience for a boy, the old man said, too big for him to be at all clear about until later on in life. All he understood at the time was that he had somehow managed to get life all wrong. Like all boys he thought he'd got to know what was what, but as he stood there in the dark and watched Bandy and Myrtle he understood that he had a lot to learn. He'd been taken in, he thought. It wasn't a pleasant thought, the old man said.

And that seems to be the end of the old man's story. He stops talking and begins to fold up his newspaper. But his listener, the narrator, is not satisfied:

What happened? I said.

Oh, the old man said, my uncle caught the pair of them in Bandy's room one night, and the girl got packed off back where she'd come from.

I see, I said, and the old man got up to go.

And what about Bandy? I said, and I got up to kick the piece of buttered bread over to the seagulls.

Oh, the old man said, one morning when he was supposed to be milking the cows Bandy hanged himself in the cowshed.

So 'The Old Man's Story' ends. By any standard, it must be one of the finest stories of our time, so skilfully are the old man's memories rendered. And one may note the brilliance with which Sargeson picks up and isolates a seemingly irrelevant detail, the gulls squabbling over a slice of buttered bread. When it is first mentioned, in the second paragraph, it seems no more than a piece of casual observation. And in fact it is not referred to again until the penultimate paragraph: 'I got up to kick the piece of buttered bread over to the seagulls.' It works like a splash of colour, unexpected in tone but recognized as absolutely right when seen in its context, which seems to bring the canvas to life.

And there is something else, which makes it paradigmatic of Sargeson's work as a whole and, for that matter, of most good fiction. The newspaper reports a situation to which the responses of us all are severely conditioned. Sargeson shows, on the evidence of one old man's experience, that the truth of the case may be nothing like that. In this, too, we can see him as a liberator, as indeed in a social sense every honest short-story writer or novelist must be.

Patrick White, who was awarded the Nobel Prize for literature in 1973, was the first Australian writer to gain international acclaim. He came to the short story relatively late in his career, his only collection, *The Burnt Ones*, appearing in 1964, twenty-five years after the publication of his first novel. The stories in it fall into two groups, one dealing with Australian life as lived for the most part in or near an outer suburb of Sydney White calls Sarsaparilla, the other with the lives of modern Greeks. Those in the first group tend to be critical, existing on the edge of satire, those in the second psychological, their province personal relations. Of these latter, perhaps the most remarkable is 'A Glass of Tea'. Vastly different as it is in setting, characters, and characterization from 'Mrs Bathurst', it is as baffling as Kipling's story, as modern in its methods of narration, and as little amenable to précis and paraphrase.

It begins with a Greek gentleman, Malliakas, about to visit an aged compatriot named Philippides to whom he has a letter of introduction from an English friend. At Philippides', he discovers the 'shrivelled, yet very bright old man' sitting in a little garden-house as frail as himself. He invites Malliakas to drink tea and apologizes for the absence of his wife, whose style and personality he conjures up in a sentence: 'Constantia – would you believe it? – learnt to shoot out a candle flame while standing at the opposite end of the court. With the ivory pistol her uncle gave her.'

He then begins to tell the story of a set of twelve glasses which he had bought from a Russian and which his wife had saved, in a cardboard box, when they fled in a French destroyer from Smyrna as the Turks burned it. Afterwards, he had been told by a gipsy that he would live till the last of the glasses broke. All are broken now except the one he is drinking from.

What is particularly noteworthy is the technical adeptness with which White tells his story. We have Philippides' words, which are in fact link words, for the story is told in the third person with him as a character in it. What is extraordinarily difficult to determine is whether what we are told takes place in Philippides' mind or is what Malliakas weaves in his imagination from what the old man tells him. We have the following paragraph, for instance:

'I remember a storm was brewing the night Kyria Assimina broke the Sèvres dishes. A shutter kept on banging. Constantia was ailing. It was her time of life. Though she was always quick-tempered, I can tell you! She said she would go away to Athens. And stay. Well, she went. When she came back – as I knew she would – she brought a girl. A young peasant from Lemnos. Aglaia, too, broke one of the glasses, but that was later.'

A few lines later,

Malliakas leaned forward. He heard the shutter banging. In Chios. Or was it inside Constantia's head? It was most important that he should hear, see, all. And as he sipped his tea out of the opalescent cup, Philippides wove the muslin gauzes, only too willingly. Stirring his dead glass.

So, by a method of Impressionism, obliquely and indirectly allusive, a way of life, more than one milieu, and a complex relation are revealed. In a page or so, the destruction of Smyrna is wonderfully evoked and so, equally subtly and brilliantly, is the quality of life on the island of Chios, which is as distinct from it as is that of Athens, whither the Philippideses next move. And always there is the relation, baffling, half-destructive, between Philippides and Constantia.

It is late when Philippides' wife returns. She conducts Malliakas to the bus stop and reveals herself to be, in fact, the second Mrs Philippides, Aglaia, Constantia's maid. Her account of the death by defenestration of the first Mrs Philippides is brilliant in its daring disjunctions and fusions of place, time, and image and is rendered in a way that owes as much to modern painting as to previous writing:

'Her health, it appears, was not of the best.'
'Oh, it was not her health!' Mrs Philippides answered. 'The *kyria* died violently. Oh, violently! I had expected it.'
And suddenly the words began to slip from this peasant throat as never before, in bursts at first, then in bitter streams, so much so that the stranger himself was caught up, and whirled with her down from the upper storey, round the spiral, and into the street.

The maid running in her slippers. Slapping the marble stairs.

It was the hour of reddish dusk, which tightens round the skull. They stood shoulder to shoulder on the pavement. He could smell the anxiety of her strong but helpless peasant body.

'*Kyria mou! Kyria!*' the maid cried.

When she stopped.

Her great buttocks were quivering distress, her great breast would have given up its breath.

Bending over the figure in the gutter.

White's finest story, however, of a kind quite different from 'A Glass of Tea', is almost certainly 'Down at the Dump', one of the Australian stories. According to Beachcroft in *The Modest Art*, it 'challenges comparison with "At the Bay" '. A number of disparate characters are brought together by virtue of an occasion which all share and which is unusual enough to reveal them in their true being. Of plot in the ordinary sense there is none. It is a totally unforced juxtaposition in place and time that links the characters.

There are in fact two sets of circumstances, two groups of characters, the Whalleys and the Hogbens and their associates. Wal Whalley decides that he and his wife should spend the day at the dump:

No one had an eye like Wal for the things a person needs: dead bat- teries and musical bedsteads, a carpet you wouldn't notice was stained, wire, and again wire, clocks only waiting to jump back into the race of time. Objects of commerce and mystery littered Whalley's back yard.

Isba Whalley agrees on the trip, mainly so that she can avoid the Hogben funeral that is to pass by their house that day.

So we are introduced to the second set of circumstances and to Myrtle Hogben. Her character and the occasion she is caught up in are swiftly sketched in the following passage, which glancingly and elliptically suggests rather than describes the scene:

It was Daise who had said: 'I'm going to enjoy the good things of life – and died in a pokey little hutch, with only a cotton frock to her back. While Myrtle had the liver-coloured home – not a single damp- mark on the ceilings – she had the washing machine, the septic, the TV, and the cream Holden Special, not to mention her husband. Les Hogben, the councillor. A builder into the bargain.

Now Myrtle stood amongst her things, and would have continued to regret the Ford the Whalleys hadn't paid for, if she hadn't been re-gretting Daise. It was not so much her sister's death as her life Mrs Hogben deplored. Still, everybody knew, and there was nothing you could do about it. . . .

After giving the matter consideration she had advertised the death in the *Herald*:

> MORROW, Daisy (Mrs), suddenly, at her
> residence, Showground Road, Sarsaparilla.

There was nothing more you could put. It wasn't fair on Les, a public servant, to rake up relationships. And the *Mrs* – well, everyone had got into the habit when Daise started going with Cunningham. It seemed sort of natural as things dragged on and on. Don't work yourself up, Myrt, Daise used to say; Jack will when his wife dies. But it was Jack Cunningham who died first. Daise said: It's the way it happened, that's all.

In every way Hogbens and Whalleys can only see each other as an affront and a scandal to everything they hold dear; the former clinging grimly to their narrow, lower middle-class notions of respectability and success; the latter boozy, rowdy, morally loose, feckless, scrounging a living from the dumps. For them, husband and wife alike, 'Daise was all right'. For the Hog-bens, Daise remains a threat. Husband and wife wonder: who will be at the funeral and, more particularly, will Ossie be there? For after Jack Cunningham's failure in death to make an honest woman of her Daise had further disgraced herself by taking up with Ossie Coogan, a scabby old deadbeat down at the fair-ground, regarded as a half-wit.

Mrs Hogben dreaded the possibility of Ossie, a Roman Catholic for extra value, standing beside Daise's grave, even if nobody, even if only Mr Brickle saw.

The Whalleys are presented equally clearly. In the utility wagon husband and wife have an argument about whether the beer is to be drunk on arrival or after they have developed a thirst:

'Keep it then!' Mum Whalley turned her back. 'What was the point of buyin' it cold if you gotta wait till it hots up? Anyways,' she said, 'I thought the beer was an excuse for comin'.'

'Arr, stuff it!' says Wal. 'A dump's business, ain't it? With or without beer. Ain't it? Any day of the week.'

He saw she had begun to sulk. He saw her rather long breasts floating around inside her dress. Silly cow! He laughed. But he cracked a bottle.

Barry said he wanted a drink.

You could hear the sound of angry suction as his mum's lips called off her swig.

'I'm not gunna stand by and watch any kid of mine,' said the wet lips, 'turn isself into a bloody dipso.'

Her eyes were at their blazing bluest. Perhaps it was because Wal Whalley admired his wife that he continued to desire her.

The Hogbens may not arouse our affection, but it is scarcely possible not to warm towards the Whalleys, who compose as unabashed a celebration of the undeserving poor as may be found in modern writing.

Whalleys and Hogbens never actually come into contact with each other as families in the story, for a 'couple of strands of barbed wire separated Sarsaparilla dump from Sarsaparilla cemetery', but their children do. On the dump Lummy Whalley meets fourteen-year-old Meg Hogben, an old enemy but also in incipient revolt against her parents and their values. They talk. She tells him that she is going to write a poem about her aunt Daise, 'like she was', gathering carnations in the dew. She encourages him to tell her his ambitions of having his own pick-up truck. The whole passage is a beautifully delicate and convincing rendering of the dawning in two very young adolescent minds of the possibilities of love. The first thing that Mrs Hogben sees after the funeral service is over is her daughter kissing, without shame, the Whalley boy in a rubbish tip.

Mrs Hogben said, and her teeth clicked, 'You chose the likeliest time. Your aunt hardly in her grave. Though, of course, it is only your aunt, if anyone, to blame.'

Whalleys and Hogbens set out at the same time for their homes:

At the back of the ute that sulky Lum turned towards the opposite direction. Meg Hogben was looking her farthest off. Any sign of acknowledgement had been so faint the wind had immediately blown it off their faces. As Meg and Lummy sat, they held their sharp, but comforting knees. They sank their chins as low as they would go. They lowered their eyes, as if they had seen enough for the present, and wished to cherish what they knew.

The warm core of certainty settled stiller as driving faster the wind payed out over the telephone wires the fences the flattened heads of grey grass always raising themselves again again again

The most remarkable feature of this story, which is an enormously accomplished adaptation to White's own needs of Joycean methods – the Joyce of *Ulysses* not *Dubliners*, with its mingling of impressionism and expressionism, rapid cutting from one point of view to another, telescoped, syncopated way of narration, reliance on the image rather than the sentence as the main unit of composition – is the moment at the burial service when Daise rises from the dead, stands among the mourners and speaks to them. It is as successful a naturalization of the irrational, here indeed of the supernatural, though a much more daring one, as the sudden appearance among the human *dramatis personae* in 'At the Bay' of Florrie, the cat.

iii

Nothing has been more remarkable in the past half-century of writing in English throughout the world than the efflorescence of what can only be called Jewish writing. If the bulk of this has taken place in the United States it is because the United States has been the main centre of immigration and the writers overwhelmingly the grandchildren of immigrants who fled the pogroms that occurred in Russia and Central Europe in the last decades of the nineteenth century and the first decade of the twentieth. Moreover, the determination to write a literature that should be specifically Jewish in nature and content was sharpened to a greater intensity than ever before by the persecution and slaughter of the Jews in Hitler's Europe.

In the Jewish short story in English the great name must be that of Bernard Malamud, who was born in Brooklyn, New York, in 1914 and educated in the city's schools and colleges. It should be said by way of qualification that though by far the greater number of his stories are certainly on themes specifically Jewish, he has also written some stories that cannot be defined in Jewish terms and among them are some of the finest of our time. One would quote here the story 'In Retirement', which deals simply with an episode in the life of a widowed physician who has retired and gone to live in an apartment in Manhattan, an episode marked by a sudden late flaring up of lust or of the demand for love. It is written with great dignity and understanding.

It is not, however, the story one would pick out to illustrate Malamud's idiosyncrasies or his special qualities, which may seem sometimes alien and exotic to readers in an English tradition. Gerda Charles, in her introduction to *Modern Jewish Stories*, writes:

A strong delicacy of feeling is perhaps the nearest one can get to defining in a phrase the particular 'Jewishness' of Jewish writing. It is inadequate, but then so is every other attempt I have ever come across. There is also, it has been suggested, a 'particular rhythm'; or a recognizable 'angle of vision'. But whatever it is, certain components can always be felt to be there. The first is a kind of courtesy towards, a respect for, suffering. The second is a regard for 'good'. We still, in spite of everything that has happened to us, believe in it. There is therefore nearly always to be found the third quality of optimism – again in spite of everything. And this in turn gives rise to our fourth and perhaps most easily noticeable characteristic of all: humour.

The humorous story is something at which our writers have always excelled. It is – as someone else has said about it – 'at once an expression and a defiance of our fate' ... Another element, very often running side by side with comedy, is fantasy; seen at some of its contemporary best in the beautiful, sadly-comic, heart-rending stories of Bernard Malamud and Isaac Bashevis Singer ...

Reading Malamud, the reader will realize the author is grafting into his prose rhythms, images, and mannerisms of the original Yiddish-speaking immigrants, using them indeed for comic ends in much the same way as Caradoc Evans, Rhys Davies, and Dylan Thomas exploit reminiscences of Welsh syntax and speech patterns in their prose.

To see him at his most characteristic, Malamud is best approached, perhaps, through two short stories that seem to mark opposite bounds of his talents. One is 'The Jewbird', the other 'The Cost of Living'. In a way, the latter seems a variant of the familiar Depression story of the nineteen-thirties. In his time, Tomashevsky has seen what happens to small shopkeepers when bigger stores set up in competition with them, and he is terrified, for the store next door has been empty for months.

Today when he had all but laid the ghost of fear, a streamer of red cracked him across the eyes: National Grocery Will Open Another Of Its Bargain Price Stores On These Premises, and the woe went into him, and his heart bled.

He tries to fight the chain store, but all his efforts are futile, the march of National Grocery is irresistible and on the appointed day it opens. Although Sam keeps his shop open longer and longer he watches his takings dwindle from week to week. 'The store was so silent it got to be a piercing pleasure when someone opened the door.' He tries to sell it but can find no buyer and when he has it put up for auction it realizes not a quarter of the money owed to the creditors. He and Sura move out of the district and 'so long as he lived he would not return to the old neighbourhood, afraid his store was standing empty, and he dreaded to look through the window'.

'The Cost of Living' is a straightforward realistic story written with what one recognizes as an angry integrity manifesting itself in an obvious concern for the dignity of work. By contrast, in any ordinary sense, 'The Jewbird' is not realistic. The first paragraph sets the scene and establishes the tone:

The window was open so the skinny bird flew in. Flappity-flap with its frazzled black wings. That's how it goes. It's open, you're in. Closed, you're out and that's your fate. The bird wearily flapped through the open kitchen window of Harry Cohen's top-floor apartment on First Avenue near the Lower East River. On a rod on the wall hung an escaped canary cage, its door wide open, but this black-typed long-beaked bird – its ruffled head and small dull eyes, crossed a little, making it look a dissipated crow – landed if not smack on Cohen's thick lamb chop, at least on the table, close by. The frozen food salesman was sitting at supper with his wife and young son on a hot August evening a year ago. Cohen, a heavy man with hairy chest and beefy shorts; Edie, in skinny yellow shorts and red halter; and their ten-year-old Morris (after her father) – Maurie, they called him, a nice kid though not overly bright.

'Right on the table,' said Cohen, putting down his beer glass and swatting at the bird. 'Son of a bitch.'

The bird speaks to him in Yiddish.

'Wise guy,' muttered Cohen. He gnawed on his chop, then put down the bone. 'So if you can talk, say what's your business. What do you want here?'

'If you can't spare a lamb chop,' said the bird, 'I'll settle for a piece of herring with a crust of bread. You can't live on your nerve for ever.'

'This ain't a restaurant,' Cohen replied. 'All I'm asking is what brings you to this address?'

'The window was open,' the bird sighed, adding after a moment, 'I'm running. I'm flying but I'm also running.'

'From whom?' asked Edie with interest.

'Anti-Semeets.'

'Anti-Semites?' they all said.

'That's from whom.'

'What kind of Anti-Semites bother a bird?' Edie asked.

'Any kind,' said the bird, 'also including eagles, vultures, and hawks. And once in a while some crows will take your eyes out.'

'But aren't you a crow?'

'Me? I'm a Jewbird.'

And Jewbird he is, as he demonstrates by praying 'without Book or tallith, but with passion'. He asks for food, they give him marinated herring and bread and grudgingly allow him to stay. Maurie, a lonely child, enjoys playing with him, and the bird, called Schwartz, helps him with his lessons.

'If he keeps up like this,' Cohen said, 'I'll get him into an Ivy League college for sure.'

'Oh I hope so,' sighed Edie.

But Schwartz shook his head. 'He's a good boy – you don't have to worry. He won't be a shicker or a wife-beater, God forbid, but a scholar he'll never be, if you know what I mean, although maybe a good mechanic. It's no disgrace in these times.'

'If I were you,' Cohen said, angered, 'I'd keep my big snoot out of other people's private business.'

'Harry, please,' said Edie.

'My Goddam patience is wearing out. That crosseyes butts into everything.'

Schwartz irritates Cohen, who accuses him of stinking, of being a 'goddamn pest and a free loader'. He gets a cat to torment him, then does so himself. In the end, Schwartz manages to catch Cohen's nose in his beak and hang on for dear life. When he at last gets his throbbing nose free, Cohen flings the bird into the street below.

That's the end of that dirty bastard, the salesman thought and went in. Edie and Maurie had come home.

'Look,' said Cohen, pointing to his bloody nose swollen three times its normal size, 'what that sonofabitchy bird did. It's a permanent scar.'

When the winter snow melts, Maurie wanders the neighbourhood looking for Schwartz and on some waste ground near the river finds a dead black bird with wings broken, neck wrung, and both eyes plucked out. Weeping, he asks who did it. 'Anti-Semeets,' Edie says.

The fantasy in which this wholly successful fable is embodied in no way mars the sense of reality it transmits. The suspension of disbelief we accord it is entirely willing: Schwartz, the be-draggled, persecuted bird, and the Cohens, lower middle-class New York Jews, live in the same world and the whole underlines Malamud's cardinal belief summed up in his phrase, 'All men are Jews.' Schwartz, despite his incarnation as a bird, may stand as the archetype of the Malamud hero in the tribulations he suffers at the hands of circumstance and his fellow beings. In him we sense – and that this should be so is evidence of Mala-mud's weight and success both as moralist and an artist – something of the quality of Job himself.

It has been said that the first quality of Malamud's fiction is its 'goodness', which is obvious enough. As Ihab Hassan has more generally observed in *Radical Innocence*, this impression of goodness created is complex, 'a touch of Dostoevsky and Cha-gall', someone has suggested, and the names are useful as point-ing towards Malamud's affinities. Not only does he seem to hover on the verge of the magical, even the miraculous, but what his very different stories have in common is a desperate and finally invincible faith in survival, the faith of a people that has, over aeons of history, somehow prevailed.

In 'The German Refugee', which is perhaps his finest story – it is certainly his most moving – Malamud faces the worst evils of our times. It is also a rare story for Malamud in that it is written from the point of view of a first-person narrator, one, moreover, who, in the absence of biographical information, in-evitably suggests Malamud as a young man:

I was in those days a poor student and would brashly attempt to teach anybody anything for a buck an hour, although I have since learnt better. . . .

Times were still hard from the Depression but anyway I made a little living from the poor refugees. They were all over uptown Broadway in 1939. I had four I tutored – Karl Otto Alp, the former film star; Wolfgang Novak, once a brilliant economist; Friedrich Wilhelm Wolff, who had taught medieval history at Heidelberg; and after the night I met him in his disordered cheap hotel room, Oskar Gassner, the Berlin critic and journalist, at one time on the *Acht Uhr Abenblatt*. They were more accomplished than me. I had my nerve associating with them, but that's what a world crisis does for people, they get educated.

Gassner has been in New York a matter of weeks and has the

prospect of work; he is to give a course of lectures on 'The Literature of the Weimar Republic' in the autumn, but first, in order to give them at all, he has to learn English. How the young narrator, Martin Goldberg, manages by trial and error, good luck and Gassner's own passion for poetry to coax him into fluency in English enough to deliver the first lecture is absorbingly told. Gassner confesses to Goldberg that during his first week in New York he had attempted suicide, and Goldberg finds himself thinking of the possibility of his attempting it again. He wonders whether 'there could be something more than a refugee's displacement, alienation, financial insecurity, being in a strange land without friends or a speakable language'.

Gassner gives his first lecture in September, 1939. He quotes Whitman, and the narrator says:

Oskar read it as though he believed it. Warsaw had fallen but the verses were somehow protective. I sat back conscious to two things: how easy it is to hide the deepest wounds; and the pride I felt in the job I had done.

Two days later Gassner commits suicide. When Goldberg can bring himself to go through his papers he finds a recent airmail letter from Gassner's anti-Semitic mother-in-law:

She writes in a tight script it takes me hours to decipher, that her daughter, after Oskar abandons her, against her own mother's fervent pleas and anguish, is converted to Judaism by a vengeful rabbi. One night the Brown Shirts appear, and though the mother wildly waves her bronze crucifix in their faces, they drag Frau Gassner, together with the other Jews, out of the apartment house, and transport them in lorries to a small border town in conquered Poland. There, it is rumoured, she is shot in the head and toppled into an open tank ditch, with the naked Jewish men, their wives and children, some Polish soldiers, and a handful of gipsies.

Doris Lessing was born some twenty years after Plomer and Stern but similarly from circumstances of her life may be seen as a displaced person. At the age of six she was taken by her parents to Rhodesia, where her father became a farmer. After living for some years in Salisbury, she came to England in 1949 and has lived there ever since. She has written, besides a dozen novels, some half a dozen volumes of short stories. Her work is not to be interpreted autobiographically, but it has always reflected her strenuous engagement in the problems of life in the Western world today, in particular, the relations between white and black in Africa and the difficulties inherent in being a woman in a world traditionally man's.

Typical of her early work in its simplicity, directness, and poetic perception is 'The Old Chief Mshlanga'. It tells of a girl on her father's farm:

A white child, opening its eyes curiously on a sun-suffused landscape, a gaunt and violent landscape, might be supposed to accept it as her own, to take the msasa trees and the thorn trees as familiars, to feel her blood running free and responsive to the swing of the seasons.

The child could not see a msasa tree, or a thorn, for what they were. Her books held tales of alien fairies, her rivers ran slow and peaceful, and she knew the shape of the leaves of an ash or an oak, the names of the little creatures that lived in English streams, when the words 'the veld' meant strangeness, though she could remember nowhere else.

Because of this, for many years, it was the veld that seemed unreal, the sun was a foreign sun, and the wind spoke a strange language.

These paragraphs define the theme of the story, which is the growth of a white child's realization of Africa.

One evening, when she is fourteen, she sees three Africans walking steadily towards her and she is outraged, for it is 'cheek for Africans not to stand aside when they see a white man'. When the girl asks them, somewhat truculently, where they are going, one of the younger men answers in English: 'My Chief travels to see his brothers beyond the river.'

A Chief! I thought, understanding the pride that made the old man stand before me like an equal – more than an equal, for he showed courtesy, and I showed none.

The girl learns that the old man is the Old Chief Mshlanga, on whose lands her father's farm stands. During the course of that year she meets him several times and finds herself changing somehow, as though influenced by his dignity and courtesy.

. . . I thought: this is my heritage, too: I was bred here; it is my country as well as the black man's country; and there is plenty of room for all of us, without elbowing each other off the pavements and roads.

Then one day she is told that they have an important man working in their kitchen, a chief's son, who will 'boss the tribe when the old man dies'. Her mother's is the typical white reaction: 'He'd better not put on a Chief's act with me.'

Realizing that the new cook must be Mshlanga's successor, the girl decides to visit the kraal. It is some miles away, and the description of her journey is a memorable rendering of the sense of fear. When she reaches the kraal she is immediately aware that she is unwelcome, but walking back home, she finds

. . . the fear had gone; the loneliness had set into stiff-necked stoicism; there was now a queer hostility in the landscape, a cold, hard, sullen indomitability that walked with me, as strong as a wall, as intangible as smoke; it seemed to say to me: you walk here as a destroyer. I went slowly homewards, with an empty heart: I had learned that if one cannot call a country to heel like a dog, neither can one dismiss the past with a smile in an easy gush of feeling, saying: I could not help it, I am also a victim.

She has in effect passed beyond her parents' response to Africa and the Africans, which is that of the conventional white settlers. It is not quite the end of the story, for the Chief and his tribe, having quarrelled with her father over some goats that have strayed, are moved by the police two hundred miles away to a 'proper native reserve'.

The story shows that it is the impact upon her of human dignity that makes the girl see and appreciate an alien and native culture and in some sense inherit it. Doris Lessing sees black and white in Africa as trapped in a situation intolerable to both, and this sense of fairness to both sides gives her African stories dignity and because of dignity, authority.

The tribulations of the white settler are indeed a major subject of her early stories. A case in point is 'The Second Hut', a story of what may be called, perhaps, honourable defeat of a kind that many settlers in Rhodesia after the first world war must have known. Major Carruthers, 'gentleman farmer going to seed', realizes that his only hope of survival in the country is to increase his acreage of maize and to do that he must hire an assistant. He finds Van Heerden, an Afrikaner and therefore a man with whom Carruthers would normally have nothing to do. 'As for Van Heerden, he immediately recognized the traditional enemy, and his inherited dislike was strong . . . But they needed each other too badly to nurse old hatreds.'

The portrait drawn of Carruthers is of a gentle, sensitive, scrupulously honest man. He shows the Afrikaner the accommodation he can offer, a thatched hut in uncleared bush, and Van Heerden finds it satisfactory. Work goes well. Then, some two months after Van Heerden's arrival, Carruthers is astonished to see a small flaxen-haired child disappearing into the bush. He follows it, 'very angry, for he knew what he would see'. At Van Heerden's hut he finds a 'vast, slatternly woman', knowing no English, surrounded by her children. He goes in search of Van Heerden, his anger somewhat abated by his efforts to imagine what it would be like to live in such squalor, a condition into which he feels he may himself one day sink if he is too proud to borrow money from his rich brother in England.

Carruthers decides it is his plain duty to have a new hut built for the man and his family, and as he is wondering how best this can be managed, his bossboy comes to him with an ultimatum: unless the Afrikaner goes, he and his friends will. 'Dutchmen are no good,' he says simply. Carruthers manages to persuade the bossboy to change his mind, and the building of the hut is completed. Carruthers is deeply moved by Van Heerden's gratitude. Then, next day just before dawn, voices awake him. The new hut is on fire, and Carruthers arrives there to find Mrs Van Heerden clutching a tiny child that has been badly burned. It dies before Carruthers can get it to the doctor.

It is plain that the hut was fired by one of the Africans. Of the child Van Heerden says, 'one comes and another goes'.

Major Carruthers leaned against the wall of the hut and took out a cigarette clumsily. He felt weak. He felt as if Van Heerden had struck him, smiling. This was an absurd and unjust feeling, but for a moment he hated Van Heerden for standing there and saying: the grey country of poverty that you fear so much, will take on a different look when you actually enter it. You will cease to exist: there is no energy left, when one is wrestling naked with life, for your kind of fine feelings and scruples and regrets.

The Major goes into his house and writes a letter. 'Each slow difficult word was a nail in the coffin of his pride as a man.' Some minutes later he goes into his wife's bedroom and tells her: 'I've written for a job at Home.'

Doris Lessing's best-known story, conceived in irony throughout, is probably 'A Home for the Highland Cattle'. Compared with that of the earlier stories, the prose is considerably looser, more colloquial, even flippant, rather as though the manner of Lawrence after *The Rainbow* had been allowed to infect George Eliot's, probably the dominant influence on Doris Lessing's earlier prose. Mrs Lessing has said: ' "A Home for the Highland Cattle" I wrote after watching a charming, liberal lady, newly immigrant to Rhodesia, who hated the society she found herself in – but eventually succumbed. She was not strong enough to right it.' And that indeed sums up the story, which is completely convincing at the naturalistic level. Everything is built round the painting of highland cattle that hangs in Marina's rented apartment, which for her is a symbol of white Rhodesian provincialism and philistinism, a prized status symbol for her landlady and, for the old African who construes wealth in terms of so many head of cattle, an image of magical significance.

Doris Lessing's African stories notably enlarge our sympathies: overtly less powerful for obvious reasons, her English stories enlarge our understanding. 'One off the Short List' and 'The Day Stalin Died' are characteristic. The former is a wry comedy dealing with the efforts of Gabriel Spence, a television 'personality', to get a woman he interviews into bed with him. In any ordinary or simple sense, 'One off the Short List' is not a story about sex at all; whatever our interpretation of it may be, if it is to be valid it must take into account work as a factor in the individual's evaluation of himself. It is a factor that no longer has meaning for Spence. He must compensate for its lack by the sexual conquest of women who are in some sense professional rivals. Mrs Lessing emphasizes what she calls the democracy of respect in which the characters in the story hold each other's work, and it is this, together with what is implied in the notion, which lifts the story quite above the class of magazine story *a la* Maugham to which at first sight it might seem to belong.

As for 'The Day Stalin Died', in its way it might be a gloss on Auden's lines:

> About suffering they were never wrong,
> The Old Masters: how well they understood
> Its human position; how it takes place
> While someone else is eating or opening a window or just
>   walking dully along . . .

The story begins:

That day began badly for me with a letter from my aunt in Bournemouth. She reminded me that I had promised to take my cousin Jessie to be photographed at four that afternoon. So I had; and forgotten all about it.

As the woman, an uneasy member of the Communist Party, is about to begin her work, 'comrade Jean' rings up to invite herself to lunch. She arrives with her sandwiches and gives the narrator a short lecture on the necessity 'for unremitting vigilance on the part of the working class' and rebukes her for her 'present vacillating attitude towards Soviet justice'. The luncheon leaves the narrator feeling 'for one reason and another, rather depressed'.

Jean having gone, the narrator takes a taxi to meet Cousin Jessie and Aunt Emma at a dress shop. En route she has a long conversation with the driver about the cost of living and life generally.

This conversation might have gone on for some time, but I saw my cousin Jessie standing on the pavement watching us. I said goodbye to the taxi man and turned, with some apprehension, to face her.

'I saw you,' she said, 'I saw you arguing with him. It's the only thing to do. They're getting so damned insolent these days. My principle is, tip them sixpence regardless of the distance, and if they argue, let them have it. Only yesterday I had one shouting at my back all down the street because I gave him sixpence. But we've got to stand up to them.'

On the way to the photographer's studio they learn from a newspaper billboard that Stalin is dying. The narrator stops to buy a paper and chats with the newspaper-seller. She joins the others, and Aunt Emma begins to talk again about the new dress, but Cousin Jessie rebukes her for her insensitivity. 'Oh, Mummy, can't you see she's upset? It's the same for her as it would be for us if Churchill was dead.' The photographic session goes badly: Stalin is dying to the accompaniment of the constant bickering of a middle-class lady and her daughter. When the narrator gets back to her flat the telephone is ringing once again. It is Comrade Jean, who is sobbing.

'He's been murdered by capitalist agents,' she said. 'It's perfectly obvious.'
'He was 73,' I said.
'People don't die like *that*,' she said.
'They do at 73,' I said.
'We will have to pledge ourselves to be worthy of him,' she said.
'Yes,' I said, 'I suppose we will.'

Nadine Gordimer was born in the Transvaal in 1923. In the introduction to her *Selected Stories*, she tells us that 'in a certain sense a writer is "selected" by his subject – his subject being the *consciousness* of his own era', which she makes specific for herself when she says: 'My time and place have been twentieth-century Africa.' The characteristic quality of her collections of stories is her total immersion in Africa, meaning by that not South Africa only, but an older and vaster Africa of which that of Conrad's 'Heart of Darkness' is felt still to be a part, part of the ancient background to the emergent Africa of our day.

It seems relevant, too, to say that Nadine Gordimer comes from Jewish stock, for this gives her the power of seeing Africa itself in a world context. She writes, as it were, from the centre, and in this respect is South Africa's first writer of international scope.

As an example of Nadine Gordimer's treatment of Africa itself one might quote a fine story of her maturity, 'Livingstone's Companions'. Carl Church, a Western correspondent, is observing a parliamentary session of one of the new African countries:

The Speaker in his long curly wig was propped askew against the tall back of his elaborate chair. His clerk, immobile, with the white pompadour, velvet bow, and lacy jabot that were part of the investiture of sovereignty handed down from the British, was a perfect *papier maché* blackamoor from the eighteenth-century slave trader's drawing room.

Back in his office, he finds a cable from his paper instructing him to retrace Livingstone's last journey for an anniversary article. He flies to the capital of the neighbouring country, reading Livingstone's *Journals*, over which he has sat up half the night.

Our sympathies are drawn out towards our humble hardy companions by a community of interests, and, it may be, of perils, which make us all friends. The book rested on his thighs, and he slept through the hour and a half journey. Livingstone had walked it taking ten months and recording his position by the stars. This could be the lead for his story, he thought: waking up to the recognition of the habits of his mind like the same old face in the shaving mirror.

From time to time throughout the story brief passages from the *Journals* occur, in unforced contrapuntal comment.

Driving from the capital in his hired car, deciding that he will spend no more than two days in the country and will use the assignment as a peg on which to write an article on attempts to achieve a form of African socialism, Church loses his way and, almost by chance, comes across a hotel owned by a fellow-traveller on the plane. After a perfunctory search in the hotel's grounds, he fails to find the graves of Livingstone's companions which are supposed to lie there and instead spends his time skin-diving in the lake, drinking, talking. Eventually, he leaves for the capital and the airport.

Suddenly, while he is still in the grounds of the hotel, he sees the path to the graves. It seems absurd not to go and look at them, and he gets down from his car and climbs the path.

The five neat headstones of the monuments commission were surmounted each by an iron cross on a circle. The names, and the dates of birth and death – the deaths were all in the last quarter of the nineteenth century – were engraved on the granite. A yard or so away, but in line with the rest, was another gravestone. Carl Church moved over to read the inscription: *In Memory of Richard Alastair Macnab, Beloved*

Husband of Dorothy and Father of Richard and Heather, died 1957. They all looked back, these dead companions to the lake, the lake that Carl Church (turning to face as they did, now) had had silent behind him all the way up; the lake that, from here, was seen to stretch much farther than one could tell, down there on the shore or at the hotel: stretching still – even from up here – as one could see, flat and shining, a long way up Africa.

Thus beautifully the story ends. It is about white man's Africa, and the ironies speak for themselves. Yet the story sets in juxtaposition one with another the many incongruous and discordant presents of Africa – the modern capital behind the main street of which 'a native market stank of dried fish', the Arabized African fisherman with his ivory bracelets working on his nets on the beach, the weekending white hotel guests drinking and goggle-fishing – and a past Africa only a century dead but belonging to a totally different world from now, evoked by the name of Livingstone and the associations of the slave trade, exploration, and heroism that cling to it. It is a story of great resonance.

In an interview in the *London Magazine* in 1965 Nadine Gordimer said:

Although none of my books is formally political, the South African situation has conditioned me as a writer to an extent that could not have happened in any other country, through the extraordinary way in which the political situation has moulded the lives of the people round me. Not only obvious confrontations of black and white are affected; whites among themselves are shaped by their peculiar position, just as black people are by theirs. I write about their private selves; often, even in the most private situations, they are what they are because their lives are regulated and their mores formed by the political situation. You see, in South Africa, society *is* the political situation.

This seems to be an extremely accurate statement of the political nature of her stories, and how that nature comes into being is vividly shown in such a story as 'The Smell of Death and Flowers', which begins at a party:

The party was an unusual one for Johannesburg. A young man called Derek Ross – out of sight behind the 'bar' at the moment – had white friends and black friends, Indian friends and friends of mixed blood, and sometimes he liked to invite them all to his flat at once. Most of them belonged to the minority that, through bohemianism, godliness, politics, or a particularly sharp sense of human dignity, did not care about the difference in one another's skins. But there were always one or two – white ones – who came, like tourists, to see the sight, and to show that they did not care, and one or two black or brown or Indian ones who found themselves paralysed by the very ease with which the white guests accepted them.

The guests are standing talking in groups or at the bar or are dancing. A guest much discussed is Jessica Malherbe.

... Malcolm Barker's young sister-in-law, a girl who had been sitting silent, pink and gold as a porcelain figurine, on the window-sill behind his back, leaned her hand for balance on his chair and said urgently, near his ear, 'Has Jessica Malherbe really been in prison?'
'Yes, in Port Elizabeth. And in Durban, they tell me. And now she's one of the civil disobedience people – defiance campaign leaders who're going to walk into some native location forbidden to Europeans. Next Tuesday. So she'll land herself in prison again . . .'

The girl finds herself fascinated by the idea of Jessica Malherbe. She says: 'She *looks* so nice. I mean she uses good perfume, and everything. You can't imagine it.' We learn that the girl, Joyce McCoy has only just returned from five years away in England and that this is the first party of the kind she has been to. We are told that 'all her life she had suffered from this impression she made of not being quite real' and we have the sense that she is consciously measuring herself against life, against life in Johannesburg perhaps especially. She dances with Eddie Ntwaka, an African politician.

She would not let herself formulate the words in her brain: I am dancing with a black man. But she allowed herself to question, with the careful detachment of scientific enquiry, quietly inside herself: 'Do I feel anything? What do I feel? . . . Is this exactly how I always dance?' she asked herself closely. 'Do I always hold my back exactly like this, do I relax this much, hold myself in reserve to just this degree?'
She found she was dancing as she always danced.
I feel nothing, she thought. *I feel nothing.*
And all at once a relief, a mild elation, took possession of her, so that she could begin to talk to the man she was dancing with.

Later, the girl realizes she is standing near Jessica Malherbe:

'Miss Malherbe,' she said, and her blank, exquisite face might have been requesting an invitation to a garden party. 'Please. Miss Malherbe, I want to go with you next week. I want to march into the location.'

When the day comes she still wants to march into the location and she goes to the rendezvous, Jessica Malherbe's home – for she is married to an Indian – in a quarter where Indians and people of mixed blood, debarred from living anywhere better, dwell beside poor whites. The march begins. They enter the location. At the cross-roads a police car is waiting, and as they approach two smartly dressed policemen get out.

When they drew abreast, one said, as if in reflex, 'Ah – good afternoon.' But the other cut in, in an emotionless official voice, 'You are all under arrest for illegal entry into Lagersdorp Location. If you'll just give us your names . . .'

Joyce stood waiting her turn, and her heart beat slowly and evenly. She thought again as she had once before – how long ago was that party? – I feel *nothing*. It's all right. I feel *nothing*.

But as the policeman came to her and she spelled out her name for him, she looked up and saw the faces of the African onlookers who stood nearest her. Two men, a small boy, and a woman, dressed in ill-matched cast-offs of European clothing which hung upon them without meaning, like coats spread on bushes, were looking at her. When she looked back, they met her gaze. And she felt, suddenly, not *nothing*, but what they felt at the sight of her, a white girl, taken – incomprehensibly, as they were used to being taken – under the force of white men's wills, which dispensed and withdrew life, imprisoned and set free, fed or starved, like God Himself.

This story seems a wholly convincing rendering of what may be called the process of conversion of the well-born, well-educated South African girl fresh from England. The process seems oiled, indeed, by Joyce's good breeding, as though common civility itself in the traffic of life works against the policy and practice of *apartheid*. And one can only admire the fusion of empathy between black and white registered in the last sentence of the story.

Admittedly, 'The Smell of Death and Flowers' is a relatively early story; it was collected in a volume published in 1956. Ursula Laredo has said in *Contemporary Novelists*: 'Nadine Gordimer's vision of life in South Africa is uncompromising and has grown steadily bleaker over the years.' The evidence of the stories confirms this. Typical of her later stories is 'Open House', which was collected in 1972. It begins:

Frances Taver was on the secret circuit for people who wanted to find out the truth about South Africa. These visiting journalists, politicians, and churchmen all had an itinerary arranged for them by their consular representatives and overseas information services, or were steered around by a 'foundation' of South African business interests eager to improve the country's image, or even carted about to the model black townships, universities, and beerhalls by the South African State Information service itself. But all had, carefully hidden among the most private of private papers (the nervous ones went so far as to keep it in code), the short list that would really take the lid off the place: the people one must see ... Most of the names on it were white names – which was rather frustrating, when one was after the real things; but it was said in London and New York that there *were* still ways of getting to meet Africans, provided you could get hold of the right white people.
  Frances Taver was one of them. Had been for years. From the forties when she had been a trade union organizer and run a mixed union of garment workers while this was legally possible ...

Now, she is always slightly embarrassed when an English or American voice telephones out of the blue. Nevertheless, when Robert Greenman Ceretti telephones her she arranges a luncheon-party in her flat for him and rounds up African guests to meet him, Jason Madela, a business man, Edgar Xixo, an attorney, Spuds Butelezi, a newspaper reporter. It is as though a charade is being mounted which everybody taking part in it knows is a charade except the visitor.

Afterwards, carrying stuff into the kitchen, Frances finds a note that reads: HOPE YOUR PARTY WENT WELL. The servants, who have rooms at the bottom of the yard, tell her that no one has asked for her.

Her African National Congress friend from underground must have heard the voices in the quiet of the afternoon, or perhaps simply have seen the cars, and gone away. She wondered if he knew who was there. Had he gone away out of consideration for her safety? They never spoke of it, of course, but he must know that the risks she took were calculated, very carefully calculated. There was no way of disguising that from someone like *him*. Then she saw him smiling to himself at the sight of the collection of guests: Jason Madela, Edgar Xixo, and Spuds Butelezi – Spuds Butelezi, as well. But probably she was wrong, and he would have come out among them without those feelings of reproach or contempt that she read into the idea of his gait, his face. HOPE YOUR PARTY WENT WELL. He may have meant just that.

Frances telephones Robert Ceretti at his hotel to say goodbye. He is fulsome in his thanks for her introductions: on Saturday night he was out on the town with her friends. She tries to warn him and explain to him.

She said: 'You must understand. Because the corruption's real. Even they've become what they are because things are the way they are. Being phoney is being corrupted by the situation . . . and that's real enough. We're made out of *that*.'

He understands that something is wrong but assumes that it is something you have to live and die in the country to find out; and all she hears over the line is his voice assuring her: 'Everyone's been marvellous – really marvellous . . .'

How much darker Nadine Gordimer's view of life in South Africa has become over the years can be clearly seen in 'Abroad' where she is still able to extract bleak comedy out of South African ironies and contradictions.

Manie Swemmer has talked for years about going up to Northern Rhodesia for a look around. In the end he does make the journey but by then Northern Rhodesia has become Zambia. Manie, an Afrikaner of invincible ignorance, passes the time in wide-eyed wonder, standing shoulder to shoulder with black men at the bar, even accepting drinks from them.

The man had slipped off the barstool, briefcase between chest and arm. 'Enjoy your holiday . . .'

'Everything of the best!' Manie Swemmer called after him. 'I tell you something, Willie, he may be black as the ace of spades, but that's a gentleman. Eh? You got to be open-minded, otherwise you can't move about in these countries. But that's a gentleman.'

Lusaka is full for the independence anniversary celebrations, and Manie finds he must share a room with an Indian from Delhi. But when he goes up to the room after a night's hard drinking he finds the door bolted against him. As the girl at the reception desk explains, the Indian gentleman had been on his high horse when he came back and found Manie's things in his room. 'I mean,' she says, 'I don't know what the fuss was all about – as I said to him, it isn't as if we've put an African in with you, it's a white man. And him Indian himself.' Manie finds that the only accommodation he can have is a room in the old wing of the hotel. It has four beds in it and has been booked by some Africans, but it's after eleven and it's unlikely they will appear now. Reluctantly, he agrees to have it. The first thing he does when he gets into the room is 'to drive the rusty bolt home across the door'.

Dan Jacobson was born in Johannesburg in 1929 of Jewish immigrant stock from Lithuania and settled in England in 1954. Besides a number of novels, he has published three volumes of short stories which in 1973 he reduced to a single volume of sixteen stories called *Through the Wilderness*. He states in a note that two only of the stories included had been written before he came to England; and in terms of publication his work is wholly English.

Fundamental to all these stories is a quite unusual sensitivity and subtlety in reading and drawing out the implications in the anecdote on which the story has been based. Consider what is probably his best-known story, 'The Zulu and the Zeide', *zeide* being the Yiddish for grandfather. Old man Grossman speaks only Yiddish, is now senile and is more than ever a source of worry, embarrassment, and expense for his son Harry, with whose family he lives and from whose house he is constantly trying to escape. When Johannes, one of the Zulu servants, brings Paulus, a 'raw' Zulu straight from the *kraal* and utterly ignorant of white ways and city life, to the house and suggests he should be employed as the old man's servant and nurse, it 'was something in the nature of a joke – almost a joke against his father – that Harry Grossman gave Paulus his chance'.

When old man Grossman went out, Paulus went too, and there was no longer any need for the doors and windows to be watched, or the police to be telephoned. The young bearded Zulu and the old bearded Jew from Lithuania walked together in the streets of the city that was strange to them both; together they looked over the fences and large gardens and into the shining foyers of the blocks of flats; together they stood on the pavements of the main arterial roads and watched the cars and trucks rush between the tall buildings; together they walked the small, sandy parks, and when the old man was tired Paulus saw to it that he sat on a bench and rested . . . Paulus knew only Zulu, the old man knew only Yiddish, there was no language in which they could talk to one another. But they talked all the same: they both commented on or complained to each other of the things they saw around, and often they agreed with one another, smiling and nodding their heads and explaining again with their hands what each happened to be talking about.

Then one night, in Paulus's absence, the old man escapes from the house, is struck down in the road and dies a few days later. It had been Paulus's afternoon off, and Harry had come home to find the old man loudly demanding *der schwarzer*. He had done his best to make the old man understand, but the old man was inconsolable. Harry offered to be Paulus's substitute, to no avail. He walked out of the room, and it was then the old man got into the road.

A few days after the funeral, when Harry orders Johannes to tell Paulus he must go, for his work is finished, he has to be reminded that he has still to pay Paulus the savings he had kept back for him from his wages. What, he demands harshly, has Paulus been saving for, anyway?

Johannes spoke to Paulus and came back with a reply. 'He says, baas, that he is saving to bring his wife and children from Zululand to Johannesburg. He is saving, baas,' Johannes said, for Harry had not seemed to understand, 'to bring his family to this town also.'
The two Zulus were bewildered to know why it was then that Harry Grossman's clenched, fist-like features should have fallen from one another, or why he stared with such guilt and despair at Paulus, while he cried, 'What else could I have done? I did my best!' before the first tears came.

'The Zulu and the Zeide' strikes one as a profoundly Jewish story. The innocence of the relation between the old Lithuanian and the unsophisticated child of nature is a perfect foil to as well as a cause of the baffled son's sense of guilt. Yet it would be quite wrong to see Jacobson only as a South African counterpart to Malamud. They share a similar delicacy of feeling certainly but one only has to read the two stories 'Trial and Error' and 'The

Little Pet' to see that Jacobson has a sensibility that strikes one as characteristically English.

The quality of 'Trial and Error' and of Jacobson's response to common experience can best be shown by quotation. A child is born to Arnold and Jennifer Bothwell:

> 'Why don't people *write* about it more!' he used to demand of Jennifer. No one had ever warned him of the pleasure he would get from handling the baby's smooth limbs, of touching his hair, of smelling him after his bath, of just watching him eat his food, of listening to his random sighs and chuckles, of recognizing in his eyes, with their mysterious bluish irises and extraordinarily unsullied whites, the recognitions that the baby himself was making. No one had ever warned him of the tenderness he would feel at seeing the baby's shoes or trousers; of the absorption he would fall into watching the tiny, precise beauties of his face. Nor had he been told that the chores of paternity would be made easily bearable by love; so that the cleaning of a napkin was a job he grumbled at and yet could find satisfaction in, and then when he woke to the baby's cry at unearthly hours of the morning he was rewarded by the clasp in his arms of a living bundle that clung to his shoulders, and snuggled against his breast with minute, comfort-seeking movements of the loins, and thrust against him round absurd knees whose weakness made him feel weak too.

What is being described is a universal experience that has always to be discovered afresh and made personal to himself by the discoverer. No one since early Lawrence has rendered the living quality of this particular experience, in which tenderness, sensuality, and sensibility come together in a single response, as vividly as Jacobson.

'The Little Pet' with its ironical comedy will also recall Lawrence. Martha and Francis, who are described as having the 'strained and guilty air of the perpetually well-intentioned', have got a rabbit for little Francis, their son. To Martha's horror, the rabbit kills its baby, and Martha will not have it in the garden any longer; it must be returned to the pet shop. Her horror is the greater when she discovers that the little boy has known all along that the rabbit has killed its young and hasn't told his mother because he guessed she'd take it away if he did. Martha tells her husband to let the rabbit stay, to let the child have it. The story ends:

> 'All right, then,' Francis senior said, giving the hutch a parting kick. 'But you'll have to feed it and give it water and everything else.' He

began to walk after his wife. He left the hutch in the middle of the lawn.

'Yes,' the little boy said.

He waited until his father had gone in to the house, then he went on his knees in front of the hutch. He put his fingers through the wire netting. 'Come here,' he said to the rabbit. 'I'm not cross with you. I know you didn't like your baby.'

The main expression of Jacobson's sensibility however, is in the stories that explore the irrationalities and assumptions governing the behaviour people who think themselves different from and therefore in some sense intrinsically superior or inferior to their neighbours. 'A Day in the Country' deals with a chance meeting between the members of a Jewish family returning from a day in the country and the members of an Afrikaner family one of whom is tormenting a black child. The two families confront each other. They quarrel and make accusations and counter-accusations but do not fight. Nothing is resolved and the story ends:

So a sort of peace did come, and we got back into the car. No one shook hands with anyone, there had been no reconciliation to warrant that. But no blows had been struck, and no one had called anyone a bloody Dutchman or a bloody Jew, so everything was as well as could be expected. Better really, for us, because we still despised them. We despised that family: it was not our fault they misinterpreted it. And they should have known that we were as frightened of them as they were of us. We left them there, outside their whitewashed shop with the house behind it, that looked across the sand road to the railway line and the railway paddock where one chestnut horse was growing thin in transit between two lost farms.

It was a quiet journey home. Everyone was feeling depressed and beaten, though, as I have explained, the victory was ours. But we had all lost, so much, somewhere, farther back, along that dusty road.

IX

No magazine of our time has published short stories of distinction more consistently than the *New Yorker*, and the fact that over the years its regular contributors in the field have included such diverse writers as Frank O'Connor, J. D. Salinger, John O'Hara, Sylvia Townsend Warner, Isaac Bashevis Singer, V. S. Pritchett, Arturo Vivente, Peter Taylor, J. F. Powers, and Nadine Gordimer, makes it impossible to speak in any sense that has meaning of a New Yorker school of short-story writers. Nevertheless, the magazine does, very definitely, have what is called an image, exemplifying the intention of the magazine's first editor, Harold Ross, which was to appeal to 'caviare sophisticates' rather than to 'the old lady in Dubuque'. 'The magazine', says *The Oxford Companion to American Literature*, 'is noted for its crisp satirical style and sophisticated whimsy', though it should be observed that the satire is rarely fierce. It should also be said that its liberal and cultural sympathies are both wide and strong.

But if it is impossible to speak of a *New Yorker* school of short-story writers, some short-story writers seem essentially of the *New Yorker*. John Cheever is one of them. Of the ten volumes he has published three are novels and the rest are short stories, typical of which and still one of the best for all its early date is 'The Enormous Radio'. The first paragraph deftly presents the two characters:

Jim and Irene Westcott were the kind of people who seem to strike that satisfactory average of income, endeavour, and respectability that is reached by the statistical reports in college alumni bulletins. They were the parents of two young children, they had been married nine years, they lived on the twelfth floor of an apartment house in the East Seventies between Fifth and Madison Avenues, they went to the theatre on an average 10·3 times a year, and they hoped some day to live in Westchester. Irene Westcott was a pleasant, rather plain girl with soft brown hair and a wide, fine forehead upon which nothing at all had been written, and in the cold weather she wore a coat of fitch skins dyed to resemble mink. You could not say that Jim Westcott, at thirty-seven, looked younger than he was, but you could at least say of him that he seemed to feel younger. He wore his greying hair cut very short, he dressed in the kind of clothes his class had worn at Andover, and his manner was earnest, vehement, and intentionally naive. The Westcotts differed from their friends, their classmates, and their neighbours only in an interest they shared in classical music. They went to a great many concerts – although they seldom mentioned this to anyone – and they spent a good deal of time listening to music on the radio.

One Sunday afternoon in the middle of a Schubert quartet their radio gives out. Next day Jim has a new one delivered. Irene tunes in to a Mozart quintet, but the music disappears into the interference, which no amount of turning of knobs and switches can dispel.

. . . it was the noise of the elevator that gave her a clue to the character of the static. The rattling of the elevator cables and the opening and closing of the elevator doors were reproduced in her loudspeaker, and, realizing that the radio was sensitive to electrical currents of all sorts, she began to discern through the Mozart the ringing of telephone bells, the dialling of phones, and the lamentation of a vacuum cleaner. . . . The powerful and ugly instrument, with a mistaken sensitivity to discord, was more than she could hope to master, so she turned the thing off and went into the nursery to see her children.

Later she and Jim find that the radio is picking up the noises in neighbouring apartments with even greater clarity. Thus:

Jim turned to another station, and the living room was filled with the uproar of a cocktail party that had over-shot its mark. Someone was playing the piano and singing the Whiffenpoof Song, and the voices that surrounded the piano were vehement and happy. 'Eat some more sandwiches,' a woman shrieked. There were screams of laughter and a dish of some sort crashed to the floor.

'Those must be the Hutchinsons, in 15-B,' Irene said, 'I knew they were giving a party this afternoon. I saw her in the liquor store. Isn't this too divine. Try something else. See if you can get those people in 18-C.'

The Westcotts overheard that evening a monologue on salmon fishing in Canada, a bridge game, running comments on home movies of what had apparently been a fortnight at Sea Island, and a bitter family quarrel about an overdraft at the bank. They turned off their radio at midnight and went to bed, weak with laughter.

Eavesdropping on their neighbours through their radio becomes compulsive until, as the panorama of misery, illness, infidelity, and vice of all kinds unrolls before them, it turns sour. The radio is repaired again, and now music comes through as it should, without distortion or extraneous noises. But something is changed in them. They have been corrupted and they quarrel. Irene turns on the radio for comfort:

The voice on the radio was suave and noncommittal. 'An early-morning railroad disaster in Tokyo,' the loudspeaker said, 'killed twenty-nine people. A fire in a catholic hospital near Buffalo for the care of blind children was extinguished early this morning by nuns. The temperature is forty-seven. The humidity is eighty-nine.'

'The Enormous Radio' is a modern morality mirroring the involuntary crack in complacency through which intimations of the real seep into the characters' consciousness. Cheever is always a moralist, a rather old-fashioned one at that, and he has been unfailingly ingenious in devising fables to illustrate the facts of life as he sees them through the surface glitter and graciousness of existence in Commuterland, U.S.A. His comments on the foibles of his time are sharp and witty, as in 'The Brigadier and the Golf Widow', which elegantly pinpoints upper-class American fashion in the Fifties of building shelters against the atomic bomb. None is better than Charlie Pastern's, a man given to shouting in country-club locker rooms: 'Let's throw a little nuclear hardware at them and show them who's boss.' Their bomb shelter is the envy of all who see it.

They would have liked to keep it a secret; would have liked at least to soft-pedal its existence; but the trucks and bulldozers going in and out of their driveway had informed everyone. It had cost thirty-two thousand dollars, and it had two chemical toilets, an oxygen supply, and a library, compiled by a Columbia professor, consisting of books meant to inspire hopefulness, humour, and tranquillity. There were stores of survival food to last three months, and several cases of hard liquor. Mrs Pastern had bought the plaster-of-Paris ducks, the birdbath, and the gnomes in an attempt to give the lump in her garden a look of innocence; to make it acceptable – at least to herself. For, bulking as it did in so pretty and domestic a scene and signifying as it must the death of at least half the world's population, she found it, with its grassy cover, impossible to reconcile with the blue sky and the white clouds. She liked to keep the curtains drawn on that side of the house.

In his more recent work, Cheever has essayed a number of stories on the international theme, notably of expatriate Americans in Italy. By far the best of these is 'The World of Apples', the story of a veteran American poet long resident in Italy. He is presented in the first paragraph:

Asa Bascomb, the old laureate, wandered around his work house or study – he had never been able to settle on a name for a house where one wrote poetry – swatting hornets with a copy of *La Stampa* and wondering why he had never been given the Nobel Prize. He had received nearly every other sign of renown. In a trunk in the corner there were medals, citations, wreaths, sheaves, ribbons, and badges. The stove that heated his study had been given to him by the Oslo P.E.N. Club, his desk was a gift from the Kiev Writers' Union, and the study itself had been built by an international association of his admirers. The presidents of both Italy and the United States had wired their congratulations on the day he was presented with the key to the place. Why no Nobel Prize? Swat, swat.

The old poet now finds himself in the grip of an obsession to write pornography. 'Obscenity – gross obscenity – seemed to be the only fact of life that possessed colour and cheer.' He is oppressed by its boorishness and its boringness but he cannot free himself of it. 'At the end of ten days he was at the bottom of the pornographer's barrel; he was writing dirty limericks.' He goes on a pilgrimage to a shrine in the mountains. Walking back next day, hearing the sound of a waterfall, he has a vision of his father bathing in a waterfall on the edge of the farm in Vermont where he had been raised. The story ends:

Now he did what his father had done – unlaced his shoes, tore at the buttons of his shirt and knowing that a mossy stone or the force of the water could be the end of him he stepped naked into the torrent, bellowing like his father. He could stand the cold for only a minute but when he stepped away from the water he seemed at last to be himself. He went on down to the main road where he was picked up by some mounted police, since Maria had sounded the alarm and the whole province was looking for the maestro. His return to Monte Carbone was triumphant and in the morning he began a long poem on the inalienable dignity of light and air that, while it would not get him the Nobel Prize, would grace the last months of his life.

Among other things, a beautiful evocation of Italy, 'The World of Apples' is a triumphantly successful fable of rebirth that quite transcends the ordinary run of Cheever's stories.

John Updike, too, is a writer who seems essentially of the *New Yorker*. He has worked as a staff reporter on the magazine, the bulk of his short stories and verse has appeared there, and he is one of its principal book-reviewers. His work seems to divide in two: the location of his sophisticated stories is the old town in Massachusetts he calls Tarbox; the farming community in Pennsylvania he has christened Olinger seems to derive from and express his own background. Though in the following instance, 'The Family Meadow', the setting is in fact New Jersey, its background and ethos admirably suggest the Olinger community.

The meadow is set for the picnic lunch:

The eating begins. Clams steam, corn steams, salad wilts, butter runs, hot dogs turn, torn chicken shines in the savage light. Iced tea, brewed in forty-quart milk cans, chuckles when sloshed. Paper plates buckle on broad laps. Plastic butter knives, asked to cut cold ham, refuse. Children underfoot in the pleased frenzy eat only potato chips. Somehow, as the first wave of appetite subsides, the long tables turn musical, and a murmur rises to the blank sky, a cackle rendered harmonious by a remote singleness of ancestor; a kind of fabric is woven and hung, a tapestry of the family fortunes, the threads of which include milkmen, ministers, mailmen, bankruptcy, death by war, death by automobile, insanity – a strangely prevalent thead, the thread of insanity. Never far from a farm or the memory of a farm, the family has hovered in honorable obscurity, between poverty and wealth, between jail and high office. Real-estate dealers, schoolteachers, veterinarians are its noblemen; butchers, electricians, door-to-door salesmen its yeomen. Protestant, teetotalling, and undaring, ironically virtuous and mildly proud, it has added to America's statistics without altering their meaning. Whence, then, this strange joy?

Watermelons smelling of childhood cellars are produced and massively sliced. The sun passes noon and the shadows relax in the intimate grass of this antique field. To the music of reminiscence is added the rhythmic chunking of thrown quoits . . .

The passage is characteristic of Updike. The humour and wit are immediately evident; words, even in prose, dance to his music, and his choice of words is elegant to the point of being dandiacal. Present all the time is a feeling for tradition, a sense of piety towards family and place, the long-established. And the manner is relaxed; indeed, if we did not know the passage came from a short story we might assume its source was a reflective essay. We do in fact find that in Updike as in Cheever the story can come perilously close to the essay and often seems in danger of being lost in it. An example of this might be the story 'The Corner', a celebration of a street-corner in an old New England town at which traffic accidents tend to occur. The final paragraph gives the whole a sense of significance:

> The driver's story had been strange, but no stranger, to the people who live here, than the truth that the corner is one among many on the map of the town, and the town is a dot on the map of the state, and the state a mere patch on the globe, and the globe insignificant from any of the stars overhead.

Updike is always a most beguiling writer, but there are times when it is difficult not to feel that the beguilement, the fluency, and the facility are little more than a sleight of hand indulged in to mask an emptiness within. At such times it is necessary to remember the stories about youth growing up. The best known of these is probably 'A & P', which begins:

> In walks these three girls in nothing but bathing suits. I'm in the third checkout slot, with my back to the door, so I don't see them until they're over by the bread. The one that caught my eye first was the one in the plaid green two-piece. She was a chunky kid, with a good tan and a sweet broad soft-looking can with those two crescents of white just under it, where the sun never seems to hit, at the top of the backs of her legs. I stood there with my hand on a box of HiHo crackers trying to remember if I rang it up or not. I ring it up again and the customer starts giving me hell. She's one of these cash-register-watchers, a witch about fifty with rouge on her cheekbones and no eyebrows, and I know it made her day to trip me up. She'd been watching cash registers for fifty years and probably never seen a mistake before.

The narrating voice is that of Sammy, a nineteen-year-old boy who has a vacation job at a supermarket and the tone of the story has been admirably defined in the phrase 'the muted chivalry of youth'. The manager of the store, Lengel ('Lengel's pretty dreary, teaches Sunday school and the rest, but he doesn't miss that much') rebukes the girls: ' "Girls, I don't want to argue with you. After this come in here with your shoulders covered. It's our policy." '

Humiliated, the girls leave, whereupon Sammy says 'I quit', and takes off his apron and his bow tie. Patient and old and grey, Lengel sighs and speaks to him:

'You'll feel this for the rest of your life,' Lengel says, and I know it's true, too, but remembering how he had made that pretty girl blush makes me so scrunchy inside I punch the No Sale tab and the machine whirs 'pee-pu' and the drawer splats out.

He walks out of the supermarket and his job. The girls have disappeared.

Looking back in the big windows, over the bags of peat moss aluminum and lawn furniture stacked on the pavement, I could see Lengel at my place in the slot, checking the sheep through. His face was dark grey and his back stiff, as if he'd just had an injection of iron, and my stomach kind of fell as I felt how hard the world was going to be to me hereafter.

'A & P' is especially noteworthy for its fidelity and fairness, fidelity to adolescent sense of what is fitting and fairness to all concerned. Lengel, for instance, is neither a villain nor a bully, and his pathetic dignity is wonderfully well realized. Updike's art is such that justice to Lengel is achieved without the reader's having any feeling that truth to Sammy has been tampered with.

'Pigeon Feathers', one of the Olinger stories, is even more impressive, for it deals with a crisis that may be considered profound. It begins with the sentence: 'When they moved to Firetown, things were upset, displaced, rearranged.' For David, aged fourteen, the move means disorientation and violent change, which is symbolized by the shock he suffers when he dips into his mother's copy of H. G. Wells's *The Outline of History*. He has picked it up on an impulse to bridge the gap in time between himself and his parents. He begins to read.

Then, before he could halt his eyes, David slipped into Wells's account of Jesus. He had been an obscure political agitator, a kind of hobo, in a minor colony of the Roman Empire. By an accident impossible to reconstruct he (the small *h* horrified David) survived his own crucifixion and presumably died a few weeks later. A religion was founded on the freakish incident. The credulous imagination of the times retrospectively assigned miracles and supernatural pretensions to Jesus; a myth grew, and then a church, whose theology was at most points in direct contradiction of the simple, rather communistic teachings of the Galilean.

He does not believe Wells's account and marshals all the evidence he can muster against it. All the same, he is forced to admit that he cannot refute it. As Updike says:

It was as if a stone that for weeks and even years had been gathering weight in the web of David's nerves snapped them and plunged through the page and a hundred layers of paper underneath ... This was the initial impact – that at a definite spot in time and space a brain black with denial of Christ's divinity had been suffered to exist; that the universe had not spit out this ball of tar but allowed it to continue in its blasphemy, to grow old, with honours, wear a hat, write books that, if true, collapsed everything into a jumble of horrors. The world outside the deep-silled windows – a rutted lawn, a whitewashed barn, a walnut tree frothy with fresh green – seemed a haven from which he was forever sealed off.

Next day, in the catechetical class in the Lutheran church of Firetown, David tries to elicit certainty from the young minister Reverend Dobson. Pressed, Dobson says:

'David, you might think of Heaven this way: as the way the goodness of Abraham Lincoln did lives after him.'

'But is Lincoln conscious of it living on?' He blushed no longer with embarrassment but in anger; he had walked here in good faith and was being made a fool.

'Is he conscious now? I would have to say no; but I don't think it matters.' His voice had a coward's firmness; he was hostile now.

'You don't.'

'Not in the eyes of God, no.' The unction, the stunning impudence, of this reply sprung tears of outrage in David's eyes. He bowed them to his book, where short words like Duty, Love, Obey, Honour, were stacked in the form of a cross.

After the class, he walks home along the dirt road from the highway. 'His indignation at being betrayed, at seeing Christianity betrayed, had hardened him.' Back at home, his mother surprises him reading the family Bible, and he has to tell her of his encounter with the minister and he waits for the shock to strike her. It does not.

He was becoming angry, sensing her surprise at him. She had assumed that Heaven had faded from his head years ago. She had imagined that he had already entered, in the secrecy of silence, the conspiracy that he now knew to be all around him.

She tries to persuade him of her faith but to no avail. Even his father says that he welcomes death, and strangely this does not frighten the boy.

Indeed, in the man's steep self-disgust the boy felt a kind of ally. A distant ally. He saw his position with a certain strategic coldness. Nowhere in the world of other people would he find the hint, the nod, he needed to build his fortress against death. They none of them believed. He was alone. In that deep hole.

The months pass. School is some comfort, and being in crowds. And seeing clergymen cheers him, for whatever they believed, their collars are evidence that someone, somewhere, recognizes still that we cannot submit to death.

On his fifteenth birthday he is given a Remington .22, and his mother asks him to shoot and clear the pigeons from the barn. Unwillingly, he carries out the slaughter, and when it is over, digs a hole to bury them in deep enough to prevent the dog from digging them up. We are bound to recall his vision at the beginning of the story, so strong as almost to be a physical sensation, of himself being buried after death. Packing the hole with the dead birds, he finds himself examining and marvelling at the design of the birds' feathers, which seem to him executed 'in a controlled rapture'. Yet these birds breed in their millions to be destroyed as pests.

As he fitted the last two, still pliant, on the top, and stood up, crusty coverings were lifted from him, and with a feminine, slipping sensation along his nerves that seemed to give the air hands, he was robed in this certainty: that the God who had lavished such craft upon these worthless birds would not destroy His whole Creation by refusing to let David live forever.

So the story ends. It is a remarkable achievement, unlike anything else in the short story, and it is likely to remain as a classic in fiction of the bewilderment, sickness, and misery felt when religious belief has to face the first assaults on the mind of the evidence of evil and discrepancy in the world.

Alan Sillitoe gained an immediate reputation in 1958 with his first novel, *Saturday Night and Sunday Morning*, a reputation consolidated by the appearance of 'The Loneliness of the Long-Distance Runner', a long short story that was made into a successful film, a year later. In twenty years he has now published twenty-five books of fiction, verse, and travel. An early story, 'The Decline and Fall of Frankie Buller', is especially revealing. It begins:

Sitting in what has come to be called my study, a room in the first-floor flat of a ramshackle Majorcan house, my eyes move over racks of books around me. Row after row of coloured backs and dusty tops, they give an air of distinction not only to the room but to the whole flat, and one can sense the thoughts of occasional visitors who stoop down discreetly during drinks to read their titles:

'A Greek lexicon, Homer in the original. He knows Greek! (Wrong, these books belong to my brother-in-law.) Shakespeare, the Golden Bough, a Holy Bible bookmarked with tapes and paper. He even reads it! Euripides and the rest, and a dozen mouldering Baedekers. What a funny idea to collect them! Proust, all twelve volumes! I never waded through that lot. (Neither did I.) Dostoevsky. My God, is *he* still going strong?'

And so on and so on, items that have become part of me, foliage that has grown to conceal the bare stem of my real personality, what I was like before I ever saw these books, or any book at all, come to that. Often I would like to rip them away from me one by one, extract their shadows out of my mouth and heart, cut them neatly with a scalpel from my jungle-brain. Impossible. You can't wind back the clock that sits grinning on the marble shelf. You can't even smash its face in and forget it.

It is well-known that Sillitoe lived for a time in the Fifties on Majorca, and the narrator of the story is referred to as Alan. The story, indeed, is presented as a piece of autobiography, and we may see it as a gloss upon Sillitoe's progress through life. In the story, the Proustian device of the sound of a cuckoo suddenly heard projects Sillitoe back to his childhood just before the war in working-class Nottingham, when for some years he was a soldier in the local army led by Frankie Buller, a young man between twenty and twenty-five, a mental defective.

He was glad and proud of being 'like he was' because it meant he did not have to work in a factory all day and earn his living like other men of his age. He preferred to lead the gang of twelve-year-olds in our street to war against the same age group of another district.

The war begins, and soon Alan is evacuated with the other children of the city into the country and does not see Frankie again for two years. Then, he is pushing a handcart loaded with bundles of firewood. They do not find much to talk about; Frankie seems ashamed to be seen talking to one so much younger.

More than ten years pass before they meet again, outside a cinema, by which time Alan has become a writer, 'having, for some indescribable reason, after evacuation and during the later bombs, taken to reading books'.

He was not my leader any more, and we both instantly recognized the fact as we shook hands. Frankie's one-man wood business had prospered, and he now went around the streets with a pony and cart. He wasn't well-off, but he was his own employer. The outspoken ambition of our class was to become one's own boss. He knew he wasn't the leader of kindred spirits any more, while he probably wondered as we spoke whether or not I might be, which could have accounted for his shyness. . . .

''Ow are yer gooin' on these days, Frankie?' I asked, revelling in the old accent, though knowing that I no longer had the right to use it.

Frankie asks Alan to read the cinema poster for him, and when Alan tells him that it is a sort of cowboy film with a terrific train smash at the end there comes into his eyes the same glint as when, years ago, he stood with his spear and shouted 'Charge!' They part, and the story ends:

And I with my books have not seen him since. It was like saying goodbye to a big part of me, for ever.

'The Decline and Fall of Frankie Buller' is a faithful, moving and, though not executed in irony, ironical encapsulation of a universal experience of slum childhood. The point of view from which it is written, however, is odd. It is not merely that Sillitoe is torn between his childish hero-worship of Frankie and an adult's realistic appraisal of Frankie as a mental defective, but there is also a strong sense of betrayal of himself and his class through his having become a writer and thus moved himself from slum life in Nottingham. There seems a suspicion in the narrator's mind that by doing this he has somehow become less genuine. The precipitating cause of this lack of authenticity appears to be initially the ability to read; from this, everything else flows.

Now this new version of the Fall is surely naive in the extreme and liable to lead to sentimentality. Nevertheless, it must be admitted that it is useful in that it allows Sillitoe to identify himself with people who are inarticulate as well as economically and culturally dispossessed. This is seen at its most impressive in 'The Loneliness of the Long-Distance Runner'.

It is in the simplest sense an heroic story, that of one man against the world, and the one man deliberately loses, as if to echo the scriptural 'What shall it profit a man, if he shall gain the whole world, and lose his own soul?' It has the fascination, too, of seeming to throw light on the psychology of the rebel, the intransigent nonconformist in the literal sense.

The story takes the form of a retrospective account and consideration of a cross-country race run by Borstal boys. It gives essential information about the runner's life before Borstal, showing how, in some ways, Colin and the typical Sillitoe character may appear to be representations of Shaw's undeserving poor. They are completely untouched by middle-class values or by the traditional working-class aspirations. Outside the province of their own self-satisfaction, they are moved only by class rancour and the sense of solidarity with all who feel deprived or defrauded by those with superior advantages.

In this, Colin is intransigent. As he says:

> You see, by sending me to Borstal they've shown me the knife, and from now on I know something I didn't know before: that it's war between me and them. . . . Government wars aren't my wars; they've got nowt to do with me, because my own war's all that I'll ever be bothered about. I remember when I was fourteen and I went into the country with three of my cousins, all about the same age, who later

went to different Borstals, and then to different regiments, from which they soon deserted, and then to different gaols where they still are as far as I know. . . . Up Colliers' Pad we heard another lot of kids talking in high-school voices behind a hedge. We crept up on them and peeped through the brambles, and saw they were eating a picnic, a real posh spread out of baskets and flasks and towels. There must have been about seven of them, lads and girls sent out by their mams and dads for the afternoon. So we went on our bellies through the hedge like crocodiles and surrounded them, and then dashed into the middle, scattering the fire and batting their tabs and snatching up all there was to eat, then running off over Cherry Orchard fields into the woods, with a man chasing us who'd come up while we were ransacking the picnic. We got away all right, and had a good feed into the bargain, because we'd been clambed to death and couldn't wait long enough to get our chops ripping into them thin lettuce and ham sandwiches and creamy cakes.

Colin is born to theft. His father dies of cancer, and his mother collects five hundred pounds in compensation.

Night after night we sat in front of the telly with a ham sandwich in one hand, a bar of chocolate in the other, and a bottle of lemonade between our boots, while mam was with some fancy-man upstairs on the new bed she'd ordered, and I've never known a family as happy as ours was in that couple of months when we'd got all the money we needed. And when the dough ran out I didn't think about anything much, but just roamed the streets – looking for another job, I told mam – hoping I suppose to get my hands on another five hundred nicker so's the nice life we'd got used to could go on and on for ever.

One night Colin and his pal Mike break into the office of a baker's, from which they steal a money-box containing more than one hundred and fifty pounds, but they are caught and Colin is sent to Borstal.

There, he is entered by the governor to run in the Borstal Blue Ribbon Prize Cup for Long Distance Cross Country Running (All England). Though he knows it is within his power to do so, he also knows that he must not win, for to do so would be to bolster up the governor in his self-esteem, to curry favour with the class enemy. His honour is involved. As for the governor:

He got his own back right enough, or thought he did, because he had me carting dustbins about every morning from the big full-working kitchen to the garden-bottoms where I had to empty them; and in the afternoon I spread out slops over spuds and carrots growing in the allotments. In the evenings I scrubbed floors, miles and miles of them. . . . The work didn't break me; if anything it made me stronger in many ways, and the governor knew, when I left, that his spite had got him nowhere. For since leaving Borstal they tried to get me into the army, but I didn't pass the medical and I'll tell you why. No sooner was I out, after that final run and six-months hard, than I went down with pleurisy, which seems as far as I'm concerned that I lost the governor's race all right, and won my own twice over, because I know for certain that if I hadn't raced my race I wouldn't have got this pleurisy, which keeps me out of khaki but doesn't stop me doing the sort of work my itchy fingers want to do.

'The Loneliness of the Long-Distance Runner' remains Sillitoe's finest story, written, one feels, at the most favourable point in his career, for it is plain that such a writer as Sillitoe is bound, by the very passage of the years and the consequences of his own success, to change in relation to his past and become less consistent and authoritative in his assessment of it. The title story of his second collection, 'The Ragman's Daughter', offers some evidence of this.

It begins admirably in Sillitoe's most direct manner of first-person narration:

I was walking home with an empty suitcase one night, an up-to-date pigskin zip job I was fetching back from a pal who thought he'd borrowed it for good, and two plain-clothes coppers stopped me. They questioned me for twenty minutes, then gave up and let me go. While they had been talking to me, a smash-and-grab had taken place around the corner, and ten thousand nicker had vanished into the wide open spaces of somebody who needed it.

That's life. I was lucky my suitcase had nothing but air in it. Sometimes I walk out with a box of butter and cheese from the warehouse I work at, but for once that no-good God was on my side – trying to make up for the times he's stabbed me in the back maybe. But if the coppers had had a word with me a few nights later they'd have found me loaded with high-class provision snap.

Tony, the narrator, quickly establishes himself as a character. He is a petty criminal, though he does not live by crime. He works in a wholesale food warehouse but from his earliest days he has wanted to be a thief and he began at the infants' school, stealing building bricks.

Once, an uncle asked what I wanted to be when I grew up, and I answered, 'A thief.' He bumped me, so I decided, whenever anybody asked that trick question to say, 'An honest man' or 'An engine driver.'

In his youth, he discovers that he especially likes thieving with girls, and one evening he picks up Doris outside a fish-and-chip shop. When he tells her that he lives by 'nicking', she replies that though she has never stolen anything in her life, she has often wanted to. When they meet a few evenings later, at her suggestion they just prowl around until they see 'something'.

The overhead lights made us look TB, as if some big government scab had made a mistake on the telephone and had too much milk tipped into the sea. We even stopped talking at the sight of each other's fag-and-ash faces, but after a while the darker streets brought us back to life, and every ten yards I got what she'd not been ready to give on the back seat of the pictures: a fully fledged passionate kiss. Into each went all my wondering at why a girl like this should want to come out on nightwork with a lout called me.

She is the daughter of a scrap-metal dealer he has seen driving through the town in a maroon Jaguar. She herself is in her last year at a grammar school. She is obviously his superior in terms of economic class, but as they wander through the streets the sense of an easy relation between them emerges. They come to the yard of a small car-body workshop, break in, and then walk back to the street. When they inspect their booty, Doris has a bundle of pound notes and Tony a large envelope of postage stamps. They take half each, Tony sticking one or two stamps on every corner turned until they come to the banks of the river, where they make love.

So their partnership in love and thieving begins. They go on many 'expeditions', as Doris calls them; until one night, Tony is caught. Doris is not seen, but Tony is sent to Borstal for three years and, though he writes to her, receives no answer. When he is out he is able to piece things together. Doris had been pregnant by him at the time of his arrest and three months later had married a garage mechanic. Her child, who was a boy, she had called Tony. When it was two months old, she had gone out with her husband on Christmas Eve and been killed when the motorbike on which she was riding pillion crashed into a petrol tanker.

Tony steals a transistor radio from a car and is sent to prison for six months. When he is released he is able to face things again. He gets a job at a sawmill and one day sees an elderly man with a little boy dressed in a cowboy suit whacking flowers with a stick. He realizes the old man is Doris's father and the little boy his own son. The story ends:

I can watch him without wanting to put my head in the gas oven, to watch him and laugh to myself because I was happy to see him at all. He's in good hands and prospering. I'm going straight as well, working in the warehouse where they store butter and cheese. I eat like a fighting cock, and take home so much that my wife and two kids don't do bad on it either.

'The Ragman's Daughter' is, among other things, a romantic rogue's story. Tony is entirely convincing as a drawing of a young amoralist who steals for the thrill it gives him. And this is even more true of Doris. We are very near literary territory popular in the Thirties, in fictional versions, for instance, of the Leopold and Loeb murder and in the novels of André Gide and their derivatives. We might borrow a phrase from Lawrence and call 'The Ragman's Daughter' a thought-adventure but, even so, I suspect we should have to consider it decadent after 'The Loneliness of the Long-Distance Runner'.

Joyce Carol Oates was born in 1938 near Buffalo, in the north-west corner of New York State, and this region of America has been the setting of most of her stories. Since her first novel appeared in 1964 she has been an extremely prolific writer, and since she is very much in mid-career, any judgement on her work must be tentative. According to one American critic, Fred Silva, in *Contemporary Novelists*, her work recalls in style and manner both the writings of the Naturalists and of those of the Southern Renaissance, recalls, specifically, Steinbeck, Welty, Cather, Faulkner, and Dreiser. She has, too, often been labelled 'Gothic' because of the intensity of her rendering of horror and violence, and on this charge she has herself commented: 'Gothicism, what-ever it is, is not a literary tradition so much as a fairly realistic assessment of modern life.' Certainly, her work shows she is learned in American fiction and shows, too, she is steeped in the lore of American life as lived in the Fifties and Sixties. One has only to read a story like 'Where Are You Going, Where Have You Been?' to see her knowledge of the young of the time. It begins:

Her name was Connie. She was fifteen and she had a quick, nervous giggling habit of craning her neck to glance into mirrors or checking other people's faces to make sure her own was all right. Her mother, who noticed everything and who hadn't much reason any longer to look at her own face, always scolded Connie about it. 'Stop gawking at yourself. Who are you? You think you're so pretty?' she would say. Connie would raise her eyebrows at these familiar old complaints and look right through her mother, into a shadowy vision of herself as she was right at that moment: she knew she was pretty and that was everything. Her mother had been pretty once too, if you could believe those old snapshots in the album, but now her looks were gone and that was why she was always after Connie.

'Why don't you keep your room clean like your sister? How've you got your hair fixed – what the hell stinks? Hair spray? You don't see your sister using that junk.'

Joyce Carol Oates's dominant intutitions about life emerge in a story like 'Normal Love', which is written under a series of headings such as 'Downtown', 'My husband', 'My children', 'My neighborhood supermarket'. They are notes, as it were, on day-to-day living in a college town in upper New York State, beginning:

I park my car in a high-rise garage, three floors up. Everything is silent. The garage in grey, the colour of concrete blocks and metal. Many cars are parked here, in silence, but no one is around. A small tension rises in me, an alarm. Is there anyone around? Anyone? Our city is not a large city, there is no danger. There might be danger late at night for a woman alone. Now it is the winter afternoon, a weekday, overcast, too cold for anyone to make trouble. . . . I lock the car door, I put the keys in my purse, I walk quickly to the elevator and press the button for Down.

There is a man in the elevator, but he says nothing, makes no movement, though the lady's heart keeps hammering. The elevator stops, and she gets out quickly, escapes. The section ends: 'I spend the afternoon shopping. I am not followed.'

And what happens after? In a way, very little. The lady's husband, a university professor, finds a woman's purse, with the name Linda Slater in it, and takes it to the police station. Two or three days later, the dismembered, mutilated body of Linda Slater is found in the river. But what is all-important is the suspense, the menace, a feeling that cuts across the brilliant rendering of the superficies of American life.

Comparable to 'Normal Love' in its effect is 'The Children', in which the menace, the symbol of disruption, is the idiot boy Gower. He terrifies the young children:

With a high inhuman shriek he ran round the other side of the house again. The children began to cry, terrified. Rachel cried convulsively, gasping for breath, and Ginny was filled with a terrible anguish. She knelt to embrace the child. 'It's all right, darling. It's all right,' she whispered. Sobs shook Rachel's body and Ginny was overcome by a sense of the child's vulnerability; it was a terrible thing for her to understand.

Ronald her husband has a fence installed round the house, but it cannot prevent infection by the evil of which Gower is a symbol and which corrupts the little girls and then Ginny herself, though she realizes that the boy is no more than a pathetic deprived child.

Joyce Carol Oates has, so far, written no finer story than 'Waiting', which begins by plunging straight into the heart of the story:

'I wouldn't be here except for them kids,' Mr Mott said.

'Your children?'

'No, them kids, like I said, them kids out of school,' he explained, flushing. He was in his late forties and had a narrow, sullen face. From time to time his eyes lifted to Katherine's suspiciously, as if he were checking on her. Was she nervous, why hadn't she remembered about the kids who were out of school now, in June, instead of thinking Mr Mott was talking about his own children —?

'Yes, I see,' Katherine said. 'The boys who work part-time.'

'Hires them part-time and kicks me out, on account of that – that whatdyacallit, a law or something. He didn't have to pay into the thing, that state thing, with them. With me it's different, but I asked him, was that my fault? He was pretending he was laying me off and it was only temporary —'

The scene is the social welfare centre in a north American city and Katherine is a social worker, an idealistic girl from the working class who has worked in a factory to save up enough money to go to college and qualify as a social worker. Now she has a case-load of forty families; Mr Mott may stand as the archetype of them all. Hers has been and still is essentially a life of waiting. She has had to break off her engagement to a young dentist to look after her mother, now housebound and 'always greedy for bad news'.

Katherine, now twenty-six, was conscious of herself as young and oddly clean compared to this old woman. Yes, her mother had become an old woman at last. Finally, to amuse her, she told stories of the 'hillbillies' (an expression Katherine never used down at the Centre, though other people did), who used all the wrong words, who couldn't keep jobs, who had such pale, washed-out, sad, humble, dangerous faces . . . Mr X's son, who was twelve, had gone into a drug store and asked for some cream; and when he was served he was given *cream* – in a glass! (He had really wanted ice cream, Katherine explained.) So he lost his temper and started a fight, because everybody was laughing at him.

'Oh, these hillbillies! There's some of them right on this block,' Katherine's mother said.

And what about the niggers? her mother wanted to know.

'The Negroes,' Katherine said carefully, '. . . the blacks . . . are polite and quiet. They don't want any trouble.'

'Hadn't better want any,' her mother said. 'Blacks!' She snorted; she seemed pleased.

When she is in her twenty-eighth year Katherine begins to harden towards her Welfare clients, or perhaps her attitude towards them becomes more professional. She learns to talk more clearly, with greater confidence and authority to Welfare applicants, though confrontations with prostitutes applying for Welfare can still disturb her. She is promoted to supervisor. Her mother dies; she inherits the house, which she continues to occupy, though the area in which it stands has now been taken over by coloured people, meaning, Miss Oates explains, people who can afford to buy nothing better. She is in her thirties now; she still thinks of herself as young and still thinks of the man she is yet to meet, though she no longer buys nightgowns with the vague expectation of their being 'for her marriage'. A few days after her thirty-fourth birthday, leaving the Centre she is accosted by a man wearing a suit 'exactly like the kind advertised in all the fall magazines'. It is her old client Mr Mott, but a changed Mr Mott, a Mr Mott become prosperous. He has a new car and he offers to drive her home, an offer she accepts.

She invites him in for 'a minute and chat'. As he sits on the sofa he becomes slyly insulting and she has to bear his resentment for his years of attendance at the Welfare Centre. In the end he strikes her, and the story ends:

> She waited. The numbness around her eyes began to ease and turned into pain, so that she was able to weep. The sobs were violent, like blows, and her chest heaved with the effort of giving them passage, letting them free. She had not wept for years. There was a lifetime of weeping before her but she did not know why. The secret of her pain seemed to be in the long procession of sallow-faced straggly witches and broken-down men, or in this house, in the memory of her mother and father, or out dawdling along the sidewalk from the Boulevard, Katherine herself a child again with an armload of books – but she did not understand it. She did not understand Mr Mott's hatred and she did not understand the power he had, to make her feel such pain.

'Waiting' is Chekhovian not only in its compassion but in the artistry with which a life is summed up as it was in the past, is in the present, and will be in the future.

iv

From its very nature, a book of this kind, the survey of an art-form still living, unfolding, changing, can have no satisfactory ending. It can only stop, and this is likely to please neither reader nor writer. The one will expect at least an interim judgement. The writer, on the other hand, will know that at best all he can provide are informed guesses and generalizations the truth of which the unforeseen events of a year or two ahead may wholly disprove. The only safe view, he will think, is the short view.

Thus, he may well see in the present brilliance of the South African story in English a modern instance of the truth of what Abraham Cowley wrote three centuries ago: 'A warlike, various, and a tragical age is the best to write of, but the worst to write in,' but still prefer to take as a model of what the story should be the Irish story as it has existed over the past fifteen years. During that time, it has charted with the utmost delicacy and precision and in all their fluctuating subtleties of nuance the developments and changes in a people's perception of itself.

The most striking feature of the Irish story throughout its ex-istence has been pinned down by V. S. Pritchett in his preface to David Marcus's anthology of 1976, *New Irish Writing*: 'What has always struck me in Irish writing is the sense of Ireland itself, its past or its imagined future, as a presence or invisible extra char-acter in the story I am reading.' By contrast, he notes, 'Among the English the sense of England as an extra character is very rarely felt – indeed Kipling is the only writer I can think of who shows signs of this feeling.'

What the post-O'Connor Irish story records is an Ireland in rapid change, an Ireland no longer dominated overwhelmingly by the priest, an Ireland moving into a world and an age that may be represented by the twin symbols of the international airport and the international hotel, a world and an age, one is tempted to think, in which idiosyncrasy must disappear. It is able to do so because it is an immensely various story, as a brief glance at some of its manifestations will show. In the world outside Ireland, Brian Friel's *A Saucer of Larks* shows him to be a natural story-writer who has snared a great deal of Irish life in his stories, which are set in lonely cottages in Donegal, small villages in the north-west. He accepts his findings about life there without reservations and he transmits admirably the feel of ordinary life. Stories like 'The Fawn Pup' and 'My Father and the Sergeant', warm, affectionate, and without posturings of any kind, are particularly successful, and in them, as in the beautiful title-story, we are in the presence of something like Wordsworth's natural piety.

Since Friel's stories deal with a people still governed by traditional values, they make an excellent foil to the stories of Edna O'Brien. She appeared as a novelist whose essential theme seemed to be the Irish girl, whether at home or in England. Her first collection of stories, *The Love Object*, was published in 1969, and what was immediately noticeable was that it contained only one story with a specifically Irish setting, 'Irish Revel'. A young girl is invited to a party at a country hotel and cycles to it through the rain in her unfashionable borrowed finery. There, it slowly dawns on her that her role is that of unpaid skivvy. At daybreak she leaves and '. . . she wondered if and what she would tell her mother and her brothers about it, and if all parties were as bad'. 'Irish Revel' is a very tender and sympathetic story which evokes a country district, the small town that is its metropolis, and its way of life. Sad and funny, it is a memorable rendering in an Irish context of the miseries of adolescence.

Then one sets it side by side with the title-story of the volume. It is very different, a story, told from the woman's point of view, of an affair between a television announcer and a lawyer she meets at a party. The setting is London, in what one guesses to be Kensington, and the course of the affair and the woman's feelings are, it seems to me, scrupulously rendered. When these stories are placed in juxtaposition one sees what is happening not only to Miss O'Brien but perhaps to the Irish story generally. She has moved, as it were, into the international scene; or it may be that the international scene has moved into Ireland, a view confirmed in part, at least, by a reading of Tom Macintyre's collection *Dance the Dance*.

It contains two stories that are considerable achievements in their own right, and once again they make a striking contrast one with the other. 'Such a Favour' is a comedy of conventional Irish piety, the story of a boy for whom 'the year past had been troublesome for the ear: hospital, surgery, drops, powders, and ointments'. The trouble clears, and the boy, caught up in his mother's excessive devotional zeal, concludes that he has been healed by a miraculous intervention on the part of the Blessed Oliver Plunkett.

Murdered by the English. Hanged, drawn, and quartered. Horrible. Still, someday he'll be a saint. 'Two major miracles,' my mother speaking after a while, 'would do it.'

Perhaps, thinks the boy, his healing is one of them.

This is a story close to the centre of the Irish tradition. The subject is one that O'Faolain or O'Connor might have treated. The other story, 'Epithalamium', is very different and, though one could imagine a medieval equivalent, seems to me totally original, for it is a story of what might be called circumstantial impotence. A newly-married couple drive to an hotel for their honeymoon. After two nights in apparently ideal surroundings the marriage is still not consummated. On the third day, a Sunday, they go to mass and hear the priest in his sermon pronounce a rhetorical question, 'Will you never kennel the beast within you?' Next morning they bolt: to the house that is waiting for them in Dublin. There, we assume, nothing will be easier than the consummation of marriage.

Something similar to the shift one sees taking place in Edna O'Brien's and Tom Macintyre's stories is discernible in the stories in *Death of a Chieftain*, by John Montague, whose main reputation is as a poet. It appeared in 1964. The setting of most of the stories is County Tyrone and the finest of them is probably 'The New Enamel Bucket', which describes a day and a night spent at the local fair by John Rooney, a circumspect, un-aggressive man of sober habits. The time is passed in aimless (and in Rooney's case reluctant) drinking and in attempts to pick quarrels with Protestants. The story is essentially an exposure, dispassionate yet charitable, of the hopelessness and mindless violence rooted in habitual poverty.

In this story Montague is the Irish writer in his role of critic of Ireland and the Irish: 'A Change of Management', however, gives us a glimpse – ambivalent, admittedly – of an untraditional modern Ireland, discernible in 1964 and now, after she has joined the European Community, well on the way towards a flourishing existence.

John O'Shea, a civil servant, learns from his boss that the department of government he works in is about to be merged into the National Renaissance Board, which is headed by Dr William Pearse Clohessy, who, according to his old friend and colleague Tadgh Cronin, is a 'smooth bastard' who has what is necessary to get on in Ireland today – 'neck; pure, unadulterated, armour-plated, insensitive *neck*'. Lunching in a pub with Cronin, who once published a volume of verse and lives on 'the old-fashioned fidelity and the respect still paid in the community to the idea of the poet, half pure spirit, half biting satirist'. O'Shea recalls Clohessy's avowal, made many years before as an undergraduate, of his ambitions:

... in clear and precise tones, Clohessy outlined for them the shape he wished his career to follow. By twenty, he hoped to graduate with First Class Honours in Legal and Political Science; he would then enter a well-known Dublin firm as a junior executive. By twenty-two, he would be Fencing Champion of Ireland, but would give it up afterwards: it took too much time. By twenty-five he should be Assistant Manager and have his Doctorate in Economics. By thirty, he would certainly be a section head, but since he could hardly hope to rise any further in Ireland for the moment, he would probably go abroad and work for one of the big economic organizations, to gain top managerial experience. It was difficult to get a proper salary in Ireland at that level, but he felt sure that the government would ask him back before he was forty, to take charge of a national or semi-state organization. Perhaps they would even create a new one, some man-sized job commensurate with his training and abilities. ...

That evening, O'Shea meets Clohessy at an official dinner and as acquaintances they drink together afterwards. Clohessy tells O'Shea:

'When I came back to this country after the war, I saw that it had no future. My first instinct was to clear out again, and to hell with it: with my background and training I could have a comfortable life anywhere in the world. ... Then I thought that was a bit cowardly. Why not

come back and try and create a future for the country at the same
time as I was creating my own? As you know, we've had a lot of
patriots.'

'You can say that again,' said O'Shea fervently.

'But what it has never had are a group of practical, hard-headed
people who would try to put it back on its feet, like any business.
People not afraid to face the priests, the politicians, the whole vast
bog of the Irish middle class, and woo something positive out of
it. . . .'

Later, Clohessy inquires about Cronin, whom he describes as
'the original Stone-age Bohemian; in any other country he would
have been remaindered years ago'. It strikes O'Shea that never
before has he encountered 'a glance which combined affability
and threat in such proportions' as Clohessy's.

Next day, O'Shea is telephoned by Cronin, who tells him in
great excitement that he is resigning from his Department, for
he has been threatened with disciplinary action unless he con-
forms to regulations. O'Shea thereupon tells Cronin of his encounter with Clohessy;

There was a pause at the other end of the line and then Cronin's
voice came through, triumphant, low, almost a snarl.

'I was right!'

'What do you mean you were right?'

'To resign. The hour has come. *The bastards are on the march.*'

. . . O'Shea could nearly see Cronin grasping the receiver at the other
end, in his excitement. 'Since this country was founded we've had two
waves of chances. The first were easy to spot; the gunman turned
gombeen: they were so ignorant that they practically ruined themselves.
But this second lot are a tougher proposition. In fifty years they'll have
made this country just like every place else.'

'And what's wrong with that?'

'You know damn well what's wrong with that: they'll murder us
with activity! Factories owned by Germans, posh hotels catering to
the grey flannel brigade, computers instead of decent pen-pushers:
do you call that progress? If this country becomes a chancer's paradise, it will be over my dead body. *Over my dead body, do you
hear?*'

And that (repeated several times with increasing vehemance) was
Cronin's parting shot . . .

The contemporary Irish story seems to be to offer a paradigm of the condition of Ireland herself, both as she exists within herself and in relation to the world outside, and in the stories of Julia O'Faolain, the brilliant daughter of Sean, we see traditionally Irish themes merging into the Jamesean International Subject, though opening out beyond the mutual involvement of Britain and the United States.

Her range is wide. There is the story 'It's a Long Way to Tipperary', which deals with the problems of the Irishman forced, in some sense, into Englishness. Cuddahy enlists as a private in the British Army in 1914, rises to the rank of captain, and marries an English woman of better class than himself. He eventually comes back to Ireland a renegade twice over, a renegade Catholic through his wife's influence and a renegade Irishman.

'It's a Long Way to Tipperary' is at once funny almost to the point of farce, a hard-headed and moving story of a specifically Irish dilemma. Julia O'Faolain is a writer of great flexibility, reminiscent to some degree of Kipling in her diversity of scene. Thus, besides 'It's a Long Way to Tipperary', *Man in the Cellar*, the volume in which it appears, contains two other brilliant stories in modes very different from it and from each other. One is 'This Is My Body', which is set in a convent in sixth-century Gaul and is a dramatization of the impact of Christianity on people still pagan in feeling and impulse. The other is 'Man In the Cellar' itself, and here the International Subject is subsumed in another subject, one we may call in rough shorthand Women's Lib. It is an index of the story's success that it will almost certainly recall Poe. The story is in the form of a long letter to her mother-in-law written by a young Englishwoman describing the revenge she has taken on her domineering and sadistic Italian husband. 'Marriage,' writes Miss O'Faolain in her last paragraph, 'like topiary, distorts growth.'

'Romantic Ireland's dead and gone.' Certainly the Ireland of today is a different Ireland from Yeats's and Joyce's or even O'Connor's. But, as the short stories being written at the present time show, it is no less Ireland, for all that it has moved into the modern world. The Irish dimension in these stories of the Sixties and Seventies is as pronounced as it has been at any time in the history of Irish writing in English, and in this respect the contemporary Irish story may be held up as a model.

That said, we are bound to wonder whether it will always be so and immediately we find ourselves among the imponderables. It is one thing to assert that so long as men and women remain recognizably men and women they will go on telling stories, quite another to assume that the stories will be necessarily similar to those that have been the theme of this book. Those stories have been to an overwhelming degree products of the periodical press. They came into existence with the great early nineteenth-century developments in it and have remained organically linked to it: short-story writers have addressed themselves primarily to the editors and readers of newspapers and magazines, not to book publishers. It now seems probable that in the widest sense the printing press is considerably less important than it was at the beginning of the century and that for some things and in some ways it has been becoming increasingly secondary and even subsidiary to more modern media of communication, film, sound broadcasting, and television. These and other new developments in technology could lead to the cessation of publication of short stories altogether; yet it would not necessarily mean the total disappearance of the modern short story or of something very much like it. Television has shown itself particularly symbiotic upon the classic story and the adaptation to television drama of short stories by Chekhov and Maupassant, Kipling, Joyce, Fitzgerald, Lawrence, Katherine Mansfield, and Coppard has proved conspicuously successful. A few television plays, some of those of Alan Bennett in particular, owe their power to entertain and move us by qualities of a kind intrinsic to the modern short story, which makes them reminiscent, in their depiction of relationships, angle of approach, and poetry of mood, of the art of writers like Joyce, Fitzgerald, and Mansfield.

The fact remains, such plays are inevitably few and they are still plays, not stories. But this is to be too pessimistic. Reviewing what has been achieved in the modern short story in English in all its branches during the hundred and fifty years since it first appeared in Scott, one cannot believe that the form will be allowed to disappear. In the end, the real hope for its future lies in its necessity, in the unique opportunities it offers imaginative writers themselves.

Select Bibliography

Collections of Stories

The works listed below are representative of those writers dealt with in *The Short Story in English*. Collected editions, where available, are listed.

AIKEN, CONRAD, *The Collected Short Stories of Conrad Aiken*, London, 1966

ANDERSON, SHERWOOD, *Short Stories*, New York, 1962; *Winesburg, Ohio*, New York, 1919, Harmondsworth and New York, 1976

AUMONIER, STACY, *Love-a-duck, and other stories*, London, 1921; *Overheard. Fifteen Tales*, reprint of 1924 ed., New York, 1972; *Ups and Downs. A Collection of Stories*, London, 1929, 1935. Reprinted USA; *Little Windows. A Collection of Stories*, London, 1931

BATES, H. E., *Thirty-one Selected Tales*, London, 1951; *Selected Short Stories of H. E. Bates*, London, 1951; *Seven by Five. Stories. 1926–1961*, London, 1963; *Country Tales. Collected Short Stories*, Bath, 1974; *Short Stories*, London, 1975

BENNETT, ARNOLD, *Selected Tales*, London, 1928; *Tales of the Five Towns*, London, 1905, 1964, New York, 1976; *The Grim Smile of the Five Towns*, London, 1907, Harmondsworth, 1971, New York, 1976; *The Matador of the Five Towns and other stories*, London, 1912, 1972, New York, 1976

BIERCE, AMBROSE, *Collected Writings of Ambrose Bierce*, New Jersey, 1960; *Stories and Fables of Ambrose Bierce*, Maryland, 1977; *The Cynic's Wordbook*, London and New York, 1906, reissued as *The Devil's Dictionary*, Maryland, 1978

BOWEN, ELIZABETH, *Encounters*, London, 1923, 1949; *Ann Lee's and Other Stories*, London, 1926, reprint of 1926 ed., New York; *Joining Charles, and other stories*, London, 1929, 1952; *The Cat Jumps, and other stories*, London, 1934, 1949; *Look at all Those Roses. Short Stories*, London, 1941, 1951; *The Demon Lover, and other stories*, London, 1945, Harmondsworth, 1966; *Ivy Gripped the Steps, and other stories*, New York, 1946; *Selected Stories*, Dublin and London, 1946

CALDWELL, ERSKINE, *Complete Stories of Erskine Caldwell*, Boston, 1953

CALLAGHAN, MORLEY, *Morley Callaghan's Stories*, Toronto, 1967; *Stories*, London, 1962, 1964

CATHER, WILLA, *Collected Short Fiction 1892–1912*, Nebraska, 1970; *Early Stories of Willa Cather*, New York, 1957; *Uncle Valentine and other stories: Willa Cather's Uncollected Short Fiction 1915–1929*, Nebraska, 1973

CHEEVER, JOHN, *The Stories of John Cheever*, New York, 1978

CONRAD, JOSEPH, *Complete Short Stories of Joseph Conrad*, London, 1933; *Short Stories*, London, 1975; *Selected Tales*, London, 1977; *Heart of Darkness*, London, 1910, New York, 1979, Harmondsworth, 1973, 1980; *'Nigger of the Narcissus'* (1891) *and Typhoon* (1903), Harmondsworth, 1963, 1978

COPPARD, A. E., *The Collected Tales of A. E. Coppard*, New York, 1951; *Selected Stories*, London, 1972; *Collected Tales*, reprint of 1948 ed., New York, 1976; *Dusky Ruth and other stories*, London, 1972, Harmondsworth, 1974, 1977

CORKERY, DANIEL, *Hounds of Banba*, New York, 1920, Dublin, 1921; *The Wager and other stories*, Connecticut, 1950

CRANE, STEPHEN, *Great Short Works of Stephen Crane*, New York, 1965; *Stories and Tales*, New York, 1955; *Whilomville Stories*, London and New York, 1900, reprinted New York, 1972; *Sullivan County tales and sketches*, Iowa, 1968; *The Open Boat and three other tales*, London, 1898, 1968

DAVIES, RHYS, *The Collected Stories of Rhys Davies*, London, 1955; *The Darling of her Heart, and other stories*, London, 1958

DE LA MARE, WALTER, *The Collected Tales of Walter de la Mare*, New York, 1950; *Best Stories of Walter de la Mare*, London, 1942; *Some Stories*, London, 1962

DICKENS, CHARLES, *Sketches by Boz*, London, 1850, 1957, New York, 1968; *Selected Short Fiction*, Harmondsworth, 1976, 1979

EVANS, CARADOC, *My People*, London, 1915, 1967; *Capel Sion* (*Short Stories*), London, 1917; *My Neighbours: Stories of the Welsh People*, London, 1919, reprint of 1920 ed., New York; *The Earth Gives All and Takes All. Tales*, London, 1946

FAULKNER, WILLIAM, *Collected Stories of William Faulkner*, New York, 1956, 1977

FITZGERALD, F. SCOTT, *Stories of F. Scott Fitzgerald*, New York, 1951, subsequently reprinted; *Collected Stories*, Harmondsworth, 1965–1974

FLAUBERT, GUSTAVE, *Trois Contes*, Paris, 1877, translated as *Three Tales*, Harmondsworth, 1961, 1979

FORSTER, E. M., *Collected Short Stories*, Harmondsworth, 1954, 1979; *The Abinger Edition of E. M. Forster*, London, 1972–; *The Celestial Omnibus and other stories*, London, 1911, New York, 1976; *The Eter-*

nal Moment and other Stories, London, 1928, New York, 1973; *Life to Come, and other stories*, London, 1972, Harmondsworth, 1975, 1979, New York, 1976

FRIEL, BRIAN, *A Saucer of Larks*, London, 1962

GARLAND, HAMLIN, *Main-Travelled Roads*, Boston, 1891, London, 1892, New York, 1962; *Other Main-Travelled Roads*, New York and London, 1910; *Prairie Folks. Tales*, London and Chicago, 1893, subsequently reprinted, New York

GORDIMER, NADINE, *Selected Stories*, London, 1975, New York, 1976; *Face to Face. Short Stories*, Johannesburg, 1949; *The Soft Voice of the Serpent, and other stories*, London, 1953, Harmondsworth, 1962; *Six Feet of the Country. Short Stories*, London, 1956; *Friday's Footprint*, London, 1960; *Not for Publication*, London, 1965; *Livingstone's Companions: Stories*, London, 1972, Harmondsworth, 1975; *No Place Like: Selected Stories*, Harmondsworth, 1978; *A Soldier's Embrace*, London, 1980

HALWARD, LESLIE, *To Tea on Sunday*, London, 1936; *The Money's All Right and other stories*, London, 1938

HARDY, THOMAS, *Stories. New Wessex Edition*, London, 1977; *Selected Stories*, London, 1966

HARRIS, FRANK, *Elder Conklin and Other Stories*, London, 1895, 1930, New York, 1977, Philadelphia, 1978; *Montes the Matador and Other Stories*, London, 1900, 1952, New York, 1977, Philadelphia, 1978; *The Yellow Ticket and other Stories*, London, 1914

HAWTHORNE, NATHANIEL, *Complete Short Stories*, New York, 1959; *Short Stories*, New York, 1973; *Selected Tales and Sketches*, New York and London, 1970; *The Selected Works*, London, 1971

HEMINGWAY, ERNEST, *The Short Stories of Ernest Hemingway*, reprint of the 1934 ed., New York; *Selected Works*, London, 1977; *Selected Short Stories*, London, 1972; *The Nick Adams Stories*, Illinois, 1973; *In Our Time. Stories*, Paris, 1924, New York, 1977; *The Old Man and the Sea*, London, 1952, 1976

HENRY, O., *The Best of O. Henry*, London, 1929, Philadelphia, 1978; *More O. Henry*, London, 1933; *58 Short Stories*, London and Glasgow, 1956

JACOBS, W. W., *Cruises and Cargoes. A W. W. Jacobs Omnibus*, London, 1934; *Selected Short Stories*, Harmondsworth, 1959, London, 1975

JACOBSON, DAN, *Beggar My Neighbour. Short Stories*, London, 1963; *The Trap and A Dance in the Sun*, Harmondsworth, 1968; *A Way of Life and other stories*, London, 1971; *Inklings. Selected Stories*, London, 1973, this was also issued as *Through the Wilderness: Selected Stories*, New York, 1968, Harmondsworth, 1977

JAMES, HENRY, *The Complete Tales of Henry James*, London, 1962–1964; *The Bodley Head Henry James*, London, 1967–1971; *Selected Short Stories*, Harmondsworth, 1963, 1979

JEWETT, SARAH ORNE, *Best Stories*, Minnesota; *The Country of the Pointed Firs*, Cambridge, Mass., 1884, New York, 1954, 1977

JOYCE, JAMES, *Dubliners*, London, 1914, 1977, New York, 1976

KIPLING, RUDYARD, *Short Stories*, Harmondsworth, 1977; *Stories and Poems*, London, 1970, 1971

LARDNER, RING, *The Best Short Stories of Ring Lardner*, New York, 1957, London, 1959, 1974; *You Know Me, Al*, New York, 1916, 1979 (reprint of 1925 ed.); *How to Write Short Stories*, New York, 1924, Philadelphia, 1973

LAVIN, MARY, *The Stories of Mary Lavin*, London, 1964, 1974; *Collected Stories*, Boston, 1971; *The Shrine and other stories*, Boston, 1977

LAWRENCE, D. H., *Collected Short Stories*, London, 1974, 1976; *Short Stories*, Harmondsworth, 1971

LAWSON, HENRY, *Henry Lawson's best stories*, Sydney, 1966, 1968; *While the Billy Boils. 87 stories from the Prose Works of Henry Lawson*, London, 1897, 1972; *Selected Stories*, Adelaide, 1971

LESSING, DORIS, *Collected African Stories*, London, 1973; *Collected Stories*, London, 1978

LEWIS, ALUN, *The Last Inspection and other stories*, London, 1942; *In the Green Tree: Home Letters and Short Stories*, London, 1948

McCULLERS, CARSON, *Shorter Novels and Stories*, London, 1972; *The Ballad of the Sad Café, and other stories*, New York, 1951, 1967, London, 1952, Harmondsworth, 1970; *The Member of the Wedding*, New York and London, 1946, Illinois, 1969; *The Mortgaged Heart. Previously Uncollected Writings*, New York, 1971, London, 1975

MACINTYRE, TOM, *Dance the Dance*, London, 1970

McLAVERTY, MICHAEL, *The Game-Cock and other Stories*, Connecticut, 1947; London, 1949

MALAMUD, BERNARD, *The Magic Barrel*, New York, 1958, 1972, London, 1960; *Idiots First*, New York, 1963, 1975, London, 1964

MANSFIELD, KATHERINE, *The Short Stories of Katherine Mansfield*, New York, 1937; *Collected Stories*, London, 1945; *34 Short Stories*. Selected by Elizabeth Bowen, New York, 1956, London and Glasgow, 1957, London, 1974, *Short Stories*, London, 1975

MAUGHAM, W. SOMERSET, *Collected Short Stories*, London, 1975–6, New York, 1977–8

MELVILLE, HERMAN, *Great Short Works of Herman Melville*, New York, 1969; *Selected Tales and Poems*, New York, 1950; *Billy Budd, Sailor and other stories*, New York, 1968, Harmondsworth, 1970

MONTAGUE, JOHN, *Death of a Chieftain, and other stories*, London, 1964

MOORE, GEORGE, *Celibates*, London, 1895, later issued as *Celibate Lives*, London, 1968; *The Untilled Field*, London, 1903, New Jersey, 1978

MORRISON, ARTHUR, *Selected Tales*, London, 1929; *Tales of Mean Streets*, London, 1894, reprinted New York, 1921; *Fiddle O'Dreams*, London, 1933

OATES, JOYCE CAROL, *By the North Gate*, New York, 1963, 1978, London, 1975; *Upon the Sweeping Flood*, New York, 1966, 1977, London, 1973, 1975; *The Wheel of Love*, New York, 1970, 1977, London, 1971; *Marriages and Infidelities*, New York, 1972, 1978, London, 1974; *The Girl*, Cambridge, Mass., 1974; *The Poisoned Kiss and Other Portuguese Stories*, New York, 1975; *The Seduction and Other Stories*, Santa Barbara, California, 1975, 1976; *Where are You Going. Where Have You Been*, New York, 1976; *The Goddess and Other Women*, New York, 1974, 1976, London, 1975

O'BRIEN, EDNA, *The Love Object*, London, 1968, New York, 1975, Harmondsworth, 1970, 1979; *A Scandalous Woman and other stories*, London, 1974, New York, 1974, 1976, Harmondsworth, 1976, 1978

O'CONNOR, FLANNERY, *The Complete Stories*, New York, 1972; *The Artificial Nigger*, New York, 1955, reissued as *A Good Man is Hard to Find and other stories*, London, 1957, 1962, 1980, New York, 1970; *Everything that Rises Must Converge*, New York, 1965, London, 1966, Harmondsworth, 1975

O'CONNOR, FRANK, *Stories of Frank O'Connor*, New York, 1952, 1966; *Domestic Relations*, London, 1957; *Collection Two*, London, 1964; *More Stories*, New York, 1967; *Collection Three*, London, 1969; *Fish for Friday and other stories*, London, 1971; *Day Dreams and other stories*, London, 1973; *The Holy Door and other stories*, London, 1973; *My Oedipus Complex and other stories* (From *The Stories of Frank O'Connor* and *Domestic Relations*) Harmondsworth, 1963, 1979

O'FAOLAIN, JULIA, *We Might See Sights, and other stories*, London, 1968; *Man in the Cellar. Stories*, London, 1974

O'FAOLAIN, SEAN, *The Finest Short Stories of Sean O'Faolain*, Boston and Toronto, 1957, 1965; *The Stories of Sean O'Faolain* (with an introduction by the author), London, 1958; *Stories*, Harmondsworth, 1971; *I Remember! I Remember! Stories*, London, 1962; *The Heat of the Sun: stories and tales*, London, 1966; *The Talking Trees, and other stories*, London, 1971; *Foreign Affairs, and other stories*, Boston, 1976, Harmondsworth, 1976, 1978

O'FLAHERTY, LIAM, *The Short Stories of Liam O'Flaherty*, London, 1937, 1966; *Two Lovely Beasts, and other stories*, London, 1948, 1961; *The Wounded Cormorant and other stories*, New York, 1973

O'HARA, JOHN, *Great Short Stories*, New York, 1973; *And Other Stories*, New York, 1968, London, 1969; *The Doctor's Son, and other stories*, New York, 1935

PLOMER, WILLIAM, *Four Countries (Selected Stories)*, London, 1949; *I Speak of Africa*, London, 1927; *The Child of Queen Victoria, and other stories*, London, 1933; *Paper Houses*, Harmondsworth and New York, 1943; *The Dorking Thigh and other satires*, London, 1945

POE, E. A., *Complete Tales and Poems*, New York, 1975

PORTER, KATHERINE ANNE, *Collected Stories*, London, 1964, 1967, New York, 1965

POWYS, T. F., *The Left Leg*, New York, 1923, London, 1923, 1968; *The House with the Echo. 26 Stories*, London, 1928; *Fables*, London, 1929, Mississippi, 1971, reissued as *No Painted Plumage*, London, 1934; *Uncle Dottery*, Bristol, 1930; *Christ in the Cupboard*, London, 1930; *The White Paternoster and other stories*, London, 1930, subsequently reprinted, New York; *When Thou Wast Naked*, Waltham St. Lawrence, 1931; *The Tithe Barn, and the dove and the eagle*, London, 1932; *Captain Patch. Twenty one Stories*, London, 1935; *Bottle's Path, and other stories*, London, 1946; *God's Eyes A-Twinkle*, London, 1947, Bath, 1974; *Rosie Plum, and other stories*, London, 1966; *The Scapegoat*, Hastings, 1966

PRITCHETT, V. S., *Collected Stories*, London, 1956; *The Sailor, the Sense of Humour, and other stories*, New York, 1956; *When My Girl Comes Home*, London, 1961; *The Key to my Heart*, London, 1963; *Blind Love*, London, 1969; *The Camberwell Beauty and other stories*, London and New York, 1974; *Selected Stories*, New York, 1978; *On the Edge of the Cliff*, London, 1980

SAKI (H. H. MUNRO), *The Bodley Head Saki*, London, 1963; *Incredible Tales: Saki Short Stories*, New York, 1966; *Best of Saki*, London, 1976, New York, 1977; *Short Stories*, London, 1979

SANSOM, WILLIAM, *The Stories of William Sansom*, London, 1963, subsequently reprinted, New York

SARGESON, FRANK, *Collected Stories, 1935–1963*, London, 1965; *The Stories of Frank Sargeson*, Auckland, 1973, New York, 1974

SCOTT, DUNCAN CAMPBELL, *Selected Stories*, Ontario, 1972; *In the Village of Viger, and other stories*, Toronto, 1896, 1973

SCOTT, WALTER, *Short Stories*, reprint of the 1834 ed., New York; *Chronicles of the Canongate*, Edinburgh, 1827, London, 1928; *The Two Drovers*, New Jersey, 1971

SILLITOE, ALAN, *Selection*, London, 1968; *The Loneliness of the Long Distance Runner*, London, 1959, 1975, New York, 1971; *The Ragman's Daughter*, London, 1963, 1977; *Guzman Go Home*, London, 1968, 1970; *Men, Women and Children*, London, 1973

SMITH, PAULINE, *The Little Karoo*, London, 1925, New Hampshire, 1978

STERN, JAMES, *Short Stories*, London, 1968

STEVENSON, R. L., *The Works of Robert Louis Stevenson*, reprint of the 1923 ed., New York, 1975; *Novels and Stories*, London, 1945; *Selected Poetry and Prose of Robert Louis Stevenson*, Boston, 1968; *The Suicide Club, and other stories*, Oxford, 1970, 1974, Houston, 1975

TAYLOR, PETER, *The Collected Stories of Peter Taylor*, New York, 1971

THOMAS, DYLAN, *Selected Writings*, London, 1970; *The Map of Love*, London, 1939; *A Portrait of the Artist as a Young Dog*, London, 1940, 1965, New York, 1956; *Adventures in the Skin Trade and other stories*, Norfolk, Conn., and London, 1955, 1977; *A Prospect of the Sea and other stories and prose writings*, London, 1955, 1966

TURGENEV, IVAN, *Sportsman's Sketches*, 1851, translated as *Sketches from a Hunter's Album*, Harmondsworth, 1967, 1979

UPDIKE, JOHN, *Assorted Prose*, New York, 1965, London, 1965, 1966; *The Same Door*, New York, 1959, 1972, London, 1962; *Pigeon Feathers and other stories*, New York, 1962, 1978, London, 1962, Harmondsworth, 1965, 1978; *The Music School*, New York, 1966, 1977, London, 1967, 1973; *Museums and Women*, New York, 1972, 1973, London, 1973; *Too Far to Go: The Maples Stories*, New York, 1979; *Problems and other stories*, London, 1980

WARNER, SYLVIA TOWNSEND, *Some World far from Ours and 'Stay, Corydon, Thou Swain'*, London, 1929; *The Salutation*, London, 1932; *More Joy in Heaven, and other stories*, London, 1935, 1939; *A Garland of Straw: twenty eight stories*, London, 1943, subsequently reprinted, New York; *The Museum of Cheats, and other stories*, London, 1947; *Winter in the Air, and other stories*, London, 1955; *A Stranger with a Bag, and other stories*, London, 1966; *The Innocent and the Guilty*, London, 1971; *Kingdoms of Elfin*, London, 1977, 1979

WELLS, H. G., *Complete Short Stories of H. G. Wells*, London, 1927, 1966; *Selected Short Stories*, Harmondsworth, 1958, 1979

WELTY, EUDORA, *Selected Stories*, New York, 1954; *Thirteen Stories*, New York, 1965; *A Curtain of Green and other stories*, New York, 1941, London, 1943; *The Wide Net and other stories*, New York, 1943, 1974, London, 1945; *The Golden Apples*, New York, 1949; *The Bride of the Innisfallen and other stories*, New York, 1955, 1972, London, 1955

WHITE, PATRICK, *The Burnt Ones*, London, 1964, Harmondsworth, 1968, 1977; *The Cockatoos. Short novels and stories*, London, 1974, New York, 1975

WILSON, ANGUS, *Death Dance: Twenty-five Stories*, Harmondsworth, 1970; *The Wrong Set and other stories*, London, 1949, Harmondsworth, 1960, 1969; *Such Darling Dodos and other stories*, London, 1950, 1960; *A Bit off the Map and other stories*, London, 1957, Harmondsworth, 1968, 1978, New York, 1978

Critical Works

The editions cited here are those that are the most accessible. The original editions are not necessarily cited.

AIKEN, CONRAD, *A Reviewer's ABC* (on Mansfield) new ed. as *Collected Criticism*, New York, 1968

ARNOLD, MATTHEW, *Civilization in the United States*, reprint of the 1888 ed., New York, 1972

AUDEN, W. H., *Collected Shorter Poems, 1927–1957*, London, 1969

BATES, H. E., *The Modern Short Story: a critical survey*, London, 1972

BEACHCROFT, T. O., *The Modest Art, a survey of the short story in English*, London, 1968

BERRYMAN, JOHN, *Stephen Crane*, reprint of 1950 ed., New York, 1975

BOWEN, ELIZABETH, Intro. to *Stories by Katherine Mansfield*, New York, 1956

CHARLES, GERDA, Intro. to *Modern Jewish Stories*, London, 1963

CHASE, RICHARD, *The American Novel and its Tradition*, reprint of 1957 ed., New York, 1978

COOK, SYLVIA JENKINS, *From Tobacco Road to Route 66: The Southern Poor White in Fiction*, North Carolina, 1976

ELIOT, T. S., Intro. to *A Choice of Kipling's Verse*, London, 1941

FLAUBERT, GUSTAVE, *Selected Letters*, trans. by Francis Steegmuller, reprint of 1953 ed., New York

FORSTER, E. M., *Aspects of the Novel*, London, 1927, Harmondsworth, 1970

FRYE, NORTHROP, *Anatomy of Criticism*, Princeton, 1957

GEISMAR, MAXWELL, *The Last of the Provincials, the American Novel, 1915–1925* (on Willa Cather, Anderson, Fitzgerald), New York, 1959

GREENE, GRAHAM, *Collected Essays*, Harmondsworth, 1978

HASSAN, IHAB, *Radical Innocence*, Princeton, 1961, New York, 1966

HOFFMAN, DANIEL G., *Form and Fable in American Fiction*, New York, 1973

HOLLOWAY, JOHN, 'The Literary Scene' in Vol. 7 of *The Modern Age, Pelican Guide to English Literature*, Harmondsworth, 1961, 1978

HOUGH, GRAHAM, *The Dark Sun: a critical study of D. H. Lawrence*, London, 1970

JARRELL, RANDALL, Introductions to *The English in England. Short Stories by Rudyard Kipling* and *In the Vernacular, the English in India. Short Stories*, Minnesota

JONES, GWYN, Introductions to *Twenty Five Welsh Short Stories*, ed. G. Jones and I. F. Elis, Oxford, 1971 and *Welsh Short Stories*, London, 1956

LAREDO, URSULA, see *Contemporary Novelists*, London and New York, 1972, 1976

LAWRENCE, D. H. *Studies in Classic American Literature*, London, 1964, New York, 1977

LEAVIS, F. R., *D. H. Lawrence: Novelist*, Harmondsworth, 1973

LEWES, G. H., 'Dickens in Relation to Criticism', *Fortnightly Review* (February 1872); see also *Charles Dickens* by Edgar Johnson, London, 1978, Harmondsworth, 1979

LEWIS, WYNDHAM, *The Writer and the Absolute*, London, 1952, reprinted, Connecticut, 1976

LITZ, A. WALTON (ed.), *Major American Short Stories*, Oxford, 1975

MARCUS, DAVID (ed.), *New Irish Writing*, An Anthology from The Irish Press Series, Dublin, 1970 etc.

MARCUS, MORDECAI, 'Melville's Bartleby as a Psychological Double' *College English*, XXIII (Feburary 1962), reprinted in *The Dimensions of the Short Story*, New York, 1964

MILLGATE, MICHAEL, *The Achievement of William Faulkner*, Edinburgh, 1961, London, 1966, New York, 1971

O'CONNOR, FRANK, *The Lonely Voice. A Study of the short story*, London, 1965; Intro. to *Modern Irish Stories*, London, 1957

PATER, WALTER, *Studies in the History of the Renaissance*, London, 1873; *The Renaissance*, Chicago, 1977

PEARSON, NORMAN HOLMES, 'Faulkner's Three Evening Suns', *Yale University Library Gazette*, XXIX (October, 1954); see also *The Achievement of William Faulkner* by Michael Millgate, Edinburgh, 1961, London, 1966, New York, 1971

PRITCHETT, V. S., *The Living Novel* (on Scott and Morrison), London, 1966; *The Working Novelist* (on Kipling and Saki), London, 1965

SILVA, FRED, see *Contemporary Novelists*, London and New York, 1972, 1976

STEAD, C. K., 'Katherine Mansfield and the Art of Fiction', *New Review*, September 1977

STEWART, J. I. M., *Rudyard Kipling*, New York and London, 1966
TANNER, TONY, *Conrad: Lord Jim*, London, 1963
VINSON, JAMES (ed.), *Contemporary Novelists of the English Language*, London and New York, 1972, 1976
WALL, STEPHEN, 'Aspects of the Novel 1930–1960' in *The Twentieth Century*, Vol. 7 of the *Sphere History of Literature in the English Language*
WILSON, ANGUS, see *Contemporary Novelists*, London and New York, 1972, 1976
WILSON, EDMUND, *O Canada: An American's Notes on Canadian Culture*, London, 1967, New York, 1976; *The Shores of Light. A Literary chronicle of the Twenties and Thirties* (on Lardner and Hemingway), New York, 1927, 1952
WINTERS, YVOR, *In Defence of Reason*, London, 1960
WOOLF, VIRGINIA, *The Common Reader, First Series*, London, 1925, 1975; *Second Series*, London, 1932, 1974

Index